Physical Appearance, Stigma, and Social Behavior:

The Ontario Symposium, Volume 3

ONTARIO SYMPOSIUM ON PERSONALITY AND SOCIAL PSYCHOLOGY

E. T. HIGGINS, C. P. HERMAN, M. P. ZANNA, EDS.
  Social Cognition: The Ontario Symposium, Volume 1

M. P. ZANNA, E. T. HIGGINS, C. P. HERMAN, EDS.
  Consistency in Behavior: The Ontario Symposium, Volume 2

C. P. HERMAN, M. P. ZANNA, E. T. HIGGINS, EDS.
  Physical Appearance, Stigma, and Social Behavior: The Ontario Symposium, Volume 3

J. M. OLSON, C. P. HERMAN, M. P. ZANNA, EDS.
  Relative Deprivation and Social Comparison: The Ontario Symposium, Volume 4

PHYSICAL APPEARANCE, STIGMA, AND SOCIAL BEHAVIOR:

The Ontario Symposium, Volume 3

Edited by

C. Peter Herman
University of Toronto

Mark P. Zanna
University of Waterloo

E. Tory Higgins
University of Western Ontario

 LAWRENCE ERLBAUM ASSOCIATES, PUBLISHERS
1986   Hillsdale, New Jersey   London

Lawrence Erlbaum Associates, Inc., Publishers
365 Broadway
Hillsdale, New Jersey 07642

Library of Congress Cataloging-in-Publication Data
Ontario Symposium on Personality and Social Psychology
   (3rd : 1981 : University of Toronto)
   Physical appearance, stigma, and social behavior.

   Includes bibliographies and indexes.
   1. Stigma (Social psychology)—Congresses.
2. Beauty, Personal—Congresses.   3. Body image—
Congresses.   4. Stereotype (Psychology)—Congresses.
I. Herman, C. Peter, 1946–   .   II. Zanna, Mark P.
III. Higgins, E. Tory (Edward Tory), 1946–
IV. Title.
HM291.067   1986   153.7′5   86-2041
ISBN 0-89859-638-6

Printed in the United States of America
10   9   8   7   6   5   4   3   2   1

Contents

Preface   ix

I: FACIAL ATTRACTIVENESS

1. **Stereotyping Based on Physical Attractiveness: Issues and
   Conceptual Perspectives**   7
   Karen K. Dion

   Research on Physical Attractiveness Stereotyping   *7*
   Social Learning Perspective   *10*
   Conclusions and Implications   *17*
   References   *19*

2. **From the Eye of the Beholder to Behavioral Reality:
   Development of Social Behaviors and Social Relations as a
   Function of Physical Attractiveness**   23
   Judith H. Langlois

   Theoretical Overview   *23*
   Differential Expectations   *24*
   Mediating Variables and Individual Differences
      in Behavioral Expectations   *27*
   Differential Treatment and Socialization   *34*
   The Development of Differential Behavior   *40*
   Continuity of Attractiveness   *43*
   Summary   *44*
   Future Directions   *45*
   References   *47*

3. **Psychological Adjustment of Patients with Craniofacial
    Deformities Before and After Surgery**   **53**
    Arlette Lefebvre and Ian R. Munro

    The Subjects—Material and Methods   *53*
    Results   *55*
    Discussion   *59*
    Conclusion   *62*
    References   *62*

II: PHYSIQUE

4. **The Social Psychological Effects of Overweight**   **65**
    William DeJong and Robert E. Kleck

    Introduction   *65*
    References   *83*

5. **Causes and Consequences of the Current Preference for Thin
    Female Physics**   **89**
    Janet Polivy, David M. Garner, and Paul E. Garfinkel

    Sociocultural Pressures for Thinness   *91*
    Empirical Evidence for Body Size Stereotypes   *95*
    Social Attitudes as a Cause of Illness   *98*
    Consequences of Social Pressure for Thinness   *99*
    References   *108*

6. **The Psychology of Height: An Empirical Review**   **113**
    Julian V. Roberts and C. Peter Herman

    Height and Weight   *114*
    Stature   *115*
    How Tall is Tall?; How Short is Short?   *116*
    Height and Body Image   *118*
    Body Image and Self-Descriptions   *120*
    Own Height and Estimates of Population Means   *121*
    Differences Between Short and Tall People   *121*
    Perception of Height in Others   *124*
    Ascribed Social Status and Perceived Height   *126*
    Height and Attractiveness   *128*
    Height and Personal Space   *132*
    Summary   *133*
    Future Research Directions   *134*
    References   *136*

III: IMPACT ON SOCIAL BEHAVIOR

7. **Physical Appearance and Social Influence**   **143**
   Shelly Chaiken

   Physical Appearance as an Agent Variable   *147*
   Physical Appearance as a Target Variable   *161*
   Summary and Conclusions   *166*
   References   *170*

8. **The Role of Olfaction in Social Perception and Behavior**   **179**
   John M. Levine and Donald H. McBurney

   Smell Among the Senses   *181*
   Odor and Human Social Perception and Behavior   *186*
   Toward a Social Psychology of Smell   *205*
   References   *211*

IV: DEVIANCE

9. **Maturation and Social Behavior: A Framework for the
   Analysis of Deviance**   **221**
   Gregory Northcraft and Albert Hastorf

   Introduction: Studied Indifference?   *221*
   An Extended Perspective   *224*
   Deviant Maturation: A Case in Point?   *229*
   Past Efforts: Research at the Macro-Outcome Level?   *232*
   Conclusions   *239*
   References   *241*

10. **The Measurement of Attitudes Toward Physically Disabled
    Persons**   **245**
    Jerome Siller

    Measurement Considerations   *246*
    Structure of Attitudes   *252*
    Are the Physically Disabled Really Different?   *255*
    The Social Position of the Physically Disabled and
       Preference Rankings for Types of Disabilities   *263*
    Attitudes of Professionals and Rehabilitation Workers
       271
    Attitudes of Educators   *271*
    References   *280*

V: COMMENTARY

11.   The Question of the Importance of Physical Attractiveness   291
      Ellen Berscheid

         References   *298*

AUTHOR INDEX   299
SUBJECT INDEX   313

Preface

This book grew out of a symposium held in May of 1981 at the University of Toronto, under the auspices of the Ontario Symposium in Personality and Social Psychology, funded by the Social Sciences and Humanities Research Council of Canada and the University of Toronto College of Arts & Sciences. The chapters collected here formed the basis for the presentations and discussions at that symposium, and have been updated to some extent to reflect developments that have occurred since the symposium itself.

The topic of the symposium, as of this volume, was physical appearance as a determinant of personality and social behavior. There is little doubt that one's physical appearance has some impact on the way one is perceived and treated; and presumably, owing to the socially reflected nature of the self, one's personality likewise will be affected by one's appearance. The questions arising from these basic observations and assumptions are legion, and the editors felt that it was appropriate to invite various experts to discuss their research on some of the implications of individual differences in appearance as they ramify into personality and social interaction.

How do appearance-based stereotypes arise, and how are they maintained? Can they be changed? Is there a "kernel of truth" underlying appearance stereotypes; and if so, what is the causal relation of the stereotype to the "truth," and to extrapolations beyond the "truth"? Some aspects of appearance are relatively malleable—unlike some of the more traditional bases for stereotyping effects, such as gender and race—so we may ask, What sorts of efforts are expended to change one's appearance? How successful are they, and do they accomplish a corresponding alteration in the way that people are perceived and perceive themselves? Of particular interest is the question, Given that appearance is subject to change, does not one's appearance in some way authentically reflect one's personality? ("She hasn't been taking care of herself." "You look like a new person!") And as a corollary to this question, we may ask, To the extent that appearance is *not* malleable—but is perceived to be—what inferences do people draw about their own and others' personality? ("Why doesn't she do something about her weight problem?" "What's the matter with me?") These are some of the "second-order" questions that this symposium was convened to address.

A second reason for organizing the symposium—or organizing it in the particular way it emerged—was to "bridge the neck." It seemed that over the course of the '70s, two virtually independent research literatures were developing—one concerning facial attractiveness, and one concerning body image (or, more properly, body evaluation). To a great extent, each of these literatures was self-contained, and there was little consideration of how they might relate to each other. As DeJong and Kleck (this volume, p. 81) put it, "thus far the research on overweight has largely neglected the fact that bodies have heads, just as the research on physical attractiveness has ignored the fact that faces have bodies." Both literatures have concerned themselves with attractiveness, although the "body" literature has tended to be organized in terms of (deviations from) ideal body shapes, whereas the "facial" literature speaks mainly in terms of relative attractiveness, with little reference to perfection. Such minor variations aside, these two literatures share more than they have acknowledged. The relative disattention paid by those who work above the neck to those who work below, and vice versa, probably stems from each camp's guiding premise: that their domain is what counts in physical attractiveness. In any event, we thought that the time had arrived for some active cross-fertilization, since for various reasons—some dictated by the topic, some by accident—these two domains of research had developed along slightly different lines, with differing methodologies addressing different questions. It seemed likely that communication across the neck might prove to be fruitful, by encouraging people to ask old questions in new ways, or to ask new questions, or at least to remember that there is more to physical appearance than just one's face or just one's body.

Finally, of course, the symposium shared a purpose articulated by most symposium organizers—the attempt to stimulate new thinking and new research. Physical appearance research has entered its adolescence: it is now asking subtler questions, and discovering subtler relationships between variables. But obviously, it is far from mature, either in terms of its empirical knowledge base or its conceptual organization. There is no automatic mechanism to promote development in such an area; but symposia at least provide the possibility for creative expansion. The present volume, then, even if it merely highlights how much we do not know, may serve to stimulate further, more sophisticated work.

The present volume begins with a look at recent developments in the area of facial attractiveness. Karen Dion, a pioneer in this area, examines the depth and breadth of the attractiveness stereotype, extending from her original demonstration that "what is beautiful is good." She displays the robustness of this stereotype across experimental and demographic conditions, while at the same time offering some suggestions as to the cultural preconditions for the adoption of the stereotype. The attributes stereotypically associated with good looks provide additional reasons, if any are needed, to explain our attraction to facial beauty, an attraction that is so ingrained that we use the terms "attractive" and "good looking" as synonymous with "beautiful."

Judith Langlois presents a more dialectical analysis of the development and ramifications of the attractiveness stereotype. She adopts a transactional perspective, emphasizing the stereotypical expectations held by observers, their consequent behaviors toward attractive and unattractive targets, and possible behavioral and personality alterations in the targets themselves as a result of differential treatment. Langlois pays close attention to interpretive issues, including the admittedly speculative possibility that facial attractiveness may be innately associated with certain valued personality traits.

The final chapter in the first section describes some preliminary findings emerging from an ambitious program of craniofacial surgery at Toronto's Hospital for Sick Children. Dramatic improvements in facial attractiveness are occasionally achieved, and Lefebvre and Munro describe some of the psychological and social consequences of these changes. For the most part, improvements in self-rated appearance and esteem are matched by ratings by other central figures in the children's lives, with benefits accruing to all. Interestingly, however, the grotesque deformities that prompt such surgery are not infrequently accompanied by perceptual and evaluative distortions and even denial, so that surgery may "destabilize" a defensive shell that has been protecting the deformed child. Such unanticipated negative consequences are endemic to therapeutic situations where the patient and those around him or her have accommodated themselves "too well" to the problem, with the result that additional adjustments may have to be made to the new, improved condition. Such readjustments seem like a small price to pay for the remarkable changes that surgeons can now effect, bringing children who were once "monsters" into the broad range of "normal" appearance. Lives are being saved, and we are reminded—especially when we confront such extreme cases—of the power of physical appearance to make or break the individual.

The second section, on Physique, begins with a review by DeJong and Kleck of the endomorphic stereotype. Although the intensity of the negative traits assumed to characterize fat people varies somewhat across and even within cultures, the range tends to be from bad to worse. Interestingly, it appears to be worse among health professionals, who seem to regard their patients' overweight condition as a deliberate insult. DeJong and Kleck speculate that the reason for obesity being regarded more negatively than are some other forms of physical deviance is that obesity is perceived as somehow the responsibility of the fat individual, whereas those who are blind or crippled are regarded as less responsible for their unfortunate condition. The current scientific ambiguity concerning the actual determinants of obesity no doubt contributes to the attributional confusion in this area. Another interesting attributional aspect of obesity raised in this chapter is the fat person's tendency to attribute others' reactions to him/her to his/her obese state. We are warned that such overattribution effects should not blind us to the reality of actual prejudice based on physique, although the extent of such prejudice is more a matter of speculation than of established fact at present.

Polivy, Garner, and Garfinkel confirm the foregoing analysis of endomorphy by emphasizing the pressures toward ectomorphy that currently dominate our culture, especially its female component. Their review demonstrates that women do indeed aspire to thinness, although it is still not clear—despite a wealth of speculation—whether thinness is simply regarded as being more attractive, or whether the presumptive personality correlates of thinness, above and beyond attractiveness per se, are what motivates dieters. In either case, the ideal female physique is (consensually) a thin one, and women seem willing to undergo significant privations to attain it. The consequences of the cultural endorsement of dieting are profound. So-called normal dieters exhibit a surprising variety of behaviors—some involving eating, some not—that push at the boundaries of pathology, while anorexics and bulimics represent what happens when the pressure toward thinness is applied to "vulnerable" individuals. This chapter makes it clear that appearance counts—or is at least perceived to count—and that the pursuit of an ideal appearance will supersede normal goals, including health and even happiness.

While females may wish to be thinner, it appears that males wish to be taller. Of course, thinness is meaningless in isolation from height, although we usually say "overweight" rather than "underheight" when referring to the same phenomenon—presumably because we (think we) can do more about our weight than about our height. In their chapter, Roberts and Herman review the evidence that height matters to people: Dissatisfaction with one's height is almost as widespread as is dissatisfaction with one's weight. People seem to assume that "improvements" in their height will improve their prospects, but the actual evidence in support of this proposition is curiously insubstantial. Although there is considerable evidence for a positive association between perceived height and ascribed status, methodological limitations bedevil the research, and evidence that increasing one's height will increase one's social or economic power is negligible. Even the evidence that tallness is part of physical attractiveness in males is disputed, despite consensus regarding the "cardinal principle" of dating—that the male be taller than the female. This chapter demonstrates the difficulties in distinguishing between correlates of appearance and perceived correlates of appearance, especially when the correlates themselves are primarily elements of social perception and evaluation.

The third section of this volume contains two chapters that are unique in conception and impressive in execution. Chaiken deliberately sets out to "bridge" the neck by focusing not on attractiveness or physique, but on social influence as a function of appearance variables wherever they may be located. She discovers that facial attractiveness has been studied mainly as a communicator characteristic, while overweight has been studied mainly as a target characteristic. While this asymmetry prevents serious consideration of the issue "Which is more important," Chaiken rightly applauds the situation as a reflection of the theoretically based nature of the research: there are good reasons to expect attractiveness to mediate communicator effectiveness and overweight to mediate susceptibility to social influence. Chaiken explores the "second and third generation" questions concerning *why* facial attractiveness ought to affect one's power to influence, and concludes that the effect of attractiveness, while robust, may be somewhat superficial, affecting weakly held attitudes and then only under conditions of direct interaction. She also explores the basis for the overweight/influencibility association, concluding that the analysis derived from consideration of overweight as deviance may be more compelling than the analysis derived from the externality/obesity link. This chapter provides the sort of perspective from which all researchers in the area of physical appearance might benefit.

Levine and McBurney likewise provide a remarkable perspective by reminding us that appearances are not only visual. They provide a fascinating survey of the sorts of smells that people give off and how others react to them. Like other aspects of appearance, odors may be attractive or unattractive, but in addition, odors have various properties that seem to detract from the analogy with visual appearance. The authors speculate about why researchers have paid scant attention to smell as an important element in human social behavior—even though we all know that bad smells have dramatic effects—and provide convincing evidence that we ought to be much more sensitive to what is after all a fundamental sensory modality. Methodological difficulties, including our strangely inadequate vocabulary for describing smells, are fully acknowledged; but these difficulties notwithstanding, it will be a rare reader whose consciousness (of odors, at least) is not raised by reading this chapter.

Another way of approaching appearance variables in a way that integrates various elements of appearance is to focus on stigma. Here we start with a general sociological or social psychological principle and then apply it to body parts as they present themselves. In their chapter, Northcraft and Hastorf improve upon this general stigma approach to understanding the impact of physical appearance on social behavior in two respects, by taking as their example early versus late maturers. Consideration of individuals who vary from the normative developmental timeline to the point of deviance provides, first, a situation where the "whole body"—or at least, a constellation of body parts—constitutes the deviant element. Second, the deviant element is one that itself undergoes a natural change (or correction) over time, unlike the more static elements of appearance that we ordinarily encounter in the literature. The authors give detailed consideration to the sequencing of reactions to deviance, both by the deviant and by others with whom s/he interacts, and argue persuasively for the value of an "extended molecular analysis" of the processes involved. We are encouraged to work through the sequence of appearances, reactions, attributions, positive and negative feedback loops and other aspects of the complex process that leads from (perceived) deviance to social and personality outcomes.

The next chapter, by Siller, involves a shift to more traditional types of physical deviance (e.g., blindness), most of which are not simply developmental rate abnormalities. These more severe stigmata ought to produce stronger effects on social interaction, and indeed they do; but at the same time, Siller demonstrates in great detail the problems involved in treating stigma as a unitary phenomenon. As seems to be the case so often, attempts to measure a phenomenon stimulate all sorts of difficulties, which in turn promote more thoughtful consideration of that phenomenon. Siller in this instance considers the dimensionality of physical disability and our reactions to it, developmentally and professionally. Again, we are forced to consider the basis for our reactions, and how such reactions might be altered to everyone's benefit.

Finally, Ellen Berscheid offers some thoughts on the state of the art of attractiveness research. She ponders the extent to which psychologists can currently provide answers to those from other professions about the impact of physical appearance on social and personal well-being. How much do we know? What recommendations can we make? Berscheid conveys some of the frustrations that she experiences in trying to find compelling answers to practical questions, when the answers are always qualified and often uncertain.

This book demonstrates that we have come a long way in the description and explanation of the effects of physical appearance, positive and negative, on social behavior and personality development; but it also demonstrates that we have a long way to go. One can only hope that this volume, by recapitulating the past and examining the conceptual and methodological achievements and failings of the present, will help to guide future research and thinking in more productive directions.

C. P. Herman
M. P. Zanna
E. T. Higgins

Physical Appearance, Stigma, and Social Behavior:

The Ontario Symposium, Volume 3

FACIAL ATTRACTIVENESS

1 Stereotyping based on Physical Attractiveness: Issues and Conceptual Perspectives

Karen K. Dion
University of Toronto

Does an individual's physical attractiveness affect others' impressions of him or her? This question has received considerable attention in the research literature during the past decade and continuing into the present one. Several issues pertaining to stereotyping based on physical attractiveness are covered here. In the context of the present discussion, Brigham's (1971) definition of the term *stereotype* is relevant, even though he proposed this definition with reference to ethnic stereotypes. Specifically, Brigham suggested that what makes this concept distinctive is that it is not simply "a generalization . . . about a group" (p. 30), but "a generalization . . . which is considered to be unjustified by an observer" (p. 31, italics omitted).

This discussion of physical attractiveness stereotyping begins by considering two early studies. It should be noted that this chapter focuses on the facial component of physical attractiveness.

Research on Physical Attractiveness Stereotyping

To investigate whether stereotyping based on an individual's physical attractiveness occurred, Dion, Berscheid, and Walster (1972) asked male and female university students to judge stimulus persons (also young adults) who differed in physical attractiveness, on a variety of dimensions. Respondents were told that the study concerned "accuracy in person perception," specifically, a comparison of college students' accuracy with that of two other groups (graduate students in clinical psychology and clinical psychologists). The stimulus persons were ostensibly taking part in a study of personality development that would investigate their development into adulthood, thus presumably providing the opportunity to ascertain the accuracy of respondents' judgments.

7

The findings indicated support for the existence of physical attractiveness stereotyping. Specifically, physically attractive individuals of both sexes were believed to have more socially desirable personalities and more favorable experiences in several domains. One domain showed no differences as a function of the stimulus person's attractiveness: viz. expected parental competence. Overall, the general pattern of results indicated a positivity effect, with attractive individuals receiving more favorable evaluations from peers, a pattern summarized by the phrase: "What is beautiful is good."

Another early study concerning the impact of physical attractiveness on first impressions was conducted by Miller (1970). Male and female undergraduates were asked to assess stimulus persons varying in physical attractiveness on 17 personality dimensions comprising Jackson and Minton's (1963) Adjective Preference Scale. Attractiveness effects occurred on 15 of the 17 dimensions. Highly attractive persons were more favorably evaluated than individuals who were of low physical attractiveness. Sex of stimulus person interacted with the attractiveness factor on various dimensions. The pattern of findings suggested to Miller that an individual's sex was less important in affecting first impressions of highly attractive persons compared to less attractive individuals, because there were fewer differences between ratings of male versus female stimulus persons for those of high attractiveness.

In summary, these early studies found that stereotyping based on physical attractiveness occurred, with attractive young adults rated more positively on a variety of personal attributes. These findings raised several issues that have been examined in subsequent research. Two issues are of interest for this discussion of attractiveness stereotyping; viz. its generality across different age groups and its robustness.

Considering the former issue first, what impact does physical attractiveness have on impressions of individuals who are at various phases of the life-span? The stimulus persons in the early studies (Dion et al., 1972; Miller, 1970) were in late adolescence/early adulthood, raising the question of whether attractiveness might affect judgments of individuals primarily from this age group. Subsequent research, however, has found that physical attractiveness influences evaluations of stimulus persons from other age groups. In his review of this literature, Adams (1977) stated that there was "rather strong evidence for a physical attractiveness stereotype that generalizes across differing samples, contexts, and settings which reflect varying life span stage experiences" (p. 223).

The pattern of findings across a number of studies suggests that physically attractive persons are judged more positively than physically unattractive individuals on various traits, especially those traits reflecting social competence and interpersonal ease (e.g., Adams & Huston, 1975; Bassili, 1981; Dermer & Thiel, 1975; Ellis, Olson, & Zanna, 1983; Langlois & Stephan, 1977). Some researchers also have found that on traits connoting vanity and self-centeredness, attractive individuals are rated less positively than unattractive persons (Bassili,

1981; Dermer & Thiel, 1975). In summary, there is evidence that attractiveness functions as an evaluative cue influencing impressions both of young adults and of persons from other age groups.

Another issue concerns the robustness or strength of attractiveness stereotyping that some researchers have assessed by providing instructional sets to respondents that might lessen the impact of attractiveness. For example, Dermer and Thiel (1975) asked half the participants in their second experiment to rate how much confidence they had in each of their judgments about the stimulus person. The findings indicated that whether or not respondents rated their degree of confidence in their impressions had no effect on attractiveness stereotyping.

More recently, Ellis, Olson, and Zanna (1983) examined the effect that an "objective" versus a "subjective" set concerning judgments of attractiveness had on male undergraduates' personality inferences about women differing in physical attractiveness. These investigators hypothesized that differential judgments of attractive compared to unattractive women should be weakened by a "subjective" set of instructions. Men in the "subjective" condition were told that judgments about women's physical attractiveness were "primarily matters of personal taste" whereas those in the "objective" condition were informed that these judgments were "primarily determined by the target's physical characteristics." (There was in addition a control condition in which participants were not given any information concerning the presumed basis for attractiveness ratings.) Two experiments were conducted, and in each experiment the experimental manipulations were successful. The hypothesis that the men would be more likely to show a greater degree of stereotyping in the objective compared to the subjective condition, however, was not supported. Instead, a main effect for physical attractiveness occurred on several of the personality dimensions, with attractive women being evaluated more positively than unattractive women on these dimensions.

Also, in the second experiment, respondents were asked to make ratings of their confidence for each of their personality judgments. The hypothesis underlying the inclusion of this measure was that men who were led to believe that their attractiveness judgments were largely based on subjective factors might express less confidence in their impressions relative to those responding under a more objective set. This hypothesis did not receive support. Ellis (1983) and his colleagues noted that these results were "discouraging for attempts to inhibit the stereotyping process" and concluded that "the attractiveness stereotype seems to be remarkably powerful and reliable" (p. 41).

A final point is relevant to the discussion in this section. The rather elaborate instructions used by Dion and her colleagues (Dion et al., 1972) and subsequently employed by Dermer and Thiel (1975) should have lessened the likelihood of stereotyping based on attractiveness because participants in these studies were led to believe that the research concerned accuracy of person perception, with the expectation that their judgments could be assessed as to their accuracy.

Presumably, an "accuracy" set should have made individuals more cautious and careful when assessing the stimulus persons.

In summary, stereotyping based on physical attractiveness has been found in a number of studies. It is important therefore at this point in time to address the following question: Why does this phenomenon occur? Subsequent sections of this chapter consider various conceptual perspectives that deal with this question and empirical evidence pertaining to each perspective.

Social Learning Perspective

Socialization Factors.   One possibility is that as a function of their socialization history individuals learn to differentially evaluate people who differ on physical attractiveness. From this perspective, socializing agents may play an important role influencing the child's learning to judge differences in attractiveness and ultimately to associate these differences with various evaluative connotations (Dion, 1972). Considering this viewpoint, it can be asked if adults can in fact discriminate infants' and young children's physical attractiveness and if so, whether attractiveness elicits beliefs and expectations about the probable personal characteristics of attractive compared to unattractive children.

Several studies suggest that adults can judge the physical attractiveness of infants. In one study, nurses were asked to assess the physical attractiveness of premature infants (Corter, Trehub, Boukydis, Ford, Celhoffer, & Minde, 1978). Considerable consensus on the ratings occurred both among nurses who had previous responsibilities in caring for premature infants and among nurses who had little or no prior experience with premature infants. Hildebrandt and Fitzgerald (1978) found that young adults' (college students') rankings of infants' physical attractiveness were significantly interrelated for infants in two age groups (4 months and 8 months). In another study, Hildebrandt and Fitzgerald (1981) asked both mothers and women from the same age group who were not mothers for their rankings of the relative attractiveness of infants, using stimulus photographs previously judged by college students to differ in attractiveness. When judging the attractiveness of unfamiliar infants, the women from each group judged the more attractive infants (as determined by these prior ratings) to be better looking compared to the less attractive infants. Finally, Stephan and Langlois (1984) also found that infants' attractiveness was reliably rated by young adults.

Regarding the second aspect of the social learning perspective, recent evidence suggests that differential evaluation by socializing agents begins very early in an individual's life. Stephan and Langlois (1984) asked young adults (university students) from three groups (Black, Caucasian, and Mexican–American) for their first impressions of infants from these ethnic groups. Respondents' ratings of the infants were factor analyzed yielding three factors: "good baby" (including items such as cheerful, attached to mother, responsive to other people);

"active baby," and "smart–likeable baby." One item "causes parents problems" was analyzed separately because it was not found to load on any of the three factors. The findings indicated that the most physically attractive 3-month and 9-month-old infants from all three ethnic groups were for the most part regarded more favorably than the least attractive babies on three of the four measures; viz. the "good baby" index, the "smart-likeable" baby index, and the item "causes parents problems." These data are consistent with other research (Adams, 1978) examining preschool teachers' stereotypes of young children differing in attractiveness. In general, these findings concerning adults' impressions of infants and young children who differ in attractiveness suggest that adults' use of attractiveness as an evaluative cue begins very early.

Of direct relevance for the social learning perspective, not only do adults themselves show attractiveness-related stereotyping of infants and young children, Adams and Crane (1980) found that for the most part parents and teachers of preschool children expected their children to favor good-looking children and adults when judging the relative niceness of attractive versus unattractive stimulus persons. Furthermore, attractiveness stereotyping among preschool children was related to their mothers' and preschool teachers' but not their fathers' expectations, suggesting that certain socialization agents might be particularly important in influencing children's acquisition of this stereotype. Finally, the authors mentioned briefly that "subtle reinforcement" or "self-fulfilling prophecy effects" might help explain the emergence of attractiveness stereotyping in children. As Adams and Crane noted, however, direction of effect cannot be unambiguously determined from these data because, for example, the children might also affect their parents' and teachers' beliefs.

The findings discussed in this section indicate that the social learning perspective merits further consideration. If, however, individuals learn from socializing agents to differentially assess others as a function of differences in attractiveness, the manner in which this learning occurs remains to be specified. A comparison of stereotyping based on physical attractiveness with other types of stereotypes may help to provide some insights into the acquisition process. Some stereotypes such as those elicited by an individual's sex have components that reinforce particular social identities as reflected, for example, in traditional definitions of gender roles. This type of stereotype may therefore be initially learned in part as socializing agents who endorse a traditional role structure call attention to various attributes as appropriate or inappropriate depending on an individual's sex. In contrast, early learning related to the development of attractiveness stereotyping seems likely to be relatively informal and incidental, consisting of general evaluative remarks with reference to physical appearance, such as comments indicating approval of a child's appearance. This type of comment would both sensitize children to differences in attractiveness as defined by particular cultural norms as well as to suggest to a child that a more attractive appearance can evoke a favorable response from others. Apart from these kinds of comments, any more elaborate discussion of others' physical attractiveness obviously conflicts with values such as the importance of relying on more intrinsic aspects of an individual when judging him or her. Presumably most parents and other adults would endorse this value and therefore refrain from extensive comments to children about others' attractiveness, though there may well be variability on the part of adults in the extent to which they make these types of remarks. Even if parents attempt to avoid and/or minimize references to others' physical attractiveness, the child may still encounter relatives and other adults who do comment on attractiveness, either praising the child or other children (or adults) in front of the child. So far, discussion has focused on the hypothesized contribution of adults' comments to the child's learning to associate evaluative connotations with differences in attractiveness. As the child grows older, these early impressions may be reinforced and elaborated in various interaction contexts, including those involving adults outside the child's immediate family and increasingly, interaction with peers.

Discussion of the relation between attractiveness stereotyping and interpersonal behavior has suggested that this relation is bidirectional. The mechanism hypothesized to underlie this interrelation is basically the "self-fulfilling prophecy," defined by Merton (1949, 1957, 1968) in his classic discussion of this concept as "a *false* definition of the situation evoking a new behavior which makes the originally false conception come *true*" (Merton, 1968, p. 477). Both social-psychological (e.g., Berscheid & Walster, 1974; Snyder, Tanke, & Berscheid, 1977) and more developmentally oriented accounts (e.g., Adams, 1977; Langlois & Stephan, 1981) of the impact of attractiveness stereotyping have suggested that it is an important factor influencing behavior towards individuals differing in attractiveness. In turn, this differential behavior may elicit reactions from attractive versus unattractive persons that ultimately serve to substantiate the attractiveness stereotype. Attractiveness stereotyping, however, may also be affected by earlier phases of this sequence. It seems reasonable to speculate that during childhood certain types of encounters with peers may be particularly likely to influence attractiveness stereotyping (as well as to be influenced by it). For example, some children whose appearance is considered deviant by peers may be subject to teasing, name calling, or ridicule. This type of treatment has been discussed in terms of the negative effect that it may have on the individual who is the recipient of these taunts (e.g., Berscheid, Walster, & Bohrnstedt, 1973). In addition, however, these episodes might further reinforce appearance stereotyping not only in children who participate in this type of negative behavior but also among children who simply observe the encounter. To cite another example, there is evidence that physical attractiveness is positively related to older children's popularity with their peers (Kleck, Richardson, & Ronald, 1974; Salvia, Sheare, & Algozzine, 1975). If therefore attractive children receive more favorable attention from peers, such as being included in various activities, the fact that they are the focus of this attention may increase the likelihood that socially desirable characteristics will be attributed to them by other children. Both these examples illustrate situations in which attractiveness stereotyping may be further reinforced as a result of particular experiences with peers.

Finally, during childhood (and beyond this phase), another factor that may contribute to the development of attractiveness stereotyping is the portrayal of individuals differing in attractiveness by various media such as books, television, and films. Systematic study of the impact of various media on the acquisition of attractiveness stereotyping is needed because these media seem likely to be important sources. Langlois and Stephan (1981) have commented that in films, children's cartoons, and stories the hero or heroine is typically more physically attractive than the villain, thus providing another context for acquiring attractiveness stereotyping by observational learning.

Certainly various traditional stories for children contain this kind of portrayal, as shown in those stories contrasting the positive qualities of the handsome prince and the beautiful princess with the evil epitomized by the ugly witch. The history of this theme in Western literature is intriguing. To cite one instance, the depiction of beauty as associated with virtue and ugliness with vice was noted by Curry (1916, 1972) in his literary analysis of various types of medieval literature. As this example suggests, this theme has a lengthy history.

Sociocultural Factors.   As can be seen in the preceding section, from a social learning perspective the emergence of attractiveness stereotyping is hypothesized to occur through interaction with and observation of the behavior of various socializing agents. The emphasis is on the manner in which attractiveness stereotyping may be transmitted within a given society. More general questions, however, can also be raised. Is attractiveness stereotyping more likely to occur in certain societies? What is the contribution of sociocultural factors to this type of stereotyping? Most of the research on attractiveness stereotyping has been conducted in North America. In this context, there is some evidence that physical attractiveness affects impressions of others across different ethnic groups (Adams, 1978; Langlois & Stephan, 1977; Stephan & Langlois, 1984).

Although research on attractiveness stereotyping has mostly involved North American respondents, the relation between physical attractiveness and heterosexual attraction has received some attention in the cross-cultural literature. Ford and Beach (1951) suggested that across cultures, physical appearance was one important factor contributing to heterosexual attraction, with the specific characteristics that defined an attractive appearance showing considerable diversity between different cultures. However, Rosenblatt (1974) has questioned whether physical attractiveness is important in all cultures for the formation of heterosexual relationships, in particular the selection of a marital partner. He noted that in certain cultural contexts assigning importance to physical appearance might be dysfunctional because it would conflict with other norms, for example, those pertaining to the arrangement of marriages.

Earlier research conducted by Rosenblatt and Cozby (1972) provides some support for this possibility. Based on their analysis of ethnographic descriptions from a number of cultures, Rosenblatt and Cozby found that the use of "impractical grounds" to select a marital partner was positively related to the degree of freedom of choice regarding selection of a spouse. For the most part, these "impractical grounds" referred to physical attractiveness (Rosenblatt, 1974). In contrast, Rosenblatt and Cozby (1972) state: more "practical grounds" involved considerations such as "food-getting skills, value of alliances created by the marriage, . . . rank . . . health . . ." (p. 693). Rosenblatt's analysis suggests the importance of considering what function(s) attractiveness serves in different societies. This line of argument can be extended to attractiveness stereotyping. Considering Rosenblatt and Cozby's findings, for example, one can speculate that stereotyping based on attractiveness might be more likely to occur in societies where freedom of choice of a marital partner is considered important. One of its functions in adulthood might be to provide a rationale for the value of attractiveness in this particular context.

A more general cultural orientation; viz. valuing individualism, is also of interest for the present discussion. This orientation can be contrasted with one that stresses more collective or group-oriented values. It has been suggested that societies differ with respect to the relative emphasis placed on these two value orientations. Considering these two orientations, Sampson (1977), for example, argued that "self-contained individualism" was stressed in American society. Barnlund (1975) in his study of interaction styles in Japan and the United States stated that "every society creates some entity or unit that serves as . . . the ultimate source of meaning and the locus for the interpretation of events" (p. 153). Barnlund suggested that this "psychological unit" in the United States (and many other Western societies) is the individual, whereas in Japan it might include "not merely the person, but all others who make up the nuclear group" (p. 154). Barnlund's analysis of these contrasting orientations focused on their relevance for self-definition and interpersonal communication, specifically, self-disclosure.

A difference in emphasis between the individual versus the group may also, however, have implications for the types of personal characteristics that are likely to influence impressions of other people. Personal characteristics such as physical attractiveness, particularly facial attractiveness, may be more individuating compared to other personal attributes such as sex and age that are associated with various roles or social identities. Evaluating others based on physical attractiveness might be dysfunctional in cultural contexts that stress more collective values. Physical attractiveness stereotyping may therefore be more likely to occur or may occur in a stronger form in societies that value a more differentiated and distinctive identity for the individual.

In view of this speculation, findings from a recent study comparing young children's completion of human figure drawings in Japan and the United States are of interest (Steward, Furuya, Steward, & Ikeda, 1982). When middle-class preschool children from both cultures were presented with an outline drawing of a young child and asked to complete the drawing, the American preschoolers were more likely to put facial features in their finished drawings and also to include clothing detail compared to Japanese children. Steward and her colleagues proposed an interpretation of these results based on Barnlund's (1975) findings that American college students reported a greater degree of self-disclosure or in Barnlund's terms, showed a more extensive "public self" relative to Japanese college students. They noted that the North American children's greater stress on external features might be another example of this emphasis on more public self-presentation. Another interpretation is that the children's addition of facial features and clothing detail to the drawing reflected a more individualistic orientation, as mentioned in the preceding paragraph.

The discussion in this section suggests that certain sociocultural factors may be related to attractiveness stereotyping. In addition to cross-cultural comparisons, the contribution of the types of dimensions discussed in this section to attractiveness stereotyping merits investigation at the intracultural level. One might plausibly expect differing degrees of adherence to and endorsement of values such as individualism within a particular society. Individual differences on these dimensions may moderate stereotyping based on physical attractiveness.

Cognitive Perspective

Another theoretical perspective that is relevant to understanding attractiveness stereotyping focuses on the role played by cognitive processes. This perspective on stereotyping has been considered in several conceptual accounts (e.g., Allport, 1954; Hamilton, 1979; McArthur, 1982). Certain features of these analyses are of particular interest in the present context. Allport (1954) discussed categorization as a fundamental aspect of thinking and linked this process to social cognition by suggesting that observable differences in various aspects of people's physical appearance provided a basis for categorization. He referred to this tendency as "the problem of visibility" (p. 131), suggesting that "groups that look (or sound) different will seem to *be* different, often more different than they are" (p. 132). Allport proposed that this type of cue served to capture one's attention and activate categorization. These processes can be regarded therefore as underlying stereotyping, though it should be noted that for Allport the terms *category* and *stereotype* were not synonymous. He distinguished between the two concepts by defining *stereotype* as "an exaggerated belief associated with a category" (p. 191, italics omitted). He viewed stereotypes as providing rationales or justification for behavior towards members of various groups.

More recently, cognitively oriented conceptualizations of stereotyping have focused on similar processes, making explicit their hypothesized contribution to the development of stereotypes. Hamilton (1979) reviewed empirical evidence that suggested that stereotyping could be understood in part by processes such as categorization and the perceiver's tendency to pay more attention to salient features of the environment, including the more distinctive aspects of other people. Hamilton argued that although sociocultural factors were important the contribution of cognitive factors to stereotyping merited more attention than had occurred previously in most of the literature in this area. McArthur (1982) proposed a pivotal role for the influence of physical appearance on stereotyping, suggesting that "if all stereotypes were somehow erased and if all people were equal in every respect but their physical appearance, then stereotypes could nevertheless reemerge as a result of the basic cognitive processes of categorization and selective attention" (p. 150). In support of this analysis, McArthur discussed findings pertaining to a variety of appearance cues (including race, sex, physical disability, attractiveness, specific facial features) in the context of the social cognition literature.

As can be seen from the discussion in the preceding paragraphs, these cognitively oriented conceptualizations of stereotyping may offer some insights into why attractiveness stereotyping occurs. Physical attractiveness, particularly facial attractiveness, is an easily observable characteristic. There is evidence that physical appearance and physical attractiveness are salient to perceivers. For example, in their study of person perception, Livesley and Bromley (1973) asked children and adolescents to give a written description of several individuals whom they knew personally (other than a family member) and either liked or disliked. Respondents were told *not* to mention various aspects of the person's physical appearance but to "describe what sort of person they are." Even in the presence of this instructional set, references to physical appearance were made with some frequency by respondents across age groups. (Statements in the category "Appearance" included mention of specific physical features as well as statements about attractiveness.) Livesley and Bromley also reported that in samples consisting of young adults (specifically, university students), comments about physical appearance were also quite evident in the description of others.

Milord (1978) conducted a multidimensional scaling study of faces to determine what dimensions were important for perceivers. In a series of studies, undergraduates were asked to make various judgments about facial stimuli (e.g., similarity, preference) or to rate the faces on a variety of scales. Of particular interest here, for the "homogeneous set" of stimulus faces (i.e., faces that shared several attributes in common such as age and sex), the largest dimension that emerged on the similarity and on the preference judgments had a strong "attractiveness" component as shown by the pattern of correlations with ratings of the facial stimuli. For the similarity judgments, the largest dimension showed a positive correlation with both a factor reflecting general evaluation labeled "Affect" by Milord and with the ratings on the scales assessing pleasingness and beauty, respectively. The dimension that accounted for the greatest portion of the variance in the preference judgments was positively correlated with ratings of pleasingness, attractiveness, and beauty as well as related to the factor connoting general evaluation. These results suggested therefore that physical attractiveness was one important dimension used by respondents when making their judgments.

Viewing attractiveness as a salient cue, it can be asked how this salience might influence stereotyping based on attractiveness? As noted earlier, it has been suggested that differential attention to attributes that are salient contributes to stereotyping (Hamilton, 1979; McArthur, 1982). Taylor and Fiske (1978), in their analysis of the literature on the effects of stimulus salience, reviewed findings from several areas of research concerning the relation between the amount of attention paid to a stimulus and the evaluation of that stimulus. These findings suggested that stimuli that were the focus of more attention received stronger evaluations. McArthur (1981) discussed research concerning the impact of a person's salience on evaluations of him or her and concluded that a variety of different salient attributes affected the extent to which individuals received more extreme evaluations. Considering this evidence, McArthur (1981, 1982) suggested that other physical characteristics, including high and low levels of attractiveness, should elicit evaluations that were more polarized. Because attractiveness stereotyping has a strong evaluative component, the effect of physical attractiveness on attention warrants investigation as another direction for future research that may help identify the underlying processes.

Finally, although the cognitive viewpoint and the social learning viewpoint have been discussed in separate sections here, the author of the present chapter regards these perspectives as complementary, not mutually exclusive. Each of these conceptual orientations can advance our understanding of why attractiveness stereotyping occurs.

Conclusions and Implications

As discussed in the first part of this chapter, the effect of an individual's physical attractiveness on initial impressions of her or him has been the focus of considerable attention in the research literature. Stereotyping based on attractiveness has been found across a wide range of age groups. These findings are, of course, inconsistent with the belief that judgments of people should not be influenced by this type of personal characteristic. Thus, evidence that physically attractive individuals are evaluated more favorably on a variety of dimensions (e.g., Dion et al., 1972; Ellis et al., 1983; Miller, 1970) is disconcerting. As Aronson (1969) observed a number of years ago when commenting on the relative lack of research then concerning the impact of attractiveness: "It may be that, at some levels, we would hate to find evidence indicating that beautiful women are better liked than homely women—somehow this seems undemocratic" (p. 160; also cited in Dion et al., 1972, p. 286). Although Aronson's comment focuses on the inequity of regarding attractive women more positively simply because of their appearance, findings that indicate that on certain traits attractive women are viewed less positively (e.g., Dermer & Thiel, 1975) are of course also discomfit-ing. In either case, judgments about an individual's personal characteristics are being made based on appearance. Thus the remarks of a perceptive 18th-century observer (Addison, 1711, 1961) are still pertinent, in particular, his noting the "Injustice we are guilty of towards one another, when we are prejudiced by the Looks and Features of those whom we do not know."

Given these concerns, what factors might be associated with a lessening of attractiveness stereotyping? The importance of examining why stereotyping based on physical attractiveness occurs becomes particularly apparent when one attempts to identify these factors. In their discussions of stereotyping, several writers have commented on the implications of conceptualizations of this process for attempts to modify and/or eliminate stereotypes. Reviewing the literature on ethnic stereotyping, Brigham (1971) noted that various approaches to changing stereotypes might be differentially effective depending on the basis for the ster-eotype. Hamilton (1979), when discussing the difficulty of changing stereotypes, contrasted the sociocultural with the cognitive perspective. He pointed out that in the former case, modifying stereotypes depended on cultural change, a relatively lengthy process. In the latter instance, he noted that various cognitive processes are useful in helping the individual cope with a complex environment; hence to the extent that stereotyping reflects these processes, it might be quite difficult to change. Although acknowledging this difficulty given a cognitively oriented view of stereotyping, McArthur (1982) proposed several approaches that might facilitate change.

In view of these issues, what strategies might be helpful in lessening the impact of physical attractiveness on impressions of others? One can hope that informing people (e.g., in textbooks, magazine, and newspaper articles) about research findings pertaining to stereotyping based on attractiveness will foster general awareness and concern. Considering a social learning perspective, find-ings concerning adults' impressions of infants and children who differ in physical attractiveness should be of particular interest to parents and teachers. Because it was suggested in a previous section of this chapter that early learning of the evaluative connotations associated with attractiveness is probably relatively in-formal and often incidental, awareness of the research literature may help to sensitize socializing agents to the role that they may play. Another direction for change involving social learning concerns the portrayal of individuals differing in physical attractiveness in various media. As discussed earlier, systematic study of how persons varying in attractiveness are depicted should be under-taken, because informal observation suggests that these portrayals may well differ.

The effect of knowledge about attractiveness stereotyping on individuals' subsequent judgments of others merits investigation, though it will be difficult to assess because awareness of this phenomenon could result in more socially desirable responses that might not necessarily reflect a reduction in the extent to which others' physical atttactiveness actually continues to affect impressions. When considering the potential impact of informing individuals about attractiveness stereotyping, a cognitively oriented view of stereotyping offers some insights. For example, McArthur (1982) proposed that attempts to weaken stereotyping might include techniques for encouraging greater flexibility in the manner in which people categorize others and also, providing other explanations for the behavior of individuals. Using the example of stereotyping based on attractiveness, McArthur suggested drawing people's attention to the importance of environmental factors (specifically, individuals' behavior towards others differing in attractiveness) as more useful in predicting the behavior of physically attractive versus unattractive persons than dispositional attributions. As noted by McArthur, however, there may be problems in achieving this objective given biases such as the "fundamental attribution error" discussed by Ross (1977).

The difficulty in changing particular features of social cognition by providing information about them was illustrated in an experiment conducted by Wetzel, Wilson, and Kort (1981). These investigators attempted to weaken the impact of the "halo effect" on first impressions by telling respondents (university students) in certain experimental conditions about this phenomenon before they saw and evaluated a stimulus person. Moreover, in one of the experimental conditions, participants were also told earlier empirical findings ostensibly indicated that "people with above average interpersonal sensitivity, intelligence, and creativity do *not* demonstrate the halo effect" (Wetzel et al., 1981, p. 430). This additional instructional set focusing on the social undesirability of the halo effect should have further weakened it. This information did not, however, affect the extent to which respondents' judgments were influenced by the halo effect. In summary, although information about attractiveness stereotyping hopefully will help to lessen the impact of a person's physical attractiveness on inferences about her or his other attributes, the preceding discussion notes some of the difficulties that may be associated with this approach.

ACKNOWLEDGMENT

The author would like to thank Mark Zanna for his thoughtful comments on an earlier draft of this chapter.

REFERENCES

Adams, G. R. (1977). Physical attractiveness research: Toward a developmental social psychology of beauty. *Human Development, 20,* 217–239.

Adams, G. R. (1978). Racial membership and physical attractiveness effects on preschool teachers' expectations. *Child Study Journal, 8,* 29–41.

Adams, G.R., & Crane, P. (1980). An assessment of parents' and teachers' expectations of preschool children's social preference for attractive or unattractive children and adults. *Child Development, 51,* 224–231.

Adams, G. R., & Huston, T. L. (1975). Social perception of middle-aged persons varying in physical attractiveness. *Developmental Psychology, 11,* 657–658.

Addison, J. (1961). The Spectator, Number 86 (June 8, 1711). In G. Smith (Ed.), *The Spectator* (Vol. 1). London: J. M. Dent.

Allport, G. (1954). *The nature of prejudice.* Reading, MA: Addison–Wesley.

Aronson, E. (1969). Some antecedents of interpersonal attraction. In W. J. Arnold, & D. Levine (Eds.), *Nebraska Symposium on Motivation, 17,* 143–177.

Barnlund, D. C. (1975). *Public and private self in Japan and the United States.* Tokyo: The Simul Press.

Bassili, J. N. (1981). The attractiveness stereotype: Goodness or glamour? *Basic and Applied Social Psychology, 2,* 235–252.

Berscheid, E., & Walster, E. (1974). Physical attractiveness. In L. Berkowitz (Ed.), *Advances in experimental social psychology* (Vol. 7). New York: Academic Press.

Berscheid, E., Walster, E., & Bohrnstedt, G. (1973). The happy American body: A survey report. *Psychology Today, 7,* 119–131.

Brigham, J. C. (1971). Ethnic stereotypes. *Psychological Bulletin, 76,* 15–38.

Corter, C., Trehub, S., Boukydis, C., Ford, L., Celhoffer, L., & Minde, K. (1978). Nurses' judgments of the attractiveness of premature infants. *Infant Behavior and Development, 1,* 373–380.

Curry, W. (1972). *The Middle English ideal of personal beauty.* New York: AMS Press. [Reprinted from the 1916 edition, Baltimore: J.H. Furst].

Dermer, M., & Thiel, D. L. (1975). When beauty may fail. *Journal of Personality and Social Psychology, 31,* 1168–1176.

Dion, K. K. (1972). Physical attractiveness and evaluation of children's transgressions. *Journal of Personality and Social Psychology, 24,* 207–213.

Dion, K. K., Berscheid, E., & Walster, E. (1972). What is beautiful is good. *Journal of Personality and Social Psychology, 24,* 285–290.

Ellis, R. J., Olson, J. M., & Zanna, M. P. (1983). Stereotypic personality inferences following objective versus subjective judgments of beauty. *Canadian Journal of Behavioural Science, 15,* 35–42.

Ford, C. S., & Beach, F. A. (1951). *Patterns of sexual behavior.* New York: Harper.

Hamilton, D. L. (1979). A cognitive-attributional analysis of stereotyping. In L. Berkowitz (Ed.), *Advances in experimental social psychology* (Vol. 12). New York: Academic Press.

Hildebrandt, K. A., & Fitzgerald, H. E. (1978). Adults' responses to infants varying in perceived cuteness. *Behavioural Processes, 3,* 159–172.

Hildebrandt, K. A., & Fitzgerald, H. E. (1981). Mothers' responses to infant physical appearance. *Infant Mental Health Journal, 2,* 56–61.

Jackson, D. N., & Minton, H. L. (1963). A forced-choice adjective preference scale for personality assessment. *Psychological Reports, 12,* 515–520.

Kleck, R. E., Richardson, S. A., & Ronald, L. (1974). Physical appearance cues and interpersonal attraction in children. *Child Development, 45,* 305–310.

Langlois, J. H., & Stephan, C. (1977). The effects of physical attractiveness and ethnicity on children's behavioral attributions and peer preferences. *Child Development, 48,* 1694–1698.

Langlois, J. H., & Stephan, C. W. (1981). Beauty and the beast: The role of physical attractiveness in the development of peer relations and social behavior. In S. S. Brehm, S. M. Kassin, & F. X.

Gibbons (Eds.), *Developmental social psychology: Theory and research.* New York: Oxford University Press.

Livesley, W. J., & Bromley, D. (1973). *Person perception in childhood and adolescence.* London: Wiley.

McArthur, L. Z. (1981). What grabs you? The role of attention in impression formation and causal attribution. In E. T. Higgins, C. P. Herman, & M. P. Zanna (Eds.), *Social cognition: The Ontario Symposium* (Vol. 1). Hillsdale, NJ: Lawrence Erlbaum Associates.

McArthur, L. Z. (1982). Judging a book by its cover: A cognitive analysis of the relationship between physical appearance and stereotyping. In A. Hastorf, & A. Isen (Eds.), *Cognitive social psychology.* New York: Elsevier North Holland.

Merton, R. K. (1949, 1957, 1968). The self-fulfilling prophecy. In *Social theory and social structure.* New York: Free Press.

Miller, A. (1970). Role of physical attractiveness in impression formation. *Psychonomic Science, 19,* 241–243.

Milord, J. T. (1978). Aesthetic aspects of faces: A (somewhat) phenomenological analysis using multidimensional scaling methods. *Journal of Personality and Social Psychology, 36,* 205–216.

Rosenblatt, P. C. (1974). Cross-cultural perspective on attraction. In T. L. Huston (Ed.), *Foundations of interpersonal attraction.* New York: Academic Press.

Rosenblatt, P. C., & Cozby, P. C. (1972). Courtship patterns associated with freedom of choice of spouse. *Journal of Marriage and the Family, 34,* 689–695.

Ross, L. (1977). The intuitive psychologist and his shortcomings: Distortions in the attribution process. In L. Berkowtiz (Ed.), *Advances in experimental social psychology* (Vol. 10). New York: Academic Press.

Salvia, J., Sheare, J. B., & Algozzine, B. (1975). Facial attractiveness and personal–social development. *Journal of Abnormal Child Psychology, 3,* 171–178.

Sampson, E. E. (1977). Psychology and the American ideal. *Journal of Personality and Social Psychology, 35,* 767–782.

Snyder, M., Tanke, E. D., & Berscheid, E. (1977). Social perception and interpersonal behavior: On the self-fulfilling nature of social stereotypes. *Journal of Personality and Social Psychology, 35,* 656–666.

Stephan, C. W., & Langlois, J. H. (1984). Baby beautiful: Adult attributions of infant competence as a function of infant attractiveness. *Child Development, 55,* 576–585.

Steward, M. S., Furuya, T., Steward, D. S., & Ikeda, A. (1982). Japanese and American children's drawings of the outside and inside of their bodies. *Journal of Cross-Cultural Psychology, 13,* 87–104.

Taylor, S. E., & Fiske, S. T. (1978). Salience, attention, and attribution: Top of the head phenomena. In L. Berkowitz (Ed.), *Advances in experimental social psychology* (Vol. 11). New York: Academic Press.

Wetzel, C. G., Wilson, T. D., & Kort, J. (1981). The halo effect revisited: Forewarned is not forearmed. *Journal of Experimental Social Psychology, 17,* 427–439.

From the Eye of the Beholder to Behavioral Reality: Development of Social Behaviors and Social Relations as a Function of Physical Attractiveness

2

Judith H. Langlois
University of Texas at Austin

> . . . *an ugly baby is a very nasty object. . ."*
> —(Queen Victoria, 1859, cited in Fulford, 1964).

In this statement, Queen Victoria, who bore nine children, articulates what many adults believe (but rarely admit to believing) about young infants. She expresses a commonly held stereotype that there is an important connection between inner and outer beauty. Like Queen Victoria, we (Langlois & Downs, 1979; Langlois & Stephan, 1981) and others (Adams, 1977; Berscheid & Walster, 1974) argue that this stereotype can have important implications for development through a process of behavioral confirmation (Snyder & Swann, 1978). In this process, we posit that differing levels of attractiveness[1] elicit a clear and pervasive set of stereotypic behavioral expectations: Attractive children are thought to possess and exhibit more positive traits and behaviors than unattractive children. Such behavioral expectations are then supposed to lead to actual differences in the behavior of attractive and unattractive children because adults and peers treat them in a manner consistent with these stereotyped expectations. The focus of this chapter is to further explicate this theoretical account of how and why appearance may be quite important in the socialization process. Thus, the chapter proposes to evaluate Queen Victoria's "theory" about ugly babies.

Theoretical Overview

The conceptual framework underlying our view that appearance can influence development is an organismic (e.g., Bell & Harper, 1977; Lerner, 1976) and

---

[1]The research to be discussed in this chapter is limited to that concerning facial attractiveness. For a review of research dealing with body build characteristics, see Sorell and Nowak (1981).

transactional (e.g., Sameroff, 1975) model of development. In this framework, certain developmental outcomes are seen as the consequence of transactions and interactions between individuals and their social world. To the extent that appearance influences such social transactions, it can directly and indirectly influence social, personality, and perhaps intellectual development.

When this framework is applied to children, their parents, and peers, they are seen as agents affecting each other through reciprocal interchanges that are strongly influenced by the attitudes and expectations of the participants. Parental attitudes and behaviors toward their children reflect the expectations they hold for the current and future behavior and competence of the child. Children contribute significantly to their own development by coming into the world "equipped" with characteristics that elicit or consolidate the expectations of the parent. Thus, in this account, the socialization process consists of a series of intricate transactions in which parental expectations are elicited by characteristics and behaviors of the infant. These expectations will influence, in turn, how the parent treats the child. Such treatment will modify or create behavior and characteristics in the child that will then serve as a determinant of subsequent parental attitudes, expectations, and treatment, and so forth.

In the sections that follow, the empirical evidence pertinent to each component of this theoretical model is discussed in turn. Differential expectations of attractive and unattractive infants and children by adults and peers are considered first. This is followed by a discussion of individual characteristics and individual difference variables that are proposed to be important mediators of behavioral expectations. Differential treatment of attractive and unattractive children is the third element of the model to be explicated. Finally, the development of differential behavior as a function of appearance is considered.

Differential Expectations

Ethologists (e.g., Rosenblatt, 1970) have frequently noted that physical characteristics of infants of many nonhuman species can elicit and then maintain maternal behavior. The distinctive coloration or coat patterns of the young of many primate species, for example, elicit nurturance and care giving from adults (Alley, 1980). Indeed, Lorenz (1943) has suggested that specific physical characteristics of human infants—termed *babyish* features—can elicit innate and universal forms of care giving and positive affective responses in human adults. Further, that adult reactions vary as a function of the extent to which infants possess these physical characteristics is supported by the fact that such individual differences in infant babyishness predict adult evaluations of the infant's cuteness (Alley, 1981). Like Lorenz, we propose that the appearance of the human infant or child serves as a sign stimulus that releases differential expectations and affective reactions in the adult care giver. Thus, based on Queen Victoria's comment about ugly, nasty babies, we would predict that the infant she was referring to was indeed unattractive and that this infant's appearance elicited her negative expectations.

Adult Expectations.   There are considerable data available indicating that adults do indeed have such stereotyped views of the attractive and unattractive preschool and older child. Dion (1972) was one of the first to impressively demonstrate the role of attractiveness in adults' expectations for children's interpersonal behaviors. She gave adult women photographs of unfamiliar attractive and unattractive children along with a description of a transgression each child had allegedly committed. The women evaluated a transgression more negatively when it was committed by an unattractive than by an attractive child. In addition, a severe transgression was believed to be a reflection of an enduring, antisocial personality characteristic when committed by an unattractive child. In contrast, the attractive child committing the same offense was believed to be merely having an "off" day. A similar study by Rich (1975), however, obtained equivocal results when teachers rather than college women were asked to evaluate unfamiliar attractive and unattractive children. Attractive children generally received more favorable personality evaluations, but transgressions committed by unattractive children were not viewed more negatively.

Adults also hold differential expectations for the academic ability and performance of attractive and unattractive children. Clifford and Walster (1973) asked fifth-grade teachers to rate unfamiliar children on the basis of identical report cards, to which a small photograph was attached. The teachers rated attractive children as more intelligent, likely to achieve more education, and to have parents more interested in their education. These expectation data were replicated in a later study (Clifford, 1975) and similar data for elementary-school-age children have been reported by Adams (1978), Adams and Cohen (1976), and Ross and Salvia (1975).

Not only do adults hold stereotyped views of the competence and performance of school-age children but they also hold such expectations for even very young infants. Early and consistent elicitation of differential attitudes held by adults toward infants and children is an important precondition for the viability of our proposed developmental model. Suggestive data indicating that attractiveness is important early on were provided by Corter, Trehub, Bonkydis, Ford, Celhoffer, and Minde (1975). They collected attractiveness ratings and developmental prognoses from nurses attending a small sample of premature infants. Consistent with the findings for older children, infant attractiveness and intellectual prognoses were very highly related.

More systematic data have recently been reported from our laboratory (Stephan & Langlois, 1984). To determine at what age children first elicit differential expectations from adults as a function of their appearance, a sample of Black, Caucasian, and Mexican–American adults rated photographs of unfamiliar Black, Caucasian, and Mexican–American infants at three time periods in the first year of life: immediately after birth, at age 3 months, and at age 9 months. The adults were asked to assess each infant on 12 bipolar adjectives. The adjectives were reduced to four dimensions of infant behavior and competence, and a strong "beauty-is-good" (Dion, Berscheid, & Walster, 1972) stereotype was associated with three of these. For the dimension labeled *good baby*, very attractive infants were generally seen as the "best" baby at each of the three time points. The results for the "smart–likeable" baby variable showed that very attractive 3- and 9-month-olds were seen as more smart and likeable than unattractive infants. Similarly, results for both 3- and 9-month-olds on the measure labeled *causes parents problems* indicated that unattractive babies were seen as causing their parents more problems than attractive infants.

In addition to the finding that adults view even young infants differently as a function of the infant's level of attractiveness, Stephan and Langlois (1984) found that the attractiveness of the infant was a stronger predictor of adult behavioral attributions than was the infant's ethnicity: Attractive babies, regardless of race, were typically rated as "better" by adults from all ethnic groups. Thus, strong and consistent expectations for the behavior of attractive and unattractive individuals seem to be elicited at or soon after birth in Caucasian as well as non-Caucasian populations.

Finally, not only do adults have differential expectations for the behavior of unfamiliar infants and children, but even parents seem to hold behavioral stereotypes for their own children. In two related studies, Adams and Crane (1980) showed that parents, particularly mothers, expected their children to make behavioral attributions and social choices consistent with the beauty-is-good stereotype. These maternal expectations were, in turn, significantly correlated with the child's actual use of the stereotype, at least in this laboratory situation.

Peer Expectations.   The peer group, another influential socializing agent, (Hartup, 1983) has also been found to evaluate other children on the basis of physical attractiveness. Dion (1973) found that when compared with attractive children, unfamiliar unattractive children were rated by preschoolers as hitting without good reason, scaring the child raters, and likely to hurt the child raters. Attractive children were viewed as children who did not hit, who did not like to fight or shout, and who were friendly to other children. In addition, attractive children were significantly preferred as potential friends.

Such preferences for attractive peers seem to transcend race. Langlois and Stephan (1977) asked 6- and 10-year-old black, Caucasian, and Mexican–American children to make behavioral attributions and liking choices about attractive and unattractive children from these same three ethnic groups. Attractive children from all three ethnic groups were liked better, were rated as smarter and more prosocial, and were rated as less antisocial than were the unattractive children. Like the Stephan and Langlois (1984) study on infants, physical attractiveness was a more salient predictor of the children's evaluations than was ethnicity. Compatible results for 9- to 14-year-old boys have been reported by Kleck, Richardson, and Ronald (1974) in their investigation of the relationship between appearance and sociometric status in an ethnically diverse summer camp.

In addition to the Kleck et al. (1974) study, a number of other investigations have examined the role of attractiveness in peer relationships among children who are acquainted with each other. Such data are important and necessary to determine whether attractiveness is used as an evaluative cue only during the initial stage of social interaction or whether children continue to use appearance in their playmate evaluation and selection even after they are well acquainted. Both commonsense and theories of interpersonal attraction (e.g., Duck, 1973) would suggest that attractiveness should decrease in salience and importance as the acquaintance process develops and more information is acquired about the individual. Perhaps surprisingly, this does not seem to be the case: Attractiveness and positive evaluations, particularly for girls, are frequently associated even in children who know each other.

In the prototypic study of this type, Dion and Berscheid (1974) asked pre-schoolers to nominate familiar classmates they liked and disliked and to indicate which of their peers exhibited specific antisocial and prosocial behaviors. The children in the class were rated by unfamiliar adult judges for physical attractiveness. Attractive children were seen by their classmates as more self-sufficient and independent than unattractive children; in contrast, unattractive children, particularly boys, were seen as more aggressive and antisocial. Attractive children were also more popular and were selected more often as "liked" than unattractive children, with the exception of unattractive younger girls who were liked more. Similarly, Lerner and Lerner (1977) found that fourth- and sixth-grade children viewed attractive classmates more positively than unattractive ones. Low to moderate correlations between attractiveness and classmate popularity have also been reported by Cavior and Dokecki (1973), Kleck et al. (1974), and Salvia, Sheare, and Algozzine (1975). These data suggest, then, that the importance of attractiveness as an evaluative social cue is not limited to first impressions for preschool- and elementary-school-age children.

Mediating Variables and Individual Differences in Behavioral Expectations

Although all the data reviewed thus far yield fairly consistent and straightforward attractiveness effects on behavioral expectations, the picture is, in actuality, more complex. At least under certain circumstances, a number of individual difference and situational variables can mediate the effects of attractiveness on the expectancy formed for and by any particular individual.

Gender.   One such mediating variable is gender. Attractiveness seems to provide a consistent social advantage for girls but not for boys.[2] With only a few exceptions—and those only for very young ages (Dion & Berscheid, 1974; Langlois & Styczynski, 1979)—attractive girls are typically seen as more popular and are viewed more positively than their unattractive female peers by both acquainted and unacquainted age-mates (e.g., Dion, 1973; Dion & Berscheid, 1974; Langlois & Stephan, 1977; Langlois & Styczynski, 1979). Attractive boys, however, are not always rated more highly than unattractive boys, particularly by raters who know them. Langlois and Styczynski (1979) found that attractive preschool- and elementary-school-age boys were more frequently selected by their classmates as antisocial, incompetent, and disliked than were their unattractive male peers.[3] In a study comparing the behavioral attributions made by acquainted and unacquainted preschoolers, Styczynski and Langlois (1977) found that although unacquainted children of both sexes and acquainted girls generally evaluated same-age peers using the beauty-is-good stereotype, acquainted boys believed that their attractive classmates were more incompetent and less popular than unattractive peers. Similarly, Vaughn and Langlois (1983) reported that attractiveness and popularity were much more highly correlated for girls than for boys in a sample of acquainted preschoolers. Thus, from these three studies it would appear that acquainted children, particularly boys, do not necessarily view attractive children (again, particularly boys) more positively than unattractive ones. In a longitudinal study designed to examine these gender differences, Langlois and Vaughn (1983), noted that once again attractiveness was not related to social *acceptance* in acquainted preschool boys although it was negatively related to social *rejection* for these boys. The correlations for girls, on the other hand, showed that attractiveness was consistently related to acceptance but not to rejection.

There are then, a number of studies suggesting that the effects of attractiveness on children's behavioral expectations and liking are mediated by gender. Attractiveness by gender interactions are revealed most consistently in studies in

---

[2]Whether attractiveness is a long-term advantage for girls is debatable. In addition to data suggesting that beautiful women may at times be perceived as intimidating (e.g., Stokes & Bickman, 1974), and egoistic (e.g., Dermer & Thiel, 1975), other data indicate that attractive women may be suspicious of the sincerity of praise in face-to-face situations (Sigall & Michela, 1976). Both very attractive and very unattractive women may in fact come to believe that they have little impact on their environment because they are responded to frequently on the basis of their appearance rather than their competence.

[3]At the same time, however, the classmates of these attractive boys evaluated them as more popular and more prosocial, that is, attractive boys were seen as both increasingly liked and disliked, prosocial and antisocial, and competent and incompetent. Such data suggest the possibility that the behavior of attractive boys may be more salient and thus noticed more readily whether these boys are behaving in a positive or negative manner. This hypothesis is consistent with data showing that photographs of attractive children receive more visual attention from preschoolers than do photographs of unattractive children (Dion, 1977).

which children are rated by their own classmates (e.g., Langlois & Styczynski, 1979; Vaughn & Langlois, 1983) although there are exceptions to this pattern (Dion & Berscheid, 1974; Kleck et al., 1974; Lerner & Lerner, 1977). The longitudinal results of Langlois and Vaughn (1983) suggest that the discrepancy between these sets of findings may be accounted for by the timing of the assessment and by the type of assessment employed (e.g., acceptance vs. rejection).

Although the existence of a gender by attractiveness interaction warrants further research and clarification, several hypotheses can be offered as potential explanations for the finding that familiarity and beauty may sometimes breed contempt for boys on the part of their peers. First, attractive boys may be preferred, treated more leniently, and allowed to engage in antisocial behavior by adult socialization agents. For example, Dion (1974) has shown that when adult females monitor a child's performance on a picture-matching task and then administer penalties to the child for incorrect responses, they behave more leniently toward attractive boys than toward attractive girls or unattractive children of both sexes. Such preferential treatment and the resulting antisocial behavior could thus reduce the likeability of the attractive boy by their familiar classmates who have to put up with such "bad" behavior. In two studies of teacher expectations (Kehle, Bramble, & Mason, 1974; Kehle, Ware, & Guidubaldi, 1976), attractive boys were in fact rated as more uncontrolled, impulsive, and unpredictable relative to unattractive boys whereas the girls were rated in a manner consistent with the beauty-is-good stereotype.

A second hypothesis suggests that attractive boys possess behaviors that are "unattractive" to their peers but in a very different manner than that suggested by the first hypothesis. Langlois and Downs (1979), in a study of the behavioral correlates of attractiveness in preschoolers, found that attractive children of both sexes were less active and were more likely to play with quiet, feminine-sex-stereotyped toys than were unattractive children. Given prevailing sex-role stereotypes and attitudes exhibited even by very young children (Kuhn, Nash, & Brucken, 1978), "prettier" boys, although initially liked, may become less desirable as friends and perceived more negatively over the course of the school year when their male peers actually choose playmates for their rough and active games and activities. Indeed, sex-role stereotypes could function to reinforce the importance of attractiveness for girls while mitigating its impact on boys because unattractive males are perceived as having more opportunities and abilities than females to compensate for their appearance (Miller, 1970).

Cognitive Mediators.   Both the degree and the ways in which individuals form and use expectancies as a function of appearance may be associated with a number of variables related to cognition and cognitive development. Some individuals may evoke stereotypes more readily and more frequently than others when processing social information (e.g., Nisbett & Ross, 1980; Tversky & Kahneman, 1973, 1974). There are currently few data that address this issue with respect to attractiveness stereotypes, but there is no reason to expect that differences in information-processing strategies would be different for stereotypes associated with attractiveness than for other stereotypes.

Two relevant adult studies investigated the relationship between sex-role stereotyping and liking for attractive and unattractive individuals. Touhey (1979) asked college students to complete a scale assessing their degree of traditional sex-role stereotyping and to indicate how much they thought they would like an attractive or unattractive target person. Both males and females who received high scores on the sex-role stereotyping scale reported more liking for the attractive target person than did low-stereotyping individuals. Likewise, Anderson and Bem (1981) found that in contrast to androgynous individuals, sex-typed males and females were rated by blind judges as being more responsive toward allegedly attractive than allegedly unattractive targets. These data suggest that adults who are more highly stereotyped on one dimension of behavior or personality are more likely to stereotype and to use attractiveness in making judgments about others.

Further, stereotype-prone individuals may be more inclined to treat the attractive and unattractive differently, with attractive partners receiving preferential treatment. Although no relevant empirical research is yet available, Sameroff (1975) provides an example of how such individual differences in the tendency to stereotype can influence the expectancies of parents for their children. In one mode of thinking described by Sameroff, mothers differentiate characteristics of the child into domains of attributes related to the child's appearance, personality, and intelligence. This type of differentiation contributes to a static view of the child's characteristics according to Sameroff (1975):

> The child is seen as maintaining the same position on these dimensions throughout life and is given a value according to prevalent social norms. The ugly, ignorant, and obnoxious child is seen as remaining so for the rest of its years. Conversely, the beautiful, intelligent, personable child is viewed as remaining equally wonderful throughout life. (p. 70)

Individual differences in children's readiness to stereotype have not been thoroughly researched. Rather, the focus has been on age or stage differences in person perception, with cognitive-developmental theory (Piaget, 1970) providing the major theoretical backdrop for much of the work in this area. From this point of view, young children should be even more likely than adults to use physical attractiveness in evaluating others. According to Piaget (1970), the perceptual evaluations of young children override other strategies because their attention is fixed or centered on the visible, concrete, physical characteristics of objects or persons. They focus on the appearance of things and judge what is good or right on the basis of what looks good (Malerstein & Ahern, 1982). Numerous studies have documented the importance of physical characteristics in the descriptions and evaluations of liked and disliked peers (e.g., Austin & Thompson, 1948; Brierley, 1966; Flapan, 1968; Little, 1968; Watts, 1944; Yarrow & Campbell, 1963). A particularly compelling example of the importance of appearance on the social cognition of children is provided by Livesley and Bromley (1973). In spite of specific instructions not to use information about appearance in describing their friends, statements about appearance were used by all children (ages 7 to 15) and were the primary descriptors used by younger children.

With some exceptions (Cavior & Dokecki, 1973; Duck, 1975; Little, 1968), there has been little work done on the role of attractiveness on stereotyping and behavior during the adolescent period. This is surprising given the great concern most adolescents seem to feel about their appearance. Although the adolescent possesses the cognitive skills required to decenter and override perceptual evaluations, other developmental issues arise that suggest that appearance may become even more potent as a determinant of social evaluation and relations. First, as a result of newly developed abstract, formal operational reasoning ability, adolescents can now examine and think about their own thinking. Indeed, adolescents typically spend so much time thinking about their own thoughts that their newly developed formal operational skills are limited by this new form of centration. Such preoccupation leads to what Elkind (1967) has described as adolescent egocentrism.

The egocentric adolescent does not distinguish between his/her own thoughts and those of others; the adolescent assumes that peers, parents, and teachers are as obsessed with his or her appearance and behavior as he or she is (Elkind, 1967). Further, because of the rapid physiological/maturational changes that occur during this developmental period, the adolescent is likely to be especially concerned and vigilant about appearances. Indeed, because a major developmental task of adolescence is accepting one's body and appearance (Havighurst, 1972), physical attractiveness should assume a more central role in evaluating and liking others for the adolescent than even for children and adults.

Similarity.   Research with children has made little attempt to examine the influence of the subject's level of physical attractiveness on his or her evaluations of target children. The adult literature, however, suggests that the subject's level of attractiveness may well influence both behavioral expectations and liking for others. Two effects based on the subject's physical attractiveness have been distinguished. The first is that individuals who are similar in attractiveness tend to affiliate with each other (e.g., Berscheid et al., 1971; Huston, 1973; Stroebe, Insko, Thompson, & Layton, 1971). Both Murstein (1972) and Silverman (1971) found highly similar levels of attractiveness among dating partners, whereas Cash and Derlega (1978) have reported similar findings for adult same-sex friendships. Two studies suggest the existence of a second effect: jealousy. Dermer and Thiel (1975) state: "physically unattractive women may, for a number of reasons, most likely carry well-honed hatchets for attractive female targets'' (p. 1169). These authors found that, whereas both average and attractive women rated attractive female targets as having more socially desirable personalities than unattractive targets, unattractive women did not. Indicating that hatchets are not confined to the female sex, Tennis and Dabbs (1975) reported that less attractive males assigned lower attractiveness ratings to targets than did more attractive males.

The scant evidence that is available suggests that similarity of the subject's and the target's level of physical attractiveness may also be an influential determinant of interpersonal behaviors for very young children. Langlois and Downs (1979) examined behaviors emitted by and toward attractive and unattractive same-sex preschoolers and found that the level of attractiveness of both types of children in the dyad was important in the expression of behavior. Both attractive and unattractive children exhibited higher levels of positive social behavior when paired with peers who were similar in levels of attractiveness than when paired with peers dissimilar in attractiveness. Such data are consistent with previous reports suggesting that peers who are paired on the basis of similarity of gender and age exhibit differential levels of social behavior than when they are paired with peers who are not similar on these dimensions (Jacklin & Maccoby, 1978; Langlois, Gottfried, Barnes, & Hendricks, 1978; Langlois, Gottfried, & Seay, 1973).

The adult data (e.g., Berscheid et al., 1971; Cash & Derlega, 1978; Dermer & Thiel, 1975; Tennis & Dabbs, 1975) and the Langlois and Downs (1979) preschool data indicate that similarity of physical attractiveness may influence physical attractiveness ratings, behavioral expectations, as well as behaviors directed toward attractive and unattractive targets. Identifying the precise impact of similarity of physical attractiveness is worthy of future examination because it has important implications for interactions occurring in real world settings. For example, a very beautiful mother may hold different attitudes about the importance of attractiveness for her children than a less attractive mother. Consequently, the unattractive child of a beautiful mother may be treated differently than an equally unattractive child of an unattractive mother. Likewise, the highly attractive younger sibling of a less attractive firstborn may receive treatment from the sibling consistent with the "jealousy" hypothesis proposed by Dermer and Thiel (1975); a less attractive younger sibling, on the other hand, may not. A developmental approach to this issue seems particularly useful because there are developmental differences in role-taking abilities and in children's comprehension of similarity (Shantz, 1975). We might expect, then, that similarity of attractiveness may have a differential impact on evaluations of others at different stages of development.

Although another form of similarity—physical resemblance—has received almost no research attention, from a developmental point of view it should be an important mediator of expectations and behaviors. The degree to which a child shares physical features with or looks like the parent may significantly influence how a parent reacts to that child. Parents may be more likely to identify with and perhaps to overestimate the attractiveness of children who possess physical characteristics similar to their own. Sappenfield and Balogh (1970) provide empirical support for this point. They found that adults perceived others who possessed physically similar attributes to themselves as being more attractive than did dissimilar appearing adults. From a sociobiological perspective, parental solicitude toward the young should be related to the likelihood and degree of genetic relatedness (Barash, 1977). Adults may, therefore, favor those offspring who resemble them because their genetic relationship is obvious. This may be especially true for fathers because physical resemblance is the only way for a father to be sure of paternity of the infant.

Contrast Effects. The last[4] mediating influence to be considered concerns the effect of judging the attractiveness of a particular child in terms of his/her attractiveness relative to other children to whom the adult has been previously exposed. For example, if a couple has an unusually attractive firstborn child, a secondborn of average attractiveness may be perceived as relatively unattractive. Further, the mass media may influence parental appearance expectations by continuously portraying highly attractive "Gerber" babies. Kenrick and Gutierres (1980) have suggested that such exposure would produce high adaptation levels (e.g., Helson, 1964) and would result in lowered evaluations of most individuals. In three empirical demonstrations of this contrast effect, Kenrick and Gutierres (1980) showed that adults who had been exposed to television programs depicting highly attractive females (e.g., "Charlie's Angels"), rated a target female as significantly less attractive than did control groups without such prior exposure.

As we have seen, the existence and operation of appearance-based stereotypes in both adults and children are well documented. Both the research and theory, however, suggest that expectations for and reactions to the attractive and unattractive child are mediated by characteristics of both the perceiver (e.g., similarity) and the target (e.g., gender). Any account, therefore, of how attractiveness can influence a particular child's development must consider such mediating variables (see Langlois & Stephan, 1981 for an extended discussion of this point). Thus, in making predictions about the development of Queen Victoria's infant, it is important to know not only what the baby looks like but also how stereotyped the Queen's own thinking is. It is important to know whether the baby looks like the Queen, her husband, older siblings, and whether the infant is male or female because princes and princesses may well encounter different paths of socialization.

---

[4]This list of mediating variables is not meant to be exhaustive. Rather, it represents those influences most relevant to the developmental approach endorsed here.

Differential Treatment and Socialization

Once the expectations for the attractive and unattractive child have been elicited, the developmental model presented here specifies that these expectations will guide behavior toward children in a manner consistent with these expectations. The "good" and expected behavior of the attractive child will be noticed and reacted to in a favorable manner whereas the similar but unexpected behavior of the unattractive child may be ignored and perhaps even punished. The model assumes that most individuals are largely unaware of both their differential expectations for and treatment of the attractive and the unattractive. Rather, the cognitive processing involved in forming expectations and guiding behavior is automatic (Neisser, 1967) and not available to direct introspection. Judgments and behavior directed toward the attractive and unattractive are assumed here to be made primarily on the basis of apriori implicit causal theories (Nisbett & Wilson, 1977) or unconscious primitive beliefs (Bem, 1970).

Compared with the extensive literature on differential expectations associated with physical attractiveness, only limited data are available to evaluate the differential treatment component of the developmental model. There are two types of studies addressing the issue of differential treatment: those of adults directing behavior toward attractive and unattractive children who are unrelated to them and those of adults directing behavior toward their own children.

Adults' Treatment of Unrelated Children.   There have been several important laboratory studies of the behavior of adults toward unfamiliar attractive and unattractive children. In a seminal study, Dion (1974) asked college women to watch an interaction between an experimenter and a child who was made to appear either physically attractive or unattractive. The women were told that they would be monitoring a child's performance on a picture-matching task and that their task was to administer penalties (take away pennies) for incorrect responses. In reality, the women viewed one of four previously prepared videotapes in which either an 8-year-old boy or girl were made up to appear either more or less attractive. Each tape portrayed the child in the same predetermined sequence of correct and incorrect responses. A gender by attractiveness interaction was found: These women treated attractive boys more leniently than either attractive girls or unattractive children of both sexes. A second study was then conducted to determine whether males would behave differentially toward attractive and unattractive boys or girls. No differences were obtained in this second study, suggesting that the effect of appearance in eliciting differential treatment may be mediated by both the gender of the target child and that of the socializing adult.

Berkowitz and Frodi (1979) conducted two laboratory studies compatible with those reported by Dion (1974). In both investigations, college women punished unattractive girls (Study 1) and unattractive boys (Study 2) more severely than attractive children in a role-playing situation in which the women were asked to behave as if they were the child's parent. Further, in both studies, one group of women was deliberately provoked by a confederate who made disparaging remarks about the subjects' intelligence and personality. Berkowitz and Frodi (1979) reported a nonsignificant tendency for women in the provocation condition to be especially harsh toward unattractive children after presumably becoming angry as a result of their prior aversive experience. To the extent that aversive stimuli facilitate aggressive reactions in real world settings, these findings could have important implications for unattractive children. In families that experience significant levels of stress and marital discord, the presence of a relatively unattractive child may prompt intense punishment on the part of the parent. Familial stress and discord are certainly aversive and unpleasant and are certainly related to child maltreatment (Garbarino & Crouter, 1978). Thus, it may be that unattractive children in these families are selected more frequently than their attractive siblings as the object of displaced aggression and perhaps abuse.

Three studies by Hildebrandt and her colleagues (Hildebrandt & Fitzgerald, 1978, 1981; Power, Hildebrandt, & Fitzgerald, 1982) have investigated adult behavioral responses to photographs of unfamiliar infants varying in rated "cuteness." In each study, photographs of infants were shown to either nonparent college students (Hildebrandt & Fitzgerald, 1978; Power, Hildebrandt, & Fitzgerald, 1982) or to women who had at least one child (Hildebrandt & Fitzgerald, 1981). A variety of behavioral and physiological assessments were recorded: looking time, smiling, length of time between heart beats, and skin conductance responses. In all three studies, looking time, but not the other assessments, differentiated the photographs. Adults looked longer at infants perceived as cuter.

Although these results are consistent with Dion's (1977) study showing that preschoolers also look longer at photographs of attractive children, the generality of the results of these three infant studies is open to question for two reasons. First, the photographs used in all three studies were selected from the same group of infants (Power, Hildebrandt, & Fitzgerald, 1982). This suggests the possibility that the results are characteristic only of this one sample of infants. More problematic is the fact that, in each study, looking time was assessed in relation to each adult's individual cuteness rating of each infant rather than in relation to a group cuteness rating averaged across raters. Although attractiveness ratings are, in general, similar and quite robust when averaged across raters (see Hildebrandt, 1982), there can be substantial disagreements between particular individuals (e.g., Vaughn & Langlois, 1983). Therefore, it is not clear whether the observed relationship between looking time and cuteness is a general or idiosyncratic phenomenon. Indeed, in one of these three studies (Hildebrandt & Fitzgerald, 1981) adults did not differentiate between more and less attractive infants when group cuteness ratings were employed.

Teachers.   There are few well-designed studies that have examined teachers' behavior toward attractive and unattractive children. This is surprising and unfortunate given the evidence that, under certain circumstances, teacher expectations can profoundly affect children's school performance and behavior (e.g., Brophy & Good, 1974). Only one study has attempted to evaluate the relationship between a child's level of attractiveness and his/her teacher's daily behavior toward him/her. Adams and Cohen (1974) asked observers to record verbatim the content of all teacher–student interactions occurring during three 30-minute sessions conducted over a 6-month period of time. Students and teachers in three classrooms (kindergarten, fourth, and seventh grades) were observed. For the older (seventh grade) but not the younger children, a child's level of attractiveness was positively related to the amount of interaction with the teachers.

The usefulness of these data is compromised, however, by several problems. First, the grade by attractiveness interaction cannot be easily interpreted because grade and teachers were confounded. Since only one teacher was observed at each grade level, any conclusions about teachers in general or about age effects are limited. Further, the attractiveness ratings used in the assessment of the relation between teacher behavior and child attractiveness were made by the teachers themselves. Thus, for each child in the study, there is only a single attractiveness rating; That is likely to be confounded with other teacher evaluations of the children as well as being quite idiosyncratic. Although little information can be extracted from this study concerning the effects of attractiveness on teachers' interactions with their students, it could be of heuristic value to future studies in this difficult area of research.

Several studies have examined the relationship between a child's level of attractiveness and grades assigned to them by teachers. Although neither Styczynski (1976) nor Maruyama and Miller (1981) found differences in grades to be a function of attractiveness, two studies have reported such an association. Lerner and Lerner (1977) found low but significant correlations between attractiveness and grades given by teachers to fourth- and sixth-graders. Two methods were used to determine the attractiveness ratings of each child: a "live" rating given by the experimenter and the average rating of a group of 97 college students. Both methods yielded the significant, positive association. Felson (1980) similarly reported that teachers assigned higher grades to attractive children in a national sample of over 2000 10th-grade boys.

In one last study, Barocas and Black (1974) reported on the effects of children's attractiveness on teacher referrals. They found that attractive children were more frequently referred by their teachers for psychological, speech, reading, and learning disability assessments than were unattractive children. Because these referrals were for remedial services and help rather than for the control of behavior problems, Barocas and Black concluded that these teachers were more willing to help attractive than unattractive children.

Parental Treatment and Behavior.   That there are only a few studies on parental treatment and behavior is not surprising given the methodological difficulties involved in assessing parental behavior. Such studies are, however, required to test the validity of the developmental model presented here. If attractiveness has little effect on close, long-term relationships, it is doubtful that behavioral and personality characteristics would be developed and internalized as a function of differential reactions based on attractiveness that are encountered in initial or superficial interactions.

For the past several years, we have been investigating the influence of infant attractiveness on parental expectations, attitudes, and behavior. A large number (150) of families with newborns were recruited into the study, and each family was followed longitudinally for the first 9 months of the infant's life. The families were from heterogeneous social class and ethnic backgrounds and all infants were healthy, full-term, firstborns. Mothers[5] were observed in two different contexts—playing and feeding—during their hospital stay and again at 3, 6, and 9 months of infant age. The Brazelton Neonatal Assessment Scale was administered at birth, and all infants received the Bayley Scales of Infant Mental and Motor Development at the later testing sessions. Multiple photographs of each infant and parent were taken and were evaluated for level of attractiveness at each measurement session. The parents also answered questionnaires designed to tap their perceptions of their infants' behavior and characteristics and to assess their attitudes toward care giving and the parental role.

Although the final data analyses have not yet been completed, a preliminary analysis has been performed (Langlois & Casey, 1984). In this analysis, the correlations between infant attractiveness ratings (as assessed by independent judges)[6] at both the newborn and 3-month periods and maternal behavior observed at these assessments were computed. Several classes of maternal behavior—care-giving activities; holding patterns (e.g., close, cuddly vs. distant, far); visual, auditory, and tactile stimulatory behaviors—were recorded at each time point. Observer reliability was monitored throughout the study and was maintained at $r = .85$. The observed maternal behaviors were factor analyzed separately for the play and feed situation.

The significant correlations, although low to moderate in magnitude, were consistent with previous research and revealed several general as well as specific patterns of results. Generally, infant attractiveness was not associated with factors of maternal behavior involving stereotypic and routine feeding and play.

---

[5]A smaller number of fathers were also observed.

[6]It may surprise some to find that parental ratings of the attractiveness of their own children agree significantly with the ratings of independent judges. Although mothers' ratings of the attractiveness of their infants are higher than those of college students, the two sets of ratings are, nevertheless, significantly correlated (Hildebrandt, 1980).

Infant attractiveness was, however, associated with maternal behavior involving affect and interest in the baby. A second general pattern to emerge was that the correlations between infant attractiveness and maternal behavior increased in both number and magnitude as the sample was broken down into specific-gender and ethnic groups. Finally, significant correlations were more often obtained at the 3-month assessment than at the newborn assessment.

While mothers were still in the hospital with their newborn girls, infant attractiveness was significantly and negatively correlated with a factor of maternal behavior labeled *Interest in Others*. The less attractive the baby, the more the mother directed her attention to and interacted with people *other* than the baby. This pattern was quite pervasive, occurring during both the feeding and the play situations.

By 3-months, infant attractiveness and the mother's interest in others were also significantly correlated for mothers of boys. And again, the pattern occurred in both the feeding and the play contexts. For 3-month-old girls, attractiveness was related to factors of maternal behavior involving positive affect. Mothers of more attractive girls, relative to those with less attractive girls, more often kissed, cooed, and smiled at their daughters while holding them close and cuddling them.

To further explicate the behavior of the mothers in this study, maternal attitudes toward their newborn infants were examined by computing the correlation between infant attractiveness and a factor reflecting concern and disappointment from the Parental Attitude Questionnaire (Parke & Sawin, 1975) on a subset of the sample. Sample items from this factor include: disappointed in baby's behavior, doesn't enjoy feeding baby, prefers not to hold baby, worries that baby is hard to calm, feels like spanking baby. The significant correlation ($r = .43$) indicated that the mothers of less attractive infants were more concerned about and disappointed in their infants, at least at the newborn period of the infant's life.

The attitudinal and behavioral data are thus both consistent and complementary and suggest that an unattractive appearance in an infant may elicit maternal concern and anxiety about the infant's health, behavior, and future development. These attitudes may then be expressed by mothers by the way in which they behave toward their infants.

An alternative explanation, however, for the differential behavior and attitudes exhibited by mothers of less attractive infants is that there may be some behavioral difference between attractive and unattractive infants. Rather than attractiveness per se eliciting differential treatment, behavioral differences associated with attractiveness could serve as the eliciting stimuli. To examine this possibility, the correlations between infant attractiveness and infant Apgar scores (a rough index of newborn health and physiological functioning) were computed, again, on a subset of the sample. Although a significant relationship between infant attractiveness and the first Apgar score (given immediately after birth) was not obtained, the analysis did yield a significant correlation between attractiveness and the second (5-minute) Apgar score. Attractive babies received higher Apgar 2 scores than did less attractive infants.

Although these Apgar score differences may indicate that there are some slight (see footnote 7)[7] behavioral differences between attractive and unattractive infants that serve as elicitors of differential maternal treatment, there are still other rival hypotheses to be ruled out before such an interpretation can be accepted. For example, because nurses (who do the Apgar ratings) probably hold stereotypic expectations based on appearance for neonates (e.g., Corter et al., 1975; Stephan & Langlois, 1984), the correlation between infant behavior and attractiveness could be in the eye of the beholder rather than behavioral reality; that is, nurses may give higher Apgar scores to attractive infants because they expect them to be more competent and healthy rather than because these infants actually are more competent and healthy.

Although these reported relationships among the newborn's level of attractiveness, maternal behavior and attitudes, and infant competence should be regarded as preliminary and tentative until the data analyses are completed and the findings on the entire sample are replicated, there are other data currently available that are consistent with these preliminary results. Parke and Sawin (1975), for example, informally assessed the attractiveness of newborns and noted that mothers more frequently kissed and maintained more eye contact and ventral holding contact when their infants were rated as attractive compared with mothers of less attractive infants. Differential behavior as a function of infant attractiveness was also observed in fathers.

In a second study by Parke (Parke, Hymel, Power, & Tinsley, 1977), the effects of a brief film intervention on paternal attitudes and behaviors were examined immediately following the birth of the infant and again at 3 weeks and 3 months. Photographs and attractiveness ratings of a subset of the sample of infants were collected before the infant left the hopsital. The film intervention was more successful in increasing fathers' involvement with their infants when the infants were rated as more rather than less attractive. Further, fathers' expected degree of responsibility for infant care giving was significantly related to infant attractiveness: The greater the infant's rated attractiveness, the higher were fathers' expectations for involvement. The attractiveness ratings of the neonates were also positively and significantly correlated with fathers' actual participation and care-giving behaviors assessed 3 months later.

There is one study available that assessed the relationships between older attractive and unattractive children and their parents. Maruyama and Miller (1981) asked both the mothers and fathers of over 700 ethnically diverse elementary schoolchildren to rate their child on 21 semantic differential trait dimensions

---

[7]Attractive babies received more scores of 10 (a perfect score) whereas the less attractive infants were more likely to receive a "good" score of 8 or 9.

(e.g., sociable–unsociable, easy–difficult to discipline, dependent–independent). Independent judges evaluated the attractiveness of the children. Two dimensions emerged from a factor analysis performed on the parental ratings: The first was termed an evaluative factor (e.g., obedient–disobedient), and the second was labeled a motivational factor (e.g., patient–impatient; slow–quick). Both factors were related to the child's rated attractiveness for his/her father: Attractive Caucasian and Mexican–American children were rated more favorably by their fathers than were unattractive children. A similar pattern was found for mothers on the second factor.[8]

Although the Maruyama and Miller (1981) study does not provide a direct assessment of parental behavior, like the Adams and Crane (1980) study of parental expectations, it provides a necessary and important link between the laboratory studies of Dion (1974) and Berkowitz and Frodi (1979) demonstrating differential treatment of unfamiliar attractive and unattractive children by adults and the naturalistic studies of differential parenting behavior of Langlois et al. (1981) and Parke et al. (1977). Thus, evidence showing that attractive and unattractive children receive differential treatment from unfamiliar adults (e.g., Dion, 1974), familiar teachers (e.g., Lerner & Lerner, 1977), and—most important—parents (e.g., Langlois et al., 1981) is beginning to accumulate. This differential treatment seems to be mediated by differential expectations and attitudes held by many important socializing agents, including peers (e.g., Dion & Berscheid, 1974; Vaughn & Langlois, 1983), teachers (e.g., Clifford & Walster, 1973), and, again, even parents (e.g., Adams & Crane, 1980; Langlois et al., 1981; Maruyama & Miller, 1981).

The Development of Differential Behavior

As a result of differential treatment, the developmental model endorsed here further specifies that children will learn to emit those behaviors that are consistent with the expectations, attitudes, and behaviors of their parents and other socialization agents. When some children are treated *as if* they will be popular, friendly, and smart and when other children are treated *as if* they will be unpopular, aggressive, and not smart, these two groups of children may, then, come to fulfill their prophecies and begin to behave "appropriately."

> John is such a pretty boy with big old brown eyes, and he smiles all the time, even his eyes smile. Wants to please, well behaved. Really joins in with any activity that is going on, and his work has been nice. I'm expecting him to be one of the better boys. (Verbatim quote from a first-grade teacher on the third day of school. (Brophy & Good, 1974, p. 26)

---

[8]The parents of Black children differed from the others and did not evaluate attractive children more positively than unattractive children.

Academic Ability. The relationship between attractiveness and grades, discussed in the previous section on differential treatment, is also relevant to academic abilities because grades are both "given" by teachers and "earned" by students. Grades undoubtedly reflect numerous factors other than attractiveness, intelligence being the most obvious of these. Three studies have examined the relationship between attractiveness and actual IQ scores. Two of these (Clifford, 1975; Styczynski, 1976) found no significant differences between attractive and unattractive children. Maruyama and Miller (1981), however, reported a positive relationship between attractiveness and scores on the performance but not the verbal scale of the WISC. The performance scores increased linearly as level of attractiveness increased.

School achievement (apart from grades) and its relationship to attractiveness have also been investigated. Both Felson (1980) and Lerner and Lerner (1977) found that teachers rated the more attractive children in their classes as having higher academic abilities. Similarly, Styczynski (1976) found a significant relationship between attractiveness and standardized achievement test scores in fourth graders. Using the second-grade achievement test scores of these fourth graders, Styczynski also found a trend for the test scores of attractive and unattractive children to become more divergent with age: The scores of the attractive children tended to increase with age whereas the scores of unattractive children decreased. In contrast, Maruyama and Miller (1981) found a nonsignificant effect of attractiveness on both verbal and quantitative achievement test scores.

Social Behavior with Peers. The data informing us about the behavior of attractive and unattractive children interacting with their peers are not abundant. There are only two naturalistic or semi-naturalistic studies of the actual play behaviors of attractive and unattractive preschool children. Langlois and Downs (1979) observed 3- and 5-year-olds interacting in same-age and sex dyads. The children were assigned to dyads on the basis of the group attractiveness ratings of independent judges. The dyads were composed of one attractive and one unattractive child, two attractive children, or two unattractive children. To guard against potential bias due to observers' attractiveness-based stereotypes and expectations, an inference-free, high speed, molecular observational system was employed by observers naive to the purpose of the study. Positive social behaviors (e.g., smiling, talking), aggressive behaviors (e.g., hitting), activity, and sex-stereotyped play behaviors were recorded.

Attractive and unattractive children differed from each other in a number of ways. First, unattractive children, particularly girls, more often showed higher levels of active play than did attractive children. Correspondingly, attractive children were typically more often observed to engage in quiet, low-activity-level play than were unattractive children. Although all the 3-year-olds showed low levels of aggressive behavior that did not differentiate attractive from unattractive children, 5-year-old unattractive children were more aggressive against peers than were their attractive counterparts. Indeed, aggressive behaviors were observed twice as often in dyads consisting of two unattractive girls than in any other type of 5-year-old female dyad. Finally, attractive children, particularly girls but also boys, more often played with traditionally feminine sex-stereotyped toys, whereas unattractive children, particularly boys, but also girls, more often played with masculine sex-stereotyped toys.

In a second study, Trnavsky and Bakeman (1976) observed preschoolers during free play and recorded solitary, onlooker, and interactive play behaviors. The play behaviors were further categorized as negative if hitting, arguing, or other disruptive behaviors occurred. Full-length photographs of each child were rated for attractiveness by 12 college-student judges. However, the median interjudge rank correlation was only .31 for the 4-year-olds and .37 for the 5-year-olds. Only one significant difference emerged: Unattractive children spent more time than attractive children in solitary play, perhaps reflecting popularity differences between these two groups of children. The failure to find further attractiveness effects could have been due to the low reliability of the attractiveness ratings.

Dion and Stein (1978) investigated behavioral differences between attractive and unattractive children in an experimental situation. Attractive and unattractive fifth and sixth graders were asked to try to convince either a same- or opposite-sex peer from another class to eat some bad-tasting "health" crackers. The interactions between children were tape-recorded, and the manipulative influence strategies (e.g., pleading, command, bribery, threat) and interaction styles (e.g., forceful, persistent, skillful) of the children were coded. Dion and Stein (1978) found that unattractive girls were more forceful, persistent, and assertive in their influence strategies than were their attractive female peers. The attractive girls, who were the least forceful and persistent of all the groups, were, nevertheless, more successful in convincing boys to eat the bad-tasting crackers! Unattractive males paired with other males were the most successful cracker sellers: They used commands and physical threats to "convince" their male peers to eat the bad-tasting crackers. These data seem quite compatible with those of Langlois and Downs (1979); unattractive children may indeed behave more aggressively and assertively with their peers.

The existence of a link between appearance and aggressive behavior is also supported in an indirect fashion by an interesting study by Cavior and Howard (1973). They reported that facial photographs of both Black and Caucasian juvenile delinquents were rated by independent judges as significantly less attractive than were photographs of corresponding groups of nondelinquent high school students.

The potential link between aggressive behavior and appearance is very intriguing because two different etiologies are suggested by the literature. On the one hand, the Langlois and Downs (1979) data are consistent with the developmental model proposed here. The fact that attractive and unattractive 5-year-olds but not 3-year-olds were differentiated in aggressiveness suggests that unattractive children may learn, over a period of time, the behaviors associated with appearance-based stereotypes through a process of behavioral confirmation.

On the other hand, Halverson and his colleagues (Halverson & Victor, 1976; Waldrop, Bell, McLaughlin, & Halverson, 1978) compiled data suggesting the possibility of a biological link between appearance and aggressive behavior. Halverson et al. (1976, 1978) measured the presence or absence of minor physical anomalies and assessed their relationships to aggression and hyperactivity. The slight physical anomalies of these children (e.g., slight deviations in the eyes, ears, and mouth) are, in fact, similar to many of the physical characteristics found in unattractive children.[9] They found that the number of minor anomalies is significantly related to peer-nominated "meaness" for randomly selected male and female elementary schoolchildren (Halverson & Victor, 1976). Likewise, in a longitudinal study of 30 boys in which anomalies were assessed at birth and again at age 3, Waldrop et al. (1978) found that both assessments of anomalies were significantly correlated with observed peer aggression at age 3. Further, a derived measure of hyperactivity correlated .67 with the newborn anomaly score and .35 with the 3-year-old score. These data are consistent with the relationship between activity level and attractiveness noted by Langlois and Downs (1979).

The three studies that have directly assessed differential behavior with peers (Dion & Stein, 1978; Langlois & Downs, 1979; Trnavsky & Bakeman, 1976) suggest that there is a relationship between a child's behavior and his or her level of attractiveness. These results are supported by other investigations of appearance-related behaviors (e.g., Cavior & Howard, 1973; Halverson & Victor, 1976). The cumulative data base from this area of investigation points in particular to a link between appearance and aggression, although the cause of such a link is not yet known. It is very possible, however, that Queen Victoria's unattractive infant will grow up to become an unattractive and aggressive preschooler.

Continuity of Attractiveness

Although studies show that the attitudes and behaviors of adults and children vary as a function of attractiveness at any one point in time, to assert that such differential reactions can produce differences in attractive and unattractive children requires at least a moderate degree of continuity in appearance over time. Attractiveness would not be expected to exert the long-term effects on behavior here proposed if an individual's appearance changes dramatically from one time to another (Berscheid & Walster, 1974).

Four sources have provided data to address this issue. Adams (1977) collected the elementary-school photographs of 20 children and asked separate panels of

---

[9]See Waldrop and Halverson (1971) for photographic examples.

college-student raters to judge the attractiveness of each cohort of children. The average correlation between the kindergarten and first-grade ratings was $r = .79$, that between kindergarten and fourth-grade was $r = .54$, and the correlation between the kindergarten and sixth-grade ratings was $r = .42$. These correlations are impressive given that unstandardized photographs were rated by different judges for each school year. In a second study, Adams (1977) collected snapshots of 20 adults at three stages in the lifecycle: adolescence (16 to 20 years of age), young adulthood (30 to 35), and older adults (45 to 50). Again, continuity in facial attractiveness was demonstrated. The correlation between attractiveness ratings taken at the adolescent and young adulthood period was $r = .87$ for women and $r = .63$ for men. The correlation between the ratings of the photographs of the adolescent and older adult period was $r = .79$ for women and $r = .59$ for men.

Sussman, Muesser, Grau, and Yarnold (1983) recently examined the stability of facial attractiveness of 13 girls for whom first-, fourth-, seventh-, and tenth-grade photos were available. Using an analysis of variance rather than a correlational approach, Sussman et al. (1983) found that attractiveness was generally stable during the childhood period and they concluded that attractiveness could be a long-term determinant of social development and mental health. Similarly, Maruyama and Miller (1981) found significant correlations between ratings of the same child based on photographs taken at 5-year intervals for a large sample ($N = 501$) of children. Finally, we have found moderate stability in our own work with infants. After photographing 35 infants at 3 and 6 months of age, we found the correlation between these ratings to be $r = .68$.

The available evidence indicates that appearance is reasonably stable across a range of developmental periods. For most individuals, then, it would seem that appearance can exert a consistent effect on development. That this will not, however, be true for all individuals could be a considerable asset to researchers in this area. A longitudinal study of those individuals who do change in level of attractiveness would provide researchers with a natural experiment in which the antecedent and consequent effects of changes in attractiveness could be examined.

Summary

There are extensive data supporting the differential expectation component of the ontogenetic model proposed here. Attractive children are expected by both adults and by their peers to be more socially and intellectually competent and to be better liked. These differential expectations go beyond single ethnic groups and may be more powerful than ethnic stereotypes. The impact of such expectations may have its beginnings in the cradle because even 1-day-old infants are viewed differently as a function of appearance. Even parents hold expectations consistent with the beauty-is-good stereotype for the behavior of their own children.

Adults behave more positively toward attractive infants and children in laboratory situations, and some data suggest that teachers may treat attractive children preferentially. Preliminary data indicating that parents exhibit more favorable attitudes toward and treatment of attractive children are also available. Although as yet there are only a limited number of studies, the research suggests that attractive and unattractive children behave differently, especially in social interactions with peers.

Future Directions

Although each individual component of the developmental model has received some empirical support, the ontogenic links between each component have not yet been systematically examined. Thus, the *process* of development proposed here awaits future research demonstration and validation. Sameroff (1975), however, has provided an example of the course of the process:

> The mother who comes to label her infant as 'difficult' may come to treat the child as difficult irrespective of his actual behavior. The transaction then moves back toward the child. As the child advances into cognitive stages where he can recognize the value the world places on himself, he will come to accept 'difficulty' as one of the central elements in his self-image; thereby, indeed becoming the 'difficult' child for all time. (p. 73)

Snyder, Tanke, and Berscheid (1977) have recently provided an important empirical demonstration of a process of behavioral confirmation as a function of attractiveness at one point in time. Male and female adults held a telephone conversation in which the males were led to believe that the females were physically attractive or unattractive. In reality, females were assigned randomly to the attractive and unattractive conditions. Tape recordings of each participant's conversations were analyzed by naive judges for evidence of behavioral confirmation of the expectancies elicited in the males. Snyder et al. found that the men who had interacted with women they believed to be physically attractive were rated by the judges as more sociable, interesting, outgoing, humorous, and socially adept than their counterparts in the unattractive conditions. Further, the "attractive" females behaved in a friendly, likeable, and sociable manner compared with those whom the males thought to be unattractive. Thus, this study, although not developmental, illustrates how social behaviors can actually be changed and differentiated as a function of attractiveness, at least at one point in time. Further, such differential interactions seem likely to foster the perseverence of the physical attractiveness stereotype because they place limits on opportunities to learn more about behavioral similarities between attractive and unattractive persons.

Longitudinal research is now required to test the ontogenetic links between expectations, treatment, and behavior that are proposed by the developmental model presented here. At least in principle, longitudinal investigations of the influence of attractiveness could provide an important window into the process of development, a process that may resemble the view provided by the experimental work of Snyder et al. (1977) on the contemporaneous effects of attractiveness on behavior.

In addition to longitudinal research, the theoretical framework discussed here indicates several directions for future research. First, the utility of further attribution and impression formation research seems limited. Because differential expectations and attributions as a function of attractiveness have been thoroughly documented, future research would benefit by focusing on the long-term effects of attractiveness. In particular, more research on the differential treatment and behavior of the attractive and unattractive child is important and necessary to evaluate the validity of the model as well as to understand social behavior and social relationships.

In 1974, Berscheid and Walster concluded their seminal review of the physical attractiveness literature by noting that, although omnipresent, physical attractiveness as a psychologically relevant variable was "theoretically arid." Indeed, at that time and even today, the majority of investigations into the effects of attractiveness on behavior have been isolated and theoretically undirected.

A theoretical framework now exists, however, to guide systematic research investigating the influence of appearance on the socialization process and the development of social behavior. Indeed, physical attractiveness could prove to be an important and theoretically relevant variable for developmental psychologists attempting to study the process of socialization. It provides a unique opportunity to determine how infant characteristics such as attractiveness influence parental expectations and attitudes, how these expectations become translated into differential treatment, and how such treatment results in the development of differential behavior. Further, because there are at least two developmental periods (i.e., infancy and puberty) during which the level of attractiveness may change dramatically, researchers are provided with a rare natural experiment in which causal influences in the socialization process can be examined.

Compared with some other variables (e.g., gender), physical attractiveness may account for a small portion of the variance in the development of social behavior. However, as Maruyama and Miller (1981) noted, the point of both the developmental model presented here and the research necessary to evaluate the model is not to elevate or exaggerate the importance of attractiveness compared with other variables but rather to illustrate how appearance can influence development. If appearance is powerful enough to influence and modify behaviors *in any way* through the mechanisms discussed here, then it is far from being theoretically or practically unimportant. That a child's level of attractiveness may have consistent and perhaps insidious effects on his or her development makes further research in this area crucial.

ACKNOWLEDGMENTS

I thank Rita Casey, Cinda Cyrus, Dorothy Lentz, and Douglas Sawin for their helpful suggestions on this chapter.

REFERENCES

Adams, G. R. (1977). Physical attractiveness research: Toward a developmental social psychology of beauty. *Human Development, 20,* 217–239.

Adams, G. R. (1978). Racial membership and physical attractiveness effects on preschool teacher's expectations. *Child Study Journal, 8,* 29–41.

Adams, G. R., & Cohen, A. S. (1974). Characteristics of children and teacher expectancy: An extension to the child's social and family life. *Journal of Educational Research, 70,* 87–90.

Adams, G. R., & Cohen, A. S. (1976). An examination of cumulative folder information used by teachers in making differential judgments of children's abilities. *Alberta Journal of Educational Research, 22,* 216–225.

Adams, G. R., & Crane, P. (1980). An assessment of parents' and teachers' expectations of preschool children's social preference for attractive or unattractive children and adults. *Child Development, 51,* 224–231.

Alley, T. R. (1980). Infantile colouration as an elicitor of caretaking behaviour in Old World primates. *Primates, 21,* 416–429.

Alley, T. R. (1981). Head shape and the perception of cuteness. *Developmental Psychology, 17,* 650–654.

Anderson, S. M., and Bem, S. L. (1981). Sex-typing and androgyny in dyadic interaction: Individual differences in responsiveness to physical attractiveness. *Journal of Personality and Social Psychology, 41,* 74–86.

Austin, M. C., & Thompson, G. G. (1948). Children's fiendships: A study of the basis on which children select and reject their best friends. *Journal of Educational Psychology, 39,* 101–116.

Barash, D. P. (1977). *Sociobiology and behavior.* New York: Elsevier North–Holland.

Barocas, R., & Black, H. K. (1974). Referral rate and physical attractiveness in third-grade children. *Perceptual Motor Skills, 39,* 731–734.

Bell, R. Q., & Harper, L. V. (1977). *Child effects on adults.* New York: Wiley.

Bem, D. (1970). *Beliefs, attitudes, and human affairs.* Belmont, CA: Brooks/Cole.

Berkowitz, L., & Frodi, A. (1979). Reactions to a child's mistakes as affected by her/his looks and speech. *Social Psychology Quarterly, 42,* 420–425.

Berscheid, E., Dion, K. K., Walster, E., & Walster, G. W. (1971). Physical attractiveness and dating choices: A test of the matching hypothesis. *Journal of Experimental Social Psychology, 7,* 173–189.

Berscheid, E., & Walster, E. (1974). Physical attractiveness. In L. Berkowitz (Ed.), *Advances in experimental social psychology.* New York: Academic Press.

Brierley, D. W. (1966). Children's use of personality constructs. *Bulletin of the British Psychological Society, 19,* (No. 65), 72.

Brophy, J. E., & Good, T. L. (1974). *Teacher–student relationships.* New York: Holt, Rinehart, & Winston.

Cash, T. F., & Derlega, V. J. (1978). The matching hypothesis: Physical attractiveness among same-sexed friends. *Personality and Social Psychology Bulletin, 4,* 240–243.

Cavior, N., & Dokecki, P. (1973). Physical attractiveness, perceived attitude similarity, and academic achievement as contributors to interpersonal attraction among adolescents. *Developmental Psychology, 9,* 44–54.

Cavior, N., & Howard, L. R. (1973). Facial attractiveness and juvenile delinquency among black and white offenders. *Journal of Abnormal Child Psychology, 1,* 202–213.

Clifford, M. M. (1975). Physical attractiveness and academic performance. *Child Study Journal, 5,* 201–209.

Clifford, M. M., & Walster, E. (1973). Research note: The effect of physical attractiveness on teacher expectations. *Sociology of Education, 46,* 248–258.

Corter, C., Trehub, S., Bonkydis, C., Ford, L., Celhoffer, L., & Minde, K. (1975). *Nurses' judgments of the attractiveness of premature infants.* Unpublished manuscript, University of Toronto.

Dermer, M., & Thiel, D. L. (1975). When beauty may fail. *Journal of Personality and Social Psychology, 31,* 1168–1176.

Dion, K. K. (1972). Physical attractiveness and evaluations of children's trangressions. *Journal of Personality and Social Psychology, 24,* 207–213.

Dion, K. K. (1973). Young children's stereotyping of facial attractiveness. *Developmental Psychology, 9,* 183–188.

Dion, K. K. (1974). Children's physical attractiveness and sex as determinants of adult punitiveness. *Developmental Psychology, 10,* 772–778.

Dion, K. K. (1977). The incentive value of physical attractiveness for young children. *Personality and Social Psychology Bulletin, 3,* 67–70.

Dion, K. K., & Berscheid, E. (1974). Physical attractiveness and peer perception among children. *Sociometry, 37,* 1–12.

Dion, K. K., Berscheid, E., & Walster, E. (1972). What is beautiful is good. *Journal of Personality and Social Psychology, 24,* 285–290.

Dion, K. K., & Stein, S. (1978). Physical attractiveness and interpersonal influence. *Journal of Experimental Social Psychology, 14,* 97–108.

Duck, S. W. (1973). *Personal relationships and personal constructs: A study of friendship formation.* New York: Wiley.

Duck, S. W. (1975). Personality similarity and friendship choices by adolescents. *European Journal of Social Psychology, 5,* 351–365.

Elkind, D. (1967). Egocentrism in adolescence. *Child Development, 38,* 1025–1034.

Felson, R. B. (1980). Physical attractiveness, grades and teachers' attributions of ability. *Representative Research in Social Psychology, 11,* 64–71.

Flapan, D. (1968). *Children's understanding of social interaction.* New York: Columbia University Teacher's College Press.

Fulford, R. (Ed.). (1964). *Dearest child: Letters between Queen Victoria and the Princess Royal (1858–1861).* London: Evans Brothers.

Garbarino, J., & Crouter, A. (1978). Defining the community context for parent–child relations: The correlates of child maltreatment. *Child Development, 49,* 604–616.

Halverson, C. F., & Victor, J. B. (1976). Minor physical anomalies and problem behavior in elementary school children. *Child Development, 47,* 281–285.

Hartup, W. W. (1983). The peer system. In P. M. Mussen (Ed.-in-chief) and E. M. Hetherington (Ed.), *Handbook of child psychology* (Vol. 4). New York: Wiley.

Havighurst, R. J. (1972). *Developmental tasks and education.* New York: McKay.

Helson, H. (1964). *Adaptation-Level theory: An experimental and systematic approach to behavior.* New York: Harper & Row.

Hildebrandt, K. A. (1980, April). *Parents' perceptions of their infants' physical attractiveness.* Paper presented at the International Conference on Infant Studies, New Haven, CT.

Hildebrandt, K. A. (1982). The role of physical attractiveness in infant and child development. In H. E. Fitzgerald, B. M. Lester, & M. W. Yogman (Eds.), *Theory and research in behavioral pediatrics,* (Vol. 1). New York: Plenum.

Hildebrandt, K. A., & Fitzgerald, H. E. (1978). Adults' responses to infants varying in perceived cuteness. *Behavioral Processes, 3,* 159–172.

Hildebrandt, K. A., & Fitzgerald, H. E. (1981). Mothers' responses to infant physical appearance. *Infant Mental Health Journal, 2,* 56–61.

Huston, T. L. (1973). Ambiguity of acceptance, social desirability, and dating choice. *Journal of Experimental Social Psychology, 9,* 32–42.

Jacklin, C. N., & Maccoby, E. E. (1978). Social behavior at 33 months in same-sex and mixed-sex dyads. *Child Development, 49,* 557–569.

Kehle, T. J., Bramble, W. J., & Mason, E. J. (1974). Teachers' expectations: Ratings of student performance as biased by student characteristics. *Journal of Experimental Education, 43,* 54–60.

Kehle, T. J., Ware, C. L., & Guidubaldi, J. (1976, April). *Effects of physical attractiveness, sex, and intelligence on expectations for students' academic ability and personality: A replication.* Paper presented at the Annual Meeting of the American Educational Research Association, San Francisco.

Kenrick, D. T., & Gutierres, S. E. (1980). Contrast effects and judgments of physical attractiveness: When beauty becomes a social problem. *Journal of Personality and Social Psychology, 38,* 131–140.

Kleck, R. E., Richardson, S. A., & Ronald, C. (1974). Physical appearance cues and interpersonal attraction in children. *Child Development, 45,* 305–310.

Kuhn, D., Nash, S. C., & Brucken, L. (1978). Sex role concepts of two- and three-year-olds. *Child Development, 49,* 445–451.

Langlois, J. H., & Casey, R. C. (1984, April). *Baby beautiful: The relationship between infant physical attractiveness and maternal behavior.* Paper presented at the fourth biennial International Conference on Infant Studies, New York.

Langlois, J. H., & Downs, A. C. (1979). Peer relations as a function of physical attractiveness: The eye of the beholder or behavioral reality? *Child Development, 50,* 409–418.

Langlois, J. H., Gottfried, N. W., Barnes, B. M., & Hendricks, D. (1978). The influence of peer age on the social behavior of preschool children. *Journal of Genetic Psychology, 132,* 11–19.

Langlois, J. H., Gottfried, N. W., & Seay, B. (1973). The influence of sex of peer on the social behavior of preschool children. *Developmental Psychology, 8,* 93–98.

Langlois, J. H., & Stephan, C. (1977). The effects of physical attractiveness and ethnicity on children's behavioral attributions and peer preferences. *Child Development, 48,* 1694–1698.

Langlois, J. H., & Stephan, C. (1981). Beauty and the beast: The role of physical attractiveness in the development of peer relations and social behavior. In S. S. Brehm, S. M. Kassin, & F. X. Gibbons (Eds.), *Developmental social psychology: Theory and research.* New York: Oxford University Press.

Langlois, J. H., & Styczynski, L. (1979). The effects of physical attractiveness on the behavioral attributions and peer preferences in acquainted children. *International Journal of Behavioral Development, 2,* 325–341.

Langlois, J. H., & Vaughn, B. E. (1983). *Prince Charming and Cinderella: The differential role of physical attractiveness in the popularity of boys and girls.* Unpublished manuscript, University of Texas at Austin.

Lerner, R. M. (1976). *Concepts and theories of human development.* Reading: Addison–Wesley.

Lerner, R. M., & Lerner, J. V. (1977). Effects of age, sex, and physical attractiveness on child–peer relations, academic performance, and elementary school adjustment. *Developmental Psychology, 13,* 585–590.

Little, B. R. (1968). Age and sex differences in the use of psychological, role and physicalistic constructs. *Bulletin of the British Psychological Society, 21,* 34.

Livesley, W. J., & Bromley, D. B. (1973). *Person perception in childhood and adolescence.* New York: Wiley.

Lorenz, K. (1943). Die angeborenen formen moglicher arfahrung. *Zeitschrift fur Tierpsychologie, 5,* 233–409.

Malerstein, A. J., & Ahern, M. (1982). *A Piagetian model of character structure.* New York: Human Sciences.

Maruyama, G., & Miller, N. (1981). Physical attractiveness and personality. In B. A. Maher (Ed.), *Progress in experimental personality research,* (Vol. 10). New York: Academic Press.

Miller, A. G. (1970). Role of physical attractiveness in impression formation. *Psychonomic Science, 19,* 241–243.

Murstein, B. I. (1972). Physical attractiveness and marital choice. *Journal of Personality and Social Psychology, 22,* 8–12.

Neisser, U. (1967). *Cognitive psychology.* New York: Appleton–Century–Crofts.

Nisbett, R. E., & Ross, L. (1980). *Human inference: Strategies and shortcomings of social judgment.* Englewood Cliffs, NJ: Prentice–Hall.

Nisbett, R. E., & Wilson, T. D. (1977). Telling more than we can know: Verbal reports on mental processes. *Psychological Review, 84,* 231–259.

Parke, R. D., Hymel, S., Power, T., & Tinsley, B. (1977, November). *Fathers and risk: A hospital based model of intervention.* Paper presented at the Symposium on Psychosocial Risks during Infancy, University of Texas at Austin.

Parke, R. D., & Sawin, D. B. (1975, April). *Infant characteristics and behavior as elicitors of maternal and paternal responsivity in the newborn period.* Paper resented at the meeting of the Society for Research in Child Development, Denver, CO.

Piaget, J. (1970). Piaget's theory. In P. H. Mussen (Ed.), *Carmichael's manual of child psychology.* New York: Wiley.

Power, T. G., Hildebrandt, K. A., & Fitzgerald, H. E. (1982). Adults' responses to infants varying in facial expression and perceived attractiveness. *Infant Behavior and Development, 5,* 33–44.

Rich, J. (1975). Effects of children's physical attractiveness on teachers' evaluations. *Journal of Educational Psychology, 67,* 599–609.

Rosenblatt, J. S. (1970). Views on the onset and maintenance of maternal behavior in the rat. In L. R. Aronson, E. Tobach, D. S. Lehrman, & Rosenblatt (Eds.), *Development and evolution of behavior.* San Francisco: W. H. Freeman.

Ross, M. B., & Salvia, J. (1975). Attractiveness as a biasing factor in teacher judgment. *American Journal of Mental Deficiency, 80,* 96–98.

Salvia, J., Sheare, J. B., & Algozzine, B. (1975). Facial attractiveness and personal social development. *Journal of Abnormal Child Psychology, 3,* 171–178.

Sameroff, A. (1975). Transactional models in early social relations. *Human Development, 18,* 65–79.

Sappenfield, B. R., & Balogh, B. (1970). Perceived attractiveness of social stimuli as related to their perceived similarity to self. *Journal of Psychology, 74,* 105–111.

Shantz, C. U. (1975). The development of social cognition. In E. M. Hetherington (Ed.), *Review of child development research.* (Vol. 5). Chicago: University of Chicago Press.

Sigall, H., & Michela, J. (1976). I'll bet you say that to all the girls: Physical attractiveness and reactions to praise. *Journal of Personality, 44,* 611–626.

Silverman, I. (1971, September). Physical attractiveness and courtship. *Sexual Behavior,* 22–25.

Snyder, M., & Swann, W. B. (1978). Behavioral confirmation in social interaction: From social perception to social reality. *Journal of Experimental Social Psychology, 14,* 148–162.

Snyder, M., Tanke, E. D., & Berscheid, E. (1977). Social perception and interpersonal behavior: On the self-fulfilling nature of social stereotypes. *Journal of Personality and Social Psychology, 35,* 656–666.

Sorell, G. T., & Nowak, C. A. (1981). The role of physical attractiveness as a contributor to individual development. In R. M. Lerner & N. A. Busch–Rossnagel (Eds.), *Individuals as producers of their development: A life-span perspective.* New York: Academic Press.

Stephan, C., & Langlois, J. H. (1984). Baby beautiful: Adult attributions of infant competence as a function of infant attractiveness. *Child Development, 55,* 576–585.

Stokes, S. J., & Bickman, L. (1974). The effect of the physical attractiveness and role of the helper on help seeking. *Journal of Applied Social Psychology, 4,* 286–294.

Stroebe, W., Insko, C. A., Thompson, V. D., & Layton, B. D. (1971). Effects of physical attractiveness, attitude similarity, and sex on various aspects of interpersonal attraction. *Journal of Personality and Social Psychology, 18,* 79–91.

Styczynski, L. E. (1976). *Effects of physical characteristics on the social, emotional, and intellectual development of early school age children.* Unpublished doctoral dissertation, The University of Texas at Austin.

Styczynski, L., & Langlois, J. H. (1977). The effects of familiarity on behavioral stereotypes associated with physical attractiveness in young children. *Child Development, 48,* 1137–1141.

Sussman, S., Muesser, K. T., Grau, B. W., & Yarnold, P. R. (1983). Stability of females' facial attractiveness during childhood. *Journal of Personality and Social Psychology, 44,* 1231–1233.

Tennis, G. H., & Dabbs, J. M. (1975). Judging physical attractiveness: Effects of judges' own attractiveness. *Personality and Social Psychology Bulletin, 1,* 513–516.

Touhey, J. C. (1979). Sex-role stereotyping and individual differences in liking for the physical attractive. *Social Psychology Quarterly, 42,* 285–289.

Trnavsky, P. A., & Bakeman, R. (1976, August). Physical attractiveness: Stereotype and social behavior in preschool children. Paper presented at the meeting of the American Psychological Association, Washington, DC.

Tversky, A., & Kahneman, D. (1973). Availability: A heuristic for judging frequency and probability. *Cognitive Psychology, 5,* 207–232.

Tversky, A., & Kahneman, D. (1974). Judgment under uncertainty: Heuristics and biases. *Science, 185,* 1124–1131.

Vaughn, B. E., & Langlois, J. H. (1983). Physical attractiveness as a correlate of peer status and social competence in preschool children. *Developmental Psychology, 19,* 561–567.

Waldrop, M. F., Bell, R. Q., McLaughlin, B., & Halverson, C. F. (1978). Newborn minor physical anomalies predict short attention span, peer aggression, and impulsivity at age 3. *Science, 199,* 563–564.

Waldrop, M. F., & Halverson, C. F. (1971). Minor physical anomalies and hyperactive behavior in young children. In J. Hellmuth (Ed.), *Exceptional infant* (Vol. 2): *Studies in abnormalities.* New York: Brunner/Mazel.

Watts, A. F. (1944). *The language and mental development of children.* London: Harrays.

Yarrow, M. R., & Campbell, J. D. (1963). Person perception in children. *Merrill–Palmer Quarterly, 9,* 57–72.

3 Psychological Adjustment of Patients with Craniofacial Deformities Before and After Surgery

Arlette Lefebvre, M. D.
The Hospital for Sick Children, Toronto

Ian R. Munro, M.A., M.B., B. Chir.
The Hospital for Sick Children and Sunnybrook Medical Centre, Toronto

Of all the physical handicaps, none is more socially devastating than facial deformity. Rather than the sympathy or pity evoked by a crutch or a wheelchair, facial disfigurement elicits anxiety, fear, and a wish to remove it from one's sight (Belfer et al., 1979a, 1979b). Traditionally, according to historians, painters, scientists, and folklore, deformed or disfigured individuals are villains, born criminals, amoral, or (at the very least) mentally retarded. Yet, only in the past 10 years have surgical techniques offered patients with severe congenital deformities, such as the famous "Elephant Man," some hope of approaching normality (Bernstein, 1978; Berscheid & Walster, 1972; Constable & Bernstein, 1979).

At The Hospital for Sick Children in Toronto, the Craniofacial Team, led by Dr. Ian Munro, plans and carries out radical surgery resulting in complete craniofacial reconstruction. This team includes a child psychiatrist, psychologist, and social worker whose roles are to assess the impact of this surgery and of the rapid changes in objective appearance on the patient's self-esteem, intellectual functioning, and on the family dynamics, respectively.

THE SUBJECTS—MATERIAL AND METHODS

Global Study

The 250 patients with severe craniofacial deformities ranged in age from 6 weeks to 39 years of age at preoperative interview. The parents of the 215 patients who were children or adolescents were also interviewed. When appropriate, parents

53

and child were interviewed separately, then together. All interviews were conducted by a social worker and child psychiatrist, following a semistructured interview protocol that stressed social adjustment, reactions to staring and teasing, school performance, and plans for the future.

Patients who were able to do so were asked to rate their appearance according to Hay's Standardized Rating Scale of Appearance (Hay et al., 1973), which ranges from "perfect feature" (No. 1) to "very marked imperfection" (No. 9). When appropriate, parents were asked to rate their child's appearance independently. Patients or parents were also requested to rate the deformity and state their expectations from surgery according to the scale. Children too young to use the scale were usually asked to draw themselves, but self-rating was not possible for infants.

The Piers–Harris Self-esteem Inventory, which is valid in the 8- to 16-year-old range (Piers, 1969), is administered to the child while the parents are given the Family Assessment Measure.

Postoperative interviews, scheduled 1, 2, and 4 years after surgery, followed the same basic protocol of psychosocial assessment and rating of appearance and self-esteem. Patients and parents also reported the social impact of the surgery.

Pilot Project—Self-esteem Ratings

In a pilot project 34 children and adolescents, randomly selected, were asked to fill out the Piers–Harris Self-concept Scale preoperatively and 1-year postsurgery. These 34 subjects ranged in age from 8 to 17 years. They included 21 females and 13 males, and presented with either congenital disorders, such as Crouzon's Syndrome, in 21 cases, and acquired deformities, such as malocclusions, in 13. The patients were also asked to rate their appearance according to Hay's Scale preoperatively and 1-year postop.

In a second phase of this study, we asked a panel of 14 nonmedical volunteers, 7 males and 7 females, whose average age was 24.6 and 24.8, respectively, to view and rate photographs of the same patients, using the same Hay's rating scale. The photographs were black and white, 12" × 14," taken full face at two points in time, namely before surgery and 1 year after the operation. However, the order of presentation was randomized and the raters were not told which photos were pre and which ones were postoperative. They were only informed that the pictures represented surgical patients.

In a third phase of this study another panel of 16 nonmedical volunteers, consisting of 9 males and 7 females of an average age of 26.1 and 23.7 years, respectively, were asked to rank in order 4 groups of 10 photographs of the same subjects. These groups contained 5 pre and 5 postoperative photos of the same patients. The raters were asked to rank these pictures from least to most attractive on a scale from 1 to 10, without being told anything more than in the rating experiment above.

RESULTS

Diagnostic Criteria

The 250 patients were classified according to their diagnoses (Table 3.1). Congenital conditions affected 178 patients. Of these most children with autosomal dominant mutations were of normal intelligence except those with Apert's disease, which involves syndactyly, motor coordination impairment, hyperactivity, and frequently below-average intellectual capacity. Lateral Facial Dysplasia (LFD) is a term coined by our Craniofacial Team to describe unilateral hypoplasia, microtia, and partial or total deafness. Cleft lip and palate cases are the "bread and butter" of most plastic surgeons. Only the most severe residual defects require reconstructive surgery, usually during adolescence. Among the other congenital disorders was the Moebius syndrome in which complete paralysis of the facial nerves produces a striking, flat-affect appearance. Two of our patients with this syndrome presented with accompanying schizophreniform syndromes and one other had classical autism.

Patients with congenital disorders usually present at a younger age and are more severely affected than those with acquired disorders. They are more likely to require urgent neurosurgery to release prematurely fused sutures or to protect

TABLE 3.1

Classification of Disorder In 250 Patients Undergoing Craniofacial Surgery

Type	Description	No.
A. Congenital		
Autosomal dominant syndromes	Hypertelorism, Crouzon's disease, Apert's disease, Treacher–Collins syndrome	78
Lateral facial dysplasia (LFD)	Unilateral hypoplasia, microtia, and partial or total deafness	32
Cleft lip and palate	Severe residual effects	29
Miscellaneous	Facial abnormalities associated with hydrocephalus, microcephaly, cerebral palsy, thalidomide syndrome, Binder's syndrome, Goldenhar's syndrome, Moebius syndrome	39
Total Congenital		178
B. Acquired		
Severe malocclusion	Related to prognathism or retrognathism	48
Tumor	Rapidly growing, oversized hemangiomas, or slowly growing neurofibromas	12
Miscellaneous	Accidental injuries, postinflammatory, postinfectious or postburn deformities	12
Total Acquired		72

eyesight. The acquired disorders usually are mild or moderate in severity and present in adolescence or young adulthood.

Results of Self- and Parent's Ratings of Appearance Before Surgery

1. Self-ratings on Hay's Scale.   By 1980 (Lefebvre & Barclay, 1982) we had an initial group of 175 patients who were old enough to rate themselves on Hay's Scale (Table 3.2).

On the average, patients with congenital disorders rated their preoperative appearance as more imperfect than those with acquired disorders (Table 3.2). However, the difference between the two groups was not significant ($\chi^2 = 3.30$) (Table 3.3) even though the actual appearance of patients with congenital disorders was much more abnormal than that of the patients with acquired deformities. On the other hand, a much higher percentage of patients with congenital disorders had ratings between 5 and 9 (moderate to very marked imperfection) than did the group of patients with acquired disorders. However, most tumor patients (in the acquired group) also rated their appearance severely.

2. Parents' versus Patients' Ratings of Appearance.   Excluding early adolescents, most young patients rated their appearance more positively than did their parents (122 of 175). This difference was highly significant (Table 3.4). In 37 cases the ratings were the same and in 16 the parents' rating was less severe than the patient's. The results also confirmed the trend seen in an earlier pilot study (Lefebvre & Barclay, 1982) in which a close concordance between the ratings of parents and team members was found.

TABLE 3.2
Self-Ratings Of Patients

		Average Score	*% of Ratings > 5*
A.	Congenital Disorders	5.4	41
	Autosomal dominant syndromes	5.3	59
	LFD	5.5	33
	Severe cleft lip and palate	6.0	30
	Miscellaneous	5.2	24
B.	Acquired Disorders	4.3	28
	Severe malocclusion	4.0	24
	Tumor	5.0	57
	Miscellaneous	4.7	27

TABLE 3.3
Relationship Between Onset Of Deformity And
Severity Of Self-Rating

	Mild to Moderate Rating 1–5	Moderate to Marked Rating 6–9	
Congenital Disorders	105	73	178
Acquired Disorders	52	20	72
	157	93	250

$\chi^2 = 3.30$
Not Significant

3. Mother's versus Father's Ratings of Appearance.   When rating their child's appearance independently, mothers and fathers gave identical scores in 103 out of 175 cases: The mother's rating was more severe in 43 cases and the father's in 29 instances.

Ratings of Appearance After Surgery

In 202 of the 250 patients seen at least once after surgery (at the 1-year follow-up), self-rating improved by an average of three points on the scale. There was

TABLE 3.4
Relationship Between Patients' Self-Rating Versus Parents'
Ratings Of Deformity

	Rating of patient less severe than rating of parent	Rating of parent equal or more severe than rating of patient	
Children under 13	117	3	120
Patients 13 and older	5	50	55
	122	53	175

$\chi^2 = 139.6$
Highly Significant

no significant difference in improvement of self-ratings between the congenital and acquired patients (Table 3.5). Thirty-five patients rated their features as almost perfect or minimal imperfection both pre and postoperatively and seven others rated themselves as more deformed after surgery (by one point). In the six remaining cases, postoperative self-ratings were not obtained because the patients had suffered major complications, such as meningitis or brain damage, or died as a result of surgery.

Where patients were too young to rate themselves, improvement in parents' ratings was reported by only 51 of the 75 families and averaged two points. In 13 cases the parents gave the same ratings pre and postoperatively and 11 mothers rated the appearance as worse after surgery.

Psychosocial Adjustment Following Surgery

In 102 of the 250 cases the patients' change in body image was accompanied by a subjective emotional improvement, described as increased comfort in public places, diminished self-consciousness when meeting strangers, increased interest in appearance and grooming, and a general feeling of being more appealing to others. Such changes in self-image were dramatically illustrated by the self-portraits of a 6-year-old boy who had drawn himself as a frog preoperatively and as a "six billion dollar man" after surgery, or by the change in dress of a teenaged girl who came in an army uniform for her initial evaluation and reappeared in a miniskirt and see-through blouse after surgery.

In 81 of these patients, as well as subjective improvement, there was also an objective improvement in the patient's quality of life, demonstrated by improved academic or work performance, promotions, or beneficiary change of jobs and increased heterosexual activities.

Ten patients reported no change in psychosocial adjustment. However, 28 families reported increased friction between family members; in 15 of these the patient and parents were satisfied with the physical changes accomplished by surgery but the parents were displeased with the accompanying personality

TABLE 3.5
Relationship Between Onset Of Deformity And
Patients' Perceived Outcome Of Surgery

	Improved	Not Improved	
Congenital	88	12	100
Acquired	20	5	25
	108	17	125

changes (for example, the patient became more independent or left home) or disappointed by the patient's ongoing learning or social problems. In 13 families marital separation or divorce occurred within the first year after surgery. Usually this was done on the initiative of the patient's mother who claimed to have postponed dealing with an unsatisfactory marriage. Only two patients said that they would not have agreed to the surgery if they had been able to predict the results. Both were adolescents who felt they had been pressured into surgery against their will and were disappointed and angry with the physical and social results.

Results of Self-esteem Project

The majority of the patients in our sample of 34 reported dramatic improvements in their appearance, social acceptance, and self-esteem. The increase in self-esteem scores was found to be highly significant for both the acquired and congenital groups at the .001 level. The subjective improvement in the appearance score was also significant at the .001 level.

Their families concurred with these accounts of increased self-confidence, decreased self-consciousness, and a more relaxed, natural approach towards meeting strangers.

DISCUSSION

Patients with severe congenital disorders were more extreme in their self-rating of appearance, ranging from complete denial of the deformity (No. 1, perfect feature or No. 2, almost perfect feature) to self-deprecation (No. 9, very marked imperfection). Patients with acquired defects were more moderate in their self-rating.

Even more surprising is the apparent lack of correlation between the patient's rating and the actual severity of the deformity. Many investigators have assumed that a greater deformity forces a more realistic outlook on patients and their families than does a minor deformity (Hay & Heather, 1973; Lefebvre & Munroe, 1979; MacGregor, 1979), but this is not always the case. Although the toddler becomes aware of physical differences soon after he/she learns to walk and recognize his/her image, a close-knit family and small community may protect the child from the full social impact of the deformity, providing a model of denial and reaction formation (Ouellette, 1978) (for example, "a different face is more interesting.")

Belfer et al., in their studies at Harvard (Belfer et al., 1979a, 1979b), recently described the decision to undergo surgery as "that absolutely essential start of dissolution of pathological denial" (Hay & Heather, 1973). However, this leaves two unanswered questions. First, is the denial always pathological, or is a certain degree of reaction formation essential for parents to bond with a grossly deformed infant, after overcoming the initial grief process (Belfer et al., 1979a)? Could this explain why the happiest children often seem to be the most unrealistic in their self-rating? Second, is the decision in favor of surgery really a sign that truly pathological denial has ceased or merely been replaced by the unrealistic expectation that the child will become completely normal? In our experience, the prospect of yet another operation was often reassuring to parents or patients because it kept them from despairing about reality (MacGregor, 1979). The lay press often depicts the reconstructive facial surgeon as a "miracle worker" that further perpetuates the myth of magical solutions to long-term social problems.

We were also surprised to find that patients, except adolescents, usually rated their appearance as less deformed than their parents did, because we had assumed that parental love would turn a blind eye to stares and comments and focus on the child's positive physical attributes. Indeed, parents did frequently comment that they "no longer see the deformity" or "consider the child is perfect in their eyes," before going on to give us their usually realistic ratings. This rating scale often prompted them to describe vividly their anguished feelings of hurt, anger, and guilt when strangers stared or laughed at their child. The more sensitive they were to this social ostracism, the more severe their ratings of the deformity.

Most preschool and latency-aged children were remarkably able to shut out offending comments, avoid threatening situations (occasionally at the cost of social isolation), and rationalize their attitudes with far less guilt and anxiety than their parents. Adolescence, with its critical peer group conformity and self-deprecation, shattered the remnants of the fortress of parental-anxious reaction formation and the child's security denial, often breaking through the conspiracy of silence about the facial disfigurement for the first time. The result was often a disturbance of precarious family equilibrium and a power struggle between over-protective parents and independence-hungry, and often resentful, adolescents.

The enthusiasm of most patients about the results far exceeded the Craniofacial Team's expectations, albeit concurring with the findings of other authors (Phillips & Whitaker, 1979). Phillips and Whitaker surveyed 50 patients who had undergone craniofacial surgery and found that 90% of these patients would make the same decision again. Ouellette (1978) reported 93% satisfaction with combined orthodontic and facial treatment.

Our breakdown of psychosocial changes postoperatively (87% subjective improvement and 39% objective and subjective improvement) is similar to the results of Phillips and Whitaker (1979) (50% objective improvement) and Ouellette (1978) (37% moderate and 23% extreme life changes). Our slightly lower proportion of objective improvement is accounted for by the greater proportion of school- or preschool-aged children in our sample who are not in a position to make measured alterations (for example, change jobs or get married). However, many of these children were considered more intelligent by their teachers when their faces were more normal.

The 35 patients whose self-ratings of appearance did not change had given unrealistic appraisals of their deformity before surgery. Three were young children coming from very overprotective families prone to denial, all were anxious about the procedure of surgery (Foust, 1980) and all had minimal life changes as a result of surgery.

The seven patients who were disappointed with the physical outcome of surgery had been ambivalent or unrealistic preoperatively, either feeling pressured into surgery or expecting it to erase all problems. Phillips and Whitaker (1979) also noticed that adolescents were more prone to postoperative disappointment (45%), especially if they had not been involved in the decision to have surgery.

The remaining 28 families who were satisfied with the technical outcome of surgery but experienced increased family difficulties (occasionally culminating in divorce) immediately after surgery remain a source of great concern to us. There is no doubt that in some cases these family problems were a reaction to the patient's or one parent's growth in self-esteem and assertiveness, and represented a healthy identity crisis. Similarly, Belfer et al. (1979a, 1979b) reported divorces in four cases after cosmetic surgery in adults (Bernstein, 1976). However, we cannot help but wonder whether additional counseling and community support would have helped resolve long-standing family tensions and possibly prevent family breakdown in some of our cases. Hopefully, earlier diagnosis of congenital disorders, greater community understanding, and more thorough preoperative investigation of the patient's and family's strengths and difficulties will improve the timing of and expectations for drastic reconstructive surgery in each child. We are counting on the recently formed Craniofacial Family Association to provide continuing support for these patients and their families.

The results of our Self-esteem Pilot Project are particularly intriguing. Although it is evident that most patients who seek reconstructive surgery, and have realistic expectations about its outcome, do indeed benefit from this intervention, both in terms of self-esteem, and social competence, it appears, however, that the "man on the street" cannot usually tell the difference between a preoperative and a postoperative photograph of the same patient, and may, therefore, be expected to have the same initial subjective, negative impression of the patient's personality (Belfer et al., 1979a). This means that either our black and white, full-face photographs are poor representations of surgical results, or else the crucial variable in improving patients' social competence is their own improved self-perception and confidence rather than objective differences. Perhaps Beauty lies in the eye of the Beheld as much as in the gaze of the Beholder.

Finally, we are now gradually incorporating Steinhauer's Family Assessment Measure (J. Santa–Barbara, P.D. Steinhauer, & H. Skinner, personal communication, 1980) into our assessment protocol to evaluate the impact of these deformities and their surgical correction on the family system of the child.

CONCLUSION

Facial reconstruction of severe congenital and acquired deformities is generally very successful, providing both physical and psychosocial improvement, especially when the patient is actively involved in the decision-making process. However, we are gradually recognizing the danger signals of unrealistic preoperative expectations or unilateral decisions in favor of surgery as potential sources of family tension and patient disappointment after the operation. A more detailed analysis of data and correlation studies on this material is presently underway.

REFERENCES

Belfer, M. L., Harrison, A. M., & Murray, J. E. (1979a). Body image and the process of reconstructive surgery. *American Journal of Diseases in Childhood, 133,* 532–535.

Belfer, M. L., Mulliken, J. B., & Cochran, T. C. (1979b). Cosmetic surgery as an antecedent of life change. *American Journal of Psychiatry, 136,* 199–201.

Bernstein, N. R. (1976). *Emotional care of the facially burned and disfigured.* Boston: Little, Brown.

Berscheid, E., & Walster, E. (1972). Beauty and the best. *Psychol Today, 5*(10), 42–46, 74.

Constable, J. D., & Bernstein, N. R. (1979). Public and professional reactions to the facially disfigured which interfere with rehabilitation. *Scandinavian Journal of Plastic & Reconstructive Surgery, 13,* 181–183.

Constable, J. D., Bernstein, N. R., & Sheehy, E. (1979). Unreasonable expectations of reconstructive patients affecting rehabilitation. *Scandinavian Journal of Plastic & Reconstructive Surgery, 13,* 177–179.

Foust, L. A. (1980). The concerns of a ten-year-old boy threatened with body image disruption due to reconstructive craniofacial surgery. *Maternal Child Nursing Journal,* Spring 1980, *9*(1), 37–48.

Hay, G. G., & Heather, B. B. (1973). Changes in psychometric test results following cosmetic nasal operations. *British Journal of Psychiatry, 122,* 89–90.

Lefebvre, A., & Barclay, S. (1982). Psychosocial impact of craniofacial deformities before and after reconstructive surgery. *Canadian Journal of Psychiatry, 27,* 579–583.

Lefebvre, A., & Munro, I. (1979). The role of psychiatry in a craniofacial team. *Plastic & Reconstructive Surgery, 61,* 564–569.

MacGregor, F. C. (1979). *After Plastic Surgery: Adaptation and adjustment.* New York: Praeger.

Ouellette, P. L. (1978). Psychological ramifications of facial change in relation to orthodontic treatment and orthognathic surgery. *Journal of Oral Surgery, 36,* 787–790.

Phillips, J., & Whitaker, L. A. (1979). The social effects of craniofacial deformity and its correction. *Cleft Palate Journal, 16,* 7–15.

Piers, E. V. (1969). *Manual for the Piers–Harris Children's Self-Concept Scale (The Way I See Myself).* Nashville: Counselor Recordings and Tests.

PHYSIQUE

4 The Social Psychological Effects of Overweight

William DeJong
Education Development Center, Newton, Massachusetts

Robert E. Kleck
Dartmouth College

INTRODUCTION

The perception that one is overweight is a highly aversive state, particularly for females. In the United States, for example, literally billions of dollars are spent each year, mostly by women, on diet books, pills, exercise machines, salons, and low calorie foods. Persons who are massively overweight readily undergo major surgery, despite the serious mortality risks and bothersome side effects associated with that surgery, in the hopes of achieving a more "normal" body weight (e.g., Quaade, 1979; Solow, 1977).

It is plausible that the motivation supporting this effort and expense stems directly from the aversiveness of the physical state itself. The additional energy required to move a larger body mass, the discomfort experienced in small chairs or architectural spaces, and the often cited medical risks associated with excess body fat may all contribute to the overweight individual's herculean efforts to get and stay slimmer. Though we would acknowledge that such factors probably play some role in weight control attempts, particularly for dramatically overweight persons, they are, in our view, relatively trivial compared to the *social* pressures stemming from our culture's view of what constitutes acceptable or desirable human form.

In this sense, being overweight shares some similarities with other forms of body stigma (Goffman, 1963). Like persons with facial scars, missing limbs, and other physical "handicaps," overweight persons may be precluded from full social acceptance. What is different about their social condition, however, is the perception that they could escape their deviant status if only they could muster sufficient willpower. The overweight not only do not have an acceptable physical appearance but are also perceived as characterologically flawed for not being able to resist the temptations of food.

In the first section of this chapter we review the data on attitudes and dispositions toward the overweight. Second, we discuss how these attitudes may translate into discriminatory behavior toward the overweight thereby complicating and contaminating their social experiences. Third, we consider how the social reality of an individual may be constructed with weight as an organizing concept. The potential implications of such constructions for the perceptions and social behavior of overweight persons also are examined. Finally, we briefly discuss productive directions for future research efforts in this domain.

Throughout this discussion, we employ the term *overweight* in preference to the more common, but negatively connoted and frequently ill-defined term *obesity*. This is not to ignore that these terms are occasionally used within the medical literature to refer to quite different conditions of the human body. The former is often used to denote excess weight for a given height whereas the latter describes excess adipose tissue or body fat. Many psychologists and sociologists have used measures of weight but have referred to them as measures of obesity. For purposes of this chapter, we are more concerned with how body weight is *perceived,* both by self and by others, than with its reliable measurement.[1] Indeed, many individuals, particularly women, consider themselves overweight even though they fall within or below "normal" ranges as indexed by various actuarial or medical criteria (e.g., Stewart & Brook, 1983). As we argue later in the chapter, the belief that one is overweight may have an impact on how social outcomes are perceived and interpreted independent of one's actual weight status.

Attitudes Toward the Overweight

The most frequently used method for assessing dispositions toward the overweight is a picture-ranking task developed by Richardson, Hastorf, Goodman, and Dornbusch (1961). These investigators were interested in measuring children's dispositions toward a number of obvious forms of physical deviance in same-sex peers. The stimuli are six line drawings that show the same boy (or girl) as physically normal and with each of five physical "disabilities," including an obvious level of overweight. The drawings are arranged in random order before an individual subject who is asked to select the one he or she likes best. The selected drawing is laid aside and the question is repeated until a preference rank-ordering has been established for the set of six stimuli. With few exceptions, all replications have used the same stimuli and the same choice procedure.

---

[1]Those interested in the various approaches to the measurement of overweight and obesity should consult Bray (1979) or Stewart, Brook, and Kane (1980) for extended discussions of the issues.

In their original study, Richardson et al. (1961) asked 10- and 11-year-olds of various ethnic and socioeconomic backgrounds to rank-order the six drawings. The drawing of the child with no physical handicap was consistently preferred. Quite surprisingly, examination of the mean ranks for the five remaining drawings showed that they were ordered in the same sequence by all groups of subjects: The child with the leg brace and crutches was ranked second, followed by the child confined to a wheelchair, the hand amputee, the child with a facial disfigurement, and, finally, the overweight child. This sequence emerged across the subject variables of sex, race, socioeconomic background, and rural versus urban residence.

Nearly all subsequent studies have found the physically normal child to be most preferred, but the rank-order for the drawings of the physically deviant children has varied somewhat. Even so, the drawing of the overweight child usually is ranked last or next to last by American subjects (Alessi & Anthony, 1969; Giancoli & Neimeyer, 1983; Goodman, Richardson, Dornbusch, & Hastorf, 1963; Maddox, Back, & Liederman, 1968; Richardson 1970; Richardson & Emerson, 1970; Richardson & Royce, 1968).

This does not mean that the rank-preference position of the overweight child is unaffected by other variables. Nineteen of Maddox et al.'s (1968) 199 subjects, for example, reported wanting to gain weight. This group ranked the drawing of the overweight child third. Likewise, in the Goodman et al. (1963) study, lower class Jewish girls moved the overweight child up to the fourth position, which reflected, according to the investigators, somewhat more positive subcultural attitudes toward food consumption and its implications for body weight.

There are several published reports of replications carried out in countries other than the United States (Chigier & Chigier, 1968; Richardson, 1971, 1977; Richardson & Green, 1971). Two dominant themes emerge from this body of work. First, the available evidence suggests that the least accepting attitudes toward overweight peers, relative to other forms of physical deviance, are found in industrialized, Western cultures. This is underscored by the results for a large Israeli sample (Chigier & Chigier, 1968). Those children whose fathers came from English-speaking or Western European countries ranked the overweight child fifth or sixth, whereas those with Middle Eastern or North African parentage were more accepting. A plausible interpretation of this finding is that overweight is less negatively valued under conditions of occasional food scarcity (Powdermaker, 1962). If not everyone can get access to food in sufficient quantities to become overweight, excess body weight may become associated with high status and even beauty (DeGarine, 1972; Rudofsky, 1971).

Second, almost without exception, females are less accepting of overweight peers than are males (Richardson, 1977). In many cases where the overall rank given to the drawing of the overweight child was the same for the two sexes, the females still assigned a lower mean rank than did males. This sex difference is found across several cultures and a broad age range. Before making too much of this gender difference, however, it is important to note that its interpretation is complicated by the fact that studies employing the picture-ranking procedure have usually had subjects rank only same-sex drawings. Thus, the finding could reflect less acceptance of overweight female peers generally, less acceptance of overweight others by females, or both.

Although the results of the many studies using the Richardson picture-ranking task have been informative regarding the social acceptability of overweight individals, the paradigm has a number of limitations. The use of line drawings rather than more life-like representations, though it provides a well-controlled manipulation of various forms of physical deviance (Richardson, 1983), may nevertheless seriously constrain the generalizability of the results (Yuker, 1983). A more important criticism is that all of this research (save Richardson, 1971) has used but a single set of drawings, even when the subjects differed greatly in age or cultural background from the depicted individuals. This leaves open the possibility that the observation of low social acceptability of overweight persons is a function of the specific age period represented in these drawings (approximately 10 to 12 years of age).

A degree of reassurance is provided on this last point in a recent study in Harris and Smith (1983). These investigators had 447 children and adults of both sexes and of various ethnic backgrounds and weights respond to 12 line drawings of individuals depicted to vary in age, sex, and weight. Their findings show that perceivers, independent of their own characteristics, negatively value overweight in both children and adults. Underweight stimuli fared better than overweight, but were themselves more negatively evaluated than normal-weight individuals.

It is important to note that we have little information on either how individuals perceived the stimuli used in these studies or the possible rationales underlying their expressed preferences. Maddox et al. (1968) conducted the only study in which this latter issue was systematically examined. After subjects had established a rank preference order for the drawings, they were asked to explain on what basis they had selected the picture. The largest number (38%) reported considering which children were physically in the worst condition while assigning ranks; these individuals placed the overweight child third. One-fourth said they ranked the pictures by how much pity they evoked; this group placed the overweight child fourth (males) or fifth (females). Fourteen percent focused on facial appearance; males who did this placed the overweight child fifth, whereas females ranked it sixth. The dimensions used by the remaining 13% of the subjects were not reported. It would clearly be informative to systematically instruct subjects to adopt certain sets toward the stimuli prior to establishing their preference rankings.

None of the studies that have used the Richardson drawings have asked their subjects what degree of overweight they associated with these stimuli. In order to provide some data on this issue, male and female adults were shown the physically normal and overweight drawings and were asked to rate them on the weight dimension (Kleck, 1984). The results reveal that the Richardson "obese" stimuli depict individuals who are perceived to be moderately overweight (mean rating = 10.6 on a 14-point scale ranging from 0 = extremely underweight to 13 = extremely overweight) and to exceed "normal" weight by an average of 32%. Sex of perceiver is important only in that females tend to perceive the overweight female as less extreme on this dimension than do males.

One final methodological concern with the picture-ranking paradigm needs to be acknowledged. Alessi and Anthony (1969) have noted that the preference orders cited in most published reports are based on the mean ranks assigned to each drawing. This can mean, of course, that no individual subject actually assigns ranks to all six pictures that are the same as those attributed to the subject sample as a whole (a result these investigators obtained with a sample of 42 boys and girls at a summer camp). They propose that authors report the number of subjects giving a certain rank to each stimulus figure. They note, for example, that 71% of their subjects, all of whom were physically handicapped, placed the overweight child fifth or sixth.

A direct implication of the total set of picture-ranking studies is that overweight children will be less preferred as friends than will more normal-weight individuals. Unfortunately, the number of studies that have attempted to assess the sociometric status of actual overweight children is remarkably small and their results equivocal. Studies by Staffieri (1967) and Sallade (1973) illustrate this state of affairs. Staffieri asked boys and girls from grades 1 through 5 to list the classmates who were their five best friends. Peers who had previously been classified as overweight on the basis of a ponderal index were selected least often as best or second-best friends.

Sallade used height–weight norms and triceps skinfold measurements to identify 30 overweight and 30 normal-weight students of both sexes. Their classmates were then asked to place them and other students on a sociometric scale. Unlike Staffieri, Sallade found no differences in the social acceptability of overweight and normal-weight peers. At the very least, the latter result suggests that interpersonal dispositions toward the overweight may be overwhelmed by or interact with situational or behavioral variables. Research by Borjeson (1962), for example, indicates that males' preferences for overweight peers may vary directly as a function of the context in which the association occurs. What is needed are more studies that examine overweight in the context of other variables. We return to this issue in the final section of this chapter.

The Fat-Person Stereotype

A great deal of research demonstrates that physical characteristics of persons can serve as focal points around which common impressions or stereotypes are elaborated. Knowing only that a person is physically attractive (Berscheid &

Walster, 1974) or malformed (Mussen & Barker, 1944), perceivers confidently speculate about that person's personality. Wright (1960) argues that physical characteristics elicit this kind of stereotypical elaboration because "physique is so intrinsically connected with the identity of persons" (p. 118). Not only is physical appearance information usually the first that is available to the perceiver, but its continuous availability during an interaction does not depend, as does attitudinal or personality information, on complex information processing and retrieval (Kleck & Rubenstein, 1975).

A number of investigators have addressed the issue of whether an elaborated stereotype is associated with excess body weight. Staffieri (1967), for example, showed 90 elementary-school-aged boys full-body silhouettes of a mesomorph (muscular), an endormorph (fat), and an ectomorph (thin). Each boy was asked to assign each of 39 adjectives to the silhouette it best described. The endomorphic silhouette was least frequently described as "best friend" and as having "lots of friends," and it was described most frequently as "gets teased." In addition, the endomorph received the most frequent endorsement for the descriptors lazy, stupid, sloppy, dirty, naughty, mean, and ugly. Similar results for elementary-school-aged girls have been reported by both Caskey and Felker (1971) and Staffieri (1972).

There are several methodological limitations to this approach. First, the use of silhouette cutouts as stimuli, although providing a degree of standardization, brings the generalizability of these results into question. Other investigators concerned with stereotyping of the overweight have used similarly deficient stimuli, such as written physical descriptions (Strongman & Hart, 1968) and profile drawings (e.g., Hinsdale, 1976; Lerner, Knapp, & Pool, 1974). Others have used photographs (e.g., Lerner, 1969b; Powell, Tutton, & Stewart, 1974), but in several cases the faces have been masked (e.g., Stewart, Powell, & Tutton, 1973). When photographs of real persons have been used, however, more than one photo of each body type is rarely used, thus bringing into question whether the reported results are tied to those particular stimuli.

A second criticism of these studies concerns the use of a forced-choice procedure. In effect, subjects are asked to evaluate all three stimuli, assigning each body type a score of one ("best fit") or zero ("not best fit") for each adjective. The use of this within-subjects design, coupled with the type of stimuli most often used and the failure to provide any kind of deceptive cover story, would make the investigators' hypotheses transparent to many subjects. Equally important, a forced-choice methodology is insensitive to the magnitude of perceived differences between the three body types. For example, although most subjects may indicate that a mesomorph rather than an endomorph "best fits" the descriptor "successful," the difference in real perceptions may be trivially small (see Lerner et al., 1974).

A forced-choice procedure has not been employed by all investigators. Alternatively, subjects have been shown all three stimuli and asked to rate each on a series of bipolar scales (e.g., Dibiase & Hjelle, 1968; Miller, Kiker, Watson, Frauchiger, & Moreland, 1968; Wells & Siegel, 1961), or subjects have been asked to rank-order six stimuli (two photographs of each type) on each of the listed traits (e.g., Powell et al., 1974; Stewart et al., 1973). In general, these studies have also found more negative evaluations of the endomorph. It must be noted, however, that these again make use of a within-subject design, and demand characteristics are again possible. Only one study used a between-subjects design, but it relied on written descriptions of the stimuli, as already noted (Strongman & Hart, 1968).

A third general criticism is that there has been no systematic selection of traits for subjects to use in judging these stimuli. Rather, most investigators have simply drawn up their own lists of items. These lists have sometimes been egregious; Stewart et al. (1973), for example, asked their subjects to rank-order six photographs of females from most to least fitting on the concepts of alcoholic, prostitute, and homosexual, among others. In other cases, specific items are not examined, but only a composite index is formed (e.g., Felker, 1972). Obviously, these differences in measurement make comparisons across studies problematic.

A favorable aspect of these studies is their inclusion of the ectomorph (thin) body type as part of the stimulus set. In several cases, it is found that the endomorph and ectomorph are nominated equally often for a particular trait (e.g., Harris & Smith, 1983; Lerner, 1969a, 1969b). Thus, differences between the mesomorph and the endomorph that might otherwise be attributed to a fatness stereotype can sometimes be seen to be the result of physical deviance per se.

Despite the methodological deficiencies of these studies, and occasional incomplete data reporting, a tentative outline of the fatness or overweight stereotype can be drawn: (1) Several studies suggest that endomorphs are viewed as less intelligent than mesomorphs or ectomorphs (e.g., Caskey & Felker, 1971; Lerner et al., 1974; Miller et al., 1968; Staffieri, 1967, 1972); (2) endomorphs are least often chosen as friends and least often thought to have many friends (e.g., Caskey & Felker, 1971; Lerner, 1969b; Powell et al., 1974; Staffieri, 1967, 1972). These studies also indicate that people do believe that fat individuals suffer from this rejection; labels such as *lonely, shy, greedy for affection,* and *dependent* are used to describe endomorphs (e.g., Caskey & Felker, 1971; Dibiase & Hjelle, 1968; Staffieri, 1972; Strongman & Hart, 1968; Wells & Siegel, 1961); (3) the view that the overweight are lazy is expressed by many groups of subjects (Caskey & Felker, 1971; Lerner et al., 1974; Staffieri, 1967, 1972; Wells & Siegel, 1961).

One surprising outcome of these studies involving American subjects is that as a group they do not constitute strong evidence for the "jolly" fat-person stereotype. Two investigations did report such evidence (Strongman & Hart, 1968; Wells & Siegel, 1961) but they are in the minority. Unfortunately, other studies that could have provided data on this issue did not list traits that tapped this aspect of the overweight stereotype directly. A recently completed study by DeJong (1980) showed that high school girls rated an overweight peer to be unhappier than one who was normal weight; no differences between the two were found on the traits of warmth or friendliness.

It is clear that studies employing more sophisticated and well-controlled methodologies are needed to better define the popular stereotype associated with overweight. In addition, a more systematic effort must be made to map out age and sex differences in perceptions of overweight individuals. The broad array of methodologies used makes this impossible in terms of the current data set.

One advantage of the forced-choice procedure is its easy application to cross-cultural comparisons. In contrast to the picture-ranking studies, however, this methodology has rarely been used with non-American populations. Lerner and Pool (1972) did show 10- to 13-year-old Mexican school children profile drawings of adult males; according to the authors' summary of that study, the endomorph was more often assigned the descriptors "mean," "cheats," "selfish," "talks a lot," and "gets teased."

Iwawaki and Lerner (1974), using photographs of adult males, discovered that male and female Japanese university students had the most negative view of the ectomophic stimulus, which was selected most often for the descriptors "has fewest friends," "least preferred as a personal friend," and "poor father." The endomorph, in contrast, was viewed relatively positively, though not so favorably as the mesomorph. Females chose the endomorph most often for the descriptor, "has many friends," whereas males chose that stimulus and the mesomorph equally often. However, males did choose the endomorph most often for "poorest doctor." In terms of a personality stereotype, the only item picked most often for the endomorph was "least aggressive."

Finally, Antons–Brandi (1972) asked female patients at a West German clinic to assign one of five silhouettes as a "best fit" for each of 13 descriptors. The two heaviest figures were most frequently nominated for both "most sociable" and "will liven up a party" and were picked as often as the middle-weight figure for the item, "gets the most joy out of life." In addition, the two endomorphic figures were also most often selected as an "authoritarian boss." Two other negative descriptors were shared equally by the endomorphic and ectomorphic figures: "gives up on a hard assignment" and "least like to work with."

The medical profession's involvement in the treatment of overweight has created a special interest in the stereotypes that physicians and other health professionals may hold for overweight persons. Mayer (1968) and Cahnman (1968) have both chastised the medical profession for its subscription to a "moralistic diagnosis" of obesity and overweight. Their complaint is echoed by Kurland (1970): "Most physicians regard obesity as a sin and treat fat patients with disdain befitting a moral leper. . . . Failure to lose weight is immediately regarded as little more than concrete evidence of moral turpitude" (p. 20). Brewer, White, and Baddeley (1974) report that they hear physicians criticise the use of jejunoileal bypass surgery because the operation supposedly rescues the massively overweight from the consequences of their lack of self-control.

In an attempt to systematically explore stereotypes toward overweight among health professionals, Maddox and Liederman (1969) asked physicians, house officers, and student clerks working in a public outpatient medical clinic to complete scale ratings of several target persons. The majority of those responding described obese patients as "ugly" and "weak-willed." Breytspraak, McGee, Conger, Whatley, and Moore (1977) had first-year medical students look at a videotape of a simulated patient interview. Two versions of the tape were made, one with the normal-weight confederate appearing as herself, and the other with her using padding to look overweight. During the 6-minute interview, the woman told her doctor that even though her test results were negative, she still sometimes felt irritable or nervous. Those seeing the overweight target described her as more nervous, more incompetent, and less likeable. Additionally, she was thought to be less likely to benefit from counseling and more likely to have continuing problems without counseling.

How might these negative attitudes or stereotypes affect the doctor–patient relationship? Maddox, Anderson, and Bogdonoff (1966) looked at records for the screening examinations given to new patients at a medical outpatient clinic. Among overweight patients (i.e., those 20% or more overweight according to height–weight norms), less than half had their weight problem noted by their physicians in chart entries. If it were noted, there was still only a 50% chance that a weight management program was suggested to the patients. Interestingly, the physicians were much more likely to make a notation of a weight problem and to recommend a management program for women patients than for men.

It is important to note that a relatively small percentage of persons who consider themselves overweight, or who have been told by medical professionals that they are overweight, actually seek medical care for this condition. A large-scale, cross-sectional study conducted by Stewart and Brook (1983) found that fewer than 7% of those who perceived that they are overweight were under a doctor's care for weight loss. Unfortunately, those who were not being seen by a physician were not asked to explain why they had not obtained medical assistance.

There are at least two factors that may be operating to keep those concerned about a weight problem off the doctor's appointment list. First, overweight individuals may avoid medical treatment for their condition because they are aware of negative attitudes on the part of medical professionals toward individuals such as themselves (e.g., Vener, Krupka, & Gerard, 1982). Second, medical professionals may directly express their disinterest in managing overweight patients (Maddox & Liederman, 1969) or may convey their sense of futility regarding the effectiveness of any weight-loss regime in the face of the patients' presumed lack of willpower (Stunkard & McLaren–Hume, 1959). Additional studies are required to clarify these important issues.

The Issue of Responsibility

Goffman (1963), like other writers (e.g., Sagarin, 1975), differentiates between three categories of stigma: (1) the physical deformities, or what he calls the "abominations of the body"; (2) the "tribal stigmata" of race, religion, or social class; and (3) the "blemishes of individual character," such as addiction, alcoholism, or homosexuality. Langer, Taylor, Fiske, and Chanowitz (1976) note that those who possess a characterological stigma are often explicitly derogated, whereas those who are physically deviant are not. This difference supposedly stems from the fact that those who possess a characterological stigma are assumed to have responsibility for acquiring and maintaining their deviant status (DeJong, 1980). In contrast, most physical attributes are seen as determined by forces beyond an individual's control.

There are, of course, some physical characteristics that are viewed as being under a person's direct control. These characteristics, such as personal hygiene or the growth of facial hair, are believed to reflect freely made choices. Intention to possess the characteristic is assumed unless information about coercive situational forces or uncontrollable internal forces, such as disease or bodily dysfunction, can be presented (Levine & McBurney, 1977).

Several authors have noted (e.g., Cahnman, 1968; Mayer, 1968) that the negative attitudes expressed toward the overweight seem to arise from the belief that it is caused by self-indulgence, gluttony, or laziness. In short, excessive weight is viewed as "a self-induced condition" (Mayer, 1968, p. 85). In this respect then, the overweight have much in common with those possessing a characterological stigma. A simple study by Maddox et al. (1968) highlights this point. Their subjects were asked to indicate to what extent an individual would be responsible for possession of each of 24 traits. Although only 2% said a blind person is responsible for that characteristic, 76% felt that a "man with a flabby body" was responsible for that condition, and 84% indicated that a "woman needing a girdle" was responsible.

Under the guise of a getting-acquainted study, DeJong (1980) had high school girls look at a folder containing a photograph and a statement of introduction that a girl from a previous experiment supposedly had written. Half of the subjects were shown a photograph of an overweight peer; the others saw a picture of a normal-weight girl. As a cross-dimension, half the subjects were told the girl had a thyroid problem, a condition that explained either her weight, or, in the case of the normal-weight target, her slight "paleness." The other subjects were told nothing about a glandular disorder. Subjects were asked to give their first impressions of the girl by rating her on a number of personality dimensions and to indicate how much they liked her. As predicted, the overweight girl with no thyroid condition was seen as lazier and was less liked than both the normal-weight girl with no thyroid condition and the overweight girl with a glandular problem. In a second study, DeJong found that an overweight girl who reported a recent weight loss, as well as one citing a thyroid disorder, was rated more positively. DeJong and Nackman (1979) showed high school girls a videotape of either an overweight or normal-weight peer. Consistent with the results of the previous study, subjects rated the overweight girl to be more self-indulgent and less self-disciplined than the normal-weight girl, except when her weight was said to result from a glandular disorder.

In another demonstration of the characterological implications of being overweight (Vann, 1976), undergraduate males participated in a bogus learning experiment with an overweight male confederate. Subjects were told that the study was concerned with how a teacher's knowledge about his pupil can affect that teacher's ability to communicate. The confederate, picked to be the pupil through a rigged drawing, was then asked to talk about himself. The confederate's discussion of his weight condition constituted the independent variable. In the high-responsibility condition he said he chose to be fat; he reported that he had dieted and lost weight in the past, but that it was not worth the sacrifice. He concluded by saying, "I don't care what people think. I eat because I really enjoy good food. So it looks like I'm gonna be fat." In contrast, in the low-responsibility condition, the confederate quickly asserted that he had a glandular disorder and would not be fat if he had any choice about it. Obviously, this manipulation of responsibility is far more elaborate than the one employed by DeJong (1980).

As the teacher, the subject's job was to help the confederate learn a predetermined sequence of lights by using electric shock to inform him of his errors. The apparatus measured which shock intensities the subject chose, how hard he pressed the shock buttons, and how long they were held down. Immediately following the "teaching" segment, the subject judged the confederate on several rating scales, many of which were then combined into an overall evaluation index. As predicted, subjects in the high-responsibility condition gave the overweight confederate more shock, as measured by how hard they pressed; there was also a nonsignificant tendency for those subjects to administer shocks of longer duration. As expected, these subjects judged the confederate more harshly on the evaluation index than did those in the low-responsibility condition.

Yet further evidence on the responsibility issue comes from a study by Northcraft (1980). Subjects were shown a set of cards, each listing a particular type of stigmatized person, and asked to rate the similarity of all possible pairings of those cards. A cluster analysis of the data revealed one set of items that had in common the presumption of the individual's responsibility for possession of the stigmatizing characteristic: (1) someone who has syphilis, (2) an exconvict, (3) a drug addict, (4) an alcoholic, (5) someone with ulcers, and (6) someone who is overweight. Thus, rather than being associated with other kinds of physical deviance (e.g., someone who has to use a wheelchair or is abnormally short), overweight appears to be grouped with the so-called characterological stigmata.

Recent medical insights into the various causes of overweight tend to under-mine the notion that the condition grows primarily out of a lack of willpower or is directly the "fault" of the overweight person. Harris (1983) reasoned, therefore, that the more informed persons are regarding the results of this research, the less they should hold overweight persons accountable for their condition and the less negatively disposed toward them they should be. She did, in fact, find a signifi-cant correlation between knowledge about obesity and positive attitudes toward the overweight for a group of 222 Australian college students. The author notes that the subject sample as a whole scored at a chance level on the eight item, true–false knowledge test.

It can be concluded, then, that the inference of perceived responsibility does play an important role in dispositions toward the overweight. It is not the mere fact that such persons are physically deviant that causes them to be derogated, but that they are assumed to be guilty of self-indulgence, gluttony, or a failure of willpower. At the same time, relieving the overweight individual of responsibil-ity for his or her physical deviance through manipulations of the sort employed by DeJong (1980) may not fully remove the stigma associated with this physical characteristic.

Overweight and Social Outcomes

Despite the various methodological limitations of the research reviewed here, it is clear that individuals report less liking for and ascribe more negative traits to overweight compared to normal-weight individuals. Though many investigators presume direct causal links between such attitudes and how overweight indi-viduals are treated, such a presumption is not justified in the absence of an empirical test of those links (Fazio & Zanna, 1981; Fishbein & Azjen, 1975). Overweight individuals in this society do report direct experience with discrimi-nation in such areas of life as the quality of medical care, employment oppor-tunities, income levels, and health and life insurance costs, to name just a few (Allon, 1982; Louderback, 1970; Millman, 1980). Empirical documentation of these claims is problematic, however, as only a very small amount of empirical research has focused on this issue.

Perhaps the most widely cited studies purported to document active discrimi-nation are those of Canning and Mayer. Though high school records of over-weight and normal-weight students were found to be very similar, and though both groups appeared equally intent upon going to college (Canning & Mayer, 1967), nevertheless, a smaller percentage of overweight individuals were admit-ted (Canning & Mayer, 1966). This was particularly true for females among whom nearly equal percentages applied (56.3% normal and 55.4% overweight), but many fewer of the overweight were admitted (31.6% vs. 51.9%). Because the authors could not detect a negative bias in how high school teachers graded the overweight, they felt that admissions interviewers were the most likely source of prejudice. Canning and Mayer (1966) also report data indicating that the prevalence of overweight among high school seniors is greater than among college freshmen. They take this as further evidence of discrimination in college admissions. This neglects the possibility that once overweight students are admitted to college they become motivated to lose weight (Larkin & Pines, 1979).

Employment is another area where blatant discrimination against the overweight has been alleged (e.g., Louderback, 1970). Larkin and Pines (1979), in an attempt to get systematic data on this issue conducted two related studies. The first established that the overweight stereotype includes trait ascriptions that would make them less desirable employees than normal-weight or under-weight individuals (e.g., "less productive," "not industrious," "disorganized," and "indecisive"). In the second study, male and female young adults saw a videotape of either an overweight or normal-weight peer performing two job selection tasks. As a cross-dimension, half of the subjects saw a female job applicant, and half saw a male applicant. Task performances of the confederates were held constant across the experimental conditions. After viewing the tapes, subjects were asked how strongly they would recommend the applicant for a job requiring skills similar to those involved in the tasks they saw the individual perform. Overweight job applicants of both sexes were less highly recommended than were the normal-weight confederates. Impressions of the applicants' job-related trait characteristics generally replicated the findings of the first study, that is, the overweight job applicant was rated as less productive, energetic, ambitious, etc.

In a related field study, Benson, Severs, Tatgenhorst, and Loddengaard (1980) created a bogus cover letter and resume from an undergraduate seeking "career guidance" in the public health field. In her letter, she asked for suggestions for graduate programs, what her chances might be for getting into a good program, and what her opportunities were for obtaining a good job in this field after getting her degree. Eighty percent of the resumes included a photograph of either of two confederates in their normal-weight condition (125 lbs, 5'6") or with padding added to give the appearance of overweight (185 lbs, 5'6"). Twenty percent of the resumes did not contain a picture and made no reference to the weight of the supposed letter writer. The materials were sent to 70 male public health administrators who did not realize that the inquiry was bogus.

Forty-six percent of the total mailing elicited a response. For those inquiries that contained a picture of an overweight woman, 25% were answered, whereas for the normal-weight condition, 57% elicited an answer. The public health professionals were much less optimistic when they thought the individual was overweight in terms of both her chances of getting into a good graduate program (29% for overweight; 81% for normal) and in terms of her chances for getting a good job after completing her training (29% for overweight; 56% for normal). The authors acknowledge that their ability to generalize from their findings is limited by the low rate of return in the overweight condition. Moreover, the health professionals were all males, and the inquiries were perceived as coming from females. They (Benson et al., 1980) suggest that this particular combination of sex of subject and sex of target "probably maximizes the effect of body-build" (p. 94).

The possible relationship between weight and earning power has received a great deal of media attention in the past several years, largely as a consequence of a report by the Robert Half Personnel Agencies (e.g., Allon, 1982). The report has been widely cited as documenting that executives sacrifice $1000 in yearly salary for each pound they are overweight. McLean and Moon (1980) used data from the National Longitudinal Survey of Mature Men to examine this earnings–obesity hypothesis. For the 2356 men in the sample (ages 51 to 65) they found a *positive* correlation between wages and overweight as indexed by the Metropolitan Life Insurance Company's tables. The authors (McLean & Moon, 1980) note that for males at least, "large size may generate a 'nonverbal signal' of power, strength, or capability" (p. 1009). It is obvious that we need much more data, particularly on women, before we can say anything definitive concerning the relationship between overweight and job or income discrimination.

Despite the protestations by overweight adults that they are the target of active discrimination and rejection, there is relatively little data, then, to empirically verify this claim. Jarvie, Lahey, Graziano, and Framer (1983) note that the overt rejection of overweight children implied by the many attitudinal studies has likewise not been corroborated by observations of exchanges between overweight and normal-weight children. This is not to argue that discrimination does not occur, but only that investigators have yet to seriously address this issue.

Overweight: The View From Inside

Independent of the actual role played by overweight in biasing social outcomes, there are reasons for expecting overweight individuals to nevertheless *perceive* such a bias. It has been argued elsewhere (Kleck & Strenta, in press) that if one is physically deviant in some manner (e.g., facially scarred, paraplegic, or overweight) it will be difficult to objectively assess the impact of that deviance on one's social experiences. This difficulty stems in part from the physically deviant individual's inability to use Kelley's (1967, 1971) principle of covariation. If one wished to know how responses to his or her person might be affected by two different styles of dress, for example, those styles could be systematically varied over time and peoples' responses to the two styles compared. If, on the other hand, the characteristic is something that must be taken into every interaction (such as obvious overweight), then a definitive test will not be possible and the individual is left with the hypothesis that the characteristic is playing a role in how others are responding to him or her.

This hypothesis can quickly turn into reality if overweight individuals also *expect* their weight to make a difference in how others treat them or regard them. A growing body of research demonstrates that expectancies can seriously bias both what perceivers pay attention to in social interaction as well as what meaning is attributed to any particular behavior (e.g., Duncan, 1976; Nisbett & Ross, 1980; Snyder & Frankel, 1976; Strenta & Kleck, 1984). Further, Snyder (1981) has argued that the most common strategy for perceivers to employ in testing interpersonal hypotheses is to search for information that may serve to confirm those expectancies.

In attempting to explore further the conditions under which perceivers would readily see their own physical characteristics as pivotal to their treatment by others, Kleck and Strenta (1980) lead subjects to believe that others thought they had epilepsy, an allergy, or a facial scar. The general hypothesis guiding the research was that negatively valued characteristics (epilepsy and facial scars) would be readily implicated in others' treatment of you whereas more neutral characteristics (allergy) would not.

Young adult females came to the laboratory expecting to have a conversation with a same-sex peer. Prior to the arrival of the other individual, each subject was told that the experimenters were interested in what effect, if any, a specific physical characteristic might have on her partner's behavior and disposition toward her. For the allergy and epilepsy conditions the woman was asked to include bogus medical information on the characteristic in a biographical sheet to be shared with the other person prior to the start of the interaction. This information was, in fact, deleted from the sheet before the other person saw it. In the facial scar condition, a substance was placed on the subject's face to simulate facial scars in a manner used in dramatic productions. After the subject had looked in a mirror to confirm that she had an authentic looking facial disfigurement, the experimenter applied a "moisturizing" cream that removed the "scar" without her awareness. The subject then interacted with one of several confederates who had no knowledge of the purposes of the study or of the manipulations being used.

As expected, subjects in the scar and epilepsy conditions perceived that these physical characteristics strongly influenced how much the other individual liked them and how she behaved during the exchange. Those subjects who thought the other viewed them as having an allergy, which is an evaluatively neutral characteristic, perceived that it had little impact on her liking for them or on her behavior during their conversation. When scar subjects subsequently viewed a videotape that had been candidly made of the confederate, they readily found evidence in her gaze behavior to document their assertion that the disfigurement had upset her and that she was having trouble dealing with it. Epilepsy subjects thought that their partner was distressed by having to interact with an epileptic and cited various body behaviors as indicative of that tension.[2]

---

[2]Three further studies conducted with this general paradigm (1) replicated the findings of the first study, (2) demonstrated that observers are prone to make the same sorts of attribution errors as are actors, and (3) ruled out experimenter demand and self-fulfilling prophecy explanations of the results.

What is important about this study is that it demonstrates how easily perceivers can become convinced that a characteristic they presume they have but do not, is a key determinant of another person's behavior and disposition toward them. The results offer strong testimony to Hamilton's (1981) assertion that we tend to find in the behavior of others what we expect to see there. For reasons of practicality this study was done with forms of physical deviance that could be readily manipulated within a laboratory context. There is every reason to expect, however, that overweight would result in the same sort of expectancy–confirming perceptions.

Direct evidence that overweight is a personal physical characteristic to which social outcomes are readily attributed comes from studies by Rodin and Slochower (1974) and Stunkard and Mendelson (1961). In the latter study, adults undergoing treatment for their weight problems were interviewed concerning their perceptions of their overweight. The investigators discovered that a number of these persons were prone to articulate their view of the world and their social outcomes primarily in terms of their weight. The main focus of the Rodin and Slochower study was to examine the relationship between weight and responsiveness to salient cues. Within the context of this study, confederates treated overweight and normal-weight females in a pleasant, neutral, or nasty manner. According to Rodin and Slochower (1974), when asked at the end of the study why the confederate acted toward them as she did, normal-weight subjects gave many different explanations, whereas overweight individuals "overwhelmingly attributed the confederate's behavior to their obesity" (p. 563).[3]

It is important to note that we are not arguing that the perception of prejudicial treatment is simply a social construction based on overweight individuals' expectations of how they will be treated. Indeed, as noted earlier in this chapter, there is a great deal of evidence that attitudes toward the overweight are prejudicial and, at least under some circumstances, these attitudes appear to produce overt discriminatory behavior. What we are suggesting is that a negatively valued physical characteristic, particularly one that is always on display to others, can easily lead the possessor to *overattribute* the impact that characteristic may have on social interaction outcomes.

Some Unresolved Issues

Jarvie et al. (1983), subsequent to an excellent review of the stigmatizing nature of childhood obesity, note that many important questions regarding this condi-

---

[3]It is interesting to note that within the context of this same experiment, the compliance behavior of the normal-weight females was less responsive to the weight status of the confederate (overweight or normal) than was the compliance of the overweight subjects. This raises the possibility that weight is a more central determinant of how overweight individuals respond to others than it is for the responses of normal-weight persons.

tion remain unanswered or unresearched. This observation holds for our understanding of the social psychological consequences of overweight generally, not just its developmental implications. Our suggestions of research issues therefore overlap with those of Jarvie and his colleagues to some extent. Just as we have not attempted to comprehensively review all of the work on the social stigma of overweight (cf. Allon, 1982, and Jarvie et al., 1983, for somewhat different perspectives), so in what follows we have not attempted to be exhaustive or comprehensive:

The Stimulus of Overweight.   Investigators concerned with attitudes and dispositions toward body weight have given remarkably little attention to degree of overweight or to the precise way overweight is interpreted in their photographs, line drawings, or verbal descriptions (see Borjeson, 1962, and Powell et al., 1973, for exceptions). Because of this, it is difficult to compare results across studies and impossible to assess whether the degree or the specific nature of the overweight are important variables. As noted in regard to the Richardson stimuli, this is not because the relevant data cannot be collected, but only because investigators have failed to do so.

Weight in the Context of Other Appearance and Behavioral Cues.   Thus far the research on overweight has largely neglected the fact that bodies have heads, just as the research on physical attractiveness has ignored the fact that faces have bodies. Both the facial attractiveness literature (e.g., Adams, 1982; Hildebrandt, 1982) and the research on overweight have convincingly documented that these physical characteristics have implications for how we view and treat others. What is missing from the analyses are studies that examine the interactive effects of these aspects of appearance on social outcomes (Jarvie, et al., 1983). Further, the analysis of appearance variables like overweight must be extended to incorporate the behavior of the overweight individual as well.

The results of a study by Young and Avdzej (1979) illustrate this last point. These investigators had male and female children of various ages view overweight and normal-weight male peers who either did or did not respond to an adult female's request for assistance in moving a piece of furniture. The results replicate the now familiar finding that children form more negative impressions of an overweight peer and prefer him less as a friend. It is also the case, however, that the observed behavioral compliance or noncompliance with an adult's request had a greater impact on their interpersonal dispositions toward the peer than did his weight status. The demonstrations that static physical characteristics like overweight can have an impact on various attitudinal and behavioral measures, with other variables held constant or trivialized, are all well and good. What is needed now, however, is research that allows one to assess the *relative* robustness of overweight as a determinant of social outcomes, as well as the ways in which its effects may interact with or be modified by other variables.

Research of the sort cited above may be important for reasons that extend beyond its contribution to a more complete scientific analysis of the issues. We argued earlier that one mechanism by which overweight becomes a social psychological variable of importance is through its impact on the expectations individuals have concerning how they will be regarded or treated by others. Being overweight may cause a person to expect rejection and this expectation may lead directly to the perception of rejection by others (e.g., Kleck & Strenta, in press). These expectations may also cause the individual to behave in such a way as to actually elicit rejection via a self-fulfilling prophecy dynamic. An important question, then, is how do these expectations develop in the overweight and what sustains them?

Part of the answer to the question, and the only one that will concern us here, rests with the nature of the scientific literature itself. One of the items on the Harris (1983) eight item, true–false "knowledge of obesity" test is: "Unfavorable attitudes toward obese persons have been shown in numerous studies of children and adults from a number of different cultures." It was one of only two items on which university students scored above chance. Although these students might have encountered this information in their course work, it has also been widely reported in popular treatments of obesity (e.g., Louderback, 1970; Millman, 1980). What is missing in these reports, and indeed largely in the literature upon which they are based, is any recognition of how negative attitudes or treatment of the overweight may be modified or ameliorated by such factors as the age of onset of the overweight, level of social competence of the overweight person, and the nature of the social relationship in which the overweight person is participating. The essential point is that a reading of the literature on the social psychological implications of overweight that does not take into account where that literature is in its own development may well serve to reinforce the tendency to over-attribute social outcomes to weight.

The Antecedents and Consequences of Dispositions Toward the Overweight. The social psychological literature on overweight has been more concerned with documenting that this characteristic is stigmatizing than with exploring why this might be the case. Some exceptions to this neglect include the work on perceived responsibility (e.g., DeJong, 1980; Harris, 1983), the analysis of the relationship between food availability and attitudes toward the overweight (e.g., Powdermaker, 1962), and analyses of media portrayals (or lack of them) of overweight persons (e.g., Wooley & Wooley, 1979). Clearly this work needs to be extended, particularly if one wishes to create a knowledge base sufficient for developing interventions aimed at reducing negative attitudes toward overweight individuals.

As noted elsewhere in this chapter, the number of studies that actually examine overt discrimination against overweight individuals is very small. Rather than presuming widespread discrimination on the basis of the attitudinal studies, we need to examine the conditions under which it does or does not occur and how it is perceived and responded to by the overweight. Langer et al. (1976) have argued, for example, that individuals will more readily discriminate against the overweight than against persons who are physically handicapped. To our knowledge there are no direct tests of this assertion. We agree with Jarvie et al. (1983) that studies in this domain should move toward "nonintrusive, in vivo, observations" of actual social exchanges and away from an emphasis on a "check-list methodology" or a reliance upon self-report measures.

ACKNOWLEDGMENTS

Preparation of this chapter was supported in part by National Institute of Mental Health Grant MH29446 to the second author. We are grateful to A. Christopher Strenta and Jane Giffin for their helpful comments.

REFERENCES

Adams, G. R. (1982). Physical attractiveness. In A. G. Miller (Ed.), *In the eye of the beholder: Contemporary issues in stereotyping* (pp. 253–304). New York: Praeger.

Alessi, D. F., & Anthony, W. A. (1969). The uniformity of children's attitudes toward physical disabilities. *Exceptional Children, 35,* 543–545.

Allon, N. (1982). The stigma of overweight in everyday life. In B. B. Wolman & S. DeBerry (Eds.), *Psychological aspects of obesity: A handbook* (pp. 130–174). New York: Van Nostrand Reinhold.

Antons–Brandi, V. (1972). Attitudes toward body weight: Why overweight persons prefer to remain fat: A social-psychological study on attitudes regarding body weight. *Zeitschrift fur Psychosomatische Medizin und Psychoanalyse, 18,* 81–94.

Benson, P. L., Severs, D., Tatgenhorst, J., & Loddengaard, N. (1980). The social costs of obesity: A non-reactive field study. *Social Behavior and Personality, 8,* 91–96.

Berscheid, E., & Walster, E. (1974). Physical attractiveness. In L. Berkowitz (Ed.), *Advances in experimental social psychology* (Vol. 7, pp. 157–215). New York: Academic Press.

Borjeson, M. (1962). Overweight children. *Acta Paediatrica* (Suppl. 132). 1–76.

Bray, G. A. (1979). *The obese patient.* Philadelphia: Saunders.

Brewer, C., White, H., & Baddeley, M. (1974). Beneficial effects of jejunoileostomy on compulsive eating and associated psychiatric symptoms. *British Medical Journal, 4,* 314–316.

Breytspraak, L. M., McGee, J., Conger, J. C., Whatley, J. L., & Moore, J. T. (1977). Sensitizing medical students to impression formation processes in patient interviews. *Journal of Medical Education, 52,* 47–54.

Cahnman, W. J. (1968). The stigma of obesity. *Sociological Quarterly, 9,* 283–299.

Canning, H., & Mayer, J. (1966). Obesity: Its possible effect on college acceptance. *New England Journal of Medicine, 275,* 1172–1174.

Canning, H., & Mayer, J. (1967). Obesity: An influence on high school performance. *American Journal of Clinical Nutrition, 20,* 352–354.

Caskey, S. R., & Felker, D. W. (1971). Social stereotyping of female body image by elementary age girls. *Research Quarterly, 42,* 251–255.

Chigier, E., & Chigier, M. (1968). Attitudes to disability in the multi-cultural society of Israel. *Journal of Health and Social Behavior, 9,* 310–317.

DeGarine, I. (1972). Socio-cultural aspects of food. *Ecology of Food and Nutrition, 1,* 143–163.

DeJong, W. (1980). The stigma of obesity: The consequences of naive assumptions concerning the causes of physical deviance. *Journal of Health and Social Behavior, 21,* 75–87.

DeJong, W., & Nackman, D. M. (1979). *[The issue of responsibility in the stigma of obesity].* Unpublished raw data.

Dibiase, W. J., & Hjelle, L. A. (1968). Body-image stereotypes and body-type preferences among male college students. *Perceptual and Motor Skills, 27,* 1143–1146.

Duncan, B. L. (1976). Differential social perception and the attribution of intergroup violence: Testing the lower limits of stereotyping of blacks. *Journal of Personality and Social Psychology, 34,* 590–598.

Fazio, R. H., & Zanna, M. P. (1981). Direct experience and attitude-behavior consistency. In L. Berkowitz (Ed.), *Advances in experimental social psychology* (Vol. 14, pp. 161–202). New York: Academic Press.

Felker, D. W. (1972). Social stereotyping of male and female body types with differing facial expressions by elementary age boys and girls. *Journal of Psychology, 82,* 151–154.

Fishbein, M., & Azjen, I. (1975). *Belief, attitude, intention and behavior: An introduction to theory and research.* Reading, MA: Addison–Wesley.

Giancoli, D. L., & Neimeyer, G. J. (1983). Liking preferences toward handicapped persons. *Perceptual and Motor Skills, 57,* 1005–1006.

Goffman, E. (1963). *Stigma: Notes on the management of spoiled identity.* Englewood Cliffs, NJ: Prentice–Hall.

Goodman, N., Richardson, S. A., Dornbusch, S., & Hastorf, A. H. (1963). Variant reactions to physical disabilities. *American Sociological Review, 28,* 429–435.

Hamilton, D. (1981). *Cognitive processes in stereotyping and intergroup behavior.* Hillsdale, NJ: Lawrence Erlbaum Associates.

Harris, M. B. (1983). Eating habits, restraint, knowledge and attitudes toward obesity. *International Journal of Obesity, 7,* 271–286.

Harris, M. B., & Smith, S. D. (1983). The relationship of age, sex, ethnicity, and weight to stereotypes of obesity and self-perception. *International Journal of Obesity, 7,* 361–371.

Hildebrandt, K. A. (1982). The role of physical appearance in infant and child development. In H. E. Fitzgerald, B. M. Lester, & M. W. Yogman (Eds.), *Theory and research in behavioral pediatrics* (Vol. 1, pp. 181–218). New York: Plenum.

Hinsdale, G. (1976). *Body build stereotypes and self-identification in three age groups of females.* Unpublished master's thesis, Colgate University, Hamilton, New York.

Iwawaki, S., & Lerner, R. M. (1974). Cross-cultural analyses of body-behavior relations: I. A comparison of body build stereotypes of Japanese and American males and females. *Psychologica, 17,* 75–81.

Jarvie, G. J., Lahey, B., Graziano, W., & Framer, E. (1983). Childhood obesity and social stigma: What we know and what we don't know. *Developmental Review, 3,* 237–273.

Kelley, H. H. (1967). Attribution theory in social psychology. In D. Levine (Ed.), *Nebraska Symposium on Motivation.* Lincoln: University of Nebraska Press.

Kelley, H. H. (1971). *Attribution in social psychology.* Morristown, NJ: General Learning Press.

Kleck, R. E. (1984). *(Weight rating data on the Richardson drawings.)* Unpublished raw data.

Kleck, R. E., & Rubenstein, C. (1975). Physical attractiveness, perceived attitude similarity, and interpersonal attraction in an opposite-sex encounter. *Journal of Personality and Social Psychology, 31,* 107–114.

Kleck, R. E., & Strenta, A. (1980). Perceptions of the impact of negatively valued physical characteristics on social interaction. *Journal of Personality and Social Psychology, 39,* 861–873.

Kleck, R. E., & Strenta, A. C. (in press). Physical deviance and the perception of social outcomes. In J. A. Graham & A. M. Kligman (Eds.), *The psychology of cosmetic treatments*. New York: Praeger.

Kurland, H. D. (1970). Obesity: An unfashionable problem. *Psychiatric Opinion, 7,* 20–24.

Langer, E. J., Taylor, S. E., Fiske, S., & Chanowitz, B. (1976). Stigma, staring, and discomfort: A novel-stimulus hypothesis. *Journal of Experimental Social Psychology, 12,* 451–463.

Larkin, J. E., & Pines, H. A. (1979). No fat persons need apply. *Sociology of Work and Occupations, 6,* 312–327.

Lerner, R. M. (1969a). The development of stereotyped expectancies of body build-behavior relations. *Child Development, 40,* 137–141.

Lerner, R. M. (1969b). Some female stereotypes of male body build-behavior relations. *Perceptual and Motor Skills, 28,* 363–366.

Lerner, R. M., Knapp, J. R., & Pool, K. B. (1974). Structure of body-build stereotypes: A methodological analysis. *Perceptual and Motor Skills, 39,* 719–729.

Lerner, R. M., & Pool, K. B. (1972). Body build stereotypes: A cross-cultural comparison. *Psychological Reports, 31,* 527–532.

Levine, J. M., & McBurney, D. H. (1977). Causes and consequences of effluvia: Body oder awareness and controllability as determinants of interpersonal evaluation. *Personality and Social Psychology Bulletin, 3,* 442–445.

Louderback, L. (1970). *Fat power: Whatever you weigh is right.* New York: Hawthorne Books.

Maddox, G. L., Anderson, C. F., & Bogdonoff, M. D. (1966). Overweight as a problem of medical management in a public outpatient clinic. *American Journal of Medical Science, 252,* 394–403.

Maddox, G. L., Back, K., & Liederman, V. (1968). Overweight as social deviance and disability. *Journal of Health and Social Behavior, 9,* 287–298.

Maddox, G. L., & Liederman, V. (1969). Overweight as a social disability with medical implications. *Journal of Medical Education, 44,* 210–220.

Mayer, J. (1968). *Overweight: Causes, cost, and control.* Englewood Cliffs, NJ: Prentice–Hall.

McLean, R. A., & Moon, M. (1980). Health, obesity and earnings. *American Journal of Public Health, 70,* 1006–1009.

Miller, A. R., Kiker, V. L., Watson, R. A. R., Frauchiger, R. A., & Moreland, D. B. (1968). Experimental analyses of physiques as a social stimulus: Part II. *Perceptual and Motor Skills, 27,* 355–359.

Millman, M. (1980). *Such a pretty face: Being fat in America.* New York: Norton.

Mussen, P., & Barker, R. (1944). Attitudes toward cripples. *Journal of Abnormal and Social Psychology, 39,* 351–355.

Nisbett, R. E., & Ross, L. (1980). *Human inference: Strategies and shortcomings in social judgment.* Englewood Cliffs, NJ: Prentice–Hall.

Northcraft, G. B. (1980, May). *The perception of disability.* Paper presented at the meeting of the Western Psychological Association, Los Angeles.

Powdermaker, H. (1962). An anthropological approach to the problem of obesity. *Bulletin of the New York Academy of Medicine, 36,* 286–295.

Powell, G. E., Tutton, S. J., & Stewart, R. A. (1974). The differential stereotyping of similar physiques. *British Journal of Social and Clinical Psychology, 13,* 421–423.

Quaade, F. (1979). Jejunoileal bypass for morbid obesity: A bibliographic study and a randomized clinical trial. *Surgical Clinics of North America, 59,* 1055–1069.

Richardson, S. A. (1970). Age and sex differences in values toward physical handicaps. *Journal of Health and Social Behavior, 11,* 207–214.

Richardson, S. A. (1971). Research report: Handicap, appearance, and stigma. *Social Science and Medicine, 5,* 621–628.

Richardson, S. A. (1977). *Sex differences in values toward obesity: A cross-cultural study.* Unpublished manuscript, Albert Einstein College of Medicine, New York.

Richardson, S. A. (1983). Children's values in regard to disabilities: A reply to Yuker. *Rehabilitation Psychology, 28,* 131–140.

Richardson, S. A., & Emerson, P. (1970). Race and physical handicap in children's perference for other children: A replication in a southern city. *Human Relations, 23,* 31–36.

Richardson, S. A., & Green, A. (1971). When is black beautiful? Colored and white children's reactions to skin color. *British Journal of Educational Psychology, 41,* 62–69.

Richardson, S. A., Hastorf, A. H., Goodman, N., & Dornbusch, S. M. (1961). Cultural uniformity in reaction to physical disabilities. *American Sociological Review, 26,* 241–247.

Richardson, S. A., & Royce, J. (1968). Race and physical handicap in children's preferences for other children. *Child Development, 39,* 467–480.

Rodin, J., & Slochower, J. (1974). Fat chance for a favor: Obese-normal differences in compliance and incidental learning. *Journal of Personality and Social Psychology, 29,* 557–565.

Rudofsky, B. (1971). *The unfashionable human body.* Garden City, NY: Doubleday.

Sagarin, E. (1975). *Deviants and deviance.* New York: Praeger.

Sallade, J. (1973). A comparison of the psychological adjustment of obese and nonobese children. *Journal of Psychosomatic Research, 17,* 89–96.

Snyder, M. (1981). On the self-perpetuating nature of social stereotypes. In D. L. Hamilton (Ed.), *Cognitive processes in stereotyping and intergroup behavior.* Hillsdale, NJ: Lawrence Erlbaum Associates.

Snyder, M. L., & Frankel, A. (1976). Observer bias: A stringent test of behavior engulfing the field. *Journal of Personality and Social Psychology, 34,* 857–864.

Solow, C. (1977). Psychosocial aspects of intestinal bypass surgery for massive obesity: Current status. *American Journal of Clinical Nutrition, 30,* 103–108.

Staffieri, J. R. (1967). A study of social stereotype of body image in children. *Journal of Personality and Social Psychology, 7,* 101–104.

Staffieri, J. R. (1972). Body build and behavioral expectancies in young females. *Developmental Psychology, 6,* 125–127.

Stewart, A. L., & Brook, R. H. (1983). Effects of being overweight. *American Journal of Public Health, 73,* 171–178.

Stewart, A. L., Brook, R. H., & Kane, R. L. (1980). *Conceptualization and measurement of health habits for adults in the health insurance study: Overweight* (Vol. 2). Santa Monica, CA: Rand.

Stewart, R. A., Powell, G. E., & Tutton, S. J. (1973). The oral character: Personality type or stereotype? *Perceptual and Motor Skills, 37,* 948.

Strenta, A. C., & Kleck, R. E. (1984). Physical disability and the perception of social interaction: It's not what you look at but how you look at it. *Personality and Social Psychological Bulletin, 10,* 279–288.

Strongman, K. T., & Hart, C. J. (1968). Stereotyped reactions to body build. *Psychological Reports, 23,* 1175–1178.

Stunkard, A., & McLaren-Hume, M. (1959). The results of treatment for obesity. *Archives of Internal Medicine, 103,* 79–85.

Stunkard, A., & Mendelson, M. (1961). Disturbances in body image of some obese persons. *Journal of the American Dietetic Association, 38,* 328–331.

Vann, D. H. (1976). *Personal responsibility, authoritarianism, and treatment of the obese.* Unpublished doctoral dissertation, New York University, New York.

Vener, A. M., Krupka, L. R., & Gerard, R. J. (1982). Overweight/obese patients: An overview. *The Practitioner, 226,* 1102–1109.

Wells, W. D., & Siegel, B. (1961). Stereotyped somatotypes. *Psychological Reports, 8,* 77–78.

Wooley, S. C., & Wooley, O. W. (1979). Obesity and women—I. A closer look at the facts. *Women's Studies International Quarterly, 2,* 69–79.

Wright, B. (1960). *Physical disability: A psychological approach.* New York: Harper & Row.

Young, R. D., & Avdzej, A. (1979). The effects of obedience/disobedience and obese/nonobese body type on social acceptance by peers. *Journal of Genetic Psychology, 134,* 43–49.

Yuker, H. E. (1983). The lack of a stable order of preference for disabilities: A response to Richardson and Ronald. *Rehabilitation Psychology, 28,* 93–103.

5 Causes and Consequences of the Current Preference for Thin Female Physiques

Janet Polivy
David M. Garner
Paul E. Garfinkel
Toronto General Hospital

Physical appearance is dictated to a great extent by societal preferences. In this chapter we focus on one aspect of appearance that receives particular attention in current Western society, body size and shape. We document a recent, marked shift to a preference for thinness, especially for women's bodies, and attempt to identify causes of the present pursuit of slimness. An interest in the sources of this emphasis on slimness is more than academic, as is shown in the latter part of this chapter where we discuss some of the effects of society's pressure on people (especially women) to be thin.

Traditionally, Western society has preferred a rounded, relatively plump shape. This is evident in classical Greek, Renaissance, and 17th Century (Rubenesque) art (Clark, 1980). Until the 20th century, Venus, the goddess of love, was almost invariably depicted as plump and curvaceous (Beller, 1977). In economies more oriented to subsistence than abundance, a plump figure was a sign of wealth, health and youth. For instance, a biographer of the Krupp dynasty assumed that its founder must have been portly, because successful businessmen of the 16th century displayed their wealth by eating prodigious (and expensive) amounts, thus becoming overweight (Manchester, 1968). Ford and Beach (1952) pointed out that for many societies plumpness in females is not only considered attractive but is often actually deemed a secondary sexual characteristic.

Since the early 1960's there has been a shift toward an idealization of thinness for women. Evidence for this was presented by Garner, Garfinkel, Schwartz, and Thompson (1980). They collected data from two groups of American women who might be said to represent cultural ideals for feminine appearance, Playboy Magazine centerfolds and Miss America Pageant contestants. Comparing height, weight, and body measurements of the playmates from 1959 through 1978, they found that height increased over the 20 years and percentage of average weight (for age and height) decreased significantly. Furthermore, bust and hip measurements decreased significantly whereas waists became larger (either because a generally more tubular appearance was being selected or because the taller, less voluptuous women tended to have this less curvaceous build.) The playmates were about 91% of average weight in 1959 and only 84% in 1978. Similar results were obtained for Miss America Pageant contestants during that same period. Their average weight declined over the years, and for winners this decline was even more marked. Prior to 1970, contestants weighed 87.6% of (the 1959) average, whereas after 1970 this declined to 84.6%. Before 1970, the winners of the pageant weighed about the same as the other contestants (87.7% of average), but since 1970 the winners have tended to be even thinner than the average contestant (82.5% of average). Over that same period (from 1959 to 1979) the actual weight (at all levels of height) of women under age 30 has increased by an average of 5 pounds, according to the Society of Actuaries' 1979 norms (possibly because of generally improved nutrition). An examination of a related measure, the number of articles on dieting published in six leading women's magazines during those 20 years, indicates that diet articles have proliferated as the ideal female shape has contracted (a mean of 17.1 diet articles per year appeared in these magazines from 1959–1968, whereas the mean per year was 29.6 from 1969–1978). Thus, over the last 20 years, converging evidence indicates that the ideal female shape has changed to a taller, slimmer, less rounded one, and because younger adult women have actually been getting somewhat heavier, there has been a growing focus on dieting to lose weight. Garner et al. (1980) concluded that their data reflected conservative estimates of the pressure on women to emulate slimmer role models, because the high fashion models decorating the pages of magazines women read appear to be even slimmer than are Playboy playmates or Miss America.

The impact of this changing ideal for feminine beauty is exemplified by the increasing pervasiveness of dieting among women, especially young women. Polls conducted in the early 1960s (Wyden, 1965) on a nation-wide sample of adults found that over 30% of adults with a weight problem (i.e., overweight) were not especially concerned about weight. Only 10% of overweight adults were dieting, another 20 per cent were trying not to gain any more, and the other 40 percent were concerned but not doing anything about it. A separate poll by the same author showed that such concern rarely led to corrective measures (Wyden, 1965). In contrast, Heuneman, Shapiro, Hampton, and Mitchell (1966) reported that as many as 70% of high school girls were dissatisfied with their bodies and wanted to lose weight. Dwyer, Feldman, and Mayer (1967, 1969, 1970) found that 30% of high school girls and 6% of boys were dieting on the day they were studied, although only 15% of the girls but 19% of the boys were overweight. Furthermore over 80% of the girls but less than 20% of the boys expressed a desire to weigh less, and over 40% of the girls had been on diets by their senior year in high school whereas only 24% of their male cohorts had ever dieted. By 1977, the percentage of college women either on diets or consciously trying to control their eating in order to keep their weight down was up to 82%, according to Jakobovits, Halstead, Kelley, Roe, and Young. Thus, girls seem more likely to diet than boys regardless of whether or not they are overweight, and more likely to diet since the mid-1960s than previously. Herman and Polivy (1980; 1983) have consistently found (since 1975) that females report more dieting behavior than males.

SOCIOCULTURAL PRESSURES FOR THINNESS

Females in our society thus appear to have accepted this new standard of beauty, and are actively engaged in dieting (even if they are not overweight) to attain it. Why an increased emphasis on dieting should have occurred through the last twenty years is not known. Several factors may play a role, including:

1. Emulation of the higher social classes.
2. Health consciousness and fears about obesity.
3. A growing preoccupation with body images and a quest for youth.
4. Overvaluation of a sense of personal control, or ascetic ideal.
5. Social roles for women which have evolved over the 1960s and 1970s.

It is quite possible that several or all of these have been important, but to our knowledge there have been no studies to evaluate this possibility.

The fashions of the higher classes tend to be adopted by society as a whole, and concepts of the ideal feminine appearance have often been tied to social class factors. Apart from the fact that women of the highest social classes have traditionally been the only ones with the time and means to cultivate their appearance, attributes chosen for admiration by society as a whole have often been implicit reflections of wealth and leisure. The shift in styles for skin tone reflects this. Traditionally, beautiful women were required to wear broad-brimmed hats or carry parasols to protect their delicate white complexions from the sun. It was deemed unattractive to have tanned or freckled skin, probably because in the agricultural societies of the past, only the rich never worked outdoors. Pale skin, which was considered one attribute of beauty, was thus an indication that the bearer was wealthy enough to avoid the sun. The industrial revolution radically changed this, however. Now that most people work indoors rather than out, pale complexions are the norm. It is only those wealthy enough to travel to warm climates who can present tanned skin all year long. Accordingly, current standards of beauty call for tanned skin, and we find sun worshippers on the beaches with mirrored reflectors catching every precious ray (Beller, 1977).

Similarly, the long-standing preference for robust female bodies changed as industrialized societies moved from relative scarcity of food supplies to plenty. With abundant food, plumpness no longer indicates wealth, especially because cheaper, starchier foods tend to be the more fattening ones. Furthermore, advances in medical knowledge have also eliminated the health advantages of a cushion of fat. Thus, a thin body no longer necessarily reflects poverty and/or disease. In fact, in Western industrialized society, overweight has almost become the norm. The rich now flock to health spas and reducing farms.

It is not surprising, then, to learn that for North American women in the late 20th century, thinness and dieting are related to higher social status, (Dwyer & Mayer, 1970; Goldblatt, Moore, & Stunkard, 1965; Stunkard, 1975). With slenderness replacing curves as a criterion of beauty among the wealthy, one might expect society in general to adopt this value before long. Dwyer and Mayer (1970) report a survey taken in the early 1950s that showed that as social class rose, so did the number of women who saw themselves as overweight, whether or not they actually were. In their own (later) studies, this association between social class and excessive concern with thinness held only for older women. They suggest that this indicates that weight norms are becoming more homogeneous throughout the population, with the formerly upper class value spreading through all social strata. The Duchess of Windsor's oft repeated observation that "no woman can be too slim or too rich" is apparently becoming a societal credo. As early as 1959, Calden, Lundy, and Schlafter reported that Western adolescent females reported more positive attitudes toward a small size for all body parts except busts (see also Berscheid, Walster, & Bohrnstedt, 1973a, 1973b). Moreover, reported satisfaction decreased as one's body size deviated from this social stereotype (Calden et al. 1959; Nylander, 1971). Thus the societal demands for slimness may partially be tied to an initial emulation of the upper classes, which has now become universal throughout the levels of society.

A flurry of medical reports from the 1950s and 60s linking obesity with heart disease (see Bray, 1976, for a review) and early mortality (Society of Actuaries 1959) may also have contributed to the denigration of overweight and increased value of slenderness. Although more recent medical reports question whether overweight per se is actually implicated in such health problems (see Bray, 1976; or Polivy & Herman, 1983, for a review) and even suggest that *underweight* may itself pose a health hazard (e.g., Sorlie, Gordon, & Kannel, 1980) these reports have not received the attention and publicity of the earlier ones. The image of fat as unhealthy persists and perhaps adds impetus to societal pressures on people to lose weight. However, the possible unhealthy effects of overweight seemed to be more marked in men than in women, so health-motivated pressure to reduce should focus more on males than females.

The current demand for slenderness in women seems to reflect more than a concern with new fashion or health. Shainess (1979) argues that this is only the superficial aspect of society's preoccupation with body images and growing narcissism. A compulsive quest for youth may well underly societal attitudes toward food, feeding, and body image (Shainess, 1979). Evidence shows that thinness delays pubertal maturation (Frisch & Revelle, 1970), and patients with the self-starvation syndrome of anorexia nervosa are posited to be avoiding adulthood (Crisp, 1970, 1980). Thinness may be seen as being more childlike or youthful and thus striven for in our youth-worshipping society.

A different explanation proposed for the present emphasis on slenderness concerns a response to reduced controls in other spheres of life (Garner, Garfinkel & Olmsted, 1983; Wooley & Wooley, 1980). Increased sexual permissiveness and self indulgence have caused this to be labeled the *Me generation* or *Now Society.* As limits have loosened in other areas of self-control, however, the demand for strengthened control over eating and weight has increased. A similar phenomenon occurred in the 1920s when social limits on behavior also lessened and there was a concomitant rise in pressure for slenderness and self-control over eating. The Great Depression of 1929 brought the era of the "Roaring Twenties" to an abrupt and sober end. In our current era of "moral laxness," it has more than once been observed that gluttony is the last remaining vice. The idealization of a slim body may thus reflect a search for internal controls in a time of lessened external control.

A further important source for the change in idealized body shape may stem from new social roles for women that have evolved over the last 2 decades. Beller (1977) has observed that the new ideal for women conforms more closely to a masculine physique than a feminine one and may thus have been embraced more enthusiastically by women for their own ideal than by men; that is, although Playboy playmates are getting thinner, they're still more rounded than the fashion models admired and emulated by women. Beller (1977) has suggested that the adoption of this tubular, masculine-looking physique as the ideal of feminine form may reflect the recognition by women that men have power in our society and an unconscious identification with the power-status symbol. The coincident wave of feminism with this shift away from an image of sexually productive female beauty may thus be a related phenomenon. It is important to note, however, as she points out, that this change of preference to a more slender physique is in some sense being imposed upon women by women. Regardless of what fashion designers of either sex decree, recent history has demonstrated that women select only those fashions that somehow appeal to them and are quite capable of rejecting fashion edicts not to their taste.

Selvini-Palazzoli (1974) has described the conflicted role of both assertion and passivity required of young women in current society. This may lead to conflicts between the traditional holdouts (often their own parents) and the contemporary demand for more active behavior, but at times without any real autonomy.

Orbach (1978) similarly has observed that women are given double messages: They should both blend in and stand out. But beyond these ambiguities, the modern mania for slenderness can be seen partially as a way of enhancing one's sense of personal control and thus competing in traditional masculine pursuits that relate to a professional career and the power of position. By being as slim as possible, a woman both increases her chances of attracting a man—by becoming, presumably, maximally attractive—and at the same time makes herself look more masculine, perhaps to erase traditional feminine stereotypes, so as to compete in the male world of business, profession, and power. The dual pressure—to be both super wife and mother while at the same time having a successful career—has been suggested to play some role in the increased incidence of eating and food-related disorders like anorexia nervosa (Selvini-Palazzoli, 1974) but this has not been adequately studied. Morover, Selvini-Palazzoli (1974) has observed one of the glaring contradictions of our culture, that an affluent society forces women to attempt various uncomfortable and even dangerous dietetic and ascetic practices, thus discouraging them from satisfying their appetites although surrounded by plenty. It is surprising in the face of this kind of double message, she maintains, that so few women develop anorexia nervosa.

Orbach (1978) has also asserted that disordered eating is a response by women to their position and role in our society, as well as to societal demands that women be thin. She has provided an in-depth analysis of the prevailing stereotypes of fatness and thinness and the broader social implications of such stereotypes. For example, she has noted that the general societal stereotype of "thin" is as feminine, delicate, and ideal. At the same time, thinness is actually preadolescent, less curvy, and thus actually less feminine (especially when taken to anorexic proportions). When women are asked to describe what "thin" means, they think of responses like emotionally cold, competitive, sexy, and admired. But this also makes them feel compelled to fit some cultural norm, and thus constrained. Orbach (1978) concludes that women are expected to be "petite, demure, giving, passive, receptive in the home, and above all, attractive" (p. 168). At the same time, they are "discouraged from being active, assertive, competitive, large, and above all unattractive" (p. 168). Getting large or fat is then for some women, a way of escaping the "straight jacketed stereotypes." Psychologically, defying the thinness stereotype allows them to feel important and have impact in the world, avoid intrusions of sexual matters, and compensate or give them the "strength" for the constant giving required of them. The current social stereotype of fat supports this by defining fat as unattractive, not sexy, not feminine, jovial, sloppy, and imperfect. Fat may become, for some women, a protective device, an excuse for all their mistakes, a way to avoid competing with other women, and a source of space in which to hide and to have their own feelings. Eating thus becomes a symbolic way of dealing with what Orbach describes as "an oppressive social role." Similarly, Bennett and Gurin (1982) link a preference for thinness to female sexual liberation. Given these attributes connected to body size it is not surprising that many women in our society ascribe magic properties to thinness and fatness. Thinness represents perfection, so its achievement means that life will be perfect. Fatness, on the other hand, although abhorred and to be avoided, at least at a conscious level, becomes a scapegoat on which to blame one's imperfections and problems while giving the strength to do all the myriad of tasks expected of today's "superwoman."

EMPIRICAL EVIDENCE FOR BODY SIZE STEREOTYPES

Recent research provides some support for Orbach's clinical observation of the pervasive importance of body size to social perception. Several investigations of social stereotypes associated with fat and thin physiques have been carried out and the general conclusion is that a negative stereotype is associated with over-weight. The fat person tends to be seen as self-indulgent, hedonistic, friendless and sedentary (Brodsky, 1954; Lawson, 1980; Lerner, 1969a, 1969b; Sleet, 1969; Staffieri, 1967 and 1972; Strongman & Hart, 1968). Normal-weight people have been seen most positively whereas thin people in these studies were seen as nervous and unaggressive.

A closer examination of such studies, however, suggests that the picture is more complicated than the general conclusions indicate. The more detailed picture lends some support not only to the negative stereotype of fatness that seems to pervade the current culture, but also to the kind of ambivalent and/or positive attitudes toward thinness noted by clinician-observers like Orbach. Much of this research has been done using only male subjects or targets, especially in the earlier studies (e.g., Johnson & Staffieri, 1971; Lerner, 1969 a, b; Lerner & Korn, 1972; Sleet, 1969; Staffieri, 1967; Strongman & Hart, 1968; Wells & Siegel, 1961). Boys and men consistently rated figures of average sized or mesomorphic (male) physiques most favorably and fat or endomorphic types most negatively. Thin or ectomorphic physiques were rated as intermediate, though generally more negative than positive, especially in submissive, nervous qualities. Females also showed a preference for average-sized bodies rating them most favorably and an aversion for fat physiques, rating them as bad and undesir-able (Lawson, 1980; Lerner, 1969b; Lerner & Gellert, 1969; Staffieri, 1972). However, although showing the positive view of average-sized bodies and rejection of fat shown by males, females seem to hold a different opinion of thin physiques than do males. When boys were asked which body type they themselves would like to have, a few boys chose the fat body, the vast majority chose inconsistently (on two trials) or chose the average-sized body, and a few chose the thin one (Lerner & Gellert, 1969; Lerner & Korn, 1972; Staffieri, 1967). Girls making the same choice *never* chose the fat physique and were about half as likely to choose the thin body as the average one (Lerner & Gellert, 1969; Staffieri, 1972). The attitudes of girls toward people with thin bodies also seems more favorable than that of boys. Although thin people were rated as submissive by girls as well as by boys, for girls, the submissiveness was accompanied by positive traits like quiet, clean, honest, and unworried (unlike the boys' ratings of thin men as likely to have a nervous breakdown, afraid, sneaky, worried, and friendless or lonely). Lerner and Gellert (1969) also found girls to be better able to identify their own and their peers' body types. They suggest that this reflects a cultural emphasis on appearance for girls. They find support for their contention that the superior body identifications of the girls and the rejection of fat shown by both sexes is culturally transmitted in the fact that a higher proportion of subjects showed an aversion to fat figures than the number actually able to identify which of their peers are fat. Thus, even when unable to label real people accurately as fat or thin, subjects knew that the fat silhouette was to be rejected.

Roberts and Herman (1980) found similar results with a different kind of methodology. They had subjects rate job applicants whose weight, sex, and height were embedded in a form containing other (neutral) items of personal information. Weight was found to be the most important variable in determining a person's ratings. Again, a negative stereotype for fatness appeared, with fat people, regardless of height or sex, seen as significantly less attractive, less self-controlled, less self-confident, less outgoing, and less fashionable, though more good humored. In this study some evidence of a preference for thinness was also found. Thin people not only scored higher than fat people on the aforementioned adjectives but also were seen as more self-confident and more outgoing than were average-weight people. The fact that these stereotypic findings emerged in a situation like this, where information about physique was deliberately made less salient than usual, implies that such stereotypes are very powerful.

These experimental results documenting current body size stereotypes accord well with the findings of several large-scale surveys of attitudes toward body weight and size, and respondants' corresponding behaviors (i.e., dieting). Dwyer, Feldman, Seltzer, and Mayer (1969) surveyed graduating high school students in a suburban community outside Boston. As in the similar surveys cited earlier (e.g., Dwyer et al., 1967, 1970; Jakobovits et al., 1977; Wyden, 1965), most girls wanted to weigh less, whereas, except for the most obese, boys wanted to weigh more. The authors surmise that this may result from a different interpretation by boys and girls of what weight represents, with boys seeing it as reflecting muscle and bone whereas girls connect weight with fatness. Girls reported weighing themselves more frequently than did boys but were less accurate in reporting their weights, perhaps reflecting their greater concern with overweight. The body regions reported as being furthest from subjects' ideal size differed by sex, too. Females expressed concern about overly large waists, hips, buttocks, thighs, and body weights, and to a lesser extent, girth of upper arm, calves, ankles, and feet. The only body measurements girls wanted to increase were bust, leg length, and height. Boys, on the other hand, were more concerned with increasing their height, weight, shoulders, upper arm girth, and chest cage measurements as well as wanting larger wrists, hands, calves, and ankles. Boys did show a moderate desire to decrease their waists, hips, and buttocks. The choice of ideal male and female silhouettes also differed by sex, especially for the ideal female. Girls overwhelmingly chose the two thinnest silhouettes as "most feminine" and ideal, whereas males were more likely to choose only the second thinnest figure as the most feminine. For masculine physiques, the extreme mesomorph was seen as most masculine by 86% of the boys but only 59% of the girls, though only 54% of the boys actually wanted to look like the extreme mesormorph. Thus, girls seem to think they should be thinner than they are and see the ideal female as somewhat thinner than boys do, whereas boys are over-concerned with increasing their size and muscularity. Dwyer and Mayer (1970) found similar trends in three nationwide polls and further documented the association between concern with overweight and sex, education, and socioeconomic class. Different body size norms for men and women and the increased expectation for thinness in upper class women appeared to be responsible for the heightened perception of overweight and dieting reported by women, especially those of higher socioeconomic status. Dwyer (1973) explains the heightened preoccupation with overweight of the females she has surveyed in terms of "the reality that obesity is penalized more heavily in females than in males by society" (p. 102).

Berscheid, Walster, and Bohrnstedt (1973a, 1973b) had a national sample of adults report their body satisfaction, physical attractiveness, and self-esteem. In keeping with previous findings and with the suggestion of stereotyping studies, self-esteem was connected to feelings about their bodies for both sexes, but weight was important for self-esteem and perceived physical attractiveness only for females (Berscheid et al., 1973a). They concluded that "a woman's self-esteem relates to her feeling pretty and slim; a man's self-esteem relates to being handsome and having a muscular chest" (Berscheid et al., 1973b, p. 123). The more global emphasis on women's whole bodies, as opposed to men's chest size, may reflect both sex differences in body fat distribution, and fashions in clothing. As Dwyer (1973) points out, normal adult females have twice as much body fat as do males and it is distributed on conspicious body parts like hips, chest, and extremities where attention is automatically drawn to it. Fashions, designed in the last few decades for a slim ideal, are meant to call attention to the female body. Even if the less slender woman can find clothes to fit her, she is less likely to look well in fashions designed to flatter a different shaped physique. In contrast to the visibility of female fat and the enhancement of this attention by fashion, men's bodies tend to accumulate fat more centrally where it is less noticeable, and male clothing, dominated by utility and status factors rather than by seductiveness, is usually shapeless enough to mask all but the grosser deviations from normal body shapes.

Thus both laboratory and survey research document the powerful influence of physique on evaluations of people in our society. The stereotypic rejection of fatness applies to both sexes, but a preference for thinness seems to apply only to females.

Further support for these stereotypes can be found in an examination of cultural phrases and slogans. "Fat slob" is an ephithet hurled by children at people they dislike, but to call someone a "thin slob" would be somehow ludicrous. An advertising campaign claimed that "The best cigarettes are like women, slim and rich," but it is difficult to imagine a similar campaign for "fat and rich" cigars. Shakespeare warned 17th-century readers of Cassius' "lean and hungry look" but today's villains are "fat cat" businessmen.

The message is clear. For whatever reasons—emulation of rich, upper class elegance or masculine power, compensation for lack of external controls, a quest for health and youth, or a relection of the conflicts and ambiguities in societal roles,—thin is in and fat is out. For many people being, becoming, or trying to become thin evolves into a way of life. They meet weekly with others in weight-loss groups or overeaters groups. Hardly a week goes by without some form of media attention to eating, its control, and pathology—newspapers, television, and magazines alternate articles and stories on how to diet with those on anorexia nervosa. For some, this institutionalization of concern with thinness even goes beyond their personal lives and dominates their professional lives. Research has shown that in ballet and modeling there is an increased risk of pathologic dieting or actual anorexia nervosa (Garner & Garfinkel, 1980). The concern with slim-ness thus dominates the lives of some women.

More commonly, however, this societal preoccupation is reflected in less extreme manifestations. Herman and Polivy (1980), found dieting and disor-dered eating behavior to be present, at least in some circumstances, throughout their generally college-aged sample of both women and men. Dieting, self-control, and the side effects of both seem to be significant aspects of the lives of many if not most contemporary North American women and men. Thus, cultural pressures on people to be thin appear to be forcing a large proportion of society to spend varying degrees of effort, attention, and money on attempts to conform.

SOCIAL ATTITUDES AS A CAUSE OF ILLNESS

Cultural attitudes about appearance play a role in facilitating some illnesses and idealizing others. There are examples of these in Western and other societies. For centuries Chinese women of the upper classes were forced to bind their feet from girlhood on so they would be "fashionably" tiny. The fact that this practice was quite painful and caused clubfoot was overridden by the cultural preference for tiny feet in women. This was largely related to its status value because it showed that the husband was wealthy and that his wife was not required to work. But it also severly limited her mobility and restricted her social involvements. Foot-binding died out entirely only in the early 20th century (Lyons & Petrucelli, 1978). The wearing of corsets is another example of potentially unhealthy behav-iors that were instituted to make women conform to an idealized appearance.

Apart from the extreme discomforts, these corsets of the 19th-century could cause injury from splitting of steel stays and also interfered with gastric motility and digestion. Even when these dangers had been recognized, the wearing of corsets continued because of the connotation of promiscuity associated with being uncorseted (Vincent, 1979).

At other times particular illnesses have been romanticized. Sontag (1978) documents this well in *Illness as Metaphor*. Tuberculosis was thought to make the person feel euphoric and also to act as an aphrodisiac (Sontag, 1978). It was thought to be caused by too much passion, striking sensual, reckless people or sensitive, passive victims. Sontag points out that the ethereal and the earthy are combined in the popular conception of TB as causing a beautific, serene death while at the same time making the sufferer beautiful and sexy. By the mid-18th-century, TB had become one index of gentility and sensitivity, resulting in the "fashion" for a tubercular appearance, especially among "snobs, parvenus, and social climbers" (Sontag, 1978, p. 27). Sontag (1978) suggests that "the romanticizing of TB is the first widespread example of that distinctive modern activity, promoting the self as an image. The tubercular look had to be considered attractive once it came to be considered a mark of distinction, of breeding" (p. 28). This look symbolic of an attractive vulnerability and superior sensitivity, gradually became the ideal for women. Thus the appearance that results from illness may become idealized and social customs may also cause illness. Today's social emphasis on thinness and dieting may similarly cause significant disorder.

CONSEQUENCES OF SOCIAL PRESSURE FOR THINNESS

Restrained Eating

The pressure for a slim body has resulted in the proliferation of what Herman and Polivy (1975, 1980) call restrained eating. Restrained eaters are defined as people who are concerned about their weight and eating and try to limit (or restrain) both (Herman & Polivy, 1980). Evidence of such restrained eating is measured by responses to a brief questionnaire (the Restraint Scale—see Table 1). Investigations of these restrained eaters have indicated that chronic dieting has effects beyond slenderness. The eating behavior of people constantly struggling to be thinner shows some strange and ironic deviations from that of normal nondieters. For one thing, restrained eaters seem inclined to overeat or "binge" under a variety of conditions that normally reduce intake. For example, Herman and Mack (1975) found that giving two milkshakes to restrained college co-eds led them to eat more ice cream afterward than did giving them only one or even none. Nondieters naturally ate less ice cream after one milkshake and much less after two. The restrained eaters, it should be noted, in keeping with their attempt to lose weight, ate less than normal when not forced to consume anything first (i.e., in the "no milkshake" condition). College men showed a similar response whether they were overweight, average weight, or underweight—those who were dieters ate significantly more after two (than zero) milkshakes whereas the nondieters significantly reduced their intake (Hibscher & Herman, 1977). Studies examining this counterregulatory response further have shown that the actual number of calories ingested prior to the test situation is unimportant. The trigger for the "binge" is whether or not the dieter believes s/he has just consumed something high in calories (i.e., was the preload enough to "ruin one's diet," has one already "overeaten"?) Regardless of the actual number of calories ingested, restrained eaters who believed they had a "high calorie" preload overate subsequently compared either to unrestrained eaters after a high calorie load or restrained eaters eating the *same* preload but convinced that it was "low calorie" or "dietetic" (Polivy, 1976; Ruderman & Wilson, 1979; Spencer & Fremouw, 1979; Woody, Costanzo, Leifer, & Conger, 1980). It seems then, that after being forced to consume a preload, dieters who think they have "blown" their diets eat more than either nondieters or dieters who believe they are still within their calorie limits for the day. For dieters, then, overeating seems to engender more overeating.

Herman and Polivy (1975) speculated that this counterregulatory behavior, or "bingeing," was a reflection of the results of disinhibiting the dieter's restrained eating. The restraint involved in maintaining a diet and losing weight is disrupted by the high calorie preload. The diet is ruined, at least for that day, so it no longer pays to restrain oneself. Following similar reasoning, they predicted that other forms of disinhibition should also produce overeating in chronic dieters. Accordingly, they searched for other means of disinhibiting dietary restraint. Previous studies on obese and normal-weight subjects (McKenna, 1972; Schachter, Goldman, & Gordon, 1968) had shown that although normal-weight people eat less when they are made anxious, obese people do not. Herman and Polivy (1975) replicated this finding using normal-weight restrained and unrestrained subjects and showed that, like the obese, restrained subjects ate slightly more when anxious than when they weren't anxious. (Having found 90% of the obese people they tested to be restrained, Herman and Polivy (1980) have claimed that so-called obese–normal differences in behavior are probably really restrained–unrestrained differences). They interpreted these results as another example of disinhibition of restrained eating. Anxiety, they pointed out, disrupts cognitive self-control processes, leading to an increase in normally inhibited behaviors, in this case, eating by dieters. Because unrestrained eaters do not inhibit their eating, they do not exhibit suppressed behavior. Their eating was thus a reflection of their internal state. Because anxiety stimulates sympathetic nervous system responses, these internal "cues" should presumably have been those of satiation, not hunger, and unrestrained eaters reduced their intake accordingly.

A similar explanation was offered for Polivy and Herman's (1976a) finding that clinical depression, which causes weight loss in normal nondieters, is associated with weight gain in restrained eaters. Like anxiety, the emotional turmoil characteristic of depression is thought to cause sympathetic nervous system arousal to which unrestrained eaters would respond by eating less and eventually losing weight. Restrained eaters, on the other hand, might find their usual restraint disrupted, producing disinhibited eating and weight gain.

Although emotionality has certainly been described as a disinhibitor, a more obvious and well-known disinhibitor is alcohol. Polivy and Herman (1976b, 1976c) thus performed a series of experiments in which they administered alcohol (in various guises) to restrained and unrestrained eaters and then allowed them to eat ad lib. The results were more complicated than originally anticipated because alcohol acted as a disinhibitor only under certain conditions (i.e., when subjects were aware that they were ingesting alcohol). However, when the appropriate conditions were met, restrained eaters showed "disinhibited eating" in response to alcohol and overate, whereas unrestrained eaters, responding perhaps to the 300 to 400 calories in the alcohol, ate less.

These studies demonstrate that people who attempt to restrict their caloric intake are prone to episodes of overeating triggered by a variety of events. Looking at more serious disturbances in eating behavior, a recent study showed that regardless of weight, it is the restrained eaters who report "bingeing," food cravings, and problems stopping eating (Wardle, 1980). Furthermore, Wardle (1980) points out that the order of appearance of symptoms in clinical disorders that include bulimia argues against the possibility that "bingers" are simply more likely to begin to diet and suggests the reverse, that dieting leads to "bingeing" (see Polivy & Herman, 1985, for an elaboration of this position). The evidence thus indicates that one side effect of succumbing to the new societal pressure to be thin is the development of an abnormal eating pattern characterized by periodic episodes of overeating that may reach the proportions of bulimia in response to a variety of events. In order to become thinner, people are forced to reduce their caloric intake, which involves restraining their normal appetites. Situations that then combine a disinhibitor with the opportunity to eat are apparently capable of disrupting restraint and causing overeating.

Another eating abnormality exhibited by restrained eaters is eating normally in social situations and then overeating as soon as they are alone. Often characteristic of psychiatric patients with serious eating disorders like bulimia or anorexia nervosa, this behavior was observed in a population of "normal" college co-eds in the laboratory. Herman, Polivy, and Silver (1979) found that although the eating behavior of unrestrained eaters was unaffected by the presence of an observer, either while she was there or after she left, restrained eaters showed a marked response. While the observer watched them the restrained eaters abandoned their usual counterregulatory behavior and ate "normally" (that is, more after a small preload and less after a large one). As soon as she left them alone, however, these subjects overate in direct proportion to the amount they had eaten while under observation.

Almost any situation investigated in the laboratory seems to disrupt restraint and cause overeating. Only when nothing is done to them do restrained eaters seem able to maintain their dieting behavior. A few ways have been found to contribute to their undereating and help them maintain their diets. One way is simply to pair a dieter with a confederate who models the behavior of dieting; that is, she eats very little (Polivy, Herman, Younger, & Erskine, 1979). Both restrained and unrestrained subjects ate less when eating with a light-eating model. Restrained subjects ate less than unrestrained subjects regardless of how much the model ate, apparently maintaining their diets very well. If the model not only ate only a small amount but also identified herself as dieting, consumption for all subjects was reduced still further. In another study, Polivy, Herman, and Hackett (1980) manipulated how self-conscious subjects felt about their eating and how aware they were of how much they were consuming. Although the combination of both of these factors was required to effect a reduction in intake for unrestrained subjects, restrained subjects were more sensitive to these manipulations and ate less under one or both conditions. In general, then, the eating behavior of people trying to be thinner seems more sensitive to the social situation as well as any kind of disinhibitory state.

This disordered eating pattern is not the only concomitant of attempted weight suppression. An increasing store of data indicates that restrained eaters are distractable (perform poorly when distracted), and are hyperemotional, or overreactive to emotion-inducing stimuli, as compared with unrestrained eaters (Herman & Polivy, 1975; Herman, Polivy, Pliner, Munic, & Threlkeld, 1978; Polivy, Herman, & Warsh, 1978). Because dieting is itself stressful and frustrating, it is not surprising that dieters appear to have fewer resources available to cope with additional stresses and thus find them more distressing (Herman & Polivy, 1980). Moreover, dieting and weight loss have frequently been linked with the precipitation of depressive episodes (see Stunkard & Rush, 1974, for a review). Finally, evidence is accumulating that implicates weight loss in heart and gallbladder disease (Roncari, 1980) and a myriad of other medical problems (see Marliss, 1978; Polivy & Herman, 1983, and Stunkard & Rush, 1974, for reviews).

Anorexia Nervosa

A more serious consequence of the sociocultural emphasis on thinness in women may be the proliferation of anorexia nervosa among young women. Anorexia nervosa is a syndrome of self-imposed starvation and relentless pursuit of thinness to the point of emaciation. Although the ''causation of anorexia nervosa remains unknown'' (Russell, 1973, p. 44), there have been many attempts to explain this puzzling disorder. The classical psychoanalytic interpretation has viewed anorexia nervosa as regression to more primitive oral functioning in response to overwhelming demands of mature genitality. (Nicolle, 1938; Sours, 1974; Szyrynski, 1973; Waller, Kaufman, & Deutsch, 1940). Similarly, Crisp (1965, 1970, 1980) has viewed the disorder as a regressive response to maturational crisis where the adolescent feels unable to meet the psycho-social demands of puberty. Through the mechanism of dieting the anorexic may assume a prepubertal body shape and hormonal status, thereby avoiding conflicts at adolescence. Recent psychodynamic explanations of anorexia nervosa derived from ego psychology and object relations theory (Ehrensing & Weitzman, 1970; Goodsitt, 1969, 1977; Masterson, 1977; Selvini–Palazzoli, 1974; Sours, 1974, 1980; Story, 1976) have emphasized disturbances in early mother–child interactions resulting in the child's failure to separate and develop an independent identity. Bruch (1973, 1978) has described specific ego deficits related to: (1) body image, (2) internal perceptions of affective and visceral sensations, and (3) feelings of ineffectiveness. Weight control becomes part of a struggle to gain control and competence. According to a "family systems" framework, anorexia nervosa is an interpersonal problem that must be understood within the context of the family communicational network (Caille, Abrahamsen, Girolami, & Sorbye, 1977; Conrad, 1977; Minuchin, Rosman, & Baker, 1978; Selvini–Palazzoli, 1974). Others have suggested that the family's overconcern with achievement, dieting, weight, and food (Bruch, 1973; Crisp, 1980; Kalucy, Crisp, & Harding, 1977) plays a role in the disorder. Finally, anorexia nervosa has been conceptualized as a heterogeneous disorder (Casper, Eckert, Halmi, Goldberg, & Davis, 1980; Garfinkel, Moldofsky, & Garner, 1980; Russell, 1979) that may be multidetermined (Garfinkel & Garner, 1982; Garner & Garfinkel, 1980).

There is a growing consensus that the incidence of anorexia nervosa has increased over the past several decades (Crisp, Palmer, & Kalucy, 1976; Duddle, 1973; Halmi, 1974; Ikemi, Ago, Nakagawa et al., 1973; Jones, Fox, Babigian et al., 1980; Sours, 1969, 1980; Theander, 1970). In a survey of nine schools in England, Crisp et al. (1976) have found the disorder to be relatively common in high school girls, particularly those of upper social class. They discovered one severe case in every 100 upper class girls over 16 years of age. Including schools representing varying social strata, one new case was found in every 250 girls surveyed. This and other recent reports have confirmed Fenwick's (1980) observation that anorexia nervosa is overrepresented in upper social classes (Bruch, 1973; Crisp, 1965; Jones et al., 1980; Morgan & Russell, 1975; Sours, 1980). It is well known that the disorder occurs more often with females, primarily during adolescence. These observations that anorexia nervosa occurs with a particular age, sex, and social class distribution as well as its increasing incidence suggest that sociocultural factors may be related to its expression.

The apparent increase in the prevalence of anorexia nervosa has been paralleled by our culture's aesthetic preference for thinness in women. Bruch (1978) has suggested that one of the factors responsible for this shift is "the enormous emphasis Fashion places on slimness" (p. viii). The impact of this thin idealized shape is evident in the pervasiveness of dieting among women. Nylander (1971) has argued that "what begins as simple dieting can, in fact, lead to the development of anorexia nervosa" (p. 25). In an epidemiological study of 2370 Swedish adolescents, Nylander found a .6% incidence of serious cases of anorexia nervosa. Moreover, the majority of the girls surveyed "felt fat" and this increased with age. Almost 20% of these were below the mean weight for their height and were actively dieting, whereas this tendency to diet was seldom reported by boys. According to Nylander (1971), when dieting is prolonged and sufficiently intense, starvation symptoms develop and actually lead to the expression of anorexia nervosa. There is thus increasing evidence that the pressure on women to diet and be thin may be at least a contributor to the increasing incidence of anorexia nervosa.

If increased pressure to diet and be thin contributes to the development of serious eating disorders, then groups in which this pressure is augmented could be expected to have a greater incidence of anorexia nervosa. Previous descriptive studies of professional ballet dancers have indicated disturbed body image perception, excessive dieting, vomiting to control weight, and frank cases of anorexia nervosa in some females (Druss & Silverman, 1979; Vincent, 1979). As Gordon (1981) points out:

> Ballerinas in America today are expected to conform to an ideal of womanhood that . . . seems intent on punishing women for the very qualities that make them womanly. Young ballet dancers learn that they must be thin if they are to succeed in their art, and many are led to believe that the thinner they become, the more successful they will be. (p. 43)

She cites evidence to the effect that the result of this pressure to be thin is "an alarming number of cases" of anorexia nervosa among ballerinas.

Garner and Garfinkel (1980) systematically studied such groups who by career choice experience intense pressure to diet. Female professional dance ($N = 183$) and modeling students ($n = 56$) were administered a questionnaire, "The Eating Attitudes Test (EAT)," which is designed to assess the symptoms of anorexia nervosa (Garner & Garfinkel, 1979). Other psychometric and demographic data were also obtained. Subjects with high EAT scores, or those with secondary amenorrhea were clinically interviewed to determine if they had anorexia nervosa. Twelve unequivocal cases (6.5% incidence) were detected in the dance sample. Furthermore, dancers from the more competitive and professionally oriented programs were more likely to develop the disorder than those from the less stringent settings (High competitive = 8% vs Low competitive = 5%). The incidence with the modeling students was similar to that for the dancers from the less competitive environment. These data suggest that both pressures to be slim and achievement expectations are risk factors in the development of anorexia nervosa.

Nylander (1971) originally suggested that the symptoms of anorexia nervosa occur on a continuum with the classical syndrome representing the extreme point. This view has been supported by others who describe the existence of "mild" or "forme fruste" anorexia nervosa (Fries, 1977; Russell, 1973). In the Garner and Garfinkel (1980) study, 31% of the entire dance sample reported significant symptoms of anorexia nervosa on the EAT scale but failed to meet all dimensions of the rigorous diagnostic criteria of Feighner et al. (1972). Many had not lost a sufficient amount of weight (25%) to justify a positive diagnosis, however, their morbid fear of weight gain and drive for thinness were significant indeed. Some resorted to vomiting, laxative abuse, and extreme dieting measures to control their weight. Furthermore, a recent investigation of so-called normal college students found that 12% of the females reported significant eating pathology (including vomiting to control weight) and also showed nonfood related attitudes and feelings similar to those of anorexic patients (i.e., problems with affective and visceral labeling, regressive wishes, self-disparagement, a lack of interpersonal trust, desires for perfectionism and excessive control, and intense body dissatisfaction; Garner, Polivy, & Olmsted, 1981). These data offer some support for the argument that anorexia nervosa does occur on a continuum with only the most serious cases receiving medical attention.

As Bruch (1978) suggests, the recent increase or "epidemic" of anorexia nervosa "must be attributed to psychosociological factors" (p. vii). The changing trend toward a thinner ideal shape for women (Garner et al., 1980) may be one cultural determinant of the disorder. In fact, it has been shown that friends and relatives of anorexic patients actually appear to admire their emaciated appearance in some cases (Branch & Eurman, 1980). Other sociocultural changes in the role of women in society have also been implicated. The increased performance expectations as well as the greater sexual freedom for women may be overwhelming for some vulnerable adolescents (Bruch, 1978). Selvini–Palazzoli (1974) has indicated that these increased demands for vocational excellence have been added to, rather than exchanged for, traditional role expectations for women. Thus, many of the posited contributors to the increased societal emphasis on slimness also seem to be implicated in the development of anorexia nervosa. However, although contemporary sociocultural pressures on women do appear to play a role in the recent increase in the disorder, they must be considered within the context of other individual and familial predisposing factors to such pathology (Garfinkel & Garner, 1982; Garner & Garfinkel, 1980).

Bulimia and Dietary Chaos

The overeating described previously in laboratory studies of presumably nonpathological restrained college students (Herman & Mack, 1975; Herman, Polivy, & Silver, 1979; Hibscher & Herman, 1977; Polivy, 1976; Ruderman & Wilson, 1979; Spencer & Fremouw, 1979) also has its analogue in the clinical population suffering from eating disorders. Described variously as bulimia (Russell, 1979), bulimarexia (Boskind–Lodahl, 1976; Boskind–Lodahl & Sirlin, 1977) or the dietary chaos syndrome (Palmer, 1979), this disorder involves the ingestion of prodigious quantities of food in one or more eating "binges," usually followed by attempts to purge oneself or rid the body of food (through vomiting, laxative and/or diuretic abuse, hyperexercising, or fasting). Unless the sufferer has previously exhibited a full-blown anorexia nervosa, she is likely to escape medical/psychiatric attention. As long as the purging attempts are successful, the bulimic may even manage to lose weight or maintain a fashionably low weight. As with anorexia nervosa, this dietary chaos syndrome is most likely to appear in young women. We discuss it here because, as with anorexia nervosa, there is some support for the idea that bulimia is facilitated by dieting and this in turn is related to the societal emphasis on slimness (Polivy & Herman, 1985). Just as investigations of restrained eating indicate that it is the dieters, not the nondieters, who "counterregulate" (Herman & Polivy, 1980), the clinical literature on bulimia indicates that the syndrome is almost always preceded by caloric restriction either as a diet (Boskind–Lodahl & Sirlin, 1977) or outright anorexia nervosa (Beaumont, George, & Smart, 1976; Palmer, 1979; Russell, 1979). However, it must be noted that there have actually been few studies of bulimia in nonanorexic groups. No clear understanding of the pathogenesis of bulimia is yet available. Like anorexia nervosa, bulimia probably results from various predisposing events. In particular, significant biological predispositions (e.g., frontal lobe tumor, hypothalamic disease) may be associated with bulimia. There may also be particular individual psychological predispositions, but these have not been properly studied. It has also been suggested (Wardle, 1980) that the alternation between starving and bulimia by young women may reflect conflict between acceptance and rejection of societal pressure to be thin. In studies of clinical populations (which may be highly biased), Orbach (1978) has linked compulsive eating with "the search for love, comfort, warmth, and support—for the indefinable something that seems never to be there" (p. 32).

Although anorexia nervosa, bulimia, and even restrained eating are probably multidetermined, societal emphasis on slimness, especially for women, does appear to be a contributor. It is interesting to note a number of parallels between aspects of anorexia nervosa and current societal trends. The increased incidence of anorexia nervosa appears to be paralleled by an increased focus by society in general on issues considered to be symptomatic in the anorexic patient. For example, anorexic patients are described as being preoccupied with food and eating, yet obsessed with weight (Bruch, 1973). They often collect and exchange recipes and take jobs that involve preparing or serving food, while at the same time they struggle to keep their weights constantly declining. The proliferation of gourmet-oriented cooking courses, magazines, stores, equipment, and newspaper columns bears abundant testimony to our society's similar preoccupation with food and eating. The accompanying increase in the prevalence of books and articles on dieting (Garner et al., 1980) likewise reflects society's obsession with weight. Anorexics also suffer from a fear of fatness and "relentless pursuit of thinness" (Bruch, 1973). Not since the Romans (and perhaps not even then) has a society been as afraid of fat as ours. Anorexics often are hyperactive and exercise excessively to lose weight (Bruch, 1973). The number of books, magazines, articles on jogging, tennis, skiing, and other forms of exercise has risen as quickly as the ones on dieting. Anorexics are notoriously prone to strange diets and food fads (Bruch, 1973). In recent years, there have been vogues in our society for grapefruit diets, banana diets, all protein diets, low or no carbohydrate diets, and so on, ad infinitum. Furthermore, health food stores and vegetarianism have proliferated. We have discussed the presence of bingeing and purging in anorexics, bulimics, and to some extent in so-called normals—again, the symptom seems to be widespread in the general population. Finally, one of the hallmark symptoms of anorexia nervosa is the denial of illness and insistence that the pursuit of thinness is "normal." Our society certainly seems to concur with this attitude—it is fatness that is seen as pathologic. It certainly seems, then, that society's attitudes and behaviors connected with food, eating, and body weight are not unlike those of an anorexic patient.

In conclusion, societal values and attitudes can contribute to illness. The current cultural pressures on people to be thin are eliciting compliance to a surprising, and possibly unhealthy degree. Restrained eating, one route chosen by many to achieve societally acceptable weight levels, may not be pathologic in and of itself, but it does seem to have correlates (like bouts of overeating, distractibility, and emotionality) that are less than desirable. Furthermore, the widespread pressure to be thin seems to be a contributor to the increased incidence of the syndromes of bulimia and anorexia nervosa. Although it is clear that disorders like bulimia and anorexia nervosa are precipitated by a number of factors in any individual patient, societal attitudes certainly have an impact on the individual both directly and indirectly (by influencing the actions of family members and peers). The behaviors and attitudes of these patients are possibly condemned as pathological because they are pursued with a singlemindedness not displayed by the majority of society; certainly most patients receive praise and reinforcement for such "symptoms," at least initially (e.g., Branch & Eurman, 1980). To the extent that societal attitudes and behaviors parallel symptoms of pathology, one might argue that they are not a healthy influence for suggestible or susceptible members of that society.

ACKNOWLEDGMENTS

The writing of the chapter was supported by grants from the Natural Sciences & Engineering Research Council of Canada (to the first author), the Medical Research Council of

Canada (to the second author), and the Ontario Mental Health Foundation (to the third author).

REFERENCES

Beaumont, P. J. V., George, G. C. W., & Smart, D. E. (1976). 'Dieters' and 'vomiters and purgers' in anorexia nervosa. *Psychological Medicine, 6*, 617–622.

Beller, A. S. (1977). *Fat and thin—A natural history of obesity.* New York: Farrar, Straus and Giroux.

Bennett, N. B., & Gurin, J. (1982). The dieter's Dilemma. New York: Basic Books.

Berscheid, E., Walster, E., & Bohrnstedt, G. W. (1973). Body image, physical appearance, and self-esteem. Paper presented at the American Sociological Association Meetings, New York.

Berscheid, E., Walster, E., & Bohrnstedt, G. W. (1973, November). The happy American body: A survey report. *Psychology Today*, pp. 119–123, 126–131.

Boskind-Lodahl, M. (1976). Cinderella's & stepsisters: A feminist perspective on anorexia nervosa and bulimia. *Signs: Journal of Women in Culture and Society, 2*, 342–356.

Boskind-Lodahl, M., & Sirlin, J. (1977, March). The gorging-purging syndrome. *Psychology Today*, pp. 50–52, 82, 85.

Branch, C. H. H., & Eurman, L. J. (1980). Social attitudes toward patients with anorexia nervosa. *American Journal of Psychiatry, 137*, 631–632.

Bray, G. (1976). *The obese patient.* Toronto: W. B. Saunders Company.

Brodsky, C. M. (1954). A study of norms for body form-behaviour relationships. *Anthropological Quarterly, 27*, 91–101.

Bruch, H. (1973). *Eating disorders.* New York: Basic Books.

Bruch, H. (1978). *The golden cage.* Cambridge: Harvard University Press.

Caille, P., Abrahamsen, P., Girolami, C., & Sorbye, B. (1977). A systems theory approach to a case of anorexia nervosa. *Family Press, 16*, 455–456.

Calden, G., Lundy, R. M., & Schlafer, R. J. (1959). Sex differences in body concepts. *Journal of Consulting Psychology, 27*, 115–222.

Casper, R. C., Eckert, E. D., Halmi, K. A., Goldberg, S. C., & Davis, J. M. (1980). Bulimia: Its incidence and clinical importance in patients with anorexia nervosa. *Archives of General Psychiatry, 37*, 1030–1035.

Clark, K. (1980). *Feminine Beauty.* New York: Rizzoli International Publications, Inc.

Conrad, D. E. (1977). A starving family—An interactional view of anorexia nervosa. *Bulletin of the Menninger Clinic, 41*, 487–495.

Crisp, A. H. (1965). Some aspects of the evolution, presentation and follow up of anorexia nervosa. *Proceedings of the Royal Society of Medicine, 58*, 814–820.

Crisp, A. H. (1970). Anorexia nervosa: 'Feeding disorder,' nervous malnutrition or weight phobia? *World Review of Nutrition, 12*, 452–504.

Crisp, A. H. (1980). *Anorexia nervosa—Let me be.* New York: Grune and Stratton.

Crisp, A. H., Palmer, R. L., & Kalucy, R. S. (1976). How common is anorexia nervosa? A prevalence study. *British Journal of Psychiatry, 218*, 549–554.

Druss, R. G., & Silverman, J. A. (1979). Body image and perfectionism of ballerinas:comparison and contrast with anorexia nervosa. *General Hospital Psychiatry, 1*, 115–121.

Duddle, M. (1973). An increase of anorexia nervosa in a university population. *British Journal of Psychiatry, 123*, 711–712.

Dwyer, J. T. (1973, March). Psychosexual aspects of weight control and dieting behavior in adolescents. *Medical Aspects of Human Sexuality*, 82–108.

Dwyer, J. T., Feldman, J. J., & Mayer, J. (1967). Adolescent dieters: Who are they? Physical characteristics, attitudes and dieting practices of adolescent girls. *American Journal of Clinical Nutrition, 20*, 1045–1056.

Dwyer, J. T., Feldman, J. J., & Mayer, J. (1970). The social psychology of dieting. *Journal of Health & Social Behavior, 11,* 269–287.

Dwyer, J. T., Feldman, J. J., Seltzer, C. C., & Mayer, J. (1969). Adolescent attitudes toward weight and appearance. *Journal of Nutrition Education, 1,* 14–19.

Dwyer, J. T., & Mayer, J. (1970). Potential dieters: Who are they? *Journal of the American Dietetic Association, 56,* 510–514.

Ehrensing, R. H., & Weitzman, E. L. (1970). The mother-daughter relationship in anorexia nervosa. *Psychosomatic Medicine, 32,* 201–208.

Feighner, J. P., Robins, E., Guze, S. B., Woodruff, R. A., Winokur, G., & Munoz, R. (1972). Diagnostic criteria for use in psychiatric research. *Archives of General Psychiatry, 26,* 57–63.

Fenwick, S. (1880). *On atrophy of the stomach and on the nervous affections of the digestive organs.* London: Churchill.

Ford, C. S., & Beach, F. A. (1952). *Patterns of sexual behavior.* New York: Ace Books.

Fries, H. (1977). Studies on secondary amenorrhoea, anorectic behaviour, and body image perception: Importance for the early recognition of anorexia nervosa. In R. A. Vigersky (Ed.) *Anorexia Nervosa* (pp. 163–176). New York: Raven Press.

Frisch, R. E., & Revelle, R. (1970). Height and weight at menarche and hypothesis of critical body weights and adolescent events. *Science, 169,* 397.

Garfinkel, P. E., & Garner, D. M. (1982). *Anorexia nervosa: A multidimensional perspective.* New York: Brunner/Mazel.

Garfinkel, P. E., Moldofsky, H., & Garner, D. M. (1980). The heterogeneity of anorexia nervosa. *Archives of General Psychiatry, 37,* 1036–1040.

Garner, D. M., & Garfinkel, P. E. (1979). The Eating Attitudes Test: An index of the symptoms of anorexia nervosa. *Psychological Medicine, 9,* 273–279.

Garner, D. M., & Garfinkel, P. E. (1980). Socio-cultural factors in the development of anorexia nervosa. *Psychological Medicine, 10,* 647–656.

Garner, D. M., Garfinkel, P. E., & Olmsted, M. P. (1983). An overview of sociocultural factors in the development of anorexia nervosa. In P. L. Darby, P. E. Garfinkel, D. M. Garner, & D. V. Coscina (Eds.) *Anorexia nervosa: Recent developments.* New York: Alan R. Liss, Inc.

Garner, D. M., Garfinkel, P. E., Schwartz, D., & Thompson, M. (1980). Cultural expectations of thinness in women. *Psychological Reports, 47,* 483–491.

Garner, D. M., Olmsted, M. P., Polivy, J., & Garfinkel, P. E. (1984). A comparison between weight preoccupied women and anorexia nervosa. *Psychosomatic Medicine.*

Garner, D. M., Polivy, J., & Olmsted, M. (1981, August). *Anorexia nervosa, obesity and dietary chaos: Common and distinctive features.* Presented at the American Psychological Association Convention, Los Angeles, California.

Goldblatt, P. B., Moore, M. E., & Stunkard, A. J. (1965). Social factors in obesity. *Journal of the American Medical Association, 192,* 1039–1044.

Goodsitt, A. (1969). Anorexia nervosa. *British Journal of Medical Psychology, 42,* 109–118.

Goodsitt, A. (1977). Narcissistic disturbances in anorexia nervosa. In Feinstein, S. C., & Giovacchini, P. (Eds.) Adolescent psychiatry vol. v: *Developmental and clinical studies.* New York: Jason Aronson, Inc.

Gordon, S. (1981). Art and anguish. *Geo, 3,* 40–50.

Halmi, K. A. (1974). Anorexia nervosa: Demographic and clinical features in 94 cases. *Psychosomatic Medicine, 36,* 18–25.

Herman, C. P., & Mack, D. (1975). Restrained and unrestrained eating. *Journal of Personality, 43,* 647–660.

Herman, C. P., & Polivy, J. (1975). Anxiety, restraint, and eating behavior. *Journal of Abnormal Psychology, 84,* 666–672.

Herman, C. P., & Polivy, J. (1980). Restrained eating. In A. Stunkard (Ed.) *Obesity* (pp. 208–239). Philadelphia: W. B. Saunders Company.

Herman, C. P., Polivy, J., Pliner, P., Threlkeld, J., & Munic, D. (1978). Distractibility in dieters and nondieters: An alternative view of "externality." *Journal of Personality and Social Psychology, 36,* 536–548.

Herman, C. P., Polivy, J., & Silver, R. (1979). Effects of an observer on eating behavior: The induction of sensible eating. *Journal of Personality, 47,* 85–99.

Heuneman, R. L., Shapiro, L. R., Hampton, M. C., & Mitchell, B. W. (1968). Food and eating practices of teen-agers. *Journal of the American Dietetic Association, 53,* 17–24.

Hibscher, J. A., & Herman, C. P. (1977). Obesity, dieting, and the expression of obese characteristics. *Journal of Comparative and Physiological Psychology, 91,* 374–380.

Ikemi, Y., Ago, Y., Nakagawa, S., Mori, S., Taka Lashi, N., Suematsu, H., Sugita, M., & Matsubara, H. (1974). Psychosomatic mechanism under social change in Japan. *Journal of Psychosomatic Research, 18,* 15–24.

Jakobovits, C., Halstead, P., Kelley, L., Roe, D. A., & Young, C. M. (1977). Eating habits and nutrient intakes of college women over a thirty-year period. *Journal of the American Dietetic Association, 71,* 405–411.

Johnson, P. A., & Staffieri, J. R. (1971). Stereotypic affective properties of personal names and somatotypes in children. *Developmental Psychology, 5,* 176.

Jones, D. J., Fox, M. M., Babigian, H. M., & Hutton, H. E. (1980). Epidermiology of anorexia nervosa in Munroe County, New York: 1960–1976. *Psychosomatic Medicine, 92,* 551–558.

Kalvcey, R. S., Crisp, A. H., & Harding, B. (1977). A study of 56 families with anorexia nervosa. *British Journal of Medical Psychology, 50,* 381–395.

Lawson, M. C. (1980). Development of body build stereotypes, peer ratings, and self-esteem in Australian children. *Journal of Psychology, 104,* 111–118.

Lerner, R. M. (1969a). The development of stereotyped expectancies of body build-behavior relations. *Child Development, 40,* 137–141.

Lerner, R. M. (1969b). Some female stereotypes of male body build-behavior relations. *Perceptual and Motor Skills, 28,* 363–366.

Lerner, R. M., & Gellert, E. (1969). Body build identification, preference, and aversion in children. *Developmental Psychology, 1,* 456–462.

Lerner, R. M., & Korn, S. J. (1972). The development of body-build stereotypes in males. *Child Development, 43,* 908–920.

Lyons, A. S., & Petrucelli, R. J. (1978). *Medicine: An illustrated history.* New York: Harry N. Abrams.

Manchester, W. (1968). *The arms of Krupp.* Boston: Little, Brown and Company.

Marliss, E. B. (1978). Protein diets for obesity: Metabolic and clinical aspects. *Canadian Medical Association Journal, 119,* 1413–1421.

Masterson, J. F. (1977). Primary anorexia nervosa in the borderline adolescent—An object—relations view. In Hartocollis, P. (Ed.) *Borderline personality disorders.* New York: International Universities Press.

McKenna, R. J. (1972). Some effects of anxiety level and food cues on the eating behavior of obese and normal subjects. *Journal of Personality and Social Psychology, 22,* 311–319.

Minuchin, S., Rosman, B., & Baker, L. (1978). *Psychosomatic families: Anorexia nervosa in context.* Cambridge: Harvard University Press.

Morgan, H. G., & Russell, G. F. M. (1975). Value of family background and clinical features as predictors of long-term outcome in anorexia nervosa: Four year follow-up study of 41 patients. *Psychological Medicine, 5,* 355–372.

Nicolle, G. (1938). Prepsychotic anorexia. *Proceedings of the Royal Society of Medicine, 3,* 1–15.

Nylander, I. (1971). The feeling of being fat and dieting in a school population: Epidemiologic interview investigation. *Acta Sociomedica Scandinavica, 3,* 17–26.

Orbach, S. (1978). *Fat is a feminist issue . . . the anti-diet guide to permanent weight loss.* New York: Paddington Press Ltd.

Palmer, R. L. (1979). The dietary chaos syndrome: A useful new term? *British Journal of Medical Psychology, 52,* 187–190.

Polivy, J. (1976). Perception of calories and regulation of intake in restrained and unrestrained subjects. *Addictive Behaviors, 1,* 237–243.

Polivy, J., & Herman, C. P. (1976a). Clinical depression and weight change: A complex relation. *Journal of Abnormal Psychology, 85,* 338–340.

Polivy, J., & Herman, C. P. (1976b). The effects of alcohol on eating behavior: Disinhibition or sedation? *Addictive Behaviors, 1976,1,* 121–125.

Polivy, J., & Herman, C. P. (1976). Effects of alcohol on eating behavior: Influences of mood and perceived intoxication. *Journal of Abnormal Psychology, 85,* 601–606.

Polivy, J., & Herman, C. P. (1983). *Breaking the diet habit,* New York: Basic Books, Inc.

Polivy, J., & Herman, C. P. (1985). Dieting and binging: A causal analysis. *American Psychologist, 40,* 193–201.

Polivy, J., Herman, C. P., & Hackett, R. (1980). *Self-awareness, self-consciousness, and the inhibition of eating.* Unpublished manuscript, University of Toronto.

Polivy, J., Herman, C. P., & Warsh, S. (1978). Internal and external components of emotionality in restrained and unrestrained eaters. *Journal of Abnormal Psychology, 87,* 497–504.

Polivy, J., Herman, C. P., Younger, J. C., & Erskine, B. (1979). Effects of a model on eating behavior: The induction of a restrained eating style. *Journal of Personality, 47,* 100–114.

Roberts, J. V., & Herman, C. P. (1980, June). *Physique stereotyping: An integrated analysis.* Presented at the Canadian Psychology Association Convention, Calgary.

Roncari, D. A. K. (1980). Obesity and lipid metabolism. In Ezrin, C., Godden, J. O., & Volpe, R. (Eds.) *Systematic endocrinology* (2nd ed.) New York: Harper & Rowe.

Ruderman, A., & Wilson, G. T. (1979). Weight, restraint, cognitions and counterregulation. *Behavior Research and Therapy, 17,* 581–590.

Russell, G. F. M. (1973). The management of anorexia nervosa. In *Symposium of anorexia nervosa and obesity.* Royal College of Physicians of Edinburgh.

Russell, G. F. M. (1979). Bulimia nervosa: An ominous variant of anorexia nervosa. *Psychological Medicine, 9,* 429–448.

Schachter, S., Goldman, R., & Gordon, A. (1968). Effects of fear, food deprivation and obesity on eating. *Journal of Personality and Social Psychology, 10,* 91–97.

Selvini-Palazzoli, M. (1974). *Self-starvation—From the intrapsychic to the transpersonal approach to anorexia nervosa.* London: Chaucer Publishing Co. Ltd.

Shainess, N. (1979). The swing of the pendulum—From anorexia to obesity. *The American Journal of Psychoanalysis, 39,* 225–234.

Sleet, D. A. (1969). Physique and social image. *Perceptual and Motor Skills, 28,* 295–299.

Society of Actuaries. (1959). *Build and blood pressure study.* Chicago: Author.

Sontag, S. (1978). *Illness as metaphor.* New York: Vintage Books.

Sorlie, P., Gordon, T., & Kannel, W. B. (1980). Body build and mortality: The Framingham study. *Journal of the American Medical Association, 243,* 1828–1831.

Sours, J. A. (1969). Anorexia nervosa: Nosology, diagnosis, developmental patterns and power control dynamics. In Caplan, G., & Levovici, S. (eds.) *Adolescence: Psychosocial perspectives.* New York: Basic Books.

Sours, J. A. (1974). The anorexia nervosa syndrome. *International Journal of Psychoanalysis, 55,* 567–576.

Sours, J. A. (1980). *Starving to death in a sea of objects: The anorexia nervosa syndrome.* New York: Jason Aronson.

Spencer, J. A., & Fremouw, W. J. (1979). Binge eating as a function of restraint and weight classification. *Journal of Abnormal Psychology, 88,* 262–267.

Staffieri, J. R. (1967). A study of social stereotype of body image in children. *Journal of Personality and Social Psychology, 7,* 101–104.

Staffieri, J. R. (1972). Body build and behavioral expectancies in young females: *Developmental Psychology, 6,* 125–127.

Story, I. (1976). Caricature and impersonating the other: Observations from psychotherapy of anorexia nervosa. *Psychiatry, 39,* 176–188.

Strongman, K. T., & Hart, C. J. (1968). Stereotyped reactions to body build. *Psychological Reports, 23,* 1175–1178.

Stunkard, A. J. (1975). From explanation to action in psychosomatic medicine: The case of obesity. Presidential address, 1974. *Psychosomatic Medicine, 37,* 195–236.

Stunkard, A. J., & Rush, J. (1974). Dieting and depression reexamined: A critical review of reports of untoward responses during weight reduction for obesity. *Annals of Internal Medicine, 81,* 526–533.

Szyrynski, V. (1973). Anorexia nervosa and psychotherapy. *American Journal of Psychotherapy, 27,* 492–505.

Theander, S. (1970). *Anorexia nervosa. Acta Psychiatrica Scandinavica* Suppl. 214.

Vincent, L. M. (1979). *Competing with the Sylph: Dancers and the pursuit of the ideal body form.* New York: Andrews and McMeel.

Waller, J., Kaufman, M. R., & Deutsch, F. (1940). Anorexia nervosa: Psychosomatic entity. *Psychosomatic Medicine, 2,* 3–16.

Wardle, J. (1980). Dietary restraint and binge eating. *Behavioural Analysis and Modification, 4,* 201–209.

Wells, W. D., & Siegel, B. (1961). Stereotyped somato types. *Psychological Reports, 8,* 77–78.

Woody, E. Z., Costanzo, P. R., Leifer, H., & Conger, J. (1980). *The effects of taste and caloric perceptions on the eating behavior of restrained and unrestrained subjects.* Unpublished manuscript, Duke University.

Wooley, S. C., & Wooley, O. W. (1980). Eating disorders: Obesity and anorexia. In Brodsky, A., Hare-Mustin, R. (Eds.): *Women and psychotherapy: An assessment of research and practice.* New York: Guilford Press.

Wyden, P. (1965). *The overweight society.* New York: Morrow.

6 The Psychology of Height: An Empirical Review

Julian V. Roberts
C. Peter Herman
University of Toronto

> *Has it not been shown that genius usually chooses for its physical abode extremes in human magnitude?*
>
> —Walter De La Mare (1935)

> *It is alleged that People of a Low Stature are pettish, passionate and fiery.*
>
> —Scottish proverb, circa 1721.

> *Tall men are like houses of four or five stories, wherein commonly the uppermost room is worst furnished.*
>
> —17th century proverb.

> *It is a fact of everyday experience that tall men have often a character curiously delicate and introvert.*
>
> —M. Gustav Morf (1965)

> *The ladies of the present age are strangely altered from the unpolished females who flourished in the days of Romance. What modern Parthenissa would not prefer a tall young fellow to the most beautiful dwarf of the universe?*
>
> —The Connoisseur (1754)

As one may see from the aforementioned observations, the traditional source of information about cultural stereotypes—folklore—is quite inconsistent with respect to the temperamental and intellectual correlates of stature. Nevertheless, it

113

may well be true that certain traits are reliably associated with height, in fact as well as in impression: there may be a "kernel of truth" to any stature stereotype, just as there seems to be for other variables such as facial attractiveness (Goldman & Lewis, 1977). And of course, to the extent that people share beliefs about the correlates of height, such beliefs may come to influence personality and behavior in the manner of a self-fulfilling prophecy (Jones, 1977) as well as to substantiate initial prejudices by means of biased hypothesis-testing (Snyder & Cantor, 1979). In this chapter, we review evidence pertaining to actual and perceived differences in behavior and personality as a function of height.

Although research of varying quality has been conducted on psychological aspects of height for several decades, the topic has attracted increasing attention lately. Two recent monographs (Gillis, 1982; Keyes, 1980) have addressed the role of stature in human affairs, but many unanswered questions remain. This chapter will review the scientific evidence pertaining to the psychology of height and evaluate the importance of human height as psychological variable.

Height and Weight

Of course height is not an independent dimension; for example, it is related to weight, and the high correlation between them (typically in the range of .7 to .8– e.g., Blommers & Lindquist, 1960) naturally confounds the interpretation of any effects observed. If only for this reason, we should expect the short or tall stereotype to be complex and interactive—especially when compared to more unitary social stereotypes such as beauty or race. Certainly, the confounding of height with other variables ought to be accorded considerable attention in the design and interpretation of research; such has not always been the case in the past.

Height has received nothing like the research attention that has been directed at the other primary dimension of physique—weight (e.g., Dejong, 1980; Mayer, 1968; Stunkard, 1980). There are several reasons for this imbalance. The health risks allegedly associated with the extremes of weight overshadow those attendant upon extremes in height. In addition, we can control our weights, even if we do not have as much control as has often been supposed (cf. Keesey, 1978). Height, by contrast, is far less malleable; beyond exercises designed to straighten the spinal cord (and thus gain a couple of inches) outlined in certain popular books (e.g., "Increase Your Height," Madowy, 1977), the most that we can do is accentuate our heights by the use of accoutrements such as heels, hats, and certain types of clothing. Finally, it is clear that weight is a more important component in the attractiveness equation. The prevalence of dieting habits in our culture, especially for females, attests to the importance of weight (cf. Polivy, Garner, & Garfinkel, this volume); and even a cursory glance at the paragons of beauty in Western culture reveals that despite considerable diversity in height (for both sexes), they are all uniformly slender. It has also been suggested that height is a less potent variable in determining attractiveness because it shows less variation than do other dimensions, such as weight; it seems that those appearance attributes that exhibit greater variation in the population are seen (along with their correlates) as correspondingly more capable of accounting for human differentiation.

Stature

There is a pervasive social attitude which associates tallness with positive characteristics and assigns negative attributes to shortness. (Stabler, Whitt, Morreault, D'Ercole & Underwood (1980, p. 743).

Height, or more precisely, size, has long been a metaphor for importance and power. The size of ecclesiastical (and secular) statues has often reflected the importance of the person portrayed. Physical size became in the earliest times a symbol of status or power—recall the ancient Egyptian temples at Abu Simbel. Historical figures are often described in terms that communicate their importance by allusions to size:

Why man, he doth bestride the narrow world like a colussus, and we petty men walk under his huge legs. (*Julius Caesar*, I, ii, 134)

Even the word "stature," defined as a "person's bodily height as an element in his appearance" (Oxford English Dictionary, 1971) now connotes social importance independent of its meaning, for example:

Rockefeller . . . expressed delight that a person of Mr. Kissinger's stature and achievements had agreed to lend his considerable expertise to Chase. (Heller, 1979, p. 361)

Likewise:

he is sharply contrasted with the tragic Lear, who is a towering figure, every inch a king, while Gloster is built on a much smaller scale and has infinitely less force and fire. (Bradley, 1978, p. 295)

and further

Imagination demands for Lear, even more than for Othello, majesty of stature and mien. Tourgenief felt this and made his 'Lear of the Steppes' a *gigantic* peasant. (Bradley, 1978, p. 295)

Moreover, some of the antiquated synonyms for the word "tall" throw light upon the skewed distribution of value as a function of height:

2b. comely, good, fair, handsome, elegant, fine: "That such a base slave as he should be saluted by such a tall man as I am"—Marlowe, The Jew of Malta, 1952, IV, iv.

Also:

3. good at arms, stout, brave, bold, and valiant: "If he can kill a man . . . he is called a tall man and a valiant man of his hands." Northbrooke, 1577.

and

8. lofty, grand, eminent. "Thine briefly in a tall friendship." (Lamb) quoted in the Oxford English Dictionary, Compact Edition 1971, page 3228)

"He cannot prevail with me". "Spoke like a tall man that respects thy reputation." (King Richard the Third, I, IV, 148–149)

Comparisons between physical size and social or intellectual status are not restricted to popular culture, as Krisberg (1974) points out: "often the eulogizers make reference to the large physical stature of the man in hopes of reconstituting his largeness as an intellectual force in modern social science" (p. 147). Thus it is clear that in Western culture at least, being tall is regarded more positively than being short.

How Tall is Tall?; How Short is Short?

Height is a vague and often ill-defined construct: Its importance often lies not in strictly objective terms, but in reference to the stature of the observer.[1] In this sense, *perceived* height may be more important in social interactions than are sheer centimeters. It probably makes little sense to define height simply in terms of population means or medians. It may be more useful to define height as a difference score between the heights of the interactants.

However, let us begin by asking what people mean when they describe someone as tall or short? Table 6.1 presents the means, in inches, generated by a sample of 100 adults asked to indicate quantitatively what they meant by short, medium, and tall. These subjects were drawn from a heterogeneous sample of visitors to a Toronto Science Museum (Roberts, 1977.) Of course, these subjects are not representative of the population, but their estimates provide a rough idea of what people mean when they use these terms. Although the medium catego-

---

[1]Maslow (1937) suggested that to individuals at the extremes there may be little differentiation: "To a giant all dwarfs look equally small and to a dwarf, all giants look equally tall" (p. 45).

TABLE 6.1
Mean Estimates of What Constitutes Short, Average, and Tall

Stimulus Category	Subjects	
Male	Male ($n=50$)	Female ($n=50$)
Short	61.9	63.6
Average	68.8	68.1
Tall	77.6	73.5
Female		
Short	57.9	60.0
Average	64.4	64.3
Tall	69.8	69.1

ries are very close to the U.S. population medians, (the median height of all U.S. males aged 18 to 74 years is 69 inches; for females, the median is 63.6 inches (Department of H.E.W., quoted in *U.S. News and World Report,* March 28, 1977), the mean heights for the tall and short groups are perhaps more extreme than one might expect. In fact asking ''how tall'' someone is (rather than ''how short'') also affects the height estimates: Harris (1973) found that phrasing the question the first way led to significantly higher mean estimates (75.4 vs. 68.5 inches).

There are many questions embedded within this research area, for instance: (1) Are there any stable personality differences between short and tall individuals? (2) Is there an association between social status and physical stature? (3) What stereotypes do people hold of short and tall males and females? All of these questions have been addressed to some degree by the literature; none have been resolved satisfactorily. One way of simplifying our exposition is to divide the research into the following general areas: (1) What impressions, expectations, and stereotypes do we hold regarding stature?; and (2) Is there any basis for any of these beliefs? With this division in mind, we begin by examining differences in body image as function of stature.

Height and Body Image

One way of determining the values attached to differing heights is to examine the literature on people's satisfaction with their own height. Central to popular notions of height and body image is the theme that shorter males find their stature frustrating. For example the authors (Dollard, Doob, Miller, Mower, & Sears, 1939) of the frustration–aggression hypothesis noted that: "Smaller-than-average stature is quite generally regarded by men as a disadvantage and must be in some degree frustrating. Although inferior size alone would not be expected to "produce" criminality in any given individual, it should show its influence statistically" (p. 119).[2]

Data from the body image literature reflect subjects' awareness of this notion. Work by Jourard and Secord (1954) and Secord and Jourard (1953) revealed height to be the most important variable in their body-cathexis questionnaire. (Of course the extent to which one can generalize about the present culture using data drawn from students 25 or 30 years ago is questionable.) Most males wanted to be taller: Large size was associated with strong positive feelings and small size was associated with the opposite. An early study (Smith, 1938) found that 56% of the male undergraduates surveyed reported being short was a source of feelings of inferiority. This may help to explain why individuals sometimes overestimate their own heights.[3] Dillon (1962) found that 71% of own height estimates exceeded the actual measurements. There were no differences between males and females in amount of bias displayed. However, questionnaire data from Calden, Lundy, and Schlafer's (1959) subjects showed that of the males dissatisfied with their physique all but two wished to be taller, whereas fully one half of the female sample wanted to be shorter.

Hinckley and Rethlingshafer (1951) found physique satisfaction scores to be lower for shorter subjects. Their subjects were male college students. It is probably this desire to be taller that motivated subjects to distort their estimates of the average male height: Estimates of average height were positively correlated with the subjects' own heights. Thus the judgment of the average male's height is influenced by the height of the men making the estimates (see below). The curve of satisfaction with one's height as a function of that height displayed a cur-

---

[2]There is no reliable evidence that this in fact the case.

[3]Most research upon this topic uses self-reports as a source of data. The question arises of how reliable such data are. If certain heights are more desirable than others, it is possible that people systematically overestimate (or underestimate) their own heights. Lass, Andes, McNair, Cline, and Pecora (1982) found that the correlations between self-reported and measured heights were substantial (r = .89 and .99 for females and males respectively. See also Biro, 1980 for similar results).

vilinear trajectory: Satisfaction scores increased with height up to approximately 74 inches, and then declined. Another study showed a sex difference. Stolz and Stolz (1951) found that adolescent males were more disturbed about being too short than about being too tall, whereas for girls the opposite was true.

The self-images of male adolescents who were "consistently retarded" (in growth) were significantly more negative than those of others who were "consistently accelerated"—so the problem with shortness is more than just being different from one's peers (Mussen & Jones, 1957). (See Northcraft and Hastorf, this volume, for discussions of the social adjustment problems attendant upon deviations from normal physical growth rate, either accelerated or retarded development.)

Gunderson (1965) found that for a sample of male U.S. Navy personnel, satisfaction with own height rose to a peak at 72 inches and then began to decline. We should be aware of the idiosyncratic nature of this subject population, however: This finding may have little generalizability to the much larger civilian male population.

Clifford (1971) asked 340 subjects of both sexes to rank-order their various physical dimensions in terms of satisfaction. He found that males were more dissatisfied with their heights than were females. In terms of satisfaction, height was ranked 38th (out of 45 items) for men and 22nd for women. This was true despite the remarkable degree of agreement concerning satisfaction with other physical dimensions (rho = .87, $p < .01$).

Not all the body image literature points to the importance of height as a factor in self-evaluation. This is particularly true of the more recent studies. Coopersmith's (1967) monograph on self-esteem found no association between actual height and self-esteem scores on the Coopersmith scale, using adolescent and preadolescent males as subjects. Lerner, Karabenick, and Stuart (1973) found that height ranked 14th (in importance) out of 24 variables related to physique in a sample of college students. They did find it to be quite important for women rating men: It ranked 7th. One other finding is relevant here: Height and satisfaction ratings, although uncorrelated for males, were positively correlated for females (.21, $p < .01$). At the same time, both sexes agreed that height was more important for males than for females. Mahoney and Finch (1976a, 1976b) found that height accounted for only 9% of the variance in male satisfaction scores (it was the 4th most important). Females ranked it third in importance, but it still accounted for only 11% of the variance. In the second of their reports Mahoney and Finch (1976b) demonstrate that for males at least voice was the most important body aspect correlated with self-esteem. Neither height nor weight was significantly related to self-esteem scores. For female subjects height was correlated with self-esteem, although the correlation coefficient was rather small (R = .04; see Table 6.3).

Among the more recent data are those provided by a Psychology Today survey conducted in 1973. This magazine selected a sample of 2000 respondents (approximating national sex and age distributions) from the 62,000 readers who returned a physique-related questionnarie. Two trends are apparent in the responses to the question of satisfaction regarding one's height. First, over two-thirds of both sexes (67% males; 72% females) were "quite" or "extremely" satisfied with their height. The comparable data for weight are much lower: 43% males and 31% of females were "quite" or "extremely" satisfied. In addition, for the options "quite" or "extremely" dissatisfied, the percentages are identical: 3% of each sample. Likewise when the samples are simply divided into those expressing any satisfaction versus any dissatisfaction, the distributions are also identical for both sexes: 13% any dissatisfaction, 87% any satisfaction. Naturally there are limitations to these data; the respondents may be quite unrepresentative of the North American population from which they were drawn. It seems unlikely, however, that the results from a truly random survey would be radically different.

Overall, then, height does not appear to be a source of body image dissatisfaction for most people. It may be that height, as a body-image variable, does not exert the influence upon self-evaluations that it formerly did. Although examination of advertisements for romantic partners studies show it is still relevant for certain subject groups, perhaps being tall, especially for males, does not mean as much as it did 2 or 3 decades ago.

Body Image and Self-Descriptions

Data from another area of research also speak to the relative importance of height to body image. To the extent that height is central to self-concept, one would expect it to appear in subjects' self-descriptions. McGuire and his colleagues (McGuire & McGuire, 1982; McGuire & Padawer–Singer, 1976) have used a technique in which subjects are asked to respond to the invitation "Tell us about yourself." The contents of the resulting self-descriptions are then coded for mention of physical characteristics. In the earlier study (McGuire & Padawer–Singer, 1976) 252 12-year-olds served as subjects. All physical characteristics combined (hair color, eye color, weight, height) accounted for only 5% of the total responses. Height was mentioned by 10% of the sample and weight by 11%. Thus, although height seemed almost as important as weight, neither was especially salient.

McGuire and Padawer–Singer tested another hypothesis relevant to our concerns: They hypothesized that those individuals who were distinctive in some way (those who were particularly short or tall) would be more likely to mention their height in their self-descriptions. There was no support, however, for this hypothesis in that study. McGuire and McGuire (1981) did find support for it using a larger sample of students ranging from Grades 5 through 12. In this later study height was mentioned more frequently—19% of the children mentioned their height (compared to 11% mentioning weight). Moreover if a child was particularly short or tall, he or she was more likely to mention his or her height.

These results suggest that, although height may not be central to the body image or self-concept of the average person, it may become increasingly important as the individual's height deviates further from the norm. Although height seemed at least as important as weight in terms of overall references, it still accounted for only a small percentage of total responses. On the basis of these studies, at least, it is hard to attribute a great deal of importance to height when it accounts for fewer references than eye color.

Own Height and Estimates of Population Means

It appears that one's own height affects estimates of other peoples' heights. Ward (1967) asked subjects to estimate the height of the average American male and female. The correlation between own height and estimates of the average American male was $+.32$ ($p < .01$). A similar comparison for female heights and estimates of the average American female was $+.37$, also significant at the .01 level. Dunaway's (1973, cited in Clifford & Bull, 1978) subjects, who were asked to estimate the heights of certain stimulus persons, erred by overestimating the heights of short targets and underestimating the taller ones. Once again there was a systematic bias: Short subjects especially underestimated tall targets. In a related experiment Williams (1975) had people watch a film of a staged robbery and then asked them to estimate the thief's height. A significant positive correlation emerged between the observers' heights and their estimates of the robber's stature.[4]

Differences Between Short and Tall People

Intelligence.   Adams (1980) conducted one of the few studies relating height to different personality traits. The effects of height (as an independent variable) were compared to the effects of age and weight, and Adams concluded: "While age and weight were predictive of several personality characteristics, height was predictive of more total personality indices. Taller adults were more likely than their shorter-stature peers to view themselves as sensation-seeking, likeable, and self-directive (internal locus of control), while height was observed to be negatively associated with emotional expression and belief in luck or chance in directing one's life" (pp. 290–291). While the personality traits investigated by

---

[4]In fact the area of eyewitness identification research provides a useful source of naturalistic information about the characteristics of people that are most salient to observers and therefore most frequently recalled (see Yarmey, 1979, for a review of this area). For instance in one study (Kuehn, 1974) analysis of 100 police reports of eyewitnesses minutes after the crime revealed that height was the second most frequently identified characteristic, exceeded only by gender.

Adams were not extensive (and may have been predisposed towards obtaining height effects) this study should stimulate further research into the personality traits actually associated with short and tall people.

Intelligence. Katz (1940) reported a significant correlation between IQ scores and height for young girls 3 to 5 years old. However no such correlation was found for boys. Jensen (1980) cites studies (see pp. 361–362) that establish a modest correlation between height and IQ, but as he points out (p. 361), this correlation probably represents assortative mating for both height and intelligence rather than a functional relationship between the two traits.

Dominance. One of the most frequently quoted stereotypical traits of tall individuals is dominance. It is perhaps not surprising that physical size has become associated with mental dominance. If it were in fact true, such a phenomenon could be readily explained by reference to some form of self-fulfilling prophecy, the behavior of the short or tall person being influenced by other peoples' expectations. However, the data do not clearly support differences along this dimension as a function of height. In 1957 Eisenberg reported a small but significant positive correlation between height and feelings of dominance. Fisher (1964) found that overestimation of own heights (by males only) was weakly related to achievement, dominance, and chauvinism scale scores. It was as if, to quote Fisher, "power aspirations were expressed in terms of a concept of one's size" (p. 732).

On the other hand, Eggins, Barker, and Walker (1975) studied the incidence of psychiatric problems in 346 schoolchildren and found that after variables such as social class and family size had been accounted for, neurotic boys tended to be taller. One must equate dominance with neuroticism in order to accomodate this particular finding.

Conformity and Dominance. Two recent studies have investigated the behavior of people placed in situations similar to those devised by Asch (1951) in his classic conformity research. Asch required participants to make perceptual judgments that contradicted the opinions of other subjects (confederates of the experimenter). People were said to conform to the extent that they went along with clearly erroneous judgments by the other "subjects". In Portnoy's (1973) study, the task of the subjects was to estimate the number of dots projected onto a screen. Using only males, Portnoy found the height of the 3 confederates influenced the amount of conformity displayed: Subjects conformed most in the presence of short confederates (66 inches). This result is the reverse of the prediction (derived from folk psychology) that tall individuals would induce conformity in shorter people.

There is also contradictory evidence from Loftus and Herman (1978) who measured conformity in a different way. Subjects viewed cartoons accompanied by an appropriate laugh track (congruent condition) or an inappropriate one (incongruent condition). In the latter condition—the one most like the Asch and Portnoy studies—short subjects displayed more conformity but tall subjects conformed more in the congruent condition. Once again the heights were objective measures rather than self-reports.

A possible resolution to these and other inconsistencies may take us beyond this kind of research and into the person perception literature. Ackerman and Herman (1979) effected encounters between subjects and recorded actual height, amount of behavioral dominance (in a debate format), and scores on a scale measure of dominance. These authors found no differences as a function of actual height but perceived height was related to a difference in dominance, that is to say subjects recalled a difference in dominance when they perceived a height difference between themselves and the other member of the dyad. Thus it appears from this study at least—and we return to this point later—that perceived height may be more important than physical reality. To summarize this section, we can say that one of the most intuitive aspects of the height stereotype (dominance) has received at best mixed support.

Height, Power and Income.   If there is a dominance—related component to the tall-person stereotype then we might expect tall individuals to occupy positions of power more frequently than short people. There is some basis for this expectation. In an early study Stogdill (1948) examined the relationship between height and leadership. He summarized 14 studies that had examined these two variables: Nine of them showed leaders were taller than average, two found the opposite, and three no difference. However this survey is now quite old and almost all these studies investigated leadership only in academic settings. One further study (Caldwell & Wellman) quoted by Stogdill was probably the most accurate: It investigated the leadership–height relationship and found that height was important but that it depended on the situation.

Farb (1978) reports a study in which men selected to advance in corporate management training programmes were significantly taller than the average. Kurtz (1969) asked 140 sales recruiters to choose between two equally qualified candidates for a sales position; one candidate was 73 inches, the other 65 inches in height. Seventy-two percent favored the taller applicant, 27% expressed no preference, whereas only 1% chose the shorter candidate. Two comments are worth making. The first is that these results, based on responses to a mail questionnaire may not be readily generalizable even to other positions in the business world. Second, an obtrusive questionnaire in which the hypothesis is patently obvious to the respondents is hardly the optimal research strategy to use. Moreover, because it was a hypothetical situation it was essentially a role-playing task for the respondents, with the all problems attendant upon such a procedure (see Freedman, 1969).

If taller individuals make better salespeople (as some anecdotal reports suggest), it should be possible to demonstrate this experimentally. Data from an earlier study by Baker and Redding (1962) are relevant here. Purdue undergraduates served as subjects in an experiment in which the same speech was attributed to a tall or a short speaker. There were no differences in degree of persuasion as a function of the speaker's height.

Finally in this context there are some relevant correlational data showing that the winners in Presidential campaigns were generally taller than the losers (see Gillis, 1982, p. 20).

There is further support if one wishes to associate income with power: Taller people in certain settings do seem to earn more. The starting salaries of men under 6 feet had a significantly lower mean ($701 per month) than those over 6 feet 2 inches ($788) according to a study reported by the *U.S. News and World Report* (1977). Keyes (1980) reports a telephone survey of 1067 Canadians in which men who earned less reported being shorter than the higher wage earners (p. 178). (It is possible that the high wage earners could be exaggerating both their annual incomes and their heights.)

Perception of height in others

Kassarjian (1963) hypothesized that perceptions of a political candidate's height would be related to voting intention. Just before the 1960 presidential election 3018 California voters were asked (1) which of the two candidates (Kennedy or Nixon) was taller and (2) whom did they intend to vote for in the forthcoming election. The results supported the experimental hypothesis: Voters who had selected a presidential candidate perceived him as being taller than his opponent. However, the effect was not strong. In fact, of the Nixon supporters, more thought John Kennedy was the taller candidate (he was, by an inch). Almost 70% of the Kennedy voters thought he was taller than Nixon, but this difference could reflect just increased familiarity. Furthermore, intensity of opinion did not affect amount of perceptual distortion although one would expect it to, given Kassarjian's hypothesis. It is not an impressive demonstration of a perceptual distortion; there is little evidence (from this study at least) that voting intentions affected perceptions of candidates' heights. It would have been interesting to have known about the heights of the voters in this study: Did their own stature affect either their perception of the candidates' heights or their intentions to vote one way or another?

The 1969 mayoral contest in New York City afforded another opportunity to test this hypothesis. Berkowitz, Nebel, and Reitman (1971) asked 276 voters a series of questions about their perception of the two leading candidates—incumbent John Lindsay (6'3") and his main opponent Mario Procaccino (5'6")—their preferences and their predictions for the outcome of the election. Preference for a candidate was not a significant factor in determining perceptual distortions here either but there were height differences between Lindsay supporters and those in favor of Procaccino. This in itself is not surprising because there is a confound (as the authors point out) involving ethnic affiliation. Berkowitz et al. also tested the hypothesis that there would be a relationship between height (self-reported) and voting intention. There was some evidence to support the hypothesis but only for certain groups. Once again the findings were inconsistent. Truhon and McKinney (1979) hypothesized that the size of childrens' drawings of presidential candidates would reflect childrens' preferences, but no significant effects were found: Size was unrelated to candidate preference.

Other results pertaining to this issue and reported by Ward (1967) are also equivocal. Ward asked two samples of undergraduate students to state his or her degree of liking for several politicians (including the incumbent president Johnson) and also to estimate the heights of these individuals. There were no statistically significant effects for female subjects. Demand cues would present a strong alternative interpretation had strong effects emerged. As it is this report offers little support for the liking—height estimation hypothesis.

The results of studies by Popper (1958, 1964) are consistent with the notion that a correspondence exists between height and social importance. Children were asked to estimate the heights of various adults known to them and they underestimated the heights of teachers from previous years. Their estimates were also affected by the perceived importance of the adults. Girls more than boys underestimated previous teachers' heights and also tended to overestimate the heights of male adults in general, compared to boys. Using similar measures Shaffer (1964) found that children underestimated their own heights in comparison to estimates of adults. Popper also hypothesized that one of the consequences of inducing a failure experience would be to lower childrens' estimates of their own heights. This hypothesis was only supported for male subjects. Over 1,000 people participated in a survey conducted by DeHamel (1980) who was interested in perceptions of parental height. Respondents were asked to estimate the heights of both parents. These estimates were then compared to measurements taken by the researcher. DeHamel found that while there was little difference between mens' and womens' estimates of their fathers' heights, men overestimated the height of their mothers to a significant degree. In addition this overestimation increased with age of subject. DeHamel argues that this pattern of results reflects parental importance.

Berkowitz (1969) investigated the relations among subjects' self-reported heights, the heights of friends, and certain personality variables. The perceived (i.e., reported) heights of friends were closer to the subjects' own heights than would be expected by chance. Once again it is hard to know whether this difference reflects reality, because actual heights were not recorded. There may be a tendency to assume one's friends are of approximately equal stature. None of the personality measures, including the dominance scale from the Edwards Personal Preference Schedule, were significantly associated with perceived height.

Osborn (1974) used male students in a study looking at the effects of liking for another person upon estimates of his stature. The Byrne Interpersonal Judgment

Scale was used as the primary dependent measure. Subjects estimated "liked" others to be more similar to themselves in height, and as one might expect, they judged "disliked" others to be less similar in height than they in fact were. In keeping with the results of a person perception study (Roberts, 1977) that manipulated the perceived height of people in videotapes, Osborn's subjects reacted to another's height in complex ways.

Bleda (1972) experimentally manipulated the attitude similarity of a stimulus person and asked subjects to guess his height. Attitude similarity was operationally defined as the proportion of attitude statements similar to the subject, this proportion ranging across five experimental conditions from .10 to .90. As the target person's attitudinal similarity increased so did subjects's estimates of his height. Moreover there was a statistically significant positive correlation between the attractiveness ratings of the stimulus person and height estimates. These findings were replicated in a subsequent study by Bleda and Bleda (1977).

Prieto (1975) investigated the perceptions of height and self-esteem among 69 grade-school boys. Self-evaluation of height, teacher's evaluations, and peers' evaluations were all highly correlated with self-esteem scores on the Coopersmith scale (coefficients of $+.77$; $+.82$ and $+.89$, respectively). Actual height was not significantly correlated with self-esteem scores, (this is in keeping with Coopersmiths' data to which we have already alluded) but by actual height the authors of this experiment meant self-reported height, because it was not actually measured. Still, it is interesting to note that social estimates of height are more highly correlated than own estimates with self-esteem. Once again the distinction between perceived and actual height emerges, and it seems that the former is at least as important as the latter.

In a related study Prieto (1975) found a significant negative relationship between students' reported height and their evaluation of their own social and academic performance. Prieto explained this association by means of a negative labeling process. It is rather disquieting to consider that self-fulfilling prophecies as a function of discrepancies in stature may be at work this early in school life. The same study showed that peers and teachers also associated poor social and academic performance with short stature.

Ascribed Social Status and Perceived Height

At this point we turn to the person perception literature from which the majority of the most recent research has emerged. The association of high status with height has been challenged in several experiments. This research has roots in earlier work in perception (e.g., Dukes & Bevan, 1952) that showed that children tend to overestimate the size of salient stimuli, such as favorite foods and monetary tokens. Bruner and Goodman (1947) found that objects of increased value or importance received exaggerated estimates of their size. Dannenmeir and Thumin (1964) sought to establish a similar effect with regard to human stature and social status. They hypothesized that an increase in status would lead people to perceive a stimulus person as taller than he or she actually was.

Forty-six students were asked to estimate the heights of several individuals known to them. These individuals ranged in status from a fellow student to the director of the school. Dannenmeir and Thumin then computed "distortion" scores by subtracting actual heights from estimates. There was a highly significant effect: The heights of high-status targets were overestimated whereas low-status ones, such as a fellow student, were underestimated. This demonstration, however, is far from perfect: The actual heights of these targets may have exercised an effect independent of the person's status, besides which the individuals obviously differed in other ways that may have interacted with the height estimation task.

With this criticism in mind Wilson (1968) used a single stimulus person who was introduced to five groups in a way that manipulated his ascribed status. To one class for example, he was introduced as a student, whereas another heard that he was a professor. (These two descriptions represent the range of ascribed status.) Following the introduction the target left the room and the students were asked to estimate his height. The differences among the groups as a function of the status ascribed to the target were highly significant. When he was introduced as a professor the target received a mean height estimate 2.5 inches in excess of the "student" condition.

Because the actual height of the target in the Wilson study was 73 inches, and the most accurate mean (72 inches) also emerged from the high-status group, the results are open, as Rump and Delin (1973) suggested, to an alternative explanation. Rather than just underestimating the height of the target in the lower status condition, perhaps the effect of high-status was to make the subjects more aware of his presence and therefore more accurate in their judgments. These authors tested their "differential attention" hypothesis using two targets (short and tall) and four status levels (postgraduate, lecturer, senior lecturer, and professor). They were thus predicting an interaction between actual height and ascribed status. The predicted interaction was significant and not the main effect suggested by the Wilson (1968) and Dannemeir and Thumin (1964) experiments. The tall professor received the greatest estimate and the short professor the smallest mean estimate. One other finding is of interest. The experimenter who was present while the stimulus person was introduced also had an effect upon the size estimates. It appeared that he acted as an anchor stimulus against which subjects judged the height of the target.

One additional study (Lerner & Moore, 1974) employed a design similar to Wilson's: College students saw a stimulus person for 15 seconds and were subsequently asked, under one of five ascribed status levels, to estimate his or her height. The status manipulation—in contrast to the previous studies—had no significant effects upon height estimates.

One resolution of these discrepant results is that the experiments differed in the amount of time the stimulus person was present. Wilson's subjects saw the target for only as long as it took to introduce him, perhaps, 15–20 seconds. The target in the Rump and Delin study remained in the room for a full 12 minutes.

Perhaps following a brief exposure people resort to stereotypical associations between status and height, whereas after a longer period the effect of the high-status label is to generate increased interest and hence attention to the stimulus. There is some support for this notion: Hensley and Angoli (1980) predicted that height estimates would be distorted more for novel stimulus persons. Their height estimation data supported this prediction. Finally, in the same context, one additional study (Meth, 1976) manipulated the status of a stimulus person and asked subjects to estimate the person's height. No significant effects emerged.

When subjects were asked by Lechelt (1975) to estimate the heights of male members of different occupations, they responded by generating heights that were positively associated with the status of the profession. The correlation between esteem scores and height ratings was $R = .91$ ($p < .01$) for males and a similarly high degree of association emerged for female subjects. The author (Lechelt, 1975) concluded: "The present findings show (1) ratings of physical height of men in different occupations are directly related to, and can be predicted by, the rated esteem associated with occupational roles, and (2) both men and women tend to respond in a similar fashion" (p. 946).

A study by Koulack and Tuthill (1972) investigated the effects of status-related ethnic membership and prejudice upon height perception. Subjects were shown silhouettes of individuals identified as belonging to one of several ethnic groups (American Swedish, Canadian, Indian, Hutterite, or Doukhobor) that had been previously rated on the Bogardus Social Distance Scale. The experimental task was to estimate the heights of these figures. The results demonstrated that height estimates corresponded to position on the Bogardus scale. Thus the American (high status) was estimated to be the tallest and the Hutterite shortest (lowest status). The authors were aware that actual heights of the ethnic groups may have contributed to this effect; certainly the mean height for American males is greater than that for other groups, but comparison between control and experimental groups showed that mere labeling was sufficient to change height estimates. For instance when the Hutterite figure was identified simply as a man, he was perceived as being taller than when accompanied by the ethnic label. Their secondary hypothesis, that the more highly prejudiced individuals would display a greater perceptual bias in favor of the high status group was not supported.

Height and Attractiveness

Height is frequently mentioned with reference to attractiveness. Berscheid and Walster (1974) for example in their chapter on physical attractiveness suggest that: "Despite the probability that people respond to characteristics in combination, to the complete configuration, one individual characteristic which may account for a fair proportion of attractiveness variance, particularly in men, is height'' (p. 178).

Popular opinion (at least in our culture) seems to have supported the taller-the-better principle[5] for males. (It is worth noting that this assumption also extends to social psychology research: One of the manipulations of desirability in a recent experiment (Zanna & Pack, 1975) was height, the highly desirable stimulus person was described as being 73 inches, the low desirability one as being 65 inches.)

One of the earliest investigations was conducted by Beigel (1954) who surveyed 227 males and 183 females. Response categories included appearance, social qualities, status considerations, education, intelligence, and character traits. Appearance in general accounted for 28% of the total responses; height itself accounted for 8.1% of the total responses. Most of the couples in this survey conformed to the ''male-taller'' norm: Of 192 couples only one contained a woman who was taller than her partner. Similar patterns emerged when people described their most desirable partner. In the group of 76 respondents who referred to height differences, only one man and one woman described the desirable male as short and only three males and two females described the desirable female as tall. Of the 77 males who referred to specific heights, 46% desired above-average height differences favoring the male, 20% favored the opposite, and 26 wanted average size differences between members of a couple. Of the 39 women who made specific height references, 72% desired above-average differences favoring males, 13% the opposite, and 15% average differences. Because Beigel solicited opinions and preferences in a rather haphazard way this study does not tell us all that much; moreover it is 25 years old and mate selection preferences may well have changed over the past quarter century.

Most recently Gillis and Avis (1980) uncovered evidence that supported the male-taller norm. Data from bank-account application forms revealed that the occurrence of couples with a female taller than the male was significantly less likely than would be expected by chance factors alone.

Feldman (1971) presented some informal data to support his contention that short men may have courtship problems in excess of those confronting especially tall men. Perhaps the major obstacle for short men is the previously mentioned ''cardinal principle of date selection'' (Berscheid & Walster, 1974), namely, that the man must be taller than his partner. In order to avoid violating this norm, short men (and tall women for that matter) must of necessity restrict the population from which they select their mates.

---

[5]Feingold (1982) correlated mens' heights (self-reported) with peer ratings of the attractiveness of their female companions, and found no significant relationship between the two variables. There was a small correlation between self-reported height and attractiveness of partner relative to oneself, but this is a rather different phenomenon.

Body image—but not necessarily height—is obviously important for inter-personal behaviors such as dating. It seems, from the scant published data on this topic, that height is of fundamental concern at least to those actively seeking romantic partners. Harrison and Saeed (1977) found that 72.5% of men and 82.5% of the women advertising in "Lonely Hearts" publications gave their heights. This may just mean that this particular sample of people think that height is important to others, because they did not actually request specific heights for their partners. However Cameron, Oskamp, and Sparks' (1978) analysis of advertisements in a "singles" newspaper demonstrated the importance of height and also supported what Berscheid and Walster (1974) call the "cardinal princi-ple" of date selection, namely that a man must be taller than his mate. In the Cameron et al. study, 80% of the women making a height request from potential partners wanted a man 6 feet or taller and almost all the women in this category wanted the man to be at least 4 inches taller than themselves. Of the men making height requests, 70% wanted a woman of small or medium stature, regardless of their own height. Recently Lynn and Shurgot (1984) reported an imaginative study which also used responses to 'Lonely-hearts' advertisements. These inves-tigators coded 395 advertisements in terms of the individual's gender, height, weight, hair and eye color. The dependent measure was the number of responses received by each advertiser (information provided by the magazine). There was a significant interaction effect involving height and gender: while the height of the female advertisers had no effect upon the number of responses they received, tall males received more responses than short ones.

The Lerner and Moore (1974) study already described found a significant positive correlation between height estimates and ratings of physical attrac-tiveness for the male target ($r + .37$, $p < .01$) but not the female one. Nev-ertheless the evidence to support the commonplace notion that tall males are more attractive than short- or average-sizes ones is not conclusive. Graziano, Brothen, and Berscheid (1978) provided female college students with facial photographs of men and asked them to rate these targets on a number of dimen-sions, including physical attractiveness and desirability as a date. The experi-menters manipulated the ascribed height of the males, who were given heights that were short (65–67 inches), medium (69–71 inches), or tall (72–79 inches). The prediction that women's attraction to men would be an increasing linear function of attributed height was not supported, regardless of the subject's height. When trait ratings were summed to compose a positivity score, the plot of these scores as a function of height followed a curvilinear pattern: The medium height targets were regarded most positively. Graziano et al. also presented their stimuli to male subjects and asked them to rate the targets on a number of personality traits. These authors found that regardless of the height of the subject 'short' targets received the most positive ratings. Thus for both male and female subjects the 'Taller-the-better' principle did not hold. However, data from sever-al other studies conflict with these findings. Elman (1977) also used photographs to evaluate the effect of attributed height upon attractiveness ratings. Targets were described as being 5 feet 4″ or 6 feet 4″ and the predicted effect for attractiveness emerged: the ''tall'' target was seen to be more attractive than the ''short'' one. The effect was not very strong however ($p = .05$) and Elman fails to report how many trait scales *failed* to elicit significant effects. The addition of another appearance factor—the presence or absence of spectacles—interacted with the height factor suggesting that height is not an independent dimension and may not generate main effects, unless you eliminate the possibility of interaction with other variables.

Gacsaly and Borges (1979) employed a trait-attribution task and varied the height (tall; short) and the body-build (endomorphic, mesomorphic, ectomorphic) of the male targets using a factorial design. Height alone had no significant effect, although some interactions did emerge. Roberts (1977) attempted to replicate the Graziano et al. findings using both students and members of the public. The exact same procedure and manipulation was employed. The pattern of data however, differed. No significant effect of attributed height emerged. One additional person perception study also found essentially negative results. Roth and Eisenberg investigated evaluations of competence made by teachers of students. In the first experiment there was a marginal ($p < .10$) effect: tall boys were rated more negatively. However, teachers were not differentially punitive towards short or tall boys. In the second experiment, in which female stimuli were employed, there were no significant effects of height upon teachers' attributions of competence or assignment of punishment.

The stimuli employed in the Graziano et al. study were not very representative of everyday life: We do not immediately become aware of someone's exact height in this way but rather form an impression of his or her height, usually in relation to our own. It is also true to say that these effects emerged in a rather jejune environment: Ascribed height was one of only four pieces of information available to the subjects. Perhaps in a more realistic encounter the effects of height might pale in contrast to other variables such as a person's personality or overall physique.

Roberts (1977) manipulated perceived height in a less obtrusive way, within the framework of a simulated job interview. Videotapes of three male targets were created in three conditions: The stimulus person was shorter or taller than the interviewer or was the same size. (These effects were achieved by adjusting the floor and seat levels prior to each interview.) Thus each target appeared in three nonstudent populations, then viewed a predetermined combination of these tapes (no one subject saw the same target in two different height conditions of course), and having done so formed an impression of the applicant and rated him on a number of scales, including physical attractiveness. Consistent with the employment format they were also asked questions relating to the person's potential as a co-worker and the probability of this person being offered a job.

In support of the 'Taller-the-better' principle derived from correlational research, when the stimulus person in the videotape appeared to be taller than the interviewer he received most positive ratings. However there was also a significant interaction between the manipulation of height and the personality of the target. Height did not affect subjects' responses independent of the person being rated. The emergence of an interaction both in this experiment and the Gacsaly and Borges (1979) study (see above) suggest that height may have variable effects depending upon the presence of other factors (such as information about a person's personality). In this respect it differs from weight which in the person perception literature at least typically results in strong main effects. One finding from the Roberts (1977) research was consistent with the Graziano et al. study: the height of the subject was not an important variable affecting subjects' responses.[6]

Stature is probably important to attractiveness—the studies by Cameron et al. (1978) and Harrison and Saeed (1977) attest to this—but it may well be an oversimplification to expect certain heights to be consistently more attractive to all subjects in all contexts. Moreover it is difficult to go as far as some people have gone on the basis of the research outlined earlier. Gillis (1982) for example concluded that "The bottom line is that height does have tremendous impact on our sex lives" (p. 51).

Height and Personal Space

One might expect a person's height to affect his or her behaviour regarding the personal space of other people. The few studies that have examined the relationship between height and personal space have generated mixed results. Cochran and Urbanczyk (1982) for example, examined the space requirements of adults and found no relationship between subjects' heights and their personal space requirements. Hartnett, Bailey, and Hartley (1974) investigated the effect of body height on invasions of personal space. Male and female subjects were asked to approach either a tall or a short stimulus person and to stop when they felt "uncomfortable." The height of the target produced a significant main effect: Subjects stopped further from the tall person than the short target. These authors saw this result as support for the hypothesis that physical height is a major determinant of personal space. However this may also be explained more parsimoniously by the fact that people must tilt their heads more when standing close to someone taller. The reason then for standing further away may simply be that it is physically more comfortable to converse and interact at that distance, and it may have little to do with the social implications of violating the personal space of a tall person. In addition, because they used only one tall and one short stimulus person, any height effects are also confounded with the characteristics of those particular individuals.

---

[6]Although Rapaport (1975) found that subject height did make a difference: Short subjects assigned more positive adjectives to tall stimulus persons than did tall subjects.

The same methodological deficiency is present in a study by Bailey, Caffrey, and Hartnett (1976). In this experiment size was crossed with a threat manipulation. Personal space invasion was unaffected by the height variable. Caplan and Goldman (1981) remedied the problem of a single stimulus person: Two tall targets (one male, one female) and two short targets were used. The experimental question was whether commuters would be differentially likely to invade the personal space of tall and short confederates. Height of confederate had a significant effect: Subjects of both sexes were less likely to invade the personal space of the tall individuals.

Finally, Veno (1974) varied the approach patterns of confederates in a field setting. Although height of the confederate was not a variable, height of the subject was significantly related to the way in which subjects responded to the intruder. Smaller subjects were more likely to emit what Veno described as "submissive" responses. This study tells us little about the social consequences of height however. To conclude this section, it appears that there is little evidence that height systematically affects responses related to a person's personal space.

SUMMARY

Such a diversity—of method, subject population, and experimental setting— complicates any attempt to summarize the area, nevertheless we attempt some general statements before proceeding to some suggestions for future research. This kind of view must perforce be subjective and the reader is reminded of the pitfalls of this kind of "literary" approach (Leviton, 1981). The alternative—a statistical meta-analysis—is not possible given the diverse material.

Prieto and Robbins (1975) made the following statement:

> since it can be demonstrated that this culture positively values tall stature, particularly for males, reflected in most advertising, fashion design, athletics, occupational qualifications, leadership, social status and heterosexual relationships, the consequences of short stature deserve attention from behavioural scientists. (p. 395)

In his recent book Gillis (1982) also emphasizes the importance of height: "Clearly, height and attitudes about height have important consequences for people." He further states: "This book explores some essential questions about human height. The answers that have been found could significantly alter the course of your life" (p. 5).

These are strong words, and probably an overstatement: Research in most of these areas, as we have tried to show—leadership and social status for instance—has failed to substantiate such a claim.[7] It is clear though that the culture does favor tall individuals to a degree and that this is known to its members. Tall men appear to be more satisfied then shorter man with their physique. People seem to overestimate their own heights, or at least to report figures that although highly correlated with reality, are nevertheless systematically inflated. There is also a tendency to drift towards the mean, to assume tall people are not quite so tall and to see short people as somewhat taller. This, unlike an egocentric bias (estimating population averages closer to one's own height) is probably purely a perceptual phenomenon.

No clear-cut relationship exists between height and social status, although in all probability people assume—when told nothing else—a correspondence between social importance and stature. They report size estimates that vary in accordance with the importance of the stimulus person in their lives.

The evidence to support or contradict the existence of systematic prejudices against tall or short individuals remains inconsistent. It will require further research to clarify this issue. We must also beware making generalizations across sex: Much of the research reported here has used only male stimuli. Researchers have made the assumption that stature is more important to male physique and there appears to be no empirical justification for this (see, for example, the results of the 1973 *Psychology Today* survey).

One methodological problem present in many of the studies in this area concerns the presence of demand cues (Orne, 1962). All too often the dependent measure—estimating own or a target person's height—is administered in close proximity to the independent variable. In research that correlates two variables—liking and perceived height for example—they are measured almost simultaneously. It is hard to imagine subjects not coming to an accurate estimation of the hypothesis being tested. For example, Touhey (1971) investigated the effect of a morale-raising speech on height estimation. Directly following the manipulation subjects were asked to estimate their own heights. Could the purpose have been made clearer? More rigorous attempts to mask the experimental hypothesis from the subjects would lend this literature more credibility.

FUTURE RESEARCH DIRECTIONS

The wide range of methods that have been used in height research enables the reader to draw certain conclusions regarding the most appropriate methodology.

---

[7]In this survey we have not touched upon the developmental or clinical literature pertaining to height. It is clear though that height is not a powerful variable in these domains either. For example, a recent survey (Gordon, Post, Crouthamel, & Richman, 1984) found groups of short and normal children to be comparable on a wide range of intellectual and achievement-related assessments. Gordon et al. concluded: "Contrary to the conclusions of uncontrolled studies, our data showed short and control groups to be comparable on all variables" (p. 291).

Although there are sound reasons within the traditional person perception field for techniques such as photographic stimuli, in which all variables save the one of primary experimental interest are restricted or eliminated, this is perhaps not the optimal strategy for height research. The stereotypes associated with stature have not been investigated as thoroughly as certain other components of physique such as weight or attractiveness. This is one reason why they remain somewhat undefined, especially for females.

Perhaps the first step involves defining the stereotypes and this involves two steps. First of all, what do people mean, in feet and inches, when they describe someone as being short or tall? Is there any consensus? The variance generated in response to this question (see Table 6.1) was substantial. Secondly we need to map out the nature and boundaries of any stature stereotypes using, for example, a technique such as that described by McCauley and Stitt (1978). These authors proposed a Bayesian analysis that generates an individual measure of stereotyping. There has not yet been a published study that has systematically explored the stereotypes associated with short or tall males and females. We do not therefore know how much consensus there is about which personality traits are associated with which sex and height combinations. Many researchers in this field seem to have assumed that important stereotypes exist about short and tall people and the validation of this assumption has not taken place. Until data addressing this issue are available, statements about the importance of height stereotypes are premature.

Having established the nature of a height stereotype we can then proceed to define those situations in which it exercises most influence over impressions and behavior. Some contexts are from the outset more likely to generate effects than others. And likewise in some situations stature will be relegated to secondary importance by other variables. We need to know about these different types of environments. Height should not be studied in isolation, it is a part of the total physique and we should pay more attention to the relationship between height and weight as the primary components of physique.

Differences among individuals as a function of stature are also appropriate areas for research. The work on conformity is an instance of a traditional social psychological variable that has produced interesting (although contradictory) results by using height as a naturally occurring "independent" variable. Aggression, cooperation, obedience, and group dynamics, to name a few, are also ripe for investigation. Consider the role of a member's height in determining his or her (and other's) behavior in a group setting. We already know height has effects in classroom settings—self (and other's) perceptions are affected by height, yet no research has been conducted upon the behavior of short or tall people or other's impressions of them independent of that behavior. We know that manipulating the amount of time a group member is speaking influences the group's perception of him or her and if it is true that perceived dominance is affected by height then stature may be an important variable in this context.

Height and aggression is another potentially fruitful area. Folklore occasionally suggests that short people are more aggressive to compensate for their lack of stature (witness the standard references to the stature of Alexander, Napoleon, Robespierre, etc.). Do people believe this and is there any truth to it? The height of an aggressor might affect the way in which other people view an aggressive act[8], just as it may modify the quality and quantity of any retaliatory response.

In conclusion, it appears that the empirical literature investigating the psychology of height is insufficient at present to clearly answer many of the questions that this chapter began by raising. A great deal more research is necessary before we can either understand its true role in the psychology of physique, or can attribute a great deal of importance to it as a psychological variable.

REFERENCES

Ackerman, C., & Herman, C. P. (1979). *Relative height and dominance in social interactions.* Unpublished manuscript, Department of Psychology, University of Toronto.

Adams, G. R. (1980). Social psychology of beauty: Effects of age, height, and weight on self-reported personality traits and social behaviour. *Journal of Social Psychology, 112,* 287–293.

Asch, S. (1951). Effects of group pressure upon the modification and distortion of judgments. lIn H. Guetzkow (Ed.), *Groups, leadership and men.* Pittsburgh: Carnegie Press.

Bailey, K. G., Caffrey, J. V., & Hartnett, J. J. (1976). Body size as implied threat: Effects on personal space and person perception. *Perceptual and Motor Skills. 43,* 223–230.

Baker, E. E., & Redding, W. C. (1962). The effects of perceived tallness in persuasive speaking: An experiment. *Journal of Communication, 12* (1), 51–53.

Beigel, H. G. (1954). Body height in mate selection. *Journal of Social Psychology, 39,* 257–268.

Berkowitz, W. R. (1969). Perceived height, personality and friendship choice. *Psychological Reports, 24,* 373–374.

Berkowitz, W. R., Nebel, J. C., & Reitman, J. W. (1971). Height and interpersonal attraction: The 1969 Mayoral election in New York City. *Proceedings, American Psychological Association Annual Convention,* 281–282.

Berscheid, E., & Walster, E. (1974). Physical attractiveness. In L. Berkowitz (Ed.), *Advances in experimental social psychology, (Vol. 7).* New York: Academic Press.

Biro, G. (1980). Validity of self-reported weights and heights in self-selected subjects. *Community Health Studies, 4,* 46–47.

Bleda, P. R. (1972). Perception of height as a linear function of attitude similarity. *Psychonomic Science, 27,* 197–198.

Bleda, R., & Bleda, S. (1977). Attitude similarity, attraction, perception of height and judgment of agreement. *Representative Research in Psychology, 8,* 57–61.

Blommers, P., & Lindquist, E. F. (1961). *Elementary statistical methods in psychology and education.* Boston: Houghton Mifflin.

Bradley, A. C. (1978). *Shakespearean tragedy.* New York: St. Martin's Press.

Bruner, J. S., & Goodman, C. C. (1947). Value and need as organizing factors in perception. *Journal of Abnormal and Social Psychology, 42,* 33–44.

Calden, G., Lundy, R. M., & Schlafer, R. S. (1959). Sex differences in body concepts. *Journal of Consulting Psychology, 23,* 378.

---

[8]Lester and Sheehan (1980) in a brief research note demonstrated that police supervisors view short policemen as "more aggressive law enforcers" than their tall colleagues.

Caldwell, O., & Wellman, B. (1926). Characteristics of school leaders. *Journal of Educational Research, 14,* 1–15.

Cameron, C., Oskamp, S., & Sparks, W. (1978). Courtship American style: Newspaper advertisements. *The Family Co-ordinator, 26,* 27–30.

Caplan, M., & Goldman, M. (1981). Personal space violations as a function of height. *Journal of Social Psychology, 114,* 167–171.

Clifford, B. R., & Bull, R. (1978). The psychology of person identification. London: Routledge and Kegan Paul.

Clifford, E. (1971). Body satisfaction in adolescence. *Perceptual and Motor skills, 33,* 119–125.

Cochran, C. D., & Urbanczyk, S. (1982). The effect of availability of vertical space on personal space. *Journal of Psychology, 111,* 137–140.

Coopersmith, S. (1967). *The antecedents of self-esteem.* San Francisco: Freeman.

Dannenmeir, W. D., & Thumin, P. J. (1964). Authority status as a factor in perceptual distortion of size. *Journal of Social Psychology, 63,* 361–365.

DeHamel, F. A. (1980). Parental height as perceived by men and women of an entire community. *Perceptual and Motor Skills, 51,* 1299–1306.

Dejong, W. (1980). The stigma of obesity: The consequences of naive assumptions concerning the causes of physical deviance. *Journal of Health and Social Behavior, 81,* 75–87.

De La Mare, W. (1935). Early one morning. London: Faber and Faber.

Dillon, D. J. (1962). Measurement of perceived body size. *Perceptual and Motor Skills, 14,* 191–196.

Dollard, J., Doob, L., Miller, N., Mowrer, O., & Sears, R. (1939). *Frustration and Aggression.* New Haven, CT: Yale University Press.

Dukes, W., & Bevan, W. (1952). Size estimation and monetary value: A correlation. *Journal of Psychology, 34,* 43–55.

Eggins, L., Barker, P., & Walker, R. J. (1975). A study of the heights and weights of different groups of disturbed children. *Child Psychiatry and Human Development, 5,* 203–208.

Elman, D. (1977). Physical characteristics and the perception of masculine traits. *Journal of Social Psychology, 103,* 157–158.

Farb, B. (1978). *Humankind.* Boston: Houghton Mifflin.

Feingold, A. (1982). Do taller men have prettier girlfriends? *Psychological Reports, 50,* 810.

Feldman, S. D. (1971). *The presentation of shortness in everyday life—height and heightism in American society: Toward a sociology of stature.* Paper presented to the Annual Meeting of the American Sociological Association.

Fisher, S. (1964). Power orientation and concept of self-height in men: A preliminary note. *Perceptual and Motor Skills, 18,* 732.

Freedman, J. L. (1969). Role-playing: Psychology by consensus. *Journal of Personality and Social Psychology, 13,* 107–114.

Gacsaly, S. A., & Borges, C. A. (1979). The male physique and behavioral expectancies. *Journal of Psychology, 101,* 97–102.

Gillis, J. S. (1982). *Too small, too tall.* Champaign, IL: Institute for Personality and Ability Testing.

Gillis, J. S., & Avis, W. E. (1980). The male-taller norm in mate selection. *Personality and Social Psychology Bulletin, 6,* 396–401.

Goldman, W., & Lewis, P. (1977). Beautiful is good: Evidence that the physically attractive are more socially skillful. *Journal of Experimental Social Psychology, 13,* 125–130.

Gordon, M., Post, E. M., Crouthamel, C., & Richman, R. A. (1984). Do children with constitutional delay really have more learning problems? *Journal of Learning Disabilities, 17,* 291–293.

Graziano, W., Brothen, T., & Berscheid, E. (1978). Height and attraction: Do men and women see eye-to-eye? *Journal of Personality, 46,* 128–146.

Gunderson, E. K. (1965). Body size, self-evaluation and military effectiveness. *Journal of Personality and Social Psychology, 2,* 902–906.

Harris, R. J. (1973). Answering questions containing marked and unmarked adjectives and adverbs. *Journal of Experimental Psychology, 97,* 399–401.

Harrison, A. A., & Saeed, L. (1977). Let's make a deal: An analysis of revelations and stipulations in Lonely Hearts advertisements. *Journal of Personality and Social Psychology, 35*(4), 257–274.

Hartnett, J. J., Bailey, K. G., & Hartley, C. S. (1974). Body height, position, and sex as determinants of personal space. *Journal of Psychology, 87,* 129–136.

Heller, J. (1979). *Good as gold.* New York: Simon & Schuster.

Hensley, W. E., & Angoli, M. (1980). Message valence, familiarity, sex, and personality effects on the perceptual distortion of height. *Journal of Psychology, 104,* 149–156.

Hinckley, E. D., & Rethlingshafer, D. (1951). Valid judgments of heights of men by college students. *Journal of Psychology, 31,* 257–262.

Jensen, A. R. (1980). *Bias in mental testing.* New York: Free Press.

Jones, R. A. (1977). *Self-fulfilling prophecies.* Hillsdale, NJ: Lawrence Erlbaum Associates.

Jourard, S. M., & Secord, P. F. (1954). Body Size and Body-Cathexis. *Journal of Consulting Psychology, 18,* 184.

Kassarjian, H. H. (1963). Voting intentions and political perception. *Journal of Psychology, 56,* 85–88.

Katz, E. (1940). The relationship of IQ to height and weight from three to five years. *Journal of Genetic Psychology, 57,* 65–82.

Keesey, R. E. (1978). Set points and body weight regulation. *The Psychiatric Clinics of North America.* (Vol. 1, #3), Toronto: W. B. Saunders and Co.

Keyes, R. (1980). *The height of your life.* Toronto: Little, Brown.

Koulack, D., & Tuthill, J. A. (1972). Height perception: Function of social distance. *Canadian Journal of Behavioral Science, 4,* 50–53.

Krisberg, B. (1974). The sociological imagination revisited. *Canadian Journal of Criminology and Corrections, 16,* 145–161.

Kuehn, L. (1974). Looking down a gun barrel: Person perception and violent crime. *Perceptual and Motor Skills, 39,* 1159–1164.

Kurtz, D. L. (1969, December). Physical appearance and stature: Important variables in sales recruiting. *Personnel Journal,* 981–983.

Lass, N. J., Andes, S. E., McNair, C. D., Cline, A. L., & Pecora, M. C. (1982). Correlational study of subjects' self-reported and measured heights and weights. *Perceptual and Motor Skills, 54,* 102.

Lechelt, E. C. (1975). Occupational affiliation and ratings of physical height and self-esteem. *Psychological Reports, 36,* 943–946.

Lerner, R. M., Karabenick, S. A., & Stuart, J. L. (1973). Relations among physical attractiveness, body attitudes, and self-concept in male and female college students. *Journal of Psychology, V85,* 119–129.

Lerner, R. M., & Moore, T. (1974). Sex and status effects on perception of physical attractiveness. *Psychological Reports, 34,* 1047–1050.

Lester, D., & Sheehan, D. (1980). Attitudes of supervisors toward short police officers. *Psychological Reports, 47,* 462.

Leviton, L. C. (1981). What differentiates meta-analysis from other forms of review. *Journal of Personality, 49,* 231–236.

Loftus, L., & Herman, C. P. (1978). *Height and conformity.* Unpublished manuscript, Department of Psychology, University of Toronto.

Lynn, M., & Shurgot, B. A. (1984). Responses to lonely hearts advertisements: Effects of reported physical attractiveness, physique and coloration. *Personality and Social Psychology Bulletin, 10,* 349–357.

Madowy, R. (1977). *Increase Your height.* Toronto: Coles.

Mahoney, E. R., & Finch, M. D. (1976a). The dimensionality of body-cathexis. *Journal of Psychology, 92,* 277–279.

Mahoney, E. R., & Finch, M. D. (1976b). Body cathexis and self-esteem: A re-analysis of the differential contribution of specific body aspects. *Journal of Social Psychology, 99,* 251–258.

Mayer, J. (1968). *Overweight: Causes, cost and control.* Englewood Cliffs, NJ: Prentice–Hall.

Maslow, A. H. (1937). Dominance-feeling, behaviour and status. *Psychological Review, 44,* 404–429.

McCauley, C., & Stitt, C. (1978). An individual and quantitative measure of stereotypes. *Journal of Personality and Social Psychology, 36,* 929–940.

McGuire, W. J., & McGuire, C. V. (1981). The spontaneous self-concept as affected by personal distinctiveness. In A. Nurem–Hebeisen, M. D. Lynch, & K. Gergen (Eds.), *The self-concept.* New York: Ballinger.

McGuire, W. J., & McGuire, C. V. (1982). Significant others in self space: Sex differences and developmental trends in the social self. In J. Suls (Ed.), *Psychological perspectives on the self* (Vol. 1). Hillsdale, NJ: Lawrence Associates.

McGuire, W. J., & Padawer–Singer, A. (1976). Trait salience in the spontaneous self-concept. *Journal of Personality and Social Psychology, 33*(6), 743–754.

Meth, S. (1976). An investigation of the relationship between perceptual set as to the status and role-playing by the perceived on the visual perception of the perceiver. *Dissertation Abstracts International, 37,* (2-B) 956.

Morf, M. G. (1965). *The Polish heritage of Joseph Conrad.* New York: Haskel House.

Orne, M. T. (1962). On the social psychology of the psychological experiment. *American Psychologist, 17,* 776–783.

Osborn III, D. R. (1974). Own height, similarity to others and judgment of other's height. *Dissertation Abstracts International, 4*(10A), 6746–6747.

Oxford English Dictionary, Compact Edition. (1971). New York: Oxford University Press.

Popper, J. M. (1958). Motivational and social factors in children's perceptions of height. *Dissertations Abstracts International, 18,* (2), 684.

Popper, J. M. (1964). Social and personality correlates of childrens' estimates of height. *General Psychology Monographs,* 93–134.

Portnoy, S. (1973). Height as a personality variable in a conformity situation. *Dissertation Abstracts International, 33*(10-B), 5024–5025.

Prieto, A. G. (1975). Junior high school students' height and its relationship to academic and social performance. *Dissertation Abstracts International 36,* (1-A) 222.

Prieto, A. G., & Robbins, M. C. (1975). Perceptions of height and self-esteem. *Perceptual and Motor Skills, 40,* 395–398.

Psychology Today. (1973, November). 119–126. *Body Image,* pp. 119–126.

Rapoport, R. (1975). Field dependence and male body height stereotyping. *Dissertations Abstracts International, 36,* (6-B), 3063.

Roberts, J. V. (1977). *Sizing people up: The effects of perceived height upon interpersonal judgments.* Master's thesis, Department of Psychology, University of Toronto.

Roth, K., & Eisenberg, N. (1983). The effects of children's heights on teachers' attributions of competence. *Journal of Genetic Psychology, 143,* 45–50.

Rump, E. E., & Delin, P. S. (1973). Differential accuracy in the status–height phenomenon and an experimenter effect. *Journal of Personality and Social Psychology, 28*(3), 343–347.

Secord, P. F., & Jourard, S. M. (1953). The Appraisal of Body-Cathexis: Body-Cathexis and the Self. *Journal of Consulting Psychology, 17,* 343–347.

Shaffer, J. P. (1964). Social and personality correlates of children's estimates of height. *General Psychology Monographs, 20,* 92–134.

Smith, M. E. (1938). A study of the causes of feelings of superiority inferiority. *Journal of Psychology, 5*, 315–322.

Snyder, M., & Cantor, N. (1979). Testing, hypotheses about other people: The use of historical knowledge. *Journal of Experimental Social Psychology, 15*, 330–342.

Stabler, B., Whitt, K., Moreault, D., D'Ercole, A., & Underwood, L. (1980). Social Judgements by children of short stature. *Psychological Reports, 46*, 743–746.

Stogdill, R. (1948). Personal factors associated with leadership. *Journal of Psychology, 25*, 35–71.

Stolz, H., & Stolz, L. (1951). *Somatic Development in Adolescent Boys.* New York: MacMillan.

Stunkard, A. J. (1980). (Ed.) *Obesity.* Philadelphia: Saunders.

The Connoisseur. (1754 June). In "The Connoisseur by Mr. Town", Vol. 1, No. 20, Oxford: Baldwin, 1767, p. 154.

Touhey, J. C. (1971). Distortion of self-ascribed characteristics. *Perceptual and Motor Skills, 33*, 385–386.

Truhon, S. A., & McKinney, J. P. (1979). Children's drawings of the presidential candidates. *Journal of Genetic Psychology, 134*, 157–158.

U.S. News and World Report. *(1977, March). 68.*

Veno, A. (1974). Proxemic components of agonistic behavior in adult humans: A field study. *Dissertation Abstracts International, 35*(5B), 2487.

Ward, C. D. (1967). Own height, sex, and liking in the judgment of the heights of others. *Journal of Personality, 35* 381–401.

Williams, J. (1975. *Application of signal detection parameters in a test of eyewitnesses to a crime* (Report No. CR-20). New York: Center for Responsive Psychology.

Wilson, P. R. (1968). Perceptual distortion of height as a function of ascribed academic status. *Journal of Social Psychology, 74*, 97–102.

Yarmey, A. D. (1979). *The Psychology of Eyewitness Testimony.* New York: Free Press.

Zanna, M. P., & Pack, S. J. (1975). On the self-fulfilling nature of apparent sex differences in behavior. *Journal of Experimental Social Psychology, 11*, 583–591.

III
IMPACT ON SOCIAL BEHAVIOR

7

Physical Appearance and Social Influence

Shelly Chaiken
New York University

The study of social influence processes has long been a central research area within social psychology. It seems only fitting then, that a volume devoted to the topic of physical appearance and social behavior should include at least some attention to the role that physical appearance plays in social influence. This chapter attempts to provide an integrative review of the existing literature concerning physical appearance and social influence. Reflecting the majority of empirical research in this area, this chapter focuses primarily on the role of physical attractiveness, weight, and height as they impact on social influence processes. Although attributes such as race/ethnicity or gender might possibly be considered appearance related, these variables are less explicitly related to the role that physique per se plays in social influence and, for this reason, are not addressed in this chapter. Further, to have included these variables in the current review would have proved unwieldy and, with respect to sex differences in social influence, would have duplicated recent reviews of this literature (e.g., Cooper, 1979; Eagly, 1978; Eagly & Carli, 1981).

Physical appearance represents a class of variables that may describe either the *agent* of social influence (e.g., a persuasive communicator) or the *target* of social influence (e.g., the recipient of a persuasive communication). As will be seen, some physical appearance variables considered in this chapter have received primary empirical attention as agent variables (e.g., physical attractiveness), whereas others have received primary attention as target variables (e.g., weight). Despite this constraint, this chapter, nevertheless, attempts to address two broad questions: (1) To what extent does a person's physical appearance (i.e., attractiveness, weight, height) affect his/her effectiveness as an agent of social influence?; and (2) to what extent does a person's appearance affect his/her susceptibility to social influence? Further, the chapter attempts to investigate whether the importance of physical appearance as a determinant of social influence and the psychological mechanisms that may account for appearance effects differ as a function of *type* of social influence phenomenon considered. Reflecting the majority of empirical research on social influence (and the majority of social influence research concerned with attractiveness, weight, and height), the present chapter focuses primarily on three classic social influence paradigms—persuasion, compliance, and conformity. Examining appearance effects as a function of type of influence induction may provide some insight regarding the extent to which such influence effects represent genuine changes in recipients' beliefs, attitudes, or behaviors versus more temporal and/or strategic responses to contemporaneous situational pressures. For example, if it proved to be the case that appearance-related influence effects were obtained almost exclusively in compliance paradigms, it might plausibly be argued that such effects reflect strategic responses rather than genuine changes in individuals' beliefs and attitudes.

Categorization of the Literature

Existing literature on the role of physical attractiveness, weight, and height in social influence was located by surveying *Psychological Abstracts* (1950–1982), the major social psychological journals, and, further, by examining previously located journal articles and textbooks for relevant citations (a number of unpublished studies were also located). Somewhat surprisingly, this relatively detailed literature search yielded a fairly small number of appearance studies that utilized explicit social influence paradigms.[1] Table 7.1 classifies these experiments by type of appearance variable (physical attractiveness, weight, height), type of social influence situation (persuasion, compliance, conformity/modeling), and whether the appearance variable under investigation pertained to the agent, or source, of social influence as opposed to the target, or recipient, of a social influence attempt. In addition, the *agent* studies were categorized with respect to the dimension of physical presence versus absence of the social influence agent. This dimension (that sometimes, though not always, covaries with type of social influence situation) roughly corresponds to whether or

---

[1]Only those located studies that utilized explicit social influence paradigms are listed in Table 7.1 and given detailed discussion in this chapter. Despite this focus, some attention will also be paid to experiments that could be construed as dealing with less explicit forms of influence (e.g., studies on the impact of victim attractiveness on helping) and to studies that provide either suggestive evidence regarding the impact of appearance on social influence (e.g., studies examining the correlation between height and perceptions of dominance) or data relevant to the mediation of appearance-influence effects (e.g., studies that examine the relation between physical attractiveness and perceived status, credibility, and likability).

TABLE 7.1

Categorization of Attractiveness, Weight, and Height Experiments by Type of Variable (Agent vs. Target), Presence (vs. Absence) of Social Influence Agent, and Type of Social Influence Paradigm (Persuasion vs. Compliance vs. Conformity/Modeling)

I. Appearance of Social Influence Agent

A.   Agent Absent (Nonsurveillance)

	Attractiveness	Weight	Height
Persuasion:	Blass et al. (1974) Chaiken et al. (1978, Exp. II) Chaiken (1979b) Horai et al. (1974) Howard et al. (1974) Maddux & Rogers (1980) Mills & Harvey (1972) Norman (1976) Pallak et al. (1983) Snyder & Rothbart (1971)	none	Baker & Redding (1962)
Compliance:	none	none	none
Conformity/ Modeling:	Baker & Churchill (1977) Smith & Engel (1968)	none	none

B.   Agent Present (Surveillance)

	Attractiveness	Weight	Height
Persuasion:	Chaiken et al. (1978, Exp. I) Chaiken (1979a) Dion & Stein (1978) Mills & Aronson (1965)	Chaiken (1982b)	Chaiken (1982b) Ackerman & Herman (1979)
Compliance:	Harrell (1978) Mims et al. (1975) Sigall & Aronson (1969) Sigall et al. (1971) West & Brown (1975)	Karris (1977) Rodin & Slochower (1974)	none
Conformity/ Modeling:	LaVoie & Adams (1978)	Elman et al. (1977)	Portnoy (1972)

II. Appearance of Social Influence Target

	Attractiveness	Weight	Height
Persuasion:	Dion & Stein (1978)	Glass et al. (1969) Herman et al. (1981)	none
Compliance:	none	Elman et al. (1977)	none

(continued)

Table 7.1 (*Continued*)

	Attractiveness	Weight	Height
Conformity/ Modeling:	none	Rodin & Slochower (1974) Sikes & Singh (1974) Wagener & Laird (1980) Elman et al. (1977) Stalling & Miller (1981) Stalling & Friedman (1981)	Portnoy (1972)

Note: Of the studies in Category **II**, all but the Glass et al. (1969), Stalling & Miller (1981), and Stalling & Friedman (1981) experiments were conducted under conditions of surveillance.

not a target person's response to a social influence attempt, be it the expression of a belief, or attitude, or the performance of some behavior, occurs under conditions of surveillance versus nonsurveillance by the social influence agent. *Target* studies were not categorized with respect to the surveillance dimension due to their small overall number and the fact that the vast majority were conducted under conditions of surveillance (see Note to Table 7.1).

A cursory inspection of Table 7.1 shows that experiments investigating the effect of physical attractiveness on social influence greatly outnumber those concerned with the weight–social influence relationship, which, in turn, out-number experiments dealing with the social influence effects of height. Given our journals' tendencies to publish papers reporting significant, rather than "noneffect," findings (Greenwald, 1975), these differences might be interpreted as reflecting the relative potency of attractiveness, weight, and height effects in social influence. Alternatively, these differences may simply reflect the relative popularity that these three physique variables have enjoyed among social psychologists.

Of the six categories formed by classifying experiments in terms of type of appearance variable investigated and whether that variable pertained to the agent versus target of influence, it can be seen that the majority of existing literature falls primarily into two categories: physical attractiveness as an agent, or source, variable and weight as a target, or recipient, variable. This uneven distribution of experiments, as well as the relative frequency of attractiveness, weight, and height studies noted earlier, probably reflects the (happy!) tendency for most researchers to test hypotheses that are at least vaguely derived from theory. Kelman's (1961) functional theory of social influence, for example, suggests that people may adopt the opinions or behaviors advocated by attractive/likable so-cial influence agents in order to emulate and/or facilitate a real or imagined relationship with those agents. Thus, it is not surprising that researchers (particularly those in the persuasion area where Kelman's theory has been most influential) have investigated whether physical attractiveness enhances one's effectiveness as a social influence agent. Similarly, Schachter's (1971) general proposition that the obese are more responsive than normal-weight individuals to external, or environmental, cues suggests the reasonableness of investigating differences between obese and normal-weight persons in their susceptibility to social influence inductions. The paucity of studies in the remaining four categories (attractiveness as a target variable, weight as an agent variable, and height as either an agent or target variable) is understandable because, beyond intuition, there exists little theoretical basis for expecting social influence effects of a particular form in these categories.

Given the small number of experiments directly relevant to examining the relationship between physical appearance and social influence, the tone of this chapter must be, necessarily, quite speculative. The first and major section of the chapter addresses the question of whether a social influence agent's appearance affects his/her effectiveness in influencing others and, if so, by what possible mechanisms. Reflecting the majority of studies in this category, this section focuses primarily on the role that agent physical attractiveness plays in social influence. However, some comments and speculations regarding the impact of a social influence agent's weight and height are also offered. The second section addresses the question of the extent to which the appearance of recipients of social influence attempts affects their susceptibility to these inductions and, if so, by what possible psychological mechanisms. Given the exceedingly small number of relevant studies in this category of experiments, the impressions offered in this section should be considered highly speculative.

PHYSICAL APPEARANCE AS AN AGENT VARIABLE

Physical Attractiveness

As Table 7.1 illustrates, the vast majority of experiments investigating the social influence effects of agent appearance have dealt with physical attractiveness. Although, as is discussed later, weight and, perhaps, height are not unrelated to global perceptions of physical attractiveness, none of the attractiveness studies listed in Table 7.1 manipulated agent attractiveness in terms of either weight or height. Of the 12 studies in the agent absent/attractiveness category, the majority of which are persuasion experiments, 10 manipulated communicator attractiveness via photographs (usually facial), and two utilized videotaped communicators whose attractiveness was varied by means of makeup, dress, and grooming (Blass et al., 1974; Howard et al., 1974). Of the 10 agent present/attractiveness studies, 7 utilized live confederates whose attractiveness was manipulated in terms of makeup, dress, and/or grooming (Harrell, 1978; LaVoie & Adams, 1978; Mills & Aronson, 1965; Mims et al., 1975; Sigall & Aronson, 1969; Sigall et al., 1971; West & Brown, 1975), one used facial photographs (Chaiken et al., 1978, Exp. 1), and two utilized a large number of "communicator–subjects" whose attractiveness was determined by independent judges (Chaiken, 1979a; Dion & Stein, 1978). Whereas Dion and Stein (1978) studied the persuasive effectiveness of fifth- and sixth-grade children with peer-aged targets, all the remaining attractiveness studies utilized college-aged or older social influence agents and all but one used college-aged targets as experimental subjects (Horai et al., 1974 employed ninth-grade subjects).

Although experiments reporting no significant effects due to attractiveness (Chaiken et al., 1978, Exp. 2; Maddux & Rogers, 1980; Mills & Aronson, 1965) or unpredicted and difficult to interpret interactions between attractiveness and other independent variables (Blass et al., 1974; Chaiken et al., 1978, Exp. 1; Howard et al., 1974; West & Brown, 1975) are not uncommon in this literature, agent physical attractiveness does seem to be generally associated with greater social influence effectiveness. Among the agent absent/persuasion studies, three have demonstrated that attractiveness can significantly enhance a male communicator's persuasiveness with both male and female message recipients (Horai et al., 1974; Pallak et al., 1983 ("emotional" message condition only); Snyder & Rothbart, 1971). Three experiments in this category (Chaiken, 1979b; Mills & Harvey, 1972; Norman, 1976), all of which examined the relative persuasiveness of primarily attractive (though inexpert) versus primarily expert (though unattractive) male communicators with female message recipients, indicate that the persuasive impact of a communicator's physical attractiveness may be quite independent of the specific verbal content of the communicator's message. For example, Norman (1976) found that an expert source's persuasiveness declined significantly when he did not (vs. did) provide persuasive arguments in support of his overall position, whereas a physically attractive communicator was equally persuasive regardless of whether he provided supportive argumentation. In a conceptually related study, Chaiken (1979b) found that presenting weak (vs. strong) persuasive arguments significantly inhibited the persuasive effectiveness of an expert communicator's message but did not significantly detract from an attractive communicator's persuasiveness.

In contrast to the typical persuasion experiment (where the communicator is physically and temporally absent from the situation), three attractiveness/persuasion studies (see Table 7.1) utilized communicators who presented their messages to recipients in a live, face-to-face setting (Chaiken, 1979a; Dion & Stein, 1978; Mills & Aronson, 1965) and one (Chaiken et al., 1978, Exp. 1) employed fictitious communicators who "transmitted" handwritten messages to recipients from "an adjoining laboratory cubicle." Among these agent present studies, Mills and Aronson found no overall effect of attractiveness on persuasion but, on a marginally significant basis, did find that their female communicator's expression of a desire to influence her male recipients enhanced persuasion when she was attractive (vs. unattractive). Both the Chaiken et al. (Exp. 1) study and the Dion and Stein study with children found that communicator physical attractiveness interacted with both communicator and target sex to influence persuasion. Dion and Stein's results showed that communicator attractiveness enhanced persuasion only in opposite-sex (vs. same-sex) dyads. In the Chaiken et al. (Exp. 1) experiment with college-aged subjects, this opposite-sex effect obtained only among female message recipients. Male targets were somewhat more persuaded by attractive (vs. unattractive) communicators regardless of their gender. In contrast to these laboratory experiments, Chaiken's (1979a) field study found that regardless of communicator or target sex, physically attractive (vs. unattractive) communicators induced significantly greater persuasion on both a private (anonymous opinion survey) and public (petition signing) measure of target agreement.

In compliance studies, the influence induction takes the form of a simple request on the part of the social influence agent (e.g., request for small amounts of money, West & Brown, 1975; request that subjects perform some experimental task, Mims et al., 1975; Sigall et al., 1971). Of the agent attractiveness/compliance studies shown in Table 7.1, all dealt with situations in which the social influence agent was in face-to-face contact with subjects, all utilized female social influence agents, and all but one employed male subjects only (Mims et al. included subjects of both sexes). All of these experiments found that heightened attractiveness significantly enhanced compliance, although Harrell (1978) found this effect only when the female requester disclosed (vs. did not disclose) her name to male subjects and West and Brown (1975) obtained an attractiveness effect only when the request seemed well (vs. poorly) justified. As noted earlier, all of these compliance experiments manipulated attractiveness through makeup, dress, and/or grooming. A number of other (primarily) field experiments that examined compliance as a function of the social influence agent's mode of dress and grooming (neat vs. sloppy) are not included in Table 7.1 because they provided no direct evidence that these manipulations affected targets' perceptions of agent physical attractiveness. Assuming, however, that dress and grooming do influence global perceptions of attractiveness (as indicated by the tabled compliance studies as well as other research, cf. Hamid, 1969, 1972; Perrin, 1921), these latter experiments add confidence and generality to the conclusion that heightened agent attractiveness typically enhances compliance because the modal finding in this literature is significantly greater compliance by both male and female targets with requests made by well-dressed, well-groomed persons of both sexes (e.g., Chaikin et al., 1974; Harris & Baudin, 1973; Kleinke, 1977; Raymond & Unger, 1972; Schiavo et al., 1974).

The current literature search yielded no studies relevant to the impact of agent physical attractiveness on conformity. Of the remaining studies shown in Table 7.1, two suggest that the presence of physically attractive models in advertisements may enhance consumers' evaluations of advertised products (Baker & Churchill, 1977; Smith & Engel, 1968) and one (LaVoie & Adams, 1978) suggests that people may be more likely to imitate behaviors exhibited by attractive, compared to unattractive, models. Finally, it should be noted that other research on physical attractiveness, although not explicitly concerned with active attempts to influence others is consistent with the idea that higher levels of attractiveness may lead to greater social influence effectiveness. For example, physically attractive (vs. unattractive) persons often receive more help and cooperation from others (e.g., Athanasious & Greene, 1973; Benson et al., 1976; Kahn et al., 1971); when applying for jobs, they may be more likely to be hired (e.g., Cash et al., 1977; Dipboye et al., 1975); and when in legal difficulty, they may be more likely to be treated leniently (e.g., Efran, 1974; Solomon & Schopler, 1978; Stewart, 1980; Storck & Sigall, 1979).

Mediation of agent attractiveness effects. Existing research does indicate that heightened physical attractiveness generally enhances one's effectiveness as a social influence agent. To use Zanna and Fazio's (1982) terminology, much of this research has tended to focus almost exclusively on the "first generation" question of "Does attractiveness affect social influence effectiveness." With few exceptions, however, this body of research has tended to neglect "second generation" questions such as, "When does attractiveness affect persuasion, compliance, etc." and, even more so, "third generation" questions such as "What mechanisms underly the social influence effects of attractiveness." The remainder of this section addresses these questions.

Person perception research suggests that physical attractiveness conveys information regarding warmth and social emotional competence as well as information about expertise and intellectual competence. In comparison to unattractive stimulus persons, attractive individuals are typically liked more and perceived as more friendly, interesting, sociable, perceptive, intelligent, confident, and as possessing higher status (e.g., Clifford & Walster, 1973; Dion, Berscheid, & Walster, 1972; Landy & Sigall, 1974; see Berscheid & Walster, 1974 for a detailed review of this literature). Social influence studies indicate that agent variables such as likability or friendliness, expertise or credibility, and high status generally confer greater social influence effectiveness (e.g., Baron, 1971; Chaiken, 1980; Chaiken & Eagly, 1983; Eagly & Chaiken, 1975; Eagly & Wood, 1982; Hovland & Weiss, 1951; Kelman, 1961; Regan, 1971).

Although attractive persons may sometimes be perceived as more expert than their unattractive counterparts, persuasion experiments that have obtained significant opinion change effects due to communicator physical attractiveness have generally not found corresponding attractiveness effects on targets' perceptions of the communicator's expertise or knowledgeability (e.g., Chaiken, 1979a; Horai et al., 1974; Norman, 1976; Snyder & Rothbart, 1971). Thus, it would seem that attractiveness effects in persuasion are not typically mediated by differential perceptions of attractive and unattractive communicators' credibility regarding the topic of social influence. Further, given the nature of most requests utilized in compliance experiments (e.g., requests for small amounts of money, requests for directions), perceptions of the social influence agent's general degree of knowledgeability or intellectual competence would seem largely irrelevant in affecting compliance. Although differences in perceived status might possibly contribute to the facilitative effect of agent physical attractiveness on social influence, the fact that status typically influences perceptions of expertise (cf. Berger, Conner, & Fisek, 1974; Lockheed & Hall, 1976) and, as noted earlier, the fact that attractiveness/persuasion studies do not tend to find differences in perceived expertise as a function of attractiveness suggests that differential perceptions of status also do not typically mediate the social influence impact of agent physical attractiveness.

Existing research is more congenial with the idea that differential liking underlies the greater social influence effectiveness of physically attractive individuals. As indicated previously, heightened physical attractiveness tends to lead reliably to greater liking (e.g., Insko et al., 1973; Stroebe et al., 1971) and a wide variety of social influence studies that have directly manipulated liking for the social influence agent indicate that greater likability increases individuals' persuasive effectiveness (e.g., Chaiken, 1980; Chaiken & Eagly, 1983), their effectiveness at inducing compliance (e.g., Baron, 1971; Regan, 1971), and their effectiveness as social models (e.g., Baron, 1970; Yarrow & Scott, 1972). In addition, a number of (persuasion) studies that have demonstrated heightened social influence for physically attractive influence agents have found that targets' perceptions of agent likability were also affected by the attractiveness variable (e.g., Chaiken, 1979a; Horai et al., 1974; Snyder & Rothbart, 1971); further, Snyder and Rothbart reported that the correlation between communicator attractiveness and persuasion decreased in size when subjects' perceptions of communicator likability were statistically controlled.

Underlying psychological processes.   The proposition that physical attractiveness affects social influence via its more direct impact on liking for the social influence agent does not fully answer the question of what psychological processes mediate the attractiveness-social influence relationship. Indeed, the liking-social influence relationship could be explained in terms of a number of psychological processes, including classical conditioning, social reinforcement, cognitive consistency, Kelman's (1961) identification process of social influence, and Chaiken's (1980, 1982a, in press) heuristic processing model. According to a simple classical conditioning explanation (cf. Staats & Staats, 1958), heightened social influence (e.g., attitude change in response to a persuasive message) could result from the contiguity of presentation of an affectively positive (i.e., attractive) social influence agent and the attitudinal position or behavior advocated, requested, or exhibited by that agent. Alternatively, persons might be motivated to accept influence from attractive social influence agents because of their inherent reinforcement value (cf. Berscheid & Walster, 1974; Hovland, Janis, & Kelley, 1953), or in the interest of maintaining cognitive balance (i.e., agreeing vs. disagreeing with a liked other, Heider, 1958), or, according to Kelman's (1961) functional theory, in order to emulate or establish a (real or imagined) relationship with the social influence agent. In contrast to these, primarily motivational, interpretations, Chaiken's notion of heuristic processing suggests that, at least for persuasion, the social influence impact of communicator physical attractiveness might reflect recipients' use of a simple cognitive heuristic such as "people generally agree with people they like". As Chaiken (1980, 1982a, in press) has noted, this liking/agreement heuristic may stem from a simple schema suggesting a fairly consistent association between the concepts of interpersonal liking and interpersonal similarity (cf. Stotland & Canon, 1972). The idea that individuals do perceive such an association is supported by research showing both that attitude similarity leads to liking (e.g., Byrne, 1961; Byrne & Nelson, 1964) and that liking leads to perceived attitude similarity (e.g., Granberg et al., 1979). Further, consistent with the idea that the liking/agreement heuristic may underlie the persuasive effectiveness of physically attractive communicators (presumably because of their greater likability), recent research indicates that individuals perceive greater attitudinal and personality similarity with physically attractive (vs. unattractive) others (Marks & Miller, 1982; Marks, Miller, & Maruyama, 1981).

When applied to persuasion, all of the aforementioned psychological explanations for attractiveness-influence effects share an assumption quite different from more "systematic" persuasion models (e.g., Greenwald, 1968; McGuire, 1968; see Chaiken, 1980, in press and Eagly & Chaiken, 1984 for a more detailed discussion). This assumption is that persuasion is not necessarily the outcome of people's reception (attention, comprehension), evaluation, and elaboration of persuasive argumentation. Consistent with this assumption, research on the communicator attractiveness-persuasion relationship indicates that the persuasive impact of attractiveness is not typically mediated by recipients' processing of persuasive argumentation (Chaiken, 1979b; Mills & Harvey, 1972; Norman, 1976; Pallak, 1983; Pallak et al., 1983). For example, Pallak (1983) found that when a male communicator's physical attractiveness was made highly salient for subjects, agreement with his message was high, regardless of whether he presented strong or weak persuasive arguments. Moreover, subjects' opinion judgments were more highly correlated with their perceptions of the communicator than with their message-based cognitions.

If liking underlies the greater social influence effectiveness of physically attractive persons, it might be expected that social influence effects due to the attractiveness variable should be stronger in settings that enhance the salience or vividness (cf. Nisbett & Ross, 1980; Taylor & Thompson, 1982) of the social influence agent and the consequent salience of interpersonal relations. In line with this expectation, agent attractiveness effects on social influence (particularly main effects due to the physical attractiveness variable) appear more commonly among studies in which the social influence agent has been physically present (vs. absent) from the social influence setting. The observation that attractiveness effects occur most frequently in agent-present studies, many of which are compliance experiments, and less frequently in agent-absent studies, the majority of which are persuasion experiments (see Table 7.1), however, raises the question of whether persuasion effects due to communicator attractiveness represent genuine changes in recipients' beliefs and attitudes (as is commonly assumed in the persuasion literature) or strategic, behavioral manifestations of agreement designed to ingratiate oneself with an attractive communicator. Although persuasion settings in which the communicator is both present and has surveillance over recipients' responses to the persuasive advocacy require careful scrutiny because of the possibility that these responses may sometimes reflect little more than surface agreement with the communicator, existing research supports the idea that physically attractive communicators can induce genuine changes in recipients' beliefs and attitudes. Thus, although agent attractiveness effects do appear less frequently in persuasion experiments in which the communicator is neither physically present nor privy to recipients' attitudinal responses, they do, nevertheless, occur (see earlier review of this category of experiments). Further, Chaiken's (1979a) field study of communicator attractiveness and persuasion, in which the communicator was present and had partial surveillance over recipients' responses (i.e., surveillance over one of two persuasion measures) yielded persuasion findings favoring the hypothesis that communicator physical attractiveness did actually effect genuine changes in targets' opinions.

Despite the fact that communicator physical attractiveness may sometimes, or even often, facilitate genuine changes in recipients' beliefs and attitudes, theoretical perspectives relevant to the attractiveness-social influence relationship such as Kelman's (1961) identification theory and Chaiken's (1980, in press) heuristic processing model suggest that opinion shifts induced by physically attractive communicators may exhibit little temporal persistence and, therefore, little relation to subsequent attitudinally relevant behaviors. According to Kelman, identification-based attitude changes (such as those presumably induced by attractive communicators) are not well integrated within the individual's existing cognitive structure and, although genuine, persist only to the extent that the recipient's relationship to the communicator remains salient. And, Chaiken's heuristic processing interpretation of the persuasive impact of communicator characteristics such as attractiveness and likability suggests that, because recipients may accept such communicators' messages on the basis of simple decision rules (mentioned earlier) rather than on the basis of "systematically" scrutinizing persuasive argumentation, they may lack the bolstering topic-relevant cognitions that may be a prerequisite for enduring opinion change (Chaiken, 1980, in press; Cook & Flay, 1978). Consistent with this hypothesis, heuristic (vs. systematic) processing of persuasion cues does seem to be associated with reduced attitudinal persistence (Chaiken, 1980; Chaiken & Eagly, 1983). In addition, Pallak, Murroni, & Koch (1983) recently reported findings suggesting both that communicator physical attractiveness affected persuasion via recipients' heuristic processing of this cue and that attitudes formed on this basis proved relatively unpredictive (in comparison to attitudes formed on the basis of systematic processing of persuasive message content) of recipients' intentions to engage in subsequent attitudinally relevant behavior.

The heuristic/systematic framework (Chaiken, 1980, in press) also suggests that physical attractiveness effects in persuasion are most likely to occur when communicators are attempting to influence recipients on relatively unimportant or uninvolving issues. Communicator cues such as likability and expertise, which like physical attractiveness may typically be processed in heuristic fashion, have been shown to be significant determinants of opinion change when recipients are exposed to messages concerning relatively low-involvement issues. However, these same cues tend to exert little persuasive impact when involvement is high (e.g., Chaiken, 1980; Petty, Cacioppo, & Goldman, 1981). In this regard, it is important to note that the majority of experiments that have obtained significant persuasion effects due to the communicator attractiveness variable have generally presented subjects with persuasive messages on relatively unimportant topics (e.g., whether speed limits should be changed, Snyder & Rothbart, 1971; whether the amount of meat served in dormitory dining rooms should be reduced, Chaiken, 1979a; whether campus roads should be named after University regents, Blass et al., 1974). Attractiveness/compliance studies have also tended to investigate targets' compliance with relatively trivial requests on the part of the social influence agent (e.g., requests for change, Kleinke, 1977; requests for help in an experiment, Sigall & Aronson, 1969; requests for negligible amounts of money, West & Brown, 1975). Thus, until additional research using more important or consequential issues and requests is conducted, researchers working in this area might consider the possibility that existing research, because of its reliance on relatively trivial, uninvolving attitudinal issues, may somewhat overstate the case for the importance of agent attractiveness as a determinant of social influence effectiveness.

Before turning to an examination of the impact of agent weight and height on social influence effectiveness, one additional explanation for the facilitative impact of attractiveness on social influence effectiveness should be considered. Because the vast majority of attractiveness/social influence studies have employed experimental manipulations of the attractiveness variable (e.g., varying agent attractiveness via photographs or makeup, grooming, and dress), the *style* in which the agent's persuasive message or request for compliance has been presented to subjects has remained constant across experimental attractiveness conditions. Such standardization is of obvious value when one is attempting to evaluate the previously discussed psychological mechanisms that may underly attractiveness effects in social influence (e.g., classical and operant conditioning processes, cognitive balance, identification processes, heuristic processing). Nevertheless, such experimental designs preclude from consideration the possibility that, in genuine interpersonal settings, attractive and unattractive individuals are differentially influential because they differ with respect to communication skills or other attributes that affect social influence effectiveness. Because of differing socialization experiences (e.g., Clifford & Walster, 1973; Dion, 1972), physical attractiveness may be confounded with other individual differences (e.g., intelligence, status, self-concept, personality; cf. Berscheid & Walster, 1974). Consistent with this argument, Goldman and Lewis (1977) obtained evidence suggesting that attractive persons may possess greater social skill than unattractive persons, and other research (Dion & Stein, 1978; Jackson & Huston, 1975; Langlois & Downs, 1977) suggests that attractive and unattractive persons may be differentially assertive in their interactions with others. Although only two attractiveness/social influence studies (Chaiken, 1979a; Dion & Stein, 1978) have explored the possibility that individual differences between attractive and unattractive persons contribute to their differential social influence effectiveness, both obtained findings consistent with this proposition. For example, Chaiken's (1979a) field study found not only that physically attractive (vs. unattractive) communicators were more persuasive but also that these attractive and unattractive communicators differed with respect to other personal characteristics relevant to persuasive effectiveness such as verbal fluency, speech rate, educational accomplishment, and several components of self-concept (e.g., self-perceptions of persuasiveness, attractiveness, interestingness, optimism). Further, when the influence of these individual difference measures was statistically controlled, the magnitude of the relationship between communicator physical attractiveness and persuasive effectiveness observed in this experiment was somewhat attenuated. These findings suggest, then, that in addition to the psychological mechanisms discussed earlier, future research on agent attractiveness should consider the possibility that attractive individuals may be more effective in influencing others partly because they possess social and communication skills or other characteristics that dispose them to be particularly effective social influence agents.

Agent Weight and Height

Weight.   As Table 7.1 illustrates, there currently exists little empirical evidence regarding the role of agent weight and height in social influence. With respect to weight, a field study by Karris (1977) found that a normal-weight male confederate was significantly more successful in convincing prospective landlords to rent to him than was an obese male confederate. However, because only two confederates were used, it is unclear whether the observed compliance difference reflected the impact of confderate weight or other potential idiosyncratic differences between the two confederates. In a laboratory study on compliance, Rodin and Slochower (1974) found that normal-weight (vs. obese) female confederates (classified as such on the basis of Metropolitan Life Insurance norms) induced significantly greater compliance with their requests that female subjects distribute political surveys. However, an interaction between confederate and subject weight indicated that the greater compliance induced by normal (vs. obese) confederates was primarily due to their greater influence with overweight subjects; confederate weight did not differentially affect compliance among normal-weight female subjects. In a modeling study using male confederates and subjects, Elman, Schroeder, and Schwartz (1977) examined the tendency for normal-weight and obese subjects to comply with an experimenter's request that they volunteer additional time for an experiment *after* they had observed a normal-weight (vs. obese) model comply fully with the experimenter's request for 10 additional hours. Paralleling Rodin and Slochower's findings, overweight subjects were significantly more likely to conform to the compliance behavior exhibited by the normal-weight (vs. obese) model. In contrast to the Rodin and Slochower study, however, normal-weight subjects proved significantly more likely to conform to the behavior exhibited by the *obese,* rather than normal-weight, confederate (influenceability differences as a function of target weight status are considered in a subsequent section).

Finally, in a field setting, Chaiken (1982b) examined the persuasive effectiveness of normal-weight versus obese male and female ''communicator-subjects'' (classified on the basis of Metropolitan Life Insurance norms) with male and female targets (target weight status was unknown). On a private measure of agreement with the communicator's message, a significant interaction between communicator sex and weight revealed that normal-weight (vs. obese) female communicators were *more* persuasive whereas normal-weight (vs. obese) male communicators were *less* persuasive; post hoc comparisons, however, indicated that neither of these simple effect trends was statistically reliable. On a public measure of agreement with the communicator (targets' willingness to sign the communicator's petition), however, normal-weight female communicators did prove significantly more persuasive than their overweight counterparts. Normal-weight and obese male communicators were not differentially effective in getting targets to sign their petitions although, in contrast to the trend on private agreement, obese (vs. normal-weight) male communicators elicited slightly *less* public agreement.

Height.   Popular wisdom and informal observation suggest that, at least in American society, height is a valued physical attribute that may enhance one's social influence power. In the realm of politics, Van Dalen's (1975) analysis of archival data suggested that President Lincoln's height (6'4") was used successfully to create an image of strong leadership. Lending further credence to the idea that height represents a political asset (or liability), Feldman (1971) has noted that between 1900 and 1972, the winner of every American Presidential election has been the taller of the two major candidates. Consistent with these observations, several survey studies have reported positive correlations between respondents' preferences for political candidates and their perceptions of those candidates' heights (e.g., Kassarjian, 1963; Ward, 1967). Being tall may also be an economic asset: Two Wall Street Journal surveys (cited by Feldman, 1971) suggest that shorter men (less than 6′) tend to receive lower starting salaries in business than taller men (6′2″ or taller) and, further, that shorter men may be less likely to be hired in the first place, even when it is made clear to recruiters that short and tall job candidates possess equivalent qualifications. In a more rigorous study, Curtis (1979) found, for both males and females, a positive and significant correlation between height and income after statistically controlling for extraneous variables such as age, education, and ethnic identification.

Unfortunately, the few experimental studies that have addressed the agent height/social influence relationship (see Table 7.1) indicate that, if such a relationship exists, it may be somewhat more complex than popular wisdom would suggest. Although dominance is a trait that is stereotypically associated with taller persons (e.g., Elman, 1977) and a few investigators have reported low but significant correlations (for males) between height and self-report measures of dominance (e.g., Fisher, 1964; Rees, 1950) Ackerman and Herman (1979) failed to find a significant relation (for males or females) between height and objective measures of behavioral dominance in an experimental setting in which subjects debated against one another. However, because subjects in this study were assigned to (same-sex) dyads randomly, rather than in a way which would maximize height differences, the study may have lacked adequate statistical power to detect dominance differences as a function of height. In an Asch-type conformity study, Portnoy (1972) investigated the tendency of both short and tall male subjects to conform to judgments given by either three tall (6′2″) or three short (5′6″) male confederates. Contrary to popular wisdom, this experiment revealed a significant overall tendency for subjects (regardless of their height) to conform more when confronted with the divergent opinions of short, rather than tall, confederates. Further, short (vs. tall) subjects conformed significantly less in the tall confederate condition.

One persuasion study (Baker & Redding, 1962) did obtain some support for the idea that taller (vs. shorter) communicators may be more persuasive. In this study, subjects were exposed to a persuasive message attributed to a male communicator (temporally and physically absent from the situation) who, via photographs, was made to appear either very tall or very short. Although no significant differences in postmessage agreement were found as a function of communicator height, subjects exposed to the tall communicator's message manifested a significant shift in opinions in the direction advocated by the communicator whereas subjects hearing the short communicator's message did not show a significant opinion shift. Finally, Chaiken's (1982b) field study cited earlier also examined the persuasive effectiveness of tall and short male and female communicators (tall males/females were $6'2''/5'7''$ or taller and short males/females were $5'8''/5'3''$ or shorter) with male and female targets (whose height was not recorded). In this face-to-face setting, a significant three-way interaction between communicator height, sex, and target sex on a private measure of agreement indicated that tall (vs. short) communicators were more persuasive in same-sex dyads but less persuasive in opposite-sex dyads; post hoc comparisons revealed, however, that the differential persuasiveness of tall versus short communicators was significant only in the female communicator/female target condition ($p < .05$). On the public petition signing measure employed in this study, no significant effects involving communicator height were obtained.

Weight, Height, and Attractiveness.   The small and somewhat inconsistent empirical literatures relevant to agent weight and height and social influence effectiveness do not permit any strong conclusions. In evaluating this research and speculating about the potential social influence effects of these physique variables, it seems reasonable to first entertain the idea that weight and height simply contribute, along with facial attractiveness (the focus of much agent attractiveness research), to global perceptions of physical attractiveness. Consistent with this assumption, person perception research indicates that both weight and height influence physical attractiveness ratings, although the weight-attractiveness relationship seems most clear-cut. Both children and adults tend to consistently judge overweight children and adults as less attractive than their normal-weight counterparts (e.g., Maddox & Liederman, 1969; Staffieri, 1972, 1967; Wells & Siegel, 1961). Further, paralleling research on the physical attractiveness stereotype, studies indicate that perceivers tend to regard obese (vs. normal-weight) individuals as less likable and as possessing a variety of traits that, for the most part, are considered socially undesirable in our culture (e.g., Breytspraak et al., 1977; Lerner & Korn, 1972; Maddox & Liederman, 1969; Wells & Siegel, 1961).

Although it is commonly assumed that height is positively related to global judgments of attractiveness, at least for men (e.g., Berscheid & Walster, 1974), very few studies have actually examined the height-attractiveness relationship. Lerner and Moore (1974) found that (male and female) perceivers' estimates of a male, but not a female, target's height were significantly and positively related to their perceptions of the target's physical attractiveness. In an experimental study by Elman (1977), both male and female subjects gave higher attractiveness ratings to a photograph of a male who was verbally described as being tall ($6'4''$), rather than short ($5'4''$). Finally, Graziano, Brothen, and Berscheid (1978) investigated subjects' perceptions of photographed males (preselected for their average attractiveness ratings) who were described as either tall ($6'2''-6'4''$), medium

(5'9"–5'11"), or short (5'5"–5'7"). Although female subjects rated the tall (vs. short) male as somewhat more attractive, the medium-height male was judged as most physically attractive. This curvilinear trend also obtained on females' liking for the target, their perceptions of his desirability as a date, and the positivity of their evaluation of the target on bipolar adjective scales (e.g., warm/cold). In contrast to the female data, male subjects' liking for the target and the positivity of their trait impressions were linearly related to target height, with *short* (vs. medium vs. tall) male targets receiving the *highest* ratings (male subjects' ratings of how attractive most females would perceive the target were unaffected by the height variable).

The commonsense notion that height is a more important determinant of male attractiveness is supported by the Lerner and Moore (1974) finding that perceived height was associated with perceived attractiveness for male, but not female, targets and is also consistent with research on the "male taller norm" in mate selection and research on body image and satisfaction with physique (e.g., Cameron, Oskamp, & Sparks, 1978; Clifford, 1971; Jourard & Secord, 1955). Similarly, research on sex differences in dissatisfaction with body weight and dieting (e.g., Berscheid, Walster, & Bohrnstedt, 1973; Calden, Lundy, & Schalafer, 1959; Herman & Polivy, 1980) and research on perceptions of ideal masculine and feminine physique (e.g., Dwyer, Feldman, & Mayer, 1969) suggest that, in our culture, weight may be a more important determinant of our judgments of women's (vs. men's) physical attractiveness.

Assuming, then, that weight and height affect one's social influence effectiveness primarily via their impact on target's perceptions of agent physical attractiveness, the aforementioned considerations regarding the relative contribution of weight and height to perceptions of female and male attractiveness suggest the hypotheses that weight may be a more important determinant of a woman's ability to exert social influence over others, whereas height may be a more important determinant of male social influence effectiveness. Given the paucity of studies that have investigated the role of agent weight and height in social influence, the validity of these hypotheses is, at present, uncertain. Nevertheless, the agent weight studies shown in Table 7.1 are at least not incompatible with the hypothesized greater importance of weight in affecting female social influence effectiveness. In the only study that utilized both male and female social influence agents (Chaiken, 1982b), the weight status of female communicators exerted a stronger persuasive impact than did the weight status of male communicators. Further, across all four studies in this category, normal-weight females tended to consistently effect greater social influence than their obese counterparts whereas the weight status of male social influence agents tended to exert inconsistent effects.

The hypothesis that height is a more important determinant of male (vs. female) social influence, although intuitively reasonable, merits empirical attention because only one of the four agent height studies even included female social influence agents in its design; further, although this study (Chaiken, 1982b) found that communicator height and sex (along with target sex) interacted to affect persuasion, the patterning of the data is inconsistent with the hypothesized greater importance of height in affecting male social influence effectiveness. Moreover, the fact that this study yielded trends suggesting that greater height facilitates influence in same-sex dyads but inhibits influence in opposite-sex dyads, as well as the Portnoy (1972) study that observed greater conformity on the part of subjects when confronted with the discrepant opinions of short (vs. tall) confederates indicates that being tall may be more of a liability than an advantage in some social influence contexts.

Despite the potentially positive impact of height on judgments of physical attractiveness and, perhaps, ascribed status (e.g., Lechelt, 1975; Wilson, 1968), people interacting with much taller individuals (especially tall men) who are attempting to influence them may feel physically dominated and, thus, somewhat threatened. Consistent with this idea, Hartnett, Baily, and Hartley (1974) found that both male and female subjects tended to maintain a larger distance between themselves and a tall (vs. short) male who they were asked to approach. Further, Higgins and Mancusco (1973) found that male confederates enacting an authoritarian (vs. democratic) leadership style were perceived by (both male and female) subjects as significantly taller. In face-to-face settings, particularly those in which the social influence agent makes explicit his or her intent to influence, people (particularly shorter persons) may feel that their attitudinal freedom is being threatened by taller social influence agents. In such situations, they might actively resist influence in order to assert their attitudinal or behavioral freedom (cf. Brehm, 1972). In this regard it is interesting to note that the only agent height study to obtain the "intuitively reasonable" finding that taller persons are more influential (Baker & Redding, 1962) utilized a pictured communicator who was physically and temporally absent from the social influence situation and thus had no surveillance over subjects' agreement with his persuasive message.

Summary.   The aforementioned considerations suggest that the assumption that agent height primarily affects social influence effectiveness via the impact of height on attractiveness judgments as well as the assumption that greater height should exert a uniformly positive impact on social influence are overly simplistic and incapable of explaining existing data. Additional research on agent height should attend more closely to the variety of impressions and affective reactions that people may experience when taller (or shorter) persons attempt to influence their opinions and behaviors and, further, whether these impressions and affective reactions differ as a function of type of social influence situation (e.g., persuasion vs. compliance contexts as well as situations in which the social influence agent does or does not exert surveillance over targets' responses to social influence). Existing data are more congenial to the notion that obese (vs. normal-weight) persons (especially females) are less effective in influencing others and that this lesser effectiveness may be the result of their less attractive physical appearance. Nevertheless, future research investigating the social influence impact of this physique variable could also benefit from greater attention to the variety of attributions perceivers make about obese (vs. normal-weight) persons and how these attributions might potentially interact with other variables (e.g., contextual variables such as type of social influence situation and presence vs. absence of the influence agent) to affect social influence outcome.

PHYSICAL APPEARANCE AS A TARGET VARIABLE

As noted at the beginning of this chapter, relatively few studies have investigated the role of physical appearance as a determinant of people's susceptibility to social influence. Further, as Table 7.1 indicates, all but two experiments in this category examined the social influence impact of target weight. Although the remainder of this chapter deals primarily with the weight-influenceability relationship, some speculations regarding the role of target height and facial attractiveness in social influence are also offered.

Weight and Susceptibility to Social Influence

With few exceptions, most research that has attempted to explore the impact of weight on susceptibility to social influence has been guided by Schachter's (1971; Schachter & Rodin, 1974) proposition that obese persons are generally more responsive to external/environmental (food and nonfood) cues than are normal-weight persons. Importantly, the Schachter model assumes that the hypothesized greater external responsiveness of obese (vs. normals) is, at least partially, a cause, rather than a consequence of being overweight (cf. Rodin, 1978; Rodin & Slochower, 1976).

Consistent with Schachter's theorizing, a number of researchers have reported a significant positive correlation between degree of overweight and field dependence (e.g., Comer & Rhodewalt, 1979; Costanzo & Woody, 1979; McArthur & Burnstein, 1975). In addition, Green (1974) found a significant positive relationship between obesity and subjects' scores on the Harvard Group Scale of Hypnotic Susceptibility. And Younger and Pliner (1976) found that degree of overweight was significantly associated with higher scores on Snyder's (1974) self-monitoring scale, a measure of the extent to which people tend to monitor their verbal and nonverbal behaviors as a function of situational cues such as the behavior of other persons.

Of the target weight studies shown in Table 7.1, two examined susceptibility to persuasion (Glass et al., 1969; Herman et al., 1983), three explored susceptibility to compliance pressures (Rodin & Slochower, 1974; Sikes & Singh, 1974; Wagener & Laird, 1980), two investigated susceptibility to conformity pressures

(Stalling & Miller, 1981; Stalling & Friedman, 1981), and one examined both direct compliance and modeled compliance as a function of target weight (Elman et al., 1977). Using the Janis and Field (1959) paradigm for examining general persuasibility, Glass et al. (1969) exposed male and female underweight, normal-weight, and overweight subjects (classified on the basis of life insurance norms) to a total of eight persuasive messages on four different topics. Although an overall effect due to weight status revealed significantly greater persuasion scores for obese, compared to normal-weight, subjects, underweight subjects also showed significantly greater persuasion than did normals and, further, did not differ from obese subjects. In addition, these authors found that neither individual differences in field dependence nor self-esteem mediated the impact of weight status on persuasibility. In a field study of persuasion, Herman, Olmsted, and Polivy (1983) investigated whether overweight and normal-weight diners (classified as such by two independent raters) at a French restaurant differentially ordered dessert as a function of whether their waitress–experimenter strongly recommended that they order a particular dessert versus merely asked if they desired dessert. In the latter control condition, the proportion of obese and normal-weight dinners choosing target or other desserts did not differ. However, in the experimental condition, a significantly higher proportion of obese (vs. normal-weight) diners ordered the desert promoted by their waitress.

Of three studies examining the tendencies of overweight (vs. normal-weight) subjects to comply with an experimenter's request that they volunteer for additional experimental sessions, Wagener and Laird (1980) found greater compliance on the part of obese (vs. normal-weight) subjects, whereas Sikes and Singh (1974) and Elman et al. (1977) found no differential compliance as a function of subjects' weight status. In the Rodin and Slochower (1974) compliance experiment, obese and normal-weight female subjects were asked to distribute political surveys for an obese (vs. normal-weight) female confederate. Although subjects had, in the beginning of the experiment, interacted briefly with the confederate, the actual request (a note from the no longer present confederate) was administered by the experimenter. This study found no overall compliance difference as a function of target weight status but did find (as summarized earlier) that obese subjects complied significantly more with the normal-weight (vs. obese) confederate's request, whereas the compliance rate manifested by normal-weight subjects was virtually identical regardless of confederate weight.

In an additional condition of the Elman et al. (1977) study described above, male subjects responded to the experimenter's request for further experimental sessions *after* observing an obese (vs. normal-weight) male confederate comply fully with the experimenter's request for 10 additional hours. As summarized in the section on agent weight status, obese (vs. normal-weight) subjects conformed significantly more to the behavior exhibited by the normal-weight confederate, whereas normal-weight (vs. obese) subjects manifested significantly greater conformity to the behavior modeled by the obese confederate. Two remaining conformity studies in this category investigated overweight, normal-weight, and underweight subjects' tendencies to differentially evaluate foods as a function of (fictitious) information indicating that a group of "other persons" (physically and temporally absent from the experimental situation) had rated these foods either positively or negatively (Stalling & Friedman, 1981; Stalling & Miller, 1981). In the Stalling and Miller (1981) study, subjects (gender not identified) rated the taste of various doughnuts after receiving information that "6 previous subjects" had either liked or disliked the doughnuts. Although all subjects gave more positive ratings to the doughnuts that were ostensibly preferred by these other persons, there was no significant tendency for subjects to be differentially responsive to the false consensus feedback as a function of their weight status. Finally, in the Stalling and Friedman (1981) experiment, subjects (gender again unknown) rated two different cookies after receiving information that a "group of gourmets" preferred one or the other cookie. The findings of this study indicated that the only subjects who were *not influenced* by the fictitious consensus information were those who were obese (vs. normal-weight or thin). In contrast, normals and thin subjects were significantly influenced by the ostensible preferences of the "gourmets", albeit in different ways. Whereas normal-weight subjects gave more positive ratings to cookies that the gourmets preferred, thin subjects reacted in the opposite manner by giving more positive ratings to cookies that the gourmets liked least.

Externality or deviance? With the exception of the Elman et al. (1977) finding that normal-weight (vs. obese) males conformed more to the behavior of an obese male model and the Stalling and Friedman (1981) finding that obese (vs. normal-weight or thin) subjects were less influenced by the fictitious opinions of others, the modal significant finding in this category of experiments does seem to be greater influenceability for obese (vs. normal-weight) persons. Although this modal finding is consistent with Schachter's internal-external theory of obesity, as others have argued (e.g., Elman et al., 1977; Krantz, 1978) it could also be explained in terms of deviance (cf. Festinger, 1954; Freedman & Doob, 1968). Because of the social stigma associated with obesity (cf. Allon, 1975; Dwyer & Mayer, 1975), obese persons may perceive themselves and be treated by others as social deviants and thus may be more highly concerned about the appropriateness of their behavior in social situations than are "nondeviant" normal-weight persons. Consistent with Festinger's (1954) early work on social comparison processes and Freedman and Doob's (1968) later work on experimentally induced deviance, one manifestation of this greater concern about behaving appropriately might be heightened conformity to the opinions of others. This interpretation, then, suggests that the greater influenceability of obese (vs. normal-weight) persons is a direct consequence of their status as social deviants rather than simply another manifestation of their hypothesized greater responsiveness to external cues.

In addition to serving as an alternative explanation for the modal finding of greater influenceability on the part of obese (vs. normal-weight) persons, the deviance perspective is more compatible with the overall pattern of existing data regarding the weight-influenceability relationship than is the externality perspective. For example, the Glass et al. (1969) finding that both overweight and *underweight* subjects showed significantly greater persuasion than normal-weight subjects is difficult to interpret from the externality perspective but is consistent with a deviance perspective if it is assumed that being either extremely overweight or underweight in our culture represents a form of deviance. Further, the Rodin and Slochower (1974) and Elman et al. (1977) findings indicating that obese (vs. normal-weight) subjects were more influenced by a normal-weight, but not obese, confederate are again difficult to interpret within the externality perspective but are compatible with Freedman and Doob's (1968) research that suggested that deviants (vs. nondeviants) are especially likely to comply with requests made by nondeviant (vs. deviant) others. Some deviance research also suggests that in face-to-face settings, nondeviants may be more likely to comply with requests made by deviant (vs. nondeviant) others because it is more of a "good deed" to help stigmatized others (Doob & Ecker, 1970; Freedman & Doob, 1968). Thus, the Elman et al. finding that normal-weight males were more likely to conform to the behavior exhibited by an obese (vs. normal-weight) confederate can also be interpreted within the deviance framework.

It should be noted that the deviance perspective on social influence has not, itself, been fully substantiated empirically: In a series of conformity, persuasion, and compliance studies, Freedman and Doob (1968) were only partly successful in demonstrating that experimental inductions of deviant/nondeviant status reliably affected subjects' responses to social influence attempts in the manner predicted by their framework. Nevertheless, the deviance perspective does provide a relatively parsimonius account of existing research on the weight-influenceability relationship. Further research exploring the relative merit of the deviancy perspective versus the externality perspective for understanding the weight-influenceability relationship should pay special empirical attention to the social context in which influence inductions take place. Whereas the externality perspective suggests (at least in its most straightforward application) that greater influenceability for obese (vs. normal-weight) persons should be found across a range of social influence settings, the deviance perspective articulated by Freedman and Doob (1968) suggests that the greater influenceability of "deviant" obese persons should be most likely to occur in face-to-face settings in which targets' social influence responses are public. In this regard, it should be noted that in all but three of the target weight studies reviewed previously (Glass et al., 1969; Stalling & Friedman, 1981; Stalling & Miller, 1981), subjects' responses to social influence attempts occurred in face-to-face settings under surveillance conditions. Research that manipulated the degree to which targets' perceived their social influence responses to be anonymous (vs. public) would facilitate investigating the relative validity of the externality versus deviance perspectives in understanding the weight-influenceability relationship. Further, such research might also provide an indication of the extent to which the apparently greater influenceability of obese (vs. normal-weight) persons represents genuine changes in such persons' beliefs, attitudes, or behaviors versus more temporal and/or strategic responses to contemporaneous situational pressures.

Target height and facial attractiveness

Little, if anything, can be concluded about the role of target height or facial attractiveness on susceptibility to social influence because, as shown in Table 7.1, only two studies have examined the relationship between these physique variables and influenceability. In the Dion and Stein (1978) study, male and female children who were judged (by independent raters) to be either attractive or unattractive were induced to eat crackers by an attractive or unattractive same- or opposite-sex peer. Although (as noted earlier) *communicator* attractiveness interacted with communicator sex and target sex to affect targets' influenceability, *target* attractiveness, itself, was unrelated to influenceability. With respect to height, the Portnoy (1972) conformity study reviewed earlier found no overall conformity difference between shorter and taller subjects but did find that short (vs. tall) subjects conformed significantly *less* when in the presence of three tall (vs. short) confederates.

For researchers interested in pursuing the potential relationship between these physique variables and influenceability, two theoretical perspectives seem most relevant. One might, for example, adopt an individual difference perspective that would involve exploring the degree to which either attractiveness or height covaries with other individual difference variables that are known to be or might potentially be related to influenceability (the same strategy could, of course, be applied to obesity). With respect to height, for example, the literature on satisfaction with body image (e.g., Cameron, Oskamp, & Sparks, 1978; Clifford, 1971; Jourard & Secord, 1955) suggests that, at least for males, height may be associated with global levels of self-esteem. Unfortunately, research has generally not substantiated a significant relationship (for either sex) between these two variables (e.g., Coopersmith, 1967; Prieto & Robbins, 1975). Further, even if it turned out to be the case that height was significantly correlated with self-esteem, a simple prediction regarding the impact of height on influenceability would still not be possible because theory and research on social influence processes suggests that chronic self-esteem, itself, bears no simple relationship to one's susceptibility to social influence (Eagly, 1981; McGuire, 1968; Nisbett & Gordon, 1967).

Somewhat greater empirical attention has been paid to possible individual differences as a function of facial attractiveness. As noted earlier, there is some evidence indicating that, as a product of differing socialization experiences, more attractive (vs. less attractive) individuals may develop more positive social skills (Goldman & Lewis, 1977), may be more assertive in their interactions with others (Jackson & Huston, 1975), and may possess higher self-esteem (e.g., Cavoir & Dokecki, 1973; Chaiken, 1979a; Maruyama & Miller, 1981). Although person perception research indicates that attractive (vs. unattractive) persons are perceived to possess greater feelings of power or internal control (Miller, 1970) and thus better able to resist influence from others (Miller et al., 1974), two recent studies have failed to obtain a significant relationship between individuals' levels of physical attractiveness and their scores on Rotter's (1966) locus of control scale (Chaiken, 1979a; Maruyama & Miller, 1981). As noted earlier with respect to the height-influenceability relationship, the ''personality strategy'' (Eagly, 1981) of investigating the attractiveness-influenceability relationship by examining the covariation between attractiveness and possible personality correlates of influenceability does not lead, by itself, to a simple prediction regarding the impact of attractiveness on individuals' general tendencies to accept or resist social influence attempts. Instead, once a reliable relationship between a particular physique variable (attractiveness, height, weight) and some individual difference dimension (e.g., self-esteem, locus of control, field dependence) has been established, one would next need to analyze a particular social influence setting in terms of the expected impact, if any, of the relevant individual difference dimension(s) on mechanisms that might theoretically determine influenceability in that setting (cf. Eagly, 1981; McGuire, 1968). Using this two-fold strategy, relatively precise (albeit specific) predictions could potentially be made regarding the social influence impact of particular physique variables in particular social influence settings.

As suggested by the weight-influenceability literature, a second possible approach to exploring the relationship between attractiveness and height and influenceability might be to consider these physique variables in terms of Freedman and Doob's (1968) deviance perspective. Exploring the viability of this perspective would first require investigating the degree to which extreme shortness or unattractiveness (and, perhaps, extreme tallness or attractiveness) are associated with self-perceptions and/or others' perceptions of deviance. Whether such an association would be found, however, is not clear because, unlike weight status, people may not generally be held responsible for their height or for their levels of facial attractiveness. Nevertheless, to the extent that these (or other) physique variables did prove to be related to perceptions of deviance, researchers could then construct social influence settings in which deviance-based hypotheses regarding the impact of physique on influenceability could be tested.

SUMMARY AND CONCLUSIONS

This chapter addressed two broad questions relevant to the role of physical appearance in social influence: The extent to which a person's physical appearance impacts on his or her effectiveness as an *agent* of social influence, and the extent to people might differ in their *susceptibility* to social influence as a function of their physical appearance. To answer these questions, relevant social influence studies from the psychological literature were located and critically examined. At the outset, it became clear that complete answers to these questions would not be possible given the distribution of existing literature (see Table 7.1). Thus, although a fair number of studies were located that investigated either physical attractiveness as an *agent* variable or weight as a *target* variable, very few studies were found that had examined either social influence effectiveness as a function of weight or height or susceptibility to social influence as a function of attractiveness or height.

The largest category of research reviewed dealt with the role of agent physical attractiveness. In general, this literature revealed a relatively consistent overall tendency for attractive persons to be more influencial than unattractive ones. Regarding the mediation of attractiveness effects, it was suggested that differential liking (vs. expertise or status) most often underlies the heightened social influence effectiveness of attractive individuals. Consistent with this idea, existing research indicates that agent attractiveness effects tend to be stronger in settings where the social influence agent is present (vs. absent); a condition that may enhance the salience of the agent and the consequent salience of interpersonal relations.

Regarding underlying psychological mechanisms, it was suggested that a variety of explanations, including classical conditioning, social reinforcement, cognitive consistency, Kelman's (1961) identification model, and Chaiken's (1980; in press; Eagly & Chaiken, 1984) heuristic processing model could account for the facilitative impact of attractiveness on social influence effectiveness. Several implications of this class of explanations were then explored. For example, that persuasion effects due to communicator attractiveness, while often (though not always) reflective of genuine attitudinal and behavioral change, should be relatively independent of recipients' evaluation of persuasive argumentation and, also, relatively temporal in nature. Finally, two limitations of existing research were noted. First, it was suggested that existing research, by virtue of its use of relatively uninvolving attitude topics and inconsequential compliance requests, might be somewhat biased in favor of finding attractiveness effects. Because recent persuasion research (e.g., Chaiken, 1980; Petty et al., 1981) indicates that communicator cues tend to exert only a minimal impact when more involving attitudinal topics are employed, it is likely that attractiveness (or other physique variables) may not confer much of an influence advantage when one is attempting to change opinions on more consequential issues or trying to gain compliance with more consequential requests. Second, it was noted that existing research has paid little attention to the idea that actual differences in communication, social, or other personal skills may often underly the differential social influence effectiveness of attractive and unattractive individuals. Although research designed to address this question would, necessarily, be characterized by less standardization than the typical laboratory experiment, such a sacrifice might be necessary in order to gain a richer understanding of how attractiveness and other physique variables impact on the social influence process in genuine interpersonal settings.

The fact that only a handful of agent weight and height studies were located necessitated a highly speculative review of this category of experiments. One hypothesis that was entertained suggested that both of these variables affect social influence effectiveness via their more direct impact on perceptions of physical attractiveness. Moreover, the idea that weight (height) may be a more important determinant of female (male) attractiveness led to the hypothesis that weight would be a more important determinant of female social influence effectiveness whereas height would be a more important determinant of male social influence effectiveness. The four agent weight studies that were reviewed proved compatible with this viewpoint, although their small number and lack of supporting information (i.e., lack of perceived attractiveness measures) do not permit a strong endorsement of the hypothesis. Nevertheless, across these studies, normal-weight females tended to be uniformly more effective in influencing others than did their obese counterparts. In contrast, the weight status of male social influence agents tended to exert weaker and/or inconsistent effects.

Of all the categories of experiments reviewed, the agent height studies proved to be least coherent. Indeed, only one of the four studies in this category obtained the "intuitively reasonable" finding that greater height would facilitate social influence effectiveness (Baker & Redding, 1962). Of the remaining studies, one yielded no effects due to agent height (Ackerman & Herman, 1979) one yielded weak and inconsistent findings across two different influence measures (Chaiken, 1982b), and one revealed that short people were more influential than taller ones (Portnoy, 1972)! Moreover, the inconsistency among these studies could not be attributed to any tendency for effects to be weaker or less consistent for female (vs. male) influence agents (as the sex difference hypothesis might imply) since only one of the four studies even utilized female social influence agents (Chaiken, 1982b). The lack of consistency across this group of studies suggested that the commonsense assumption that greater height (at least for males) should exert a uniformly positive impact on social influence (because of its impact on perceived attractiveness or via heightened perceptions of status) is overly simplistic and incapable of explaining the existing data. In attempting to make some sense of the findings in this area, it was suggested that height, at least for males, represents both an asset and a liability; an asset in that taller persons may often be perceived as possessing higher status and a liability in that people interacting in face-to-face settings with taller individuals may feel physically dominated and somewhat threatened. In this regard it is noteworthy that the only study to find a facilitative effect of height on influence effectiveness was a persuasion study in which the communicator was both temporally and physically absent from the influence setting (Baker & Redding, 1962). Perhaps in this study, the height-influence effect was mediated by differences in perceived status. In contrast, the remaining height studies, all of which were conducted in face-to-face settings, yielded either no effects due to height or found that greater height inhibited social influence effectiveness. Perhaps in these settings, perceptions of dominance and threat played a greater role in determining subjects' reactions to taller social influence agents. It was concluded that future research on the influence impact of height should attend more closely to the variety of impressions and affective reactions that people may experience when interacting with taller (vs. shorter) individuals and, further, whether these impressions and affective reactions differ as a function of social influence setting (e.g., situations in which the social influence agent is present versus absent and/or does versus does not exert surveillance over targets' responses to the social influence attempt as well as situations in which the agent actively versus passively attempts to exert influence).

Data relevant to the second broad question addressed in this chapter, whether physical appearance affects *susceptibility* to social influence, proved to be even more scarce than data relevant to the first question and, moreover, restricted almost exclusively to one type of physique variable, weight-status. Although the modal finding among these studies did seem to be greater influenceability on the part of overweight (vs. normal-weight) persons, as would be expected from Schachter's (1972) externality theory of obesity, it was concluded that the overall pattern of findings in this category was more consistent with the deviancy perspective outlined by Freedman and Doob (1968). According to the deviance perspective, the greater influenceability of obese persons is a direct consequence of their status as social deviants, rather than simply another manifestation of their hypothesized greater responsivity to external cues (Schachter, 1972). Future researchers interested in evaluating the relative merits of these two perspectives might consider constructing experiments in which these two perspectives could compete with one another. For example, it was noted that the externality perspective (in its most straightforward application) suggests that greater influenceability for obese persons should be found across a range of social influence settings, whereas the deviance perspective suggests that the greater influenceability of "deviant" obese persons should be most likely to occur in face-to-face settings in which targets' social influence responses are public.

Since only one study dealing with susceptibility to social influence dealt with facial attractiveness and only one with height, discussion of the role of these variables focused on suggesting relevant theory and/or research strategies for future researchers. Regarding theory, it was noted that the deviance perspective, used relatively successfully with regard to the weight-influenceability relationship, might also help set the context for research on target attractiveness and height. Finally, a two-stage "personality strategy" (Eagly, 1981) was also suggested as guide for future researchers committed to exploring the physique-influenceability relationship. First, researchers would need to establish a reliable relationship between a particular physique variable (e.g., weight) and some individual difference dimension deemed relevant to influenceability (e.g., self-esteem, field dependence). Then, particular social influence settings (e.g., persuasion settings) could be analyzed in terms of the expected impact (if any) that the relevant individual difference dimension might have on psychological processes (e.g., comprehension, yielding; cf. McGuire, 1968) that might be plausible mediators of social influence effects in that particular setting. In this fashion, relatively precise predictions might be made regarding the relation between physique and influenceability in particular social influence settings.

As suggested in the beginning of this chapter, the disproportionate number of social influence studies dealing with agent attractiveness and target weight in the literature probably reflects the positive tendency among researchers in our field to address empirical questions that are at least vaguely derived from theory. As an outgrowth of this theory-motivated approach, there now exists a moderate number of studies that suggest that these two variables do indeed impact on social influence. Subsequent research in these two areas might now profitably turn toward answering second and third generation questions (cf. Zanna & Fazio, 1982) such as *when and in what settings* are these appearance effects most likely to be obtained and *what psychological mechanisms* might most often underly these appearance effects? A major goal of this chapter has been to provide tentative answers, or hypotheses, regarding these second and third generation research questions. With respect to the remaining appearance categories addressed in this chapter, it is very clear that more first generation research of the sort, "Does height affect social influence effectiveness?" is required. By calling attention to these other categories of appearance-related social influence questions and suggesting possible conceptual frameworks for designing first generation research, it is hoped that subsequent reviewers of the intriguing area of physique and social influence will have something more conclusive to say about the status of research in these areas and more grist for speculating about possible answers to second and third generation questions.

ACKNOWLEDGMENT

Preparation of this chapter was supported in part by NSF Grant No. BNS-8309159. The author is grateful to Alice Eagly, Wendy Wood, and Mark Zanna for their comments on an earlier draft of this manuscript.

REFERENCES

Ackerman, C. A., & Herman, C. P. (1979). *Height and dominance: Do tall people push their height around?* Unpublished manuscript, University of Toronto.

Allon, N. (1975). The stigma of overweight in everyday life. In G. A. Bray (Ed.), *Obesity in perspective*. Washington, DC: U.S. Government Printing office.

Athanasious, R., & Greene, P. (1973). *Physical attractiveness and helping behavior*. In: Proceedings of the 81st Annual American Psychological Association Convention.

Baker, M. J., & Churchill, G. A. (1977). The impact of physically attractive models on advertising evaluations. *Journal of Marketing Research, 14*, 538–555.

Baker, E. E., & Redding, W. C. (1962). The effects of perceived tallness in persuasive speaking: An experiment. *Journal of Communication, 12*, 51–53.

Baron, R. A. (1970). Attraction toward the model and model's competence as determinants of adult imitative behavior. *Journal of Personality and Social Psychology, 14*, 345–351.

Baron, R. A. (1971). Behavioral effects of interpersonal attraction: Compliance with requests from liked and disliked others. *Psychonomic Science, 25*, 325–326.

Benson, P. L., Karabenick, S. A., & Lerner, R. M. (1976). Pretty pleases: The effects of physical attractiveness, race and sex on receiving help. *Journal of Experimental Social Psychology, 12*, 409–415.

Berger, J., Conner, T. L., & Fisek, M. H. (1974). (Eds.). *Expectation states theory: A theoretical research program*. Cambridge, MA: Winthrop.

Berscheid, E., & Walster, E. (1974). *Physical attractiveness*. In L. Berkowitz (Ed.), Advances in experimental social psychology (Vol. 7). New York: Academic Press.

Berscheid, E., Walster, E., & Bohrnstedt, G. (1973, November). The happy American body: A survey report. *Psychology Today, 1*, 119–131.

Blass, T., Alperstein, L., & Block, S. H. (1974). *Effects of communicator's race and beauty and of receiver's objectivity–subjectivity on attitude change*. Paper presented at meetings of the American Psychological Association, New Orleans.

Brehm, J. W. (1972) *Responses to loss of freedom: A theory of psychological reactance*. Morristown, NJ: General Learning Press.

Breytspraak, L. M., McGee, J., Conger, J. C., Whately, J. L., & Moore, J. T. (1977). Sensitizing medical students to impression formation processes in the patient interview. *Journal of Medical Education, 52*, 47–54.

Byrne, D. (1961). Interpersonal attraction and attitude similarity. *Journal of Abnormal and Social Psychology, 62*, 713–715.

Byrne, D., & Nelson, D. (1964). Attraction as a function of attitude similarity–dissimilarity: The effect of topic importance. *Psychonomic Science, 1*, 93–94.

Calden, G., Lundy, R. M., & Schalafer, R. J. (1959). Sex differences in body concepts. *Journal of Consulting Psychology, 23*, 378.

Cameron, C., Oskamp, S., & Sparks, W. (1978). Courtship American Style: Newspaper advertisements. *The Family Coordinator, 26*, 27–30.

Cash, T. F., Gillen, B., & Burns, D. S. (1977). Sexism and "beautyism" in personnel consultant decision making. *Journal of Applied Psychology, 62*, 301–310.

Cavoir, N., & Dokecki, P. R. (1973). Physical attractiveness, perceived attitude similarity, and academic achievement as contributors to interpersonal attraction among adolescents. *Developmental Psychology, 9*, 44–54.

Chaikin, A. L., Derlega, V. J., Yoder, J., & Phillips, D. (1974). The effects of appearance on compliance. *Journal of Social Psychology, 92*, 199–200.

Chaiken, S. (1979a). Communicator physical attractiveness and persuasion. *Journal of Personality and Social Psychology, 37*, 1387–1397.

Chaiken, S. (1979b). *The effect of communicator attractiveness, expertise and argument strength on persuasion*. Unpublished manuscript. University of Toronto.

Chaiken, S. (1980). Heuristic versus systematic information processing and the use of source versus message cues in persuasion. *Journal of Personality and Social Psychology, 39*, 752–766.

Chaiken, S. (1982a). *The heuristic/systematic processing distinction in persuasion.* Paper presented at Symposium on Automatic Processing, Society for Experimental Social Psychology, Nashville.

Chaiken, S. (1982b). *A field study on the impact of communicator weight and height on persuasion.* Unpublished manuscript, Vanderbilt University.

Chaiken, S. (in press). The heuristic model of persuasion. In M. P. Zanna, J. M. Olson, & C. P. Herman (Eds.), *Social influence: The Ontario Symposium* (Vol. 5). Hillsdale, NJ: Erlbaum.

Chaiken, S., & Eagly, A. H. (1983). Communication modality as a determinant of persuasion: The role of communicator salience. *Journal of Personality and Social Psychology, 45,* 241–256.

Chaiken, S., Eagly, A. H., Sejwacz, D., & Gregory, W. L. (1978). *Communicator physical attractiveness as a determinant of opinion change.* JSAS Catalogue of Selected Documents in Psychology, 8, 9–10.

Clifford, E. (1971). Body satisfaction in adolescents. *Perceptual and Motor Skills, 33,* 119–125.

Clifford, M. M., & Walster, E. (1973). The effect of physical attractiveness on teacher expectations. *Sociology of Education, 46,* 248–258.

Comer, R., & Rhodewalt, F. (1979). Cue utilization in the self-attribution of emotions and attitudes. *Personality and Social Psychology Bulletin, 5,* 320–324.

Cook, T. D., & Flay, B. R. (1978). The persistence of experimentally induced attitude change. In L. Berkowitz (Ed.), *Advances in experimental social psychology,* (Vol. 11). New York: Academic Press.

Cooper, H. M. (1979). Statistically combining independent studies: A meta-analysis of sex differences in conformity research. *Journal of Personality and Social Psychology, 37,* 131–146.

Coopersmith, S. (1967). *The antecedents of self-esteem.* San Francisco: Freeman.

Costanzo, P. R., & Woody, E. (1979). Externality as a function of obesity in children: Pervasive style or eating-specific attribute. *Journal of Personality and Social Psychology, 37,* 2286–2296.

Curtis, J. (1979). Unpublished manuscript, University of Waterloo.

Dion, K. K. (1972). Physical attractiveness and evaluations of children's transgressions. *Journal of Personality and Social Psychology, 24,* 207–213.

Dion, K. K., Berscheid, E., & Walster, E. (1972). What is beautiful is good. *Journal of Personality and Social Psychology, 24,* 285–290.

Dion, K. K., & Stein, S. (1978). Physical attractiveness and interpersonal influence. *Journal of Experimental Social Psychology, 14,* 97–108.

Dipboye, R. L., Fromkin, H. L., & Wiback, P. (1975). Relative importance of applicant sex, attractiveness and scholastic standing in evaluation of job applicant resumes. *Journal of Applied Psychology, 60,* 39–43.

Doob, A. N., & Ecker, B. P. (1970). Stigma and compliance. *Journal of Personality and Social Psychology, 14,* 302–304.

Dwyer, J. T., Feldman, J. J., & Mayer, J. (1969). Adolescent attitudes toward weight and appearance. *Journal of Nutrition Education, 1,* 13.

Dwyer, J. T., & Mayer, J. (1975). The dismal condition: Problems faced by obese adolescent girls in American society. In G. A. Bray (Ed.), *Obesity in perspective.* Washington, DC: U.S. Government Printing Office.

Eagly, A. H. (1978). Sex differences in influenceability. *Psychological Bulletin, 85,* 86–116.

Eagly, A. H. (1981). Recipient characteristics as determinants of responses to persuasion. In R. E. Petty, T. M. Ostrom, & T. C. Brock (Eds.), *Cognitive responses in persuasion.* Hillsdale, NJ: Lawrence Erlbaum Associates.

Eagly, A. H., & Carli, L. L. (1981). Sex of researchers and sex-typed communications as determinants of sex differences in influenceability: A meta-analysis of social influence studies. *Psychological Bulletin, 90,* 1–20.

Eagly, A. H., & Chaiken, S. (1975). An attribution analysis of the effect of communicator characteristics on opinion change: The case of communicator attractiveness. *Journal of Personality and Social Psychology, 32,* 136–144.

Eagly, A. H., & Chaiken, S. (1984). *Cognitive theories of persuasion.* In L. Berkowitz (Ed.), *Advances in experimental social psychology,* (Vol. 17). New York: Academic Press.

Eagly, A. H., & Wood, W. (1982). Inferred sex differences in status as a determinant of gender stereotypes about social influence. *Journal of Personality and Social Psychology, 43,* 915–928.

Efran, M. G. (1974). The effect of physical appearance on the judgment of guilt, interpersonal attraction, and severity of recommended punishment in a simulated jury task. *Journal of Research in Personality, 8,* 45–54.

Elman, D. (1977). Physical characteristics and the perception of masculine traits. *Journal of Social Psychology, 103,* 157–158.

Elman, D., Schroeder, H., & Schwartz, M. (1977). Reciprocal social influence of obese and normal-weight persons. *Journal of Abnormal Psychology, 86,* 408–413.

Feldman, S. (1971). *The presentation of shortness in everyday life—Height and heightism in American society: Toward a sociology of stature.* Paper presented at the meeting of the American Sociological Association, Chicago.

Festinger, L. (1954). A theory of social comparison processes. *Human Relations, 7,* 117–140.

Fisher, S. (1964). Power orientation and concept of self-height in men: Preliminary note. *Perceptual and Motor Skills, 18,* 732.

Freedman, J. L., & Doob, A. N. (1968). *Deviancy: The psychology of being different.* New York: Academic Press.

Glass, D. C., Lavin, D. E., Hency, T., Gordon, A., Mayhew, P., & Donohoe, P. (1969). Obesity and persuasibility. *Journal of Personality, 37,* 407–414.

Goldman, W., & Lewis, P. (1977). Beautiful is good: Evidence that the physically attractive are more socially skillful. *Journal of Experimental Social Psychology, 13,* 125–130.

Granberg, D., Cooper, H. M., & King, M. (1979). Cross-lagged panel analysis of the relation between attraction and perceived similarity. Unpublished manuscript. Center for Research in Social Behavior, University of Missouri, Columbia, MO.

Graziano, W., Brothen, T., & Berscheid, E. (1978). Height and attraction: Do men and women see eye-to-eye. *Journal of Personality, 46,* 128–145.

Green, M. S. (1974). *A comparison of obese and normal subjects on body image boundary, locus of controls, and hypnotic susceptibility.* Unpublished doctoral dissertation, Wayne State University.

Greenwald, A. G. (1968). Cognitive learning, cognitive responses to persuasion, and attitude change. In A. G Greenwald, T. C. Brock, & T. M. Ostrom (Eds.), *Psychological foundations of attitudes.* New York: Academic Press.

Greenwald, A. G. (1975). Consequences of prejudice against the null hypothesis. *Psychological Bulletin, 82,* 1–20.

Hamid, P. N. (1969). Changes in person perception as a function of dress. *Perceptual and Motor Skills, 29,* 191–194.

Hamid, P. N. (1972). Some effects of dress cues on observational accuracy, perceptual estimates, and impression formation. *Journal of Social Psychology, 86,* 279–289.

Harrell, W. A. (1978). Physical attractiveness, self-disclosure, and helping behavior. *Journal of Social Psychology, 104,* 15–17.

Harris, M. B., & Baudin, H. (1973). The language of altruism: The effects of language, dress, and ethnic group. *Journal of Social Psychology, 91,* 37–41.

Harnett, J. J., Baily, K. G., & Hartley, C. S. (1974). Body height, position, and sex as determinants of personal space. *The Journal of Psychology, 87,* 129–136.

Heider, F. (1958). *The psychology of interpersonal relations.* New York: Wiley.

Herman, C. P., Olmsted, M. P., & Polivy, J. (1983). Obesity, externality, and susceptibility to social influence: An integrated analysis. *Journal of Personality and Social Psychology, 45,* 926–934.

Herman, C. P., & Polivy, J. (1980). Restrained and unrestrained eating. In A. J. Stunkard (Ed.), *Obesity: Basic mechanisms and treatment.* Philadelphia: Saunders Co.

Higgins, E. T. & Manusco, R. P. (1973). *Height estimations as a function of leadership style.* Unpublished manuscript, Princeton University.

Horai, J., Naccari, N., & Fatoullah, E. (1974). The effects of expertise and physical attractiveness upon opinion agreement and liking. *Sociometry, 37,* 601–606.

Hovland, C. I., Janis, I. L., & Kelley, H. H. (1953). *Communication and persuasion.* New Haven: Yale University Press.

Hovland, C. I., & Weiss, W. (1951). The influence of source credibility on communication effectiveness. *Public Opinion Quarterly, 15,* 635–650.

Howard, C. R., Cohen, S. H., & Cavoir, N. (1974). More results on increasing the persuasiveness of a low prestige communicator: The effects of the communicator's physical attractiveness and sex of the receiver. *Personality and Social Psychology Bulletin, 1,* 393–395.

Insko, C. A., Thompson, V. D., Stroebe, W., Shoud, K. F., Penner, B. E., & Layton, B. D. (1977). Implied evaluation and the similarity-attraction effect. *Journal of Personality and Social Psychology, 25,* 297–308.

Jackson, D., & Huston, T. L. (1975). Physical attractiveness and assertiveness. *Journal of Social Psychology, 96,* 79–84.

Janis, I. L., & Field, P. B. (1959). A behavioral assessment of persuasibility: Consistency of individual differences. In C. I. Hovland & I. L. Janis (Eds.), *Personality and persuasibility.* New Haven: Yale University Press.

Jourard, S. M., & Secord, P. S. (1955). Body cathexis and personality. *British Journal of Psychology, 46,* 130–138.

Kahn, A., Hottes, J., & Davis, W. L. (1971). Cooperation and optimal responding in the prisoner's dilemma game: Effects of sex and physical attractiveness. *Journal of Personality and Social Psychology, 17,* 267–279.

Karris, L. (1977). Prejudice against obese renters. *Journal of Social Psychology, 101,* 159–160.

Kassarjian, H. H. (1963). Voting intentions and political perception. *Journal of Psychology, 56,* 85–88.

Kelman, H. C. (1961). Processes of opinion change. *Public Opinion Quarterly, 25,* 57–78.

Klienke, C. L. (1977). Effects of dress on compliance to requests in a field setting. *Journal of Social Psychology, 101,* 223–224.

Krantz, D. (1978). The social context of obesity research. *Personality and Social Psychology Bulletin, 4,* 177–184.

Landy, D., & Sigall, H. (1974). Beauty is talent: Task evaluation as a function of the performer's physical attractiveness. *Journal of Personality and Social Psychology, 29,* 299–304.

Langlois, J. H., & Downs, A. C. (1977). Peer relations as a function of physical attractiveness and ethnicity on children's behavioral attributions and peer preferences. *Child Development, 48,* 1694–1698.

LaVoie, J. C., & Adams, G. R. (1978). Physical and interpersonal attractiveness of the model and imitation in adults. *Journal of Social Psychology, 106,* 191–202.

Lechelt, E. C. (1975). Occupational affiliation and ratings of physical height and personal esteem. *Psychological Reports, 36,* 943–946.

Lerner, R. M., & Korn, S. J. (1972). The development of body-build stereotypes in males. *Child Development, 43,* 908–920.

Lerner, R. M., & Moore, T. (1974). Sex and status effects on perception of physical attractiveness. *Psychological Reports, 34,* 1047–1050.

Lockheed, M. E., & Hall, K. P. (1976). Conceptualizing sex as a status characteristic: Applications to leadership training strategies. *Journal of Social Issues, 32,* 111–124.

McArthur, L. Z., & Burnstein, B. (1975). Field dependent eating and perception as a function of weight and sex. *Journal of Personality, 43,* 402–420.

McGuire, W. J. (1968). Personality and susceptibility to social influence. In E. F. Borgatta & W. W. Lambert (Eds.), *Handbook of personality theory and research.* Chicago: Rand McNally.

Maddox, G. L., & Liederman, V. (1969). Overweight as a social disability with medical implications. *Journal of Medical Education, 44,* 214–220.

Maddux, J. E., & Rogers, R. W. (1980). Effects of source expertness, physical attractiveness, and supporting arguments on persuasion: A case of brains over beauty. *Journal of Personality and Social Psychology, 39,* 235–244.

Marks, G., & Miller, N. (1982). Target attractiveness as a mediator of assumed attitude similarity. *Personality and Social Psychology Bulletin, 8,* 728–735.

Marks, G., Miller, N., & Maruyama, G. (1981). Effects of targets' physical attractiveness on assumptions of similarity. *Journal of Personality and Social Psychology, 41,* 198–206.

Maruyama, G., & Miller, N. (1981). Physical attractiveness and personality. In B. A. Maher & W. B. Maher (Eds.), *Progress in experimental personality research,* (Vol. 10). New York: Academic Press.

Miller, A. G. (1970). Social perception of internal-external control. *Perceptual and Motor Skills, 30,* 103–109.

Miller, A. G., Gillen, B., Schenker, C., & Radlove, S. (1974). The prediction and perception of obedience to authority. *Journal of Personality, 42,* 23–42.

Mills, J., & Aronson, E. (1965). Opinion change as a function of the communicator's attractiveness and desire to influence. *Journal of Personality and Social Psychology, 1,* 173–177.

Mills, J., & Harvey, J. (1972). Opinion change as a function of when information about the communicator is received and whether he is attractive or expert. *Journal of Personality and Social Psychology, 21,* 52–55.

Mims, P. R., Hartnett, J. J., & Nay, W. R. (1975). Interpersonal attraction and help volunteering as a function of physical attractiveness. *Journal of Psychology, 89,* 125–131.

Nisbett, R. E., & Gordon, A. (1967). Self-esteem and susceptibility to social influence. *Journal of Personality and Social Psychology, 5,* 268–276.

Nisbett, R. E., & Ross, L. (1980). *Human inference: Strategies and shortcomings of social judgment.* Englewood Cliffs, NJ: Prentice–Hall.

Norman, R. (1976). When what is said is important: A comparison of expert and attractive sources. *Journal of Experimental Social Psychology, 12,* 294–300.

Pallak, S. R. (1983). Salience of a communicator's physical attractiveness and persuasion: A heuristic versus systematic processing interpretation. *Social Cognition, 2,* 156–168.

Pallak, S. R., Murroni, E., & Koch, J. (1983). Communicator attractiveness and expertise, emotional vs. rational appeals, and persuasion: A heuristic versus systematic processing interpretation. *Social Cognition, 2,* 120–139.

Perrin, F. A. (1921). Physical attractiveness and repulsiveness. *Journal of Experimental Psychology, 4,* 203–217.

Petty, R. E., Cacioppo, J. T., & Goldman, R. (1981). Personal involvement as a determinant of argument-based persuasion. *Journal of Personality and Social Psychology, 41,* 847–855.

Portnoy, S. (1972). *Height as a personality variable in a conformity situation.* Unpublished doctoral dissertation, Temple University.

Prieto, A. G., & Robbins, M. C. (1975). Perceptions of height and self-esteem. *Perceptual and Motor Skills, 40,* 395–398.

Raymond, B. T., & Unger, R. K. (1972). The apparel oft proclaims the man: Cooperation with deviant and conventional youths. *Journal of Social Psychology, 87,* 75–82.

Rees, L. (1950). Body build, personality and neurosis in women. *Journal of Mental Science, 96,* 426–434.

Regan, D. T. (1971). Effects of a favor and liking on compliance. *Journal of Experimental Social Psychology, 7,* 627–639.

Rodin, J. (1978). On social psychology and obesity research: A final note. *Personality and Social Psychology Bulletin, 4,* 185–186.

Rodin, J., & Slochower, J. (1976). Externality in the nonobese: the effects of environmental responsiveness on weight. *Journal of Personality and Social Psychology, 33*, 338–344.

Rodin, J., & Slochower, J. (1974). Fat chance for a favor: Obese–normal differences in compliance and incidental learning. *Journal of Personality and Social Psychology, 29*, 557–565.

Schachter, S. (1971). *Emotion, obesity and crime.* New York: Academic Press.

Schachter, S., & Rodin, J. (1974). *Obese humans and rats.* Washington, DC: Erlbaum/Halsted.

Schiavo, R. S., Sherlock, B., & Wicklund, G. (1974). Effect of attire on obtaining directions. *Psychological Reports, 34*, 245–246.

Sigall, H., & Aronson, E. (1969). Liking for an evaluator as a function of her physical attractiveness and nature of the evaluations. *Journal of Experimental Social Psychology, 5*, 93–100.

Sigall, H., Page, R., & Brown, A. C. (1971). Effort expenditure as a function of evaluation and evaluator attractiveness. *Representative Research in Social Psychology, 2*, 19–25.

Sikes, S., & Singh, D. (1974). Obesity and compliance. *Bulletin of the Psychonomic Society, 4*, 176.

Smith, G., & Engel, R. (1968). *Influence of a female model on perceived characteristics of an automobile.* Proceedings of the 76th Annual Convention of the American Psychological Association, *168*, 681–682.

Snyder, M. (1974). Self-monitoring of expressive behavior. *Journal of Personality and Social Psychology, 30*, 526–537.

Snyder, M., & Rothbart, M. (1971). Communicator attractiveness and opinion change. *Canadian Journal of Behavioral Science, 3*, 377–387.

Solomon, M. R., & Schopler, J. (1978). The relationship of physical attractiveness and punitiveness: Is the linearity assumption out of line? *Personality and Social Psychology Bulletin, 4*, 483–486.

Staats, A. W., & Staats, C. K. (1958). Attitudes established by classical conditioning. *Journal of Abnormal and Social Psychology, 57*, 37–40.

Stalling, R. B., & Friedman, L. (1981). External social cues and obesity: The influence of others' food evaluations on eating. *Obesity and Metabolism, 1*, 111–118.

Stalling, R. B., & Miller, A. (1981). Effect of fictitious food ratings on eating behavior of obese and normal people. *Obesity and Maturation, 1*, 105–110.

Staffieri, J. R. (1967). A study of social stereotype of body image in children. *Journal of Personality and Social Psychology, 7*, 101–104.

Staffieri, J. R. (1972). Body build and behavioral expectancies in young females. *Developmental Psychology, 6*, 125–127.

Stewart, J. E. (1980). Defendant's attractiveness as a factor in the outcome of criminal trials: An observational study. *Journal of Applied Social Psychology, 10*, 348–361.

Storck, J. T., & Sigall, H. (1979). Effect of a harm-doer's attractiveness and the victim's history of prior victimization on punishment of the harm-doer. *Personality and Social Psychology Bulletin, 5*, 344–347.

Stotland, E., & Canon, L. K. (1972). *Social psychology: A cognitive approach.* Philadelphia: Saunders Co.

Stroebe, W., Insko, C. A., Thompson, V. D., & Layton, B. D. (1971). Effects of physical attractiveness, attitude similarity, and sex on various aspects of interpersonal attraction. *Journal of Personality and Social Psychology*, 79–91.

Taylor, S. E., & Thompson, S. C. (1982). Stalking the elusive "vividness" effect. *Psychological Review, 89*, 155–181.

Van Dalen, D. B. (1975). Body image and the presidency: Abraham Lincoln. *Research Quarterly, 46*, 489–497.

Wagener, J. J., & Laird, J. D. (1980). The experimenter's foot-in-the-door: Self-perception, body weight, and volunteering. *Personality and Social Psychology Bulletin, 6*, 441–446.

Ward, C. D. (1967). Own height, sex and liking in the judgment of the heights of others. *Journal of Personality, 35*, 381–401.

Wells, W. D., & Siegel, B. (1961). Stereotyped somatotypes, *Psychological Reports, 8,* 77–78.

West, S. G., & Brown, T. J. (1975). Physical attractiveness, the severity of the emergency and helping: A field experiment and interpersonal simulation. *Journal of Experimental Social Psychology, 11,* 531–538.

Wilson, P. R. (1968). Perceptual distortion of height as a function of ascribed academic status. *Journal of Social Psychology, 74,* 97–102.

Yarrow, M. R., & Scott, P. M. (1972). Imitation of nurturant and nonnurturant models. *Journal of Personality and Social Psychology, 23,* 259–270.

Younger, J. C., & Pliner, P. (1976). Obese–normal differences in the self-monitoring of expressive behavior. *Journal of Research in Personality, 10,* 112–115.

Zanna, M. P., & Fazio, R. H. (1982). The attitude–behavior relation: Moving toward a third generation of research. In M. P. Zanna, E. T. Higgins, & C. P. Herman (Eds.), *Consistency in social behavior:* The Ontario symposium, (Vol. 2). Hillsdale, NJ: Lawrence Erlbaum Associates.

8 The Role of Olfaction in Social Perception and Behavior

John M. Levine
Donald H. McBurney
University of Pittsburgh

A bundle of myrrh is my wellbeloved unto me; he shall lie all night betwixt my breasts.
—The Song of Solomon (1: 13)

In the nineties the Western World was aroused by the elopement of the American 'Princess de Chimay' (nee Clara Ward of Nebraska) with the gypsy fiddler, Rigo . . . . she told a journalist that she was irresistibly attracted to this gypsy by his body odor.
—Brill (1932, p. 30)

I worked at a leading bank in Chicago for two years. My supervisor was an executive who made good money. . . . He smelled so terrible I used to go to my co-supervisor in order to avoid the skunk. He was in the elevator one day and the janitors were called to spray it with air freshener when he got off.
—Letter to Ann Landers, *Pittsburgh Post Gazette*, July 27, 1981

Among beliefs which profess to show that Negro and white people cannot intimately participate in the same civilization is the perennial one that Negroes have a smell extremely disagreeable to white people.
—Dollard (1957, pp. 379–380)

As these quotes suggest, odor has long been recognized as a powerful attractant and repellent in human relationships. Current interest in odor is dramatically demonstrated by the vast sums Americans spend on odor controllants, such as perfumes, after-shave lotions, deodorants, and air fresheners. According to Standard and Poor's Industry Surveys, 1980 sales of fragrances were approximately $1.6 billion. It is surprising, therefore, that odor has been almost totally neglected by social psychologists. Several possible reasons for this neglect can be cited. First, many social psychologists reside in North America, and, as Hall (1966) argues: "In the use of the olfactory apparatus Americans are culturally underdeveloped. The extensive use of deodorants and the suppression of odor in public places results in a land of olfactory blandness and sameness that would be difficult to duplicate anywhere else in the world" (p. 45). According to Hall, then, American investigators' impoverished olfactory environment may cause them to overlook smell as a determinant of behavior. Americans' rigorous control of odor can be thought of in control system terms. Smell may function like thermoregulation, in which very small deviations from an optimum level produce immediate and strong efforts to regain this level. A control system that shows high gain for small deviations produces a constant environment. Therefore, we may pay little attention to smell, as to thermoregulation, *not* because smell is unimportant, but because smell is so important and well regulated that we typically do not encounter substantial deviations from an optimum level. A second, and perhaps related, reason for our inattention to human odor has a linguistic basis. Although, as Moskowitz and Gerbers (1974) report, English dictionaries contain several hundred entries applicable to odor quality, our language lacks abstract verbal categories for odors (Lawless & Cain, 1975). The absence of such verbal categories, particularly if it reflects the absence of natural perceptual categories, inhibits our ability to study odor scientifically. Third, because human odors have strong hygienic and sexual connotations, behavioral scientists, like laypersons, may feel that discussion of such odors is inappropriate. Finally, even when the potential role of odor in human behavior is recognized, social psychologists may feel that odor is an obvious and trivial variable that does not warrant serious investigation. In regard to this last point, it is perhaps worth noting that until recently similar arguments were made about the role of physical attractiveness.

The goal of this chapter is to review research from several disciplines regarding the role of odor in human social perception and behavior. The chapter is organized into three major sections. Section I contains a brief overview of anatomical and phylogenetic aspects of the sense of smell. Included in this section is a discussion of the relationship of smell to other senses. In Section II, we review the available work on odor and human social perception and behavior. Finally, Section III attempts to link material in earlier sections to social psychological theory, suggests questions for further investigation, and mentions methodological issues that the social psychologists interested in odor research should keep in mind.

I. SMELL AMONG THE SENSES

Anatomical and Phylogenetic Considerations

Smell, which was probably the first distance sense to evolve (Sarnat & Netsky, 1974), has a number of primitive characteristics. For example, the olfactory receptor gives rise to the first-order neuron without a synapse, and olfactory nerve fibers are among the smallest and slowest conducting in the body. In addition, the prepyriform cortex, to which the olfactory system directly communicates, is one of the most primitive cortical areas. Finally, the olfactory system has such pronounced input into the limbic system, which is concerned with motivation and memorial functions, that the limbic structures were at one time called the rhinencephalon, or smell brain. This designation is no longer used because it is now realized that other senses influence the limbic system at least as readily as does smell.

The proportion of the brain devoted to olfaction decreases dramatically in higher organisms. Whereas the olfactory bulbs and their projections constitute a major fraction of the brain of reptiles, in more advanced forms the olfactory structures become progressively dwarfed by newer structures. However, the absolute, or even relative, size of the olfactory structures is not a foolproof indicator of the importance of olfaction to an animal. The brain of the bloodhound resembles that of the human considerably more than it does that of the alligator. Because the olfactory system comprises a much smaller fraction of the human brain than that of other animals and because humans are less sensitive to odors than are many other creatures, man is known as a microsmatic rather than a macrosmatic animal. However, it is not correct to conclude from this designation that man has a poor sense of smell. If we suffer by comparison with other animals, it is because they are so incredibly keen. It is true that the dog's olfactory system is about 100 times more sensitive than that of humans, but this is because the dog has about 100 times as many receptors (Moulton, 1977). This difference of two orders of magnitude is not particularly great as sensory thresholds go, particularly considering the variability of measured thresholds for smell (see McBurney, 1984). It is estimated that it takes only one odorous molecule to stimulate a single olfactory receptor in man, dog, or silkworm moth (Moulton, 1977). In fact, the human nose rivals the best physical systems for the detection of odorous molecules. It would seem, therefore, that the widespread belief in the dullness of the human nose is due to a pervasive myth rather than to scientific evidence.

It is well known that olfaction plays an important, and in some cases crucial, role in the social behavior of many animals. Olfaction is important in such diverse behaviors as individual, gender, group, and species recognition; territory and breeding-space marking; dominance, aggression, and alarms; mate selection, reproductive status, courtship, and mating; and maternal-infant relations (Mykytowycz, 1970, 1977; Stoddart, 1980). A vast literature exists on chemical communication in animals, and no attempt is made to review it in detail. The interested reader is referred to one of the many excellent reviews on this subject (e.g., Birch, 1974; Doty, 1976; Muller-Schwarze & Mozell, 1977; Rogel, 1978).

Two general points about animal social olfaction, however, deserve mention here. First, the concept of pheromones has had considerable influence on animal research. Pheromones were originally defined as "substances which are secreted to the outside by an individual and received by a second individual of the same species, in which they release a specific reaction, for example, a definite behaviour or a developmental process" (Karlson & Luscher, 1959, p. 55). The pheromone concept was developed to deal with chemical communication in insects, and many insect pheromones have in fact been isolated (see Cameron, 1981, for an interesting report of human contamination with a synthetic insect pheromone). The success of the pheromone concept in insect work, together with the well-known role of olfaction in mammalian social behavior, led ineluctably to the application of the term pheromone to mammals and to speculation about the existence of human pheromones (e.g., Comfort, 1971; Keverne, 1977). However, investigators have come to appreciate that the role of chemical communication in mammals is so subject to learning and context effects that the notion of pheromones, which works well for insects and simpler animals, is stretched beyond usefulness in the case of mammals (Beauchamp, Doty, Moulton, & Mugford, 1976, 1979; Engen, 1982; but see also Katz & Shorey, 1979, and Rutowski, 1981). In fact, no mammalian pheromone has yet been identified. Moreover, the lure of the human pheromone is such that it has directed the attention of investigators primarily to sexual behavior. It is true that in some species sexual behavior is the principal form of social behavior. In man, however, sex is more *primus inter pares*. Therefore, we would like to take a less adolescent approach to human social olfaction, looking beyond sex without overlooking it.

A second point about the role of olfaction in mammalian social behavior is that most behaviors, including reproduction, are under multisensory control (Mykytowycz, 1977). Partly because of the pheromone concept but more because of the behavioristic approach of many students of animal behavior, investigators tend to view olfaction as controlling behavior in a more or less reflexive manner. Many studies have approached olfactory control by attempting to determine what behavioral changes are produced by rendering an animal anosmic. Although in certain species (e.g., hamsters) an anosmic male will not copulate, most species, particularly the higher primates, are not so dependent on a single modality. For many species it seems to be as it was for Hornbostel, who said, "It matters little through which sense I realize that in the dark I have blundered into a pig-sty" (cited by Marks, 1978, p. 5).

Relationship of Smell to Other Senses

Olfaction is certainly the most hedonically potent of the senses. There is no other sense that elicits such a wide range of emotional reactions to simple stimuli that have not acquired meaning on the basis of conditioning. Thus, it is most implausible to imagine a hue or a tone of moderate intensity that could empty a building of occupants as hydrogen sulfide can or could command the high prices of some perfumes. The hedonic variability of odors is demonstrated by research indicating a pleasantness range of 125/1 between common odorants (Engen & McBurney, 1964).

Another significant aspect of olfaction is that it is both an interoceptive and an exteroceptive sense. Smell is the major component of the "taste" of foods, based on the refluxing of odors into the nasal cavity from the mouth. At the same time, smells are often localized in the environment rather than in the mouth or head, as when we smell an appetizing food or a "stinky" person. This dual function of smell, noted many years ago by Herrick (1933), leads to several intriguing ideas about smell. As an interoceptor, smell plays a crucial role in food preferences, including conditioned flavor aversions (Garcia, Hankins, & Rusiniak, 1974). The potency of food preferences can be glimpsed by recalling the central role of food in both religious and secular ceremonies. Moreover, it has been noted that food customs are the last distinctive habit to be lost when an ethnic group is assimilated into a new culture (Rozin, 1976).

Functioning as an exteroceptor, olfaction lacks the ability to localize the source of its stimulus. For this reason, Herrick speculated that olfaction recruits other exteroceptors to localize and act on the information provided by smell. Herrick proposed that olfaction serves two major functions: (1) activating the cortex so that other sensory information can be used to initiate action and (2) setting emotional tone. Herrick's ideas suggest the importance of perfumes, familiar foods, cleaning products, and other sources of odor in making a house feel like a home.

Closely related to these notions is evidence that olfactory input and experience are not well connected to the verbal system. It has been noted many times that we lack abstract words to describe olfactory quality; instead, smells are labeled in terms of olfactory sources (see Table 8.1). Further, odor quality has resisted all attempts at systematic classification. Of the many systems of classifying odors that have been proposed over the centuries (McBurney, 1984), none has ever done much for the field except decorate textbooks. Researchers disagree regarding how many categories exist and the placement of particular stimuli into categories. It has not proven possible to identify "primary" odors that can be used to generate all other odor qualities, as has been done for color vision. It appears now that no method of classifying odors into a few dimensions or categories will be possible; instead, there seems to be a multitude of odor experiences, all more or less distinct from one another. This is what one might expect

TABLE 8.1
Descriptors for Characterizing Odors

Fragrant	Oily, fatty	Aromatic	Fruity (citrus)
Sweaty	Like mothballs	Meaty (cooked)	Fruity (other)
Almond-like	Like gasoline, solvent	Sickening	Putrid, Foul, Decayed
Burnt, smoky	Cooked vegetables	Musty, earthy, moldy	Woody, resinous
Herbal, green, cut grass	Sweet	Sharp, pungent, acid	Musk-like
Etherish, anesthetic	Fishy	Camphor-like	Soapy
Sour, acid, vinegar	Spicy	Light	Garlic, onion
Like blood, raw meat	Paint-like	Heavy	Animal
Dry, powdery	Rancid	Cool, cooling	Vanilla-like
Like ammonia	Minty, peppermint	Warm	Fecal (like manure)
Disinfectant, carbolic	Sulfidic	Metallic	Floral
Perfumery	Yeasty	Eucalyptus	Strawberry-like
Malty	Cheesy	Buttery	Stale
Cinnamon-like	Honey-like	Like burnt paper	Cork-like
Popcorn	Anise (licorice)	Cologne	Lavender
Incense	Turpentine (pine oil)	Caraway	Cat-urine-like
Melony (cantaloupe, honey-dew)	Fresh green vegetables	Orange (fruit)	Bark-like, birch bark
Tar-like	Medicinal	Household gas	Rose-like
Peanut butter	Celery	Leather-like	Nutty (walnut etc.)
Violets	Burnt candle	Pear (fruit)	Fried fat
Tea-leaves	Mushroom-like	Stale tobacco smoke	Wet paper-like
Wet wool, wet dog	Pineapple (fruit)	Raw cucumber	Coffee-like
Chalky	Fresh cigarette smoke	Raw potato	Peach (fruit)
Mouse-like	Laurel leaves	Beery (beer-like)	Oak wood, cognac
Pepper-like	Scorched milk	Cedarwood-like	Grapefruit
Bean-like	Sewer odor	Coconut-like	Grape-juice-like
Banana-like	Sooty	Rope-like	Eggy (fresh eggs)
Burnt rubber	Crushed weeds	Seminal (sperm-like)	Bitter
Geranium leaves	Rubbery (new rubber)	Like cleaning fluid (carbona)	Cadaverous (like dead animal)
Urine-like	Bakery (fresh bread)	Cardboard-like	Raisin-like
Lemon (fruit)	Seasoning (meat)	Crushed grass	Maple (as in syrup)
Dirty linen-like	Apple (fruit)	Chocolate	Hay
Kippery (smoked fish)	Soupy	Molasses	Kerosene
Caramel	Grainy (as grain)	Sauerkraut-like	Clove-like

From Dravnieks (1975)

for a sensory system that is used largely to identify individual objects. The olfactory system seems to be designed to answer two main questions: What is that odor, and do I like it or not?

In a related vein, there is considerable evidence that although hundreds of different olfactory experiences can be discriminated, it is difficult to name the stimuli for these experiences. Early work found that only a few smells could reliably be named in an experimental situation (Engen & Pfaffmann, 1960). Later research showed that many more stimuli could be named if care was taken to use highly familiar stimuli, for which subjects already knew the names (Cain, 1979; Desor & Beauchamp, 1974; Rabin & Cain, 1984). Recognition tests demonstrate that something like the tip-of-the-tongue phenomenon occurs for smell. Subjects experiencing the tip-of-the-nose phenomenon can provide substantial information about an odor, such as its likely source or similar odors, but cannot name the odor (Lawless & Engen, 1977). Likewise, subjects have more difficulty associating odors than shapes or words to other stimuli in paired-associate tasks (Davis, 1975, 1977). When odors are used as stimuli in paired-associate learning, apparently the odor must elicit the name of the odor, which then is used to recall the response word, or recall does not take place (Eich, 1978). The difficulty of associating odors with words renders quite puzzling the reputedly powerful capacity of odors to resurrect dormant memory. Although some experiments suggest that memory for odor does not decay as rapidly as memory for other stimuli (Engen & Ross, 1973; Lawless & Cain, 1975), other experiments cast doubt on the generality of this finding (Davis, 1977). Our own suspicion is that this so-called Proust effect is overstated. Certainly pictures and recorded voices, as well as odors, often bring back long-dormant memories (Rubin, Groth, & Goldsmith, 1982). Perhaps we are not accustomed to using olfaction as a memorial cue and hence are surprised when it functions in this way. Or, perhaps the memories that odors arouse tend to be more emotionally laden than other memories (Lawless & Engen, 1977), and this is what surprises us.

Cain (1980) uses the term preverbal identification to refer to the way we respond to odors when we do not know their names. He points out that even when we cannot name an odor, we still can behave appropriately to it: We would not eat shoe polish or drink perfume. People may respond to odors much the way a dog responds to its olfactory world, that is, without benefit of verbal labels. The tenuous connection between olfaction and the verbal system suggests that odors influence our behavior on a less conscious level than do other sensory stimuli. Psychologists are once again entertaining the idea of nonconscious determinants of behavior, and olfaction may be a prime example of a nonverbalizable cause of behavior.

Odor is also different from the other senses in that an olfactory stimulus cannot be turned on and off quickly. Smells, unlike visual and auditory cues, cannot be "flashed," explaining why theaters have not successfully exploited "smell tracks" for movies. That smells, once produced, linger in the environment and are often difficult to localize engenders interesting interpersonal problems. Consider the following: You enter an elevator on the second floor to find that it is occupied only by a vile-smelling person, who gets off on the third floor. When another person joins you on the fourth floor, how do you indicate to him or her that you are not the source of the odor? For that matter, how do you know that the person who was on the elevator when you entered was the source of the odor and was not in the same boat you are? These kinds of problems may explain why we are so careful to control our odors. Even a relatively sudden and uncontrollable odor, such as flatus, causes us to think of the offender as a lout. We more readily excuse a word that slips out than an odor.

Finally, we might briefly mention the issue of sex differences in smell. It is often asserted that, compared to men, women are more sensitive to certain odors, particularly those of biological significance. However, sex differences also have been reported for odors that are not biologically significant, and women are more sensitive than men in a number of other sensory modalities, including taste, audition, and vision (Doty, Snyder, Huggins, & Lowry, 1981). Regarding the impact of the menstrual cycle on women's olfactory sensitivity, cyclical differences in odor perception do seem to exist (Parlee, 1983) but apparently are not related to major fluctuations in primary gonadal steroids or in pituitary gonadotropins, because they occur in women who are taking birth control pills (Doty et al., 1981). In any case, differences in olfactory thresholds between the sexes and as a function of menstrual phase in women are rather small and variable. They are close to the noise level of experimental measurement and thus should not be viewed as having much behavioral significance.

II. ODOR AND HUMAN SOCIAL PERCEPTION AND BEHAVIOR

Over the years, many authors have discussed the role of odor in human social perception and behavior. Leaving aside popular accounts (e.g., Hassett, 1978; Hopson, 1979; Winter, 1976), we are nonetheless left with a number of interesting contributions. Some of these are primarily speculative, whereas others are based on empirical research.

General Discussions of Odor and Human Behavior

Wiener (1966) provides an extensive discussion of human body odors. He conceptualizes such odors as "external chemical messengers" (ECM) through which individuals communicate with one another. In regard to emission of ECM, Wiener mentions the sensitivity of other animals (dogs, mosquitoes) to human odor and speculates about various sources of such odor, including the skin, urine, breath, saliva, and tears. Concerning reception of ECM, Wiener discusses subconscious or nonconscious responses to olfactory stimuli, likening these to responses to subtle nonverbal and paralinguistic cues (see also Wiener, 1979).

Adopting a sociological perspective, Largey and Watson (1972) note that odor has generally been ignored as a determinant of human interaction. However, these authors argue that odors are often related to moral status, in that disliked persons or groups are presumed to have offensive odor whereas the morally pure are thought to have a characteristically pleasant odor. In discussing impression management through odors, Largey and Watson distinguish between deodorizing (i.e., eliminating socially discreditable odors) and odorizing (i.e., adding accreditable odors). In the latter case, a distinction is made between perfuming one's body and odorizing one's environment (e.g., through use of incense in religious ceremonies).

Several discussions of human odor deal with sexuality. In this regard, Ellis (1928) mentions the power of smell to evoke emotionally laden memories, odor differences between racial and ethnic groups, the alleged relationship between the nose and genitalia, use of perfumes, and sexual associations to body odor. Concerning the latter issue, Ellis observes that body odor may be attractive *only* when an individual is already aroused sexually. An identical odor presented to an unaroused person may be quite repugnant. Ellis (1928) suggests that "in the oft-quoted case of the Austrian peasant who found that he was aided in seducing young women by dancing with them and then wiping their faces with a handkerchief he had kept in his armpit, we may doubtless regard the preliminary excitement of the dance as an essential factor in the influence produced" (p. 84). Ellis's paper contains several literary references to olfaction and sexual behavior. A more recent review of olfactory eroticism in literature has been offered by Kiell (1976). In this paper, Kiell mentions literary allusions to odor sensitivity (e.g., Hemingway, Orwell, Wilde), odor memory (e.g., Proust, Westcott), and the relationship of odor to sexual fantasy and behavior (e.g., Durrell, Fiedler, Joyce, Updike). Kiell uses psychoanalytic theory to interpret his literary examples, and this framework has also been employed by others to analyze the relationship between odor and sexuality. For example, Bieber (1959) discusses olfactory dreams involving incestuous objects and proposes an olfactory theory of heterosexual responsivity and the Oedipus complex. The historically minded reader will also recall Wilhelm Fliess, a close friend of Freud's, who argued for the existence of "Genitalstellen" (genital spots) in the nose, which he treated with cocaine and surgery to alleviate painful menstruation and neurotic symptoms (Sulloway, 1979). More extensive discussions of psychoanalytic thinking on odor and sexuality are presented by Kalogerakis (1963) and Brody (1975).

Psychoanalytic interpretations of olfaction and sexual behavior typically touch upon aspects of mental illness (e.g., olfactory fetishes and hallucinations). The most extensive discussion of this topic is Brill's (1932) paper, entitled "The sense of smell in the neuroses and psychoses." Brill discusses a number of interesting cases in which smell is alleged to have played an important role. He mentions, for example, a female patient who was extremely sensitive to odors and would not enter a bathroom until it had been vacant for at least an hour. According to Brill (1932), this woman "was in constant struggle with her family because she insisted on knowing when they defecated, and as she had two older brothers and a younger sister she was kept quite busy" (p. 21). Perhaps Brill's most dramatic case involved a man who entered treatment because of his desire to hug and kiss the bodies of dead women. The patient seems to have retained some contact with reality, however, because: "as the smell of a human body would attract too much attention and subsequent discovery, he finally decided to be satisfied with a dead horse. He at first knew no particular reason for selecting a horse; he thought 'The bigger the animal the more carrion; but where can one get a dead whale or elephant?' " (p. 24). The patient's family attempted to alleviate his unnatural cravings, his mother by giving him a dead chicken and his sister by offering herself sexually, but neither of these innovative therapies was successful. Space limitations preclude detailed discussion of other intriguing cases in which smell was an etiological factor, such as the unfortunate patient who was afflicted by both the constant fear that his fly was open and the sensation that one shoe was tighter than the other.

Response to Abnormal Body Odors

As Sastry, Buck, Janak, Dressler, and Preti (1980) point out, humans excrete thousands of compounds, many of which are volatile. These chemicals have a number of sources, including the scalp, breath, oral cavity, axillae, urine, genitals, and feet, and are influenced by both organismic factors (e.g., gender, race, health, reproductive state, emotional state) and environmental factors (e.g., diet, drugs, hygiene and perfume products) (Doty, 1981). It is not surprising then that smell has been used as a diagnostic instrument in detection of disease (e.g., Hayden, 1980; Liddell, 1976; Mace, Goodman, Centerwall, & Chinnock, 1976; Sastry et al., 1980).

Hayden (1980) lists several sources of "medically important" odors, including breath, urine, skin, sputum, vomitus, stool, vaginal discharge, pus, and cerumen (earwax). He also mentions a number of disorders that can be diagnosed on the basis of odor, including typhoid (freshly baked brown bread), rubella (freshly plucked feathers), scurvy (putrid), pellagra (sour or musty bread), diabetes (acetone), scrofula (stale beer), phenylketonuria (musty, mousy), and schizophrenia (unpleasant, pungent). As this list suggests, olfactory diagnosis is hindered by the ambiguity of some of the odor labels, which in turn is attributable to our poor vocabulary for categorizing odors. In addition, as Hayden notes, patients may sometimes camouflage diagnostically relevant odors by using perfumes, breath lozenges, etc. Happily, however, such camouflage techniques themselves often provide the alert clinician with useful diagnostic information, as when heavy use of mouthwash or breath lozenges suggests alcoholism ("the Cloret sign") or when excessive use of perfume or after-shave lotion indicates either anosmia or "personality disturbance with poor self-image" (Hayden, 1980, p. 115).

In order to facilitate olfactory diagnosis, Hayden suggests use of "scratch and smell" strips that contain medically important odors, and Mulder (1971) suggests that other species (dogs, eels) be used to detect human disease by smell. It should also be noted that various techniques developed to assess human odors mights be employed in medical diagnosis (e.g., Distelheim & Dravnieks, 1973; Dravnieks, 1975; Sastry et al., 1980). See Fig. 8.1 for procedures to collect odors for sensory and analytical (e.g., gas chromatography) evaluation.

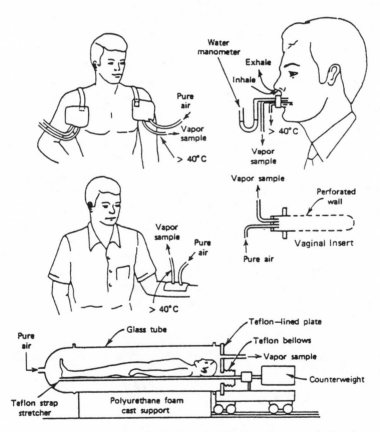

FIG 8.1.   Arrangements for vapor channeling from humans to a collecting device. (From Dravnieks, 1975.)

Response to Natural Body Odors

Skin Odor

A good deal of research has been devoted to analyzing odors arising from skin secretions. As Doty (1981) notes, there are three primary sources of odorous skin secretions: sebaceous glands, eccrine sweat glands, and apocrine sweat glands. Sebaceous glands, although located in various parts of the body, are largest and most numerous in the scalp, forehead, face, and anogenital region. These glands secrete sebum, which serves as an emollient for skin and perhaps also as a bacteriostatic and fungistatic agent. According to Montagna and Parakkal (1974), however, "the real function of sebum seems to be that of a pheromone, for even fresh sterile sebum has a distinctive odor not to be confused with that of the axillary glands" (p. 321).

Eccrine sweat glands are distributed over almost the entire body, and the number of these glands varies for different racial and ethnic groups (Montagna & Parakkal, 1974). Eccrine glands, which are primarily concerned with regulation of body temperature through evaporation of moisture, secrete a profuse watery fluid that is generally considered to be odorless. However, as Doty (1981) indicates, certain dietary factors (e.g., garlic) and metabolic diseases can influence the odor of eccrine sweat. Moreover, as discussed later, eccrine sweat may contribute to odorous properties of apocrine sweat.

Apocrine sweat glands are typically assumed to be the major source of human body odor. These glands are not dispersed over the body as are eccrine glands but instead are concentrated primarily in the axillae (armpits), anogenital region, nipples, ears, and scalp. Apocrine secretion is a viscous fluid, much less copious than eccrine secretion, that does not have a thermoregulatory function in humans. According to Doty (1981), apocrine secretions are particularly relevant to chemical communication because apocrine odor is often judged to be unpleasant in ordinary social situations and because apocrine glands (1) begin functioning at puberty and cease functioning at menopause, (2) are larger (but somewhat less numerous) in males than in females, (3) differ in size and number between various races, (4) secrete maximally during excitement and stress, and (5) produce steroids similar to those that influence behavioral and endocrine phenomena in other species.

As mentioned earlier, apocrine glands are quite prevalent in the axillary region, and the vast bulk of research on skin odor has involved this part of the body. As Montagna and Parakkal (1974) state, "considered as an odor-producing surface, the human axilla is a perfectly tailored organ. Small amounts of viscid material are secreted by the apocrine glands and dissolve in the watery eccrine sweat which spreads them over a wide surface. Axillary hairs harbor microorganisms that attack the proper substances and the whole area is kept almost constantly moist" (p. 357). Using somewhat more colloquial language, Klein (1980) refers to the axillae as "a kind of bacteria resort" (p. 20). Research indicates that fresh apocrine sweat from the axillae has no odor and that the unpleasant odor of "old" axillary sweat is due to bacterial action (Labows, McGinley, & Kligman, 1982; Shelley, Hurley, & Nicholls, 1953). In addition, as suggested by Montagna and Parakkal, axillary hairs serve as a collecting site for axillary secretion and thereby promote bacterial decomposition of this material (Shelley et al., 1953).

Cosmetic chemists have contributed greatly to our understanding of axillary odor. These researchers have developed a number of techniques for assessing axillary odor, including both sensory and analytical procedures. Each technique has its own strengths and weaknesses. For example, in discussing a sensory technique in which judges smell the axillae of stimulus persons, Whitehouse and Carter (1968) note that "evaluation of underarm odor is not for the fastidious or squeamish, and it certainly does not have the esthetic appeal of perfume or brandy smelling" (p. 68). The interested reader can consult a large literature on measurement of axillary odor and evaluation of products designed to reduce axillary secretion and odor (e.g., Bakiewicz, 1973; Dravnieks, Krotoszynski, Lieb, & Jungermann, 1968; Jungermann, 1974; Kennon, 1965; Klein, 1980; Quatrale, Stoner, & Felger, 1977; Shelley et al., 1953; Sturm, 1979; Uttley, 1972; Whitehouse & Carter, 1968).

Having presented a brief overview of the sources of skin odor, let us now examine several empirical investigations of people's reactions to such odor. With the exception of a single study on hand odor (Wallace, 1977), all the research deals with axillary odor. Most axillary odor research has involved person discrimination; recent effort has also been made to assess the role of axillary odor in menstrual synchrony.

Axillary Odor. In the first published experiment on person discrimination via axillary odor, Russell (1976) had male and female college students wear T-shirts for 24 hours (during the preceding 24 hours, subjects had washed only with clear water and had avoided perfume and deodorant). Subjects then smelled the armpit regions of three shirts (their own, a strange male's, a strange female's) and attempted to discriminate (1) their own shirt from the other two shirts and (2) the male's shirt from the female's shirt. Results indicated that 75% of subjects performed correctly on each task. Russell (1976) also reported, on the basis of informal questioning after the odor test, that "the male odours were usually characterised as musky and the female odours as sweet" (p. 521).

In another study investigating response to axillary odor, McBurney, Levine, and Cavanaugh (1977) asked male graduate students to shower and then to wear a T-shirt for 48 hours. During this period, subjects were told not to bathe or use deodorant and to engage in at least one hour of strenuous physical exercise. Afterwards, odor donors rated the unpleasantness of each shirt, using a magnitude estimation procedure, and attempted to identify their own odor. In addition, male and female undergraduates rated the odors for unpleasantness and evaluated odor donors using bipolar adjective scales. Results indicated a high degree of agreement among subjects' (graduates' and undergraduates') rankings of the unpleasantness of various odors. Correlations demonstrated that odor unpleasantness was generally associated with socially undesirable traits (e.g., dirty, unfriendly, unintelligent). However, odor unpleasantness was also associated with several positive "masculine" characteristics (e.g., active, strong, athletic). Finally, odor donors typically rated their own odor as more pleasant than did other raters and demonstrated marginal ability to detect their own odor. Subjects' lower ability to recognize their own odor in this study than in the Russell study may have been due to the difficulty of the discrimination task; that is, whereas subjects in the McBurney et al. study had to select their own odor from among 11 odors, subjects in the Russell study only had to choose from among three odors.

Porter and Moore (1981) reported two experiments in which family members were asked to identify children's odors. In both studies, children (3-to 8-years-of-age) wore a T-shirt to bed for three consecutive nights; during this period, children were not allowed to use scented soaps or perfumes. Experiment 1 indicated that both siblings and mothers of stimulus children were quite accurate in identifying their kin in a two-choice discrimination test (which paired a shirt worn by a family member with a shirt worn by an unfamiliar child of approximately the same age). Experiment 2 revealed that mothers and fathers were quite accurate in discriminating the odors produced by two of their own children.

More recent work by Porter, Cernoch, and McLaughlin (1983) and Russell, Mendelson, and Peeke (1983) indicates that mothers can recognize their neonate on the basis of odor. In one study, Porter et al. asked mothers, who had been exposed to their newborn infant for approximately 24 hours during the first 6 days of the baby's life, to identify the child in a two-choice discrimination task. Each mother was presented with two buckets, one containing a shirt worn by her own child and the other containing a shirt worn by an unfamiliar comparison child, and was asked to identify her child's shirt on the basis of odor. Sixteen of 20 mothers correctly identified the shirt worn by their own baby. In a second study, Porter et al. asked mothers, who had been exposed to their infant for only about 2 hours, to identify the child's shirt in a two-choice discrimiantion task. In this case, 13 of 17 mothers correctly identified their baby's shirt. Russell et al. (1983) asked blindfolded mothers to discriminate their own infant from two other babies on the basis of smell alone (in this study, mothers sniffed children rather than shirts). At both 6 hours and 48 hours postpartum, mothers demonstrated a statistically significant ability to identify their offspring (correct choices were made by 61% of mothers in the 6-hour group and 58% of mothers in the 48-hour group). It is important to note that mothers and infants in the 6-hour group had contact for only one-half hour immediately after the child's birth. Interestingly, only 37% of fathers who were tested 24 to 48 hours postpartum were able to identify their own baby.

Schleidt and her colleagues have conducted three experiments investigating person recognition via axillary odor. In the first, Hold and Schleidt (1977) had married couples wear cotton undershirts for seven consecutive nights. Subjects were given children's soap to wash with and were asked to refrain from using deodorant and perfume. After the odor samples were collected, subjects were asked to select their own and their partner's odor, to discriminate male from female odors, and to evaluate odors as pleasant, indifferent, and unpleasant. Results indicated that approximately 33% of the subjects correctly identified their own odor. (As in the McBurney et al. study, subjects had a relatively difficult discrimination task, in that they had to select their own odor from among 10 odors.) In addition, approximately 33% of the subjects correctly identified their partner's odor. On both recognition tasks, females were substantially more accurate than males. Regarding affective reactions to one's partner's odor, both males and females generally perceived their partner's odor as pleasant. Moreover, whereas women tended to regard their own odor as pleasant, men perceived their own odor as indifferent or unpleasant. Concerning reactions to strangers' odors, approximately 33% of the subjects correctly distinguished male from female odors; again, females were more accurate perceivers. Participants reported assuming that strong/pungent/unpleasant odors were male. Finally, both males and females judged male odors as more unpleasant than female odors.

In a follow-up study, Schleidt (1980) replicated her earlier experiment with one potentially important change: Instead of prescribing subjects' hygienic practices (e.g., a shower before the experiment, no deodorant or perfume during the experiment), subjects were allowed to follow their normal hygienic practices during the seven nights on which they wore undershirts. Compared to subjects in the earlier study, those in the second study showed approximately the same ability to detect their own and their partner's odor. Regarding affective reactions, subjects in the second study, like those in the first, judged their partner's odor as basically pleasant. Women continued to regard their own odor as predominantly pleasant in the second study, and now men also perceived their own odor as pleasant. Concerning reactions to strangers' odors, subjects in the second study were quite poor in distinguishing male from female odors. As before, however, females were more accurate perceivers than were males. Finally, in the second study both male and female odors were judged as predominantly pleasant and, overall, subjects made more indifferent and fewer unpleasant choices. Schleidt (1980) interpreted these findings as suggesting that people minimize personal odor through hygienic practices and thereby suppress the distinction between male and female odor.

In a third experiment, Schleidt, Hold, and Attili (1981) conducted a cross-cultural investigation of response to axillary odor, comparing a "noncontact" culture (Japan), a "contact" culture (Italy), and their original German data (Hold & Schleidt, 1977). Procedures were essentially identical to those in the original study. In regard to recognizing one's own and one's partner's odor, Japanese subjects were somewhat less accurate (23%) than were Germans (32%) and Italians (34%). In all three cultures, however, females were more accurate than were males. Regarding evaluation of one's partner's odor, men in all three cultures judged their partner's odor as predominantly pleasant, whereas partner odor was evaluated as pleasant by German women and as unpleasant by Japanese and Italian women. Across all cultures, women regarded their own odor as pleasant and men regarded theirs as unpleasant. Rather sizable cultural differences were obtained in ability to discriminate male from female odor: Germany (32%), Italy (20%), Japan (64%). In all cases, however, women were more accurate perceivers than were men. Finally, in all ethnic groups both men and women judged male odors as more unpleasant than female odors, and Japanese subjects tended to classify all odors as less pleasant than did German and Italian subjects. Taken as a whole, these findings suggest substantial crosscultural similarities in reaction to axillary odor (see also Schleidt & Hold, 1982). Moreover, as Doty (1981) suggests, at least some of the obtained cultural differences may reflect biases in responding to a taboo subject.

The last studies to be discussed regarding person discrimination on the basis of axillary odor were conducted by Doty and his colleagues. Doty argues that the ability to discriminate between axillary odors of males and females may be due to subjects' tendency to attribute stronger and less pleasant odors to male donors than to female donors (Doty, 1977, 1981; Doty, Orndorff, Leyden, & Kligman, 1978). This hypothesis is plausible given existing evidence that (1) males have larger apocrine glands than do females, (2) apocrine gland size correlates positively with body odor intensity, and (3) males in the U.S. are less likely than females to shave their axillae and hence males' axillary region provides a better environment for odor production.

Doty et al. (1978) conducted four experiments in which male and female odor donors wore a gauze pad taped under their armpit for several hours. Donors were instructed not to use deodorant or perfume for a week prior to the study and not to bathe for 24 hours just before the study; female donors shaved their axillae regularly. Subjects, who were not themselves donors, evaluated the intensity and pleasantness of the odorous pads, using a magnitude estimation procedure. In three studies, subjects were also asked to discriminate male from female odors. Results indicated that (1) both male and female subjects judged male odors to be stronger and more unpleasant than female odors, (2) intensity and pleasantness judgments were negatively related, and (3) the stronger and more unpleasant an odor, the more likely the odor was attributed to a male donor by both male and female subjects. Doty et al. (1978) reported that they obtained similar findings in an unpublished in vivo experiment in which blindfolded subjects smelled axillae directly. Doty (1981) concludes that: "these results suggest that the ability of humans to detect gender from axillary odors may depend on quantitative, rather than qualitative, aspects of the odors, and that strong odors are judged as having come from males and weak odors as having come from females, regardless of the true sex of the odor donor. Thus, it is likely that correct gender assignments from axillary odors are probabilistic, analogous to the estimation of gender from parameters such as height or weight'' (p. 356).

In addition to studies of person recognition via axillary odor, research has also been conducted on the role of axillary odor in menstrual synchrony. McClintock (1971) first documented menstrual synchrony in a study of the relationship between the amount of time that students at a women's college spent together and the similarity in onset of their menstrual cycles. McClintock found that, over several months, women who spent a lot of time together showed more menstrual synchrony than did random pairs of women. Efforts were made to rule out a number of factors other than time spent together that might account for the synchrony (e.g., available food, residence area, common light-dark cycles, awareness of others' menstrual periods). Graham and McGrew (1980) and Quadagno, Shubeita, Deck, and Francoeur (1981) recently replicated McClintock's findings at coeducational colleges. Although interesting, none of these studies clarifies the factor(s) responsible for menstrual synchrony (see McClintock, 1983, for a discussion of the role of pheromones in synchronizing ovarian and birth cycles). Suggestive evidence for the role of axillary odor has been provided by Russell, Switz, and Thompson (1980). In this study, axillary odor was collected from a woman who had a history of regular menstrual cycles and the ability to ''drive'' the cycle of another woman and who did not wash or shave her axillae or use deodorant during the odor collection period. Three times a week for 4 months the axillary odor (on impregnated gauze pads) was rubbed on the upper lips of several women. Subjects in a control condition were rubbed with alcohol-soaked pads. Results indicated a marked synchrony in the onset of menstruation between experimental subjects and the odor donor, whereas control subjects showed no evidence of synchrony. These findings must be viewed with caution, however, due to a number of methodological limitations of the study (Doty, 1981).

Hand Odor. The final study to be discussed in this section concerns hand, rather than axillary, odor. Like much of the aforementioned research on reaction to axillary odor, Wallace's (1977) paper on hand odor examines gender discrimination. In this experiment, blindfolded male and female subjects smelled the palms of male and female odor donors, using an olfactorium (a glass box into which donors placed their hands and subjects placed their heads). Donors prepared their palms by avoiding contact with odorous substances for 2 days prior to the study and by rinsing their hands in distilled water, ethanol, and acetone on the evening of the study. In addition, donors wore a plastic glove for 15 minutes prior to testing, which induced copious eccrine perspiration. In the first study, subjects were asked to discriminate between the odors of two males, two females, and a male and a female. More than 50% of the subjects discriminated correctly on 21 or more of the 30 trials for each task. Subjects were most accurate on the male-female discrimination, and women were generally more accurate perceivers than were men. In the second study, designed to assess the impact of genetic and dietary factors on palm odor, female subjects were asked to discriminate between two unrelated females who had been on the same diet for 3 days, identical female twins on the same diet, two female siblings on the same diet, and identical female twins on different diets. When different diets were compared, one donor ate bland foods and the other ate foods containing garlic, onions, and spices. Results indicated that unrelated donors on the same diet were easier to discriminate than were members of any related pair on the same diet. In addition, twins on different diets were easier to discriminate than were twins on the same diet.

Vaginal Odor

A good deal of research has been devoted to identifying components of vaginal odor. Doty (1981) states that the volatiles produced in the human vagina arise from several sources, including vulvar secretions from sebaceous, sweat, Batholin's and Skene's glands, exfoliated cellular debris and leukocytes, cervical mucus, endometrial and tubal fluid, transudate from the vaginal epithelium, and male semen from intercourse. The odor associated with vaginal secretion is produced by bacterial action and perhaps also by such nonbacterial causes as diet. Numerous chemical analyses of vaginal secretions have been conducted (e.g., Huggins & Preti, 1976; Michael, Bonsall, & Warner, 1974; Preti & Huggins, 1975, 1978; Preti, Huggins, & Silverberg, 1979; Sokolov, Harris, & Hecker, 1976).

Vaginal odor has been viewed as both a repellent and an attractant for humans. Regarding the former, unpleasant odor during menstruation may be an important contributor to the stigma historically associated with menses (Delaney, Lupton, & Toth, 1976). Several studies have assessed procedures for reducing vaginal odor (e.g., Keith, Dravnieks, Krotoszynski, Shah, & England, 1973), and, despite some sales drop-off in recent years, vaginal deodorants remain a big business in the United States (The Medicine Show, 1980). In contrast to this emphasis on negative reactions to vaginal odor, several authors suggest that such odors are often attractive, at least to males. Thus, Davenport (1965) reports than in one Southwest Pacific society "body odors are erotic stimulants, particularly the emanations from the woman's genitalia" (p. 183). Because of similarity between the odors of fish and vaginal secretions, men in this society "use a red ground cherry . . . to attract fish. After having caught a fish in this way, the ground cherry is believed to have power to attract women" (p. 184). Closer to home, Comfort (1972), in his popular book The Joy of Sex, discusses the powerful attractive qualities of a woman's "cassolette" (perfume box), which includes odors emanating from hair, skin, breasts, armpits, and genitals.

Most of the speculation regarding human pheromones has implicated vaginal odors, and, in spite of the problematical nature of such pheromones (see earlier discussion), several experiments have assessed reaction to vaginal odors. Of those investigating response to naturally occurring odors, two examples might be mentioned. Keith, Bush, Dravnieks, and Krotoszynski (1970) measured vaginal odor of women suffering from a number of medical conditions (e.g., hematuria, puerperal endometritis, bacterial vaginitis). Results indicated that use of nitrofurazone vaginal suppositories reduced unpleasant odors. To determine whether human vaginal odors vary over the course of the menstrual cycle, Doty, Ford, Preti, and Huggins (1975) collected vaginal secretions from four women across 15 ovulatory menstrual cycles. Odor donors were prohibited from using douches or vaginal deodorants and from eating asparagus, garlic, and onions. Male and female subjects smelled odor-impregnated tampons and judged each for intensity and pleasantness. Doty et al. found that, although secretions from the preovulatory and ovulatory phases were judged as somewhat weaker and less unpleasant than those from the menstrual, early luteal, and late luteal phases, considerable variability occurred across cycles from the same donor and different donors. The authors conlcude that, in their out-of-context in vitro situation, vaginal odors are not particularly attractive to males and that "it is unlikely that humans can use vaginal odors reliably to determine the general time of ovulation" (p. 1317).

A final study assessed the effect of "a synthetic hypothetical human female sexual pheromone" (SHHFSP) on the sexual behavior of married couples (Morris & Udry, 1978). Married couples, using contraceptive methods other than the pill or rhythm, participated for three of the wife's menstrual cycles. Each night the wife was asked to apply the contents of a small vial to her chest at bedtime. Morris and Udry state that "other methods of application were considered, i.e., in the monkey studies, the treatment was placed on the genital area. We did not choose to do this because human social interactions do not begin with the same posturing that monkey social interactions do" (p. 148). The vials contained one of four liquids: SHHFSP (alcohol, acetic acid, propionic acid, isobutyric acid, n-butyric acid, isovaleric acid, isocaproic acid); "heather" perfume and alcohol; alcohol alone; water alone. Each morning, both husbands and wives reported their sexual desire and behavior during the preceding 24 hours. Overall results indicated no treatment effects on reported desire or behavior. When only couples who reported cyclic sexual behavior (i.e., more frequent sex at midcycle than during the luteal phase) were examined, intercourse was found to be somewhat more frequent after SHHFSP than after the three remaining treatments. However, other analyses on cyclic versus non-cyclic couples failed to confirm the aforementioned finding. In view of the weak results and a number of methodological problems in the study, the authors seem correct in concluding that "we do not believe readers should hold their breaths in fear of pheromones" (p. 155).

Urinary and Fecal Odor

In addition to research on the chemical constituents of human urine (see Sastry et al., 1980), several studies have assessed reaction to urine and urine-like odors in humans. In an unpublished experiment, Beauchamp and Desor (cited by Doty, 1977) were able to train men and women to discriminate the urinary odors of male and female donors. However, these subjects were not subsequently able to identify the gender of new donors, suggesting that gender identification on the basis of urinary odor is difficult. Doty (1977) also reported a study of his own that examined the intensity and pleasantness of human female urine sampled from various stages of the menstrual cycle. Unlike the case for vaginal odors (Doty et al., 1975), intensity and pleasantness ratings of urine were not strongly and negatively related. Moreover, although intensity ratings were highest in the preovulatory phase, intensity and pleasantness ratings generally varied little across phases.

Researchers have investigated the effect of androstenol, a natural component of male urine (as well as male axillary secretion), on social perception. In one study, Cowley, Johnson, and Brooksbank (1977) had male and female college students wear paper masks impregnated with (1) androstenol, (2) a mixture of fatty acids (acetic, propionic, isobutyric, n-butyric, isovaleric) isolated from the vaginal secretions of primates, or (3) no odor (control). The ostensible purpose of the masks was to prevent subjects from observing one another's facial expressions. While wearing the masks, subjects read information about several hypothetical applicants for a campus office and then evaluated the applicants on 25 five-point scales. The applicants (three males and three females) were described as having a variety of backgrounds and interests. Perhaps at least partially because of the unsystematic manipulation of applicants' characteristics, results were complex and difficult to interpret. In general, odors had the greatest impact on females' assessments of male applicants, androstenol and the fatty acid mixture had opposite effects on females' assessments, and the odorous substances interacted with applicants' characteristics in affecting assessments.

In a second person-perception study using androstenol, Kirk-Smith, Booth, Carroll, and Davies (1978) asked male and female undergraduates to evaluate photographs of men and women (normally clothed), animals, and buildings. A within-subjects design was used, in which subjects judged the photographs while wearing either an androstenol-impregnated mask or a nonodorized (control) mask. The two judgment sessions were held one week apart. On three scales (sexy, attractive, good), photographed women were rated more positively when subjects smelled androstenol than when they did not. Similar effects were not found for the other classes of stimuli, although in the presence of androstenol "animals were judged rasher and buildings less sensitive" (p. 381). These intriguing findings must be interpreted cautiously, however, because androstenol did not produce significant effects on the majority of the 15 rating scales.

In a third study (Black & Biron, 1982), subjects interacted with an opposite-sex confederate who smelled of androstenol or Exaltolide or who wore no applied odor. Each couple interacted briefly and then watched slides of animals and flowers for 15 minutes. Subjects' judgment of the confederate's attractiveness was not influenced by his or her odor.

Finally, Kirk-Smith and Booth (1980) investigated the impact of androstenone (a compound similar to androstenol) on seating preferences in a dentist's waiting room. A target seat (that was previously avoided by women) was selected, and patients' preferences for this seat were compared on days when the seat was sprayed with varying amounts of androstenone (experimental days) and on days when the seat was unsprayed (control days). Compared to control days, on experimental days women showed increased preference for the scented seat (at two of the three concentration levels) and men showed decreased preference for the scented seat (at one concentration level).

In regard to fecal odor, we encountered little solid research. Psychoanalytic writers have discussed the role of anal odor in sexual development and neurosis (see Kalogerakis, 1963), and everyday concern about such odor is reflected in the pervasive use of bathroom fans and deodorizers. Literary allusions to one source of fecal-related odor, flatus, are rather common. Writers as diverse as Chaucer, Salinger, Barth, and Roth make humorous references to the expulsion of flatus. Some of these references suggest that flatus is not always offensive. As a character in Roth's (1974) book. *The Great American Novel,* puts it: "Mark my words: as soon as some scoundrel discovers there is a profit to be made off of the American kid's love of the fart, they will be selling artificial farts in balloons at the circus. And you can just imagine what they'll smell like too. Like *everything* artificial" (pp. 13–14).

The weight of informed opinion, however, suggests that the expulsion of flatus is an inappropriate behavior and the odor of flatus is noxious. Thus, Largey and Watson (1972) discuss the prevalent "fart taboo," which is "so widely agreed upon that formal etiquette books do not even discuss it, and certainly anyone who 'lets go a fart' in public is usually considered somewhat crass and undisciplined" (p. 1023). Given the ubiquitous negative reaction elicited by fecal odor, we might expect that adults who emit such odor would be embarrassed by it. Consistent with this speculation, Largey and Watson suggest that persons who produce flatus often try to convince onlookers that someone else is responsible. In a more serious vein, Orbach, Bard, and Sutherland (1957) report that patients with abdominal colostomies are extremely concerned about fecal odor. These authors note that "the existence of odor . . . results in an imperative necessity for many colostomy patients to remove themselves from the presence of others. Even when they are certain that the odor does not emanate from themselves, there is sometimes concern which may reach the proportions of terror that others will mistakenly identify them as the source of the odor" (p. 170).

Empirical research on reactions to the expulsion of flatus has been conducted by Lippman (1980). In an initial study, college subjects evaluated 16 flatulent individuals in a 2 X 2 X 2 X 2 X 2 design. Male and female subjects were presented with the following information: "While with a group of (acquaintances/strangers), an individual (accidentally/deliberately) produced a (rather loud/nearly silent), (very rank/almost odorless) fart" (p. 43). In the second study, a different group of college students were told to imagine that they suddenly needed to fart in a social situation. Subjects were asked how hard they would try to suppress their fart when observers were strangers or acquaintances, when observers could or could not localize the source of the fart, when the fart was loud or silent, and when the fart was odorless or rank. In the first study, ratings of the farter on the dimensions of humorousness, politeness, maliciousness, and obnoxiousness revealed a number of significant findings. For example, a farter was rated as more obnoxious when strangers were present and when the fart was deliberate, loud, and rank. In the second study, results indicated greater suppression if strangers were present and if the fart were loud and rank and could be localized. It seems fair to conclude, as does Lippman, that "the fart, despite its lowly status as a sometimes annoying by-product of metabolic maintenance, is, psychologically and socially, a complex and multidimensional event" (p. 50).

Breath Odor

In addition to the sources of human odor already discussed, the lungs and oral cavity produce breath odor (see Garfield, 1982). Such odor is attributable to a number of volatiles (Sastry et al., 1980), which arise from diverse sources (e.g., type of food and beverages consumed, oral cavity hygiene, smoking, medication intake, recent physical and/or emotional strain). Not surprisingly, analysis and control of breath odor has been of special interest to dentists. For example, Solis-Gaffar, Niles, Rainieri, and Kestenbaum (1975) used gas chromatography and flame photometric detection to assess the effectiveness of a mouthrinse on sulfur volatiles associated with mouth odor. And Jung (1976) suggested a number of prosaic remedies (e.g., brushing teeth, chewing gum) to reduce beer- and garlic-induced halitosis. It should be noted, however, that breath odor is not universally viewed as offensive. Hall (1966) states that whereas Americans prefer large interpersonal distances in part to avoid others' breath odor, Arabs prefer smaller distances because "to smell one's friend is not only nice but desirable, for to deny him your breath is to act ashamed" (p. 160).

Several authors have suggested that human breath odors may change during the menstrual cycle. Ellis (1928) asserted that menstruating girls and young women frequently have a breath odor resembling chloroform or violets. In addition, recent biochemical data on oral volatiles are consistent with the hypothesis that breath odors fluctuate during the menstrual cycle (see Doty, 1977, 1981;

Sastry et al., 1980). Unfortunately, no psychophysical studies have assessed whether breath odor in fact varies as a function of menstrual phase.

The only study we could locate on social perception and breath odor was conducted by Doty, Green, Ram, and Yankell (1982). Odor donors were male and female nonsmokers with good oral health. Donors were not allowed to use oral hygiene, to eat heavily spiced foods, or to wear perfume or after-shave lotion during the study. Prior to breakfast on 5 consecutive days, donors transmitted oral odors through glass tubes to visually isolated male and female subjects, who evaluated the odors for intensity, pleasantness, and sex of donor. Results indicated that both male and female odors were assigned correctly by the majority of subjects and that females were more accurate perceivers than were males. In addition, male odors were judged as more intense and unpleasant than female odors; female subjects rated the odors as more intense and unpleasant than did male subjects; ratings of odor intensity and pleasantness were negatively related; and the stronger and more unpleasant an odor, the more likely it was attributed to a male donor. Results of this study are similar to those obtained in experiments on axillary and hand odor.

Breast Odor

Stimulated by research indicating that many infant mammals recognize their mothers by smell, investigators have sought to determine whether human infants can recognize their mothers on the basis of breast odor (see Sastry et al., 1980, for information regarding breast milk volatiles). Russell (1976) presented healthy breast-fed infants of three ages (2 days, 2 weeks, 6 weeks) with breast pads that lactating mothers had placed inside their bras for 3 hours. Each infant was tested with his/her own mother's odor, another lactating mother's odor, and a clean moist pad. Infants, who had not been fed for 3 hours and who typically were sleeping, were tested by holding a pad near the baby's nose for approximately 30 seconds. Results indicated that at 2 days infants did not respond to any of the pads, at 2 weeks infants generally responded to both of the lactating mothers, and at 6 weeks infants typically responded to their own mother but not to the strange mother.

In a better-controlled pair of studies, MacFarlane (1975) also assessed infants' ability to recognize the odor of their mother's breast. In the first study, alert breast-fed infants who had not eaten for 3–4 hours were placed on their backs and exposed to two breast pads, one previously worn by their mother and the other a clean (control) pad. The pads were hung 1 centimeter apart above the baby's head so that pads touched the baby's cheeks on either side of the nose. In order to touch either pad with the nose, the infant had to turn his/her head 20 degrees from midline. During two 1-minute sessions, the child's orienting behavior was videotaped. Eighty-five percent of the babies spent more time turned toward the mother's pad than toward the control pad, and these babies spent approximately 75% of the time oriented toward the mother's pad. In the second study, one group of babies was tested at both 2 days and 6-days-of-age, and another group was tested at 8–10 days. Here, infants were tested with breast pads from two lactating women: their own mother and a strange mother. In terms of time spent orienting to own mother's pad as a percentage of total time spent orienting to either pad, preference for own mother increased with the baby's age (2 days: 52%, 6 days: 60%, 8–10 days: 68%). MacFarlane noted that routine hospital practices, in which mothers are encouraged to wash their breasts and to apply lanolin to their nipples, are likely to weaken results of this type of study. The factor(s) responsible for infants' ability to recognize their mothers on the basis of breast odor are not well understood. Although Russell (1983) argues for "extra-uterine" learning, Porter, Cernoch, and Balogh (1985) provide evidence suggesting that genetic factors may be important.

Response to Artificial Scents

So far, we have focused on reaction to body odor, that is, odor from volatiles excreted and secreted by the body, which often are acted upon by bacteria. As suggested in several of the earlier sections, however, people frequently seek to eliminate or alter their natural odor. In this section, we discuss the use of artificial scents to deodorize and odorize the human body.

Perfumes have played a role in human civilization for thousands of years, and several authors have traced the use of perfumes from ancient to modern times (e.g., Ellis, 1960; Genders, 1972). Thus, Genders discusses perfume use in ancient civilizations (e.g., Egypt, Persia, Greece); in Moslem and Eastern countries; in Europe from the time of Charlemagne to Napolean; in England from the Roman period through the 1800s; and in the New World. Over the centuries perfumes have been obtained from a variety of plant and animal sources and have been used for a number of purposes, including enhancing the wearer's olfactory pleasure, masking unpleasant body odors, increasing sexual attractiveness, improving health, and aiding religious and funeral rites.

As this brief discussion suggests, the science of perfumery is very old. Nevertheless, substantial contributions to perfumery are still being made, primarily by cosmetic chemists. Some of this work was cited earlier in our discussion of axillary odor. A paper by Jellinek and Koster (1979) illustrates modern research on perfumes. These investigators assessed males' and females' judgments of several odors varying in chemical complexity. The odors ranged from single odorous compounds (e.g., linalyl acetate) to complex perfumes (e.g., "Rive Gauche"). Results indicated no relationship between the chemical complexity and perceived complexity of the odors or between the perceived complexity and familiarity of the odors. However, odor preference was negatively correlated with perceived complexity for men and positively correlated with familiarity for women.

Although important, the chemical constituents of a perfume are not the only factors that influence its purchase and use. Reporting on a seminar sponsored by the Fragrance Foundation, Nemy (1981) found that executives of perfume companies view nonscent factors (e.g., advertisements, bottles) as very important to product success. Moreover, they believe that the ''concept'' of a perfume (i.e., the mood, emotion, or feeling that the fragrance projects) should guide the creation of the scent, rather than vice versa. A perfume's ability to attract members of the opposite sex is a dominant advertising theme (cf. Largey & Watson, 1972). Other advertising themes appeal to different, though perhaps related, motives. These include the desire to feel affluent (*Joy de Jean Patou*— ''The costliest perfume in the world. Imported from Paris . . . One ounce in Baccarat crystal $300'') and the desire to possess sex-appropriate characteristics (*Chaps* - ''The West. . . . It's an image of men who are real and proud. Of the freedom and independence we all would like to feel. . . . Chaps. It's the West. The West you would like to feel inside of yourself'').

In contrast to in vitro studies like that of Jellinek and Koster (1979), very few in vivo experiments have assessed reaction to persons wearing artificial scent. In one relevant study, Nesbitt and Steven (1974) investigated the impact of ''high intensity stimuli'' (i.e., bright clothing and artificial scent) on personal spacing at an amusement park. The investigators predicted and found that people waiting in line for amusement-park attractions stood farther from male and female target persons who wore bright clothing or artificial scent than from the same persons wearing conservative clothing or no scent. In another study (Baron, 1981), male subjects interacted briefly with a female confederate who either did or did not wear perfume and who was dressed either formally or informally. Results indicated that, compared to the absence of scent, perfume increased attraction to the informally-dressed confederate and decreased attraction to the formally-dressed confederate. Taken together, these two experiments suggest that artificial scent may have more complex effects than is typically assumed.

Finally, it should be noted that in some (probably infrequent) circumstances people may use artificial scent to reduce, rather than enhance, their own and others' attractiveness. Anecdotal evidence for the use of artificial scent to reduce one's own attractiveness was contained in a newspaper article about Andy Smulion, the ''human stench bomb'' (Swift, 1979). Smulion, a bill collector for a London magazine, induces debtors to pay their bills by smelling up their places of business. He impregnates his clothes with vile odors—compared to the stench of a skunk, rotten eggs, and sewage—and then sits in the office of the debtor until payment is made. Smulion reportedly is quite successful. Moreover, his employer states that, ''He has never been assaulted. Most people can't bear to approach him.'' Anecdotal evidence for the use of artificial scent to reduce others' attractiveness was provided by Stanley Lovell, head of the Research and Development Division of the Office of Strategic Services (OSS) during World War II. According to Lovell, ''to embarass the fastidious Japanese, the Research and Development Division came up with a noxious-smelling compound dubbed 'Who Me?' which was packaged in collapsible tubes and distributed to children in Japanese-occupied Chinese cities. When a Japanese officer came down the sidewalk, the little Chinese boys and girls would squirt a shot of 'Who Me?' at his trouser seat. The Japanese were horrified by the foul compound, which was virtually impossible to wash out. 'Who Me?' was no world-shaking new evolvement, but it cost the Japanese a world of face'' (Russell, 1981, pp. 108–109).

Response to Environmental Odors

In addition to altering the odor of their bodies, people often seek to alter the odor of their environments. Ellis (1960) and Genders (1972) cite many historical cases in which scent was used to manipulate environmental odor for esthetic, health, and religious reasons. Regarding more contemporary examples, Largey and Watson (1972) note that the Chicago White Sox have sprayed the odor of buttered popcorn into their stadium and that the India exhibition at the 1964–1965 World's Fair was artificially scented with the odor of curry and cows. Finally, we are all aware of the use of incense in churches and the use of air fresheners and scented candles in homes. New technology for producing environmental odors is available in the form of aroma discs, which release pleasant odors when "played" on a machine that resembles a small phonograph.

As in the case of artificial scents applied to the body, on rare occasions noxious, rather than pleasant, odors may purposely be introduced into the environment. Anecdotal evidence for deliberate "air pollution" is contained in a newspaper account of labor trouble in a high school (Stefanik, 1980). The article states that, "An unbearable stench closed Connellsville High School, Fayette County, yesterday. . . . Custodians have been on strike there since Sept. 4. . . . The odor . . . came from containers brought into the school." Noxious odor has recently been exploited to prevent rape. For $5.95, a woman can purchase a small plastic container of synthetic skunk oil ("Rapel"). When broken, the container releases a vile odor that allegedly repels would-be rapists.

Much recent attention has been devoted to malodorous air emitted by industrial and vehicular sources. Several reviews of research on measurement and control of environmental odors are available (e.g., Cain, 1974; Cheremisinoff & Young, 1975; Committee on Odors from Stationary and Mobile sources, 1980; Turk, Johnston, & Moulton, 1974). Unfortunately for present purposes, less attention has been given to the impact of malodorous air on human behavior, particularly social behavior (cf. Evans & Jacobs, 1981).

Among the very few experiments investigating social responses to environmental odor are studies by Rotton and his colleagues, which assess how unpleasant environmental odor influences interpersonal attraction and aggression. Rotton, Barry, Frey, and Soler (1978) had undergraduates evaluate attitudinally similar or dissimilar strangers while confined in a room that was polluted by ammonium sulfide or was unpolluted. Results indicated that a similar stranger in the polluted room elicited more attraction than did the three remaining strangers. The authors speculated that these results may have been due to subjects' assumption that the stranger was experiencing the same odor that they were. Therefore, Rotton et al. conducted a second study that differed from the first in two major respects: (1) subjects were told that the stranger they rated was not exposed to the environmental odor they were smelling, and (2) both butyric acid and ammonium sulfide were used as odorants. Here, results indicated that, compared to the no-odor condition, the malodorants decreased attraction toward both the similar and dissimilar strangers (see also Rotton, 1983).

In another study Rotton, Frey, Barry, Milligan, and Fitzpatrick (1979) predicted, on the basis of research on temperature and aggression, that a moderately unpleasant malodorant would produce more aggression than would an extremely unpleasant malodorant. Male undergraduates, who either were or were not exposed to an aggressive model, were given the opportunity to administer shocks to a confederate. Shocks were delivered in a room infused with an extremely unpleasant odor (ammonium sulfide), a moderately unpleasant odor (ethyl mercaptan), or no odor. Results indicated that, whereas odor did not affect shock intensity when aggressive modeling had occurred, in the no-model condition shock intensity was highest when odor was moderately unpleasant.

Finally, Baron (1980) has also examined the effect of environmental odor on aggression but has used pleasant rather than unpleasant scent. In this study, male undergraduates were angered or not angered by a male or female confederate and then were allowed to aggress against this person. The room in which subjects administered shocks had a very pleasant odor (perfume), a mildly pleasant odor (pine-scented aerosol), or no odor (the confederate was in a separate room and hence could not be perceived as the source of the odor.) On a composite index of shock intensity and shock duration, rather different results were obtained for male and female confederates. When the confederate was male, aggression was enhanced by perfume (relative to the no-scent condition) if subjects had been angered but was reduced if subjects had not been angered. When the confederate was female, aggression was enhanced by perfume in both the anger and no-anger conditions. The pine-scented aerosol had no effects. As in the case of perfumes, environmental odors appear to have complex effects on social perception and behavior.

III. TOWARD A SOCIAL PSYCHOLOGY OF SMELL

In the two previous sections, we have discussed smell as a sensory system and have reviewed research on how odor influences human social perception and behavior. In this section, we attempt to link our earlier discussion to social psychological theory, pointing out a number of unresolved issues that warrant investigation.

In attempting to conceptualize how a complex variable, such as odor, might influence social behavior, it is useful to consider various dimensions of the variable. Even though the dimensions initially identified are somewhat arbitrary and probably in need of further refinement, the effort to think in dimensional terms may have several productive consequences. One such consequence is avoiding the use of narrow operational definitions for complex conceptual variables (e.g., as when "physical attractiveness" is operationally defined as the attractiveness of a frontal photograph of a person's head and shoulders). A second and related consequence of the dimensional approach is that it provides an initial conceptual framework, which can facilitate the hypothesis generation and testing necessary for the development of an adequate theory.

Of the many dimensions of odor that might influence the impact of this variable on interpersonal perception and behavior, four seem particularly important. For purposes of simplicity, it is assumed here that each dimension can take on only two values. One dimension is the source of the odor, that is, the target person's body or the target person's environment. The second is the degree to which the target person ostensibly can control the odor; thus, an odor can be target controllable or target uncontrollable. The third dimension is the perceiver's affective reaction to the odor (positive or negative). Finally, the fourth dimension is the target's presumed belief about the perceiver's affective reaction to the odor (positive or negative); that is, does the target presumably believe that the perceiver likes or dislikes the odor? Table 8.2 presents a classification scheme based on the four dimensions mentioned above. Although it is easier to generate examples for some of the 16 cells than for others, there is heuristic utility in considering all possible combinations of the four variables.

The classification scheme suggests a number of empirically testable hypotheses regarding the effects of odor on interpersonal attraction. For example, one of the dimensions (perceiver's reaction to odor) seems likely to yield a "main effect." That is, because of classical conditioning, a target associated with a pleasant odor would be expected to elicit more attraction than a target associated with an unpleasant odor. In addition to this hypothesized main effect, a number of interactions may also occur.

Looking first at two-way interactions, it seems probable that a pleasant odor ostensibly emanating from the target's body will elicit more positive reaction than a pleasant odor arising from an environmental source, whereas an unpleasant odor emanating from the target's body will elicit more negative reaction than an unpleasant odor arising from an environmental source. This hypothesis is based on the assumptions that (1) stimuli arising from a person's body are seen as more controllable than stimuli arising from other sources; (2) the more controllable a stimulus is, the more it is perceived to reveal a person's underlying dispositions; and (3) the more a stimulus indicates underlying dispositions, the stronger

TABLE 8.2
Dimensions Underlying The Impact Of Odor On Human Social Behavior

Source of Odor	Target's Body		Target's Environment	
	Target controllable	Target uncontrollable	Target controllable	Target uncontrollable
Controllability of odor	+	+	+	–
Perceiver's reaction to odor	–	+	–	+
Target's presumed belief about perceiver's reaction	+	–	+	+

is the affective response to the stimulus.[1] Based on the latter two assumptions, we would also predict that, for both body and environmental odors, an ostensibly controllable-pleasant odor will elicit more positive reaction than an ostensibly uncontrollable-pleasant odor, whereas an ostensibly controllable-unpleasant odor will elicit more negative reaction than an ostensibly uncontrollable-unpleasant odor. Finally, one might predict than an ostensibly controllable odor that the target presumably believes the perceiver likes will elicit more positive reaction to the target than a similar uncontrollable odor, whereas an ostensibly controllable odor that the target presumably believes the perceiver dislikes will elicit more negative reaction than a similar uncontrollable odor. The assumptions underlying this hypothesis are basically the same as those offered for the previous predictions. In the former cases the target gets more "credit" for an *actual* odor when he has control over it than when he does not; in the latter case the target gets more "credit" for a *desired* odor when he has control over it than when he does not.

A three-way interaction might also be predicted. It seems likely that when an odor is perceived as unpleasant and controllable, a target who presumably is aware of the perceiver's reaction will be liked less than a target who is unaware (because the aware target is purposely offensive), whereas when an odor is perceived as unpleasant and uncontrollable, an aware target will be liked more than an unaware target (because the aware target elicits sympathy). Although not yet investigated in regard to environmental odor, this hypothesis has been confirmed for body odor (Levine & McBurney, 1977). For pleasant-controllable and pleasant-uncontrollable odors, predictions are less clear regarding the relative attractiveness of aware and unaware targets.

The aforementioned hypotheses suggest that, although pleasant and unpleasant odors may influence interpersonal attraction via simple classical conditioning mechanisms, attributions about the causes of the odor may be extremely important.[2] As mentioned earlier, the sources of odors are often difficult to localize, and this localization ambiguity presents a basic attributional problem. Probably the initial question asked by a perceiver of an odor is whether the odor emanates from a person or an environmental source. If a human source is assumed, the

---

[1] As Epictitus (circa 100 AD, cited by Cain, 1978) stated, "But who does not turn from a man who is dirty, odorous, foul-complexioned, more than from one who is bespattered with muck? The smell of the latter is external and accidental, that of the former comes from the want of tendance; it is from within, and shows a sort of inward rottenness."

[2] Baron (1980) suggests that odor may influence human social behavior by increasing general arousal, by inducing positive and negative affective states, or by affecting perceptions of the odor source. This approach is consistent with our own analysis, although, rather than viewing arousal, affect, and perception as *alternative* mechanisms by which odor influences behavior, we would like to stress the interactive relationships among the mechanisms. It seems likely that, not only are all three mechanisms frequently involved in a given situation, but the causal ordering of the mechanisms may differ across situations. For example, in some cases odor may initially influence arousal, which in turn influences affect and then perception; in other cases odor may initially influence perception, which in turn determines arousal and affect.

next question is "which human?" In general, the more people present, the more difficult the localization. The task of determining who is responsible for an odor can sometimes be eased by assumed covariations between certain odors and certain physical characteristics. Thus, fecal odor may be attributed to an infant wearing diapers, heavy perfume may be attributed to an adult female, axillary odor may be attributed to an unkempt adult male, and so on. Needless to say, although these odor stereotypes may be useful in providing probabilistic information regarding the sources of various human odors, they may often be incorrect. Even the "basic" odor stereotype, that a lone individual is responsible for any apparently human odor surrounding him or her, may be wrong, as when a lone elevator rider is "blamed" for flatus expelled by a passenger who recently left. In the case of unpleasant odors, particularly those of bodily origin, additional attributional questions arise after the odor is localized. These include, "Doesn't he/she know how bad he/she smells?" and "Can't he/she do anything about it?" The answers to these questions can substantially influence subsequent reactions to the odorous person (Levine & McBurney, 1977).

In his analyses of the attribution process, Kelley (1967, 1972) discusses additional factors that may influence reaction to odorous people. Kelley's (1967) paper suggests that, in making dispositional versus situational attributions about a person's odor, we are likely to use three types of information: consensus (the degree to which other persons emit the same odor as the target in the same situation), consistency (the degree to which the target emits the same odor at other times in the same situation), and distinctiveness (the degree to which the target emits the same odor in different situations). According to Kelley's analysis, we make an internal attribution for the odor when consensus is low, consistency is high, and distinctiveness is low. In contrast an external attribution is made when consensus, consistency, and distinctiveness are all high. In a later paper, Kelley (1972) discusses how we make attributions on the basis of a single observation of behavior (e.g., when we encounter an odorous person only once). In such situations, according to Kelley, we employ causal schemata (i.e., backlogs of previously-acquired information regarding causal relations) to infer the cause(s) of the observed behavior. Although reminiscent of the earlier point regarding the use of odor stereotypes for odor localization, we are dealing here with a different issue. That is, even after deciding on the source of an odor, an observer will often be motivated to identify the cause(s) of the odor (e.g., exercise, poor hygiene). In making this attributional analysis, the observer may rely on a schema involving, for example, multiple sufficient causes (*either* exercise or poor hygiene is sufficient to produce the odor) or multiple necessary causes (*both* exercise and poor hygiene are necessary to produce the odor).

In assessing the utility of attributional analyses of odor, two important qualifications must be kept in mind. First, not all of our interpersonal judgments and evaluations are based on reflection about the causes of behavior. Many such responses are snap judgments, based on nonreflective applications of stereotypes. Second, even when attribution does occur, the attributional process for nonverbal behavior, such as odor, may differ somewhat from that for other types of behavior (Schneider, Hastorf, & Ellsworth, 1979). Thus, compared to verbal behaviors, nonverbal behaviors are generally seen as (1) less intentional and controllable, (2) more reactive and "sincere," (3) reflecting a more limited range of events (primarily attitudes, emotions, and intentions), and (4) more ambiguous in regard to meaning. In addition, analysis of nonverbal behaviors may involve less conscious awareness than analysis of verbal behaviors (see the earlier discussion regarding cognition and smell).

Schneider et al. (1979) also point out similarities in how nonverbal and verbal cues are used in attribution. They note that for both types of cues (1) departures from norms are meaningful, (2) inconsistencies (e.g., between cue and context or between different cues) require explanation, and (3) perceivers' emotions, expectations, and goals affect their interpretations of cues. These factors seem quite relevant to reaction to odor. Thus, it seems likely that the more a body odor departs from normative expectations, the more likely is the odor to attract attention and to stimulate attributional analysis. Moreover, inconsistency between body odor and other nonverbal cues (e.g., a well-dressed person with offensive odor) may well elicit more vigorous attributional analysis than does consistency. Finally, emotional arousal may make one less accepting of persons with non-normative odor; violation of an expectation regarding odor may be attention provoking and may elicit a heightened evaluative response (either positive or negative, depending on the valence of the odor); and particular goals, such as desire for intimacy, may cause heightened responses to positive and negative odors.

If we move from snap judgments and attributions to the more general process of person perception, a number of other issues regarding reaction to odor become salient. These include developmental aspects of reactions to odors (Doty, Shaman, Applebaum, Giberson, Siksorski, & Rosenberg, 1984; Engen, 1974), the weight given to odor versus other characteristics in interpersonal judgment and evaluation, the effect of odor on self-concept and social identity (cf. Kleck & Strenta, 1980), the use of odor in impression management and interpersonal control, individual differences in response to body and environmental odor, and so on. Although space limitations do not allow discussion of these issues here, they deserve theoretical and empirical attention.

We hope that the above speculations have stimulated the reader to engage in a few thought experiments regarding odor and social behavior. Our real goal, of course, is to stimulate research conducted outside the reader's head. In light of this goal, we feel obligated to point out a few difficulties involved in carrying out in vivo experiments on odor. One problem is that body odor is a difficult independent variable to manipulate. Although at least one fragrance company formulates artificial body odor, the sample we have sniffed lacks the ineffable qualities that we associate with "true" body odor. Alternative sources of body odor (e.g., old sweat socks) pose obvious problems of standardization. Second, even with standard odors, such as perfumes and laboratory chemicals, it is difficult to calibrate atmospheric concentrations accurately. Third, odors interact with airborne chemicals in complex ways, so that it is often difficult to be sure just what subjects are smelling. Finally, people adapt to odors rather quickly, which means that the independent variable becomes weaker as the experiment proceeds. Although these problems should be kept in mind by researchers, they are not necessarily critical. For example, precise knowledge of odor concentration may be unimportant in a study comparing perfume vs. ammonium sulfide, and adaptation may not be a problem if first impressions are being assessed. In sum, then, we encourage social psychologists to employ their considerable theoretical skills and methodological ingenuity in studying odor and social behavior. Systematic work on this topic is likely to provide a breath of fresh air for our discipline.

ACKNOWLEDGEMENT

We thank R. A. Baron, W. S. Cain, R. G. Davis, R. L. Doty, and S. Tortu for helpful suggestions on an earlier draft of this paper.

REFERENCES

Bakiewicz, T. A. (1973). A critical evaluation of the methods available for measurement of antiperspirancy. *Journal of the Society of Cosmetic Chemists, 24*, 245–258.

Baron, R. A. (1980). Olfaction and human social behavior: Effects of pleasant scents on physical aggression. *Basic and Applied Social Psychology, 1*, 163–172.

Baron, R. A. (1981). Olfaction and human social behavior: Effects of a pleasant scent on attraction and social perception. *Personality and Social Psychology Bulletin, 7*, 611–616.

Beauchamp, G. K., Doty, R. L., Moulton, D. G., & Mugford, R. A. (1976). The pheromone concept in mammalian chemical communication: A critique. In R. L. Doty (Ed.), *Mammalian olfaction, reproductive processes, and behavior*. New York: Academic Press.

Beauchamp, G. K., Doty, R. L., Moulton, D. G., & Mugford, R. A. (1979). (Response to Katz and Shorey). *Chemical Ecology, 5*, 301–305.

Bieber, I. (1959). Olfaction in sexual development and adult sexual organization. *American Journal of Psychotherapy, 13*, 851–859.

Birch, M. C. (Ed.). (1974). *Pheromones*. Amsterdam: Elsevier/North Holland.

Black, S. L., & Biron, C. (1982). Androstenol as a human pheromone: No effect on perceived physical attractiveness. *Behavioral Neural Biology, 34*, 326–330.

Brill, A. A. (1932). The sense of smell in the neuroses and psychoses. *Psychoanalytic Quarterly, 1*, 7–42.

Brody, B. (1975). The sexual significance of the axillae. *Psychiatry, 38*, 278–289.

Cain, W. S. (Ed.), (1974). Odors: Evaluation, utilization, and control. *Annals of the New York Academy of Sciences, 237* (Whole).

Cain, W. S. (1978). History of research on smell. In E. C. Carterette & M. P. Friedman (Eds.), *Handbook of perception: Tasting and smelling* (Vol. 6A). New York: Academic Press.

Cain, W. S. (1979). To know with the nose: Keys to odor identification. *Science, 203,* 467–470.

Cain, W. S. (1980, April). The psychology of the sense of smell. *Aerosol Age,* 31–33.

Cameron, E. A. (1981). On the persistence of disparlure in the human body. *Journal of Chemical Ecology, 7,* 313–317.

Cheremisinoff, P. N., & Young, R. A. (1975). *Industrial odor technology assessment.* Ann Arbor: Ann Arbor Science.

Comfort, A. (1971). Likelihood of human pheromones. *Nature, 230,* 432, 433, 479.

Comfort, A. (1972). *The joy of sex: A gourmet guide to love making.* New York: Crown.

Committee on Odors from Stationary and Mobile Sources. (1980). Odors from stationary and mobile sources: Executive summary. *Journal of the Air Pollution Control Association, 30,* 13–16.

Cowley, J. J., Johnson, A. L., & Brooksbank, B. W. L. (1977). The effect of two odorous compounds on performance in an assessment-of-people test. *Psychoneuroendocrinology, 2,* 159–172.

Davenport, W. (1965). Sexual patterns and their regulation in a society of the southwest Pacific. In F. A. Beach (Ed.), *Sex and behavior.* New York: Wiley.

Davis, R. G. (1975). Acquisition of verbal associations to olfactory stimuli of varying familiarity and to abstract visual stimuli. *Journal of Experimental Psychology: Human Learning and Memory, 104,* 134–142.

Davis, R. G. (1977). Acquisition and retention of verbal associations to olfactory and abstract visual stimuli of varying similarity. *Journal of Experimental Psychology: Human Learning and Memory, 3,* 37–51.

Delaney, J., Lupton, M. J., & Toth, E. (1976). *The curse: A cultural history of menstruation.* New York: E. P. Dutton.

Desor, J. A., & Beauchamp, G. K. (1974). The human capacity to transmit olfactory information. *Perception and Psychophysics, 16,* 551–556.

Distelheim, I. H., & Dravnieks, A. (1973). A method for separating characteristics of odors in detection of disease processes. *International Journal of Dermatology, 12,* 241–244.

Dollard, J. (1957). *Caste and class in a Southern town* (3rd ed.). Garden City, New York: Doubleday.

Doty, R. L. (Ed.). (1976). *Mammalian olfaction, reproductive processes, and behavior.* New York: Academic Press.

Doty, R. L. (1977). A review of recent psychophysical studies examining the possibility of chemical communication of sex and reproductive state in humans. In D. Muller-Schwarze & M. M. Mozell (Eds.), *Chemical signals in vertebrates.* New York: Plenum.

Doty, R. L. (1981). Olfactory communication in humans. *Chemical Senses, 6,* 351–376.

Doty, R. L., Ford, M., Preti, G., & Huggins, G. R. (1975). Changes in the intensity and pleasantness of human vaginal odors during the menstrual cycle. *Science, 190,* 1316–1318.

Doty, R. L., Green, P. A., Ram, C., & Yankell, S. L. (1982). Communication of gender from human breath odors: Relationship to perceived intensity and pleasantness. *Hormones and Behavior, 16,* 13–22.

Doty, R. L., Orndorff, M. M., Leyden, J., & Kligman, A. (1978). Communication of gender from human axillary odors: Relationship to perceived intensity and hedonicity. *Behavioral Biology, 23,* 373–380.

Doty, R. L., Shaman, P., Applebaum, S. L., Giberson, R., Siksorski, L., & Rosenberg, L. (1984). Smell identification ability: Changes with age. *Science, 226,* 1441–1443.

Doty, R. L. Snyder, P. J., Huggins, G. R., & Lowry, L. D. (1981). Endocrine, cardiovascular, and psychological correlates of olfactory sensitivity changes during the human menstrual cycle. *Journal of Comparative and Physiological Psychology, 95,* 45–60.

Dravnieks, A. (1975). Evaluation of human body odors: Methods and interpretations. *Journal of the Society of Cosmetic Chemists, 26,* 551–571.

Dravnieks, A., Krotoszynski, B. K., Lieb, W. E., & Jungermann, E. (1968). Influence of an antibacterial soap on various effluents from axillae. *Journal of the Society of Cosmetic Chemists, 19,* 611–626.

Eich, J. E. (1978). Fragrances as cues for remembering words. *Journal of Verbal Learning and Verbal Behavior, 17,* 103–111.

Ellis, A. (1960). *The essence of beauty: A history of perfume and cosmetics.* New York: Macmillan.

Ellis, H. (1928). *Sexual selection in man. Studies in the psychology of sex* (Vol. 4). Philadelphia: F. A. Davis.

Engen, T. (1974). Method and theory in the study of odor preferences. In A. Turk, J. W. Johnston, & D. G. Moulton (Eds.), *Human responses to environmental odors.* New York: Academic Press.

Engen, T. (1982). *The perception of odors.* New York: Academic Press.

Engen, T., & McBurney, D. H. (1964). Magnitude and category scales of the pleasantness of odors. *Journal of Experimental Psychology, 68,* 435–440.

Engen, T., & Pfaffmann, C. (1960). Absolute judgments of odor quality. *Journal of Experimental Psychology, 59,* 214–219.

Engen, T., & Ross, B. M. (1973). Long-term memory of odors with and without verbal descriptions. *Journal of Experimental Psychology, 100,* 221–227.

Evans, G. W., & Jacobs, S. V. (1981). Air pollution and human behavior. *Journal of Social Issues, 37,* 95–125.

Garcia, J., Hankins, W. G., & Rusiniak, K. W. (1974). Behavioral regulation of the milieu interne in man and rat. *Science, 185,* 824–831.

Garfield, E. (1982). Halitosis, the silent affliction: A profile of bad-breath research. *Current Contents, 14*(44), 5–11.

Genders, R. (1972). *Perfume through the ages.* New York: Putnam.

Graham, C. A., & McGrew, W. C. (1980). Menstrual synchrony in female undergraduates living on a coeducational campus. *Psychoneuroendocrinology, 5,* 245–252.

Hall, E. T. (1966). *The hidden dimension.* Garden City, New York: Doubleday.

Hassett, J. (1978, March). Sex and smell. *Psychology Today, 40,* 42, 45.

Hayden, G. F. (1980). Olfactory diagnosis in medicine. *Postgraduate Medicine, 67*(4), 110–116.

Herrick, C. J. (1933). The functions of the olfactory parts of the cerebral cortex. *Proceedings of the National Academy of Sciences, 19,* 7–14.

Hold, B., & Schleidt, M. (1977). The importance of human odour in non-verbal communication. *Zeitschrift für Tierpsychologie, 43,* 225–238.

Hopson, J. L. (1979). *Scent signals: The silent language of sex.* New York: Morrow.

Huggins, G. R., & Preti, G. (1976). Volatile constituents of human vaginal secretions. *American Journal of Obstetrics and Gynecology, 126,* 129–136.

Jellinek, J. S., & Koster, E. P. (1979). Perceived fragrance complexity and its relation to familiarity and pleasantness. *Journal of the Society of Cosmetic Chemists, 30,* 253–262.

Jung, F. (1976). Beer and garlic sausage-induced halitosis: De gustibus non est disputandum. *Journal of the American Medical Association, 235,* 88.

Jungermann, E. (1974). Antiperspirants: New trends in formulation and testing technology. *Journal of the Society of Cosmetic Chemists, 25,* 621–638.

Kalogerakis, M. G. (1963). The role of olfaction in sexual development. *Psychosomatic Medicine, 25,* 420–432.

Karlson, P., & Luscher, M. (1959). "Pheromones": A new term for a class of biologically active substances. *Nature, 183,* 55–56.

Katz, R. A., & Shorey, H. H. (1979). In defense of the term "pheromone." *Chemical Ecology, 5,* 299–301.

Keith, L., Bush, I. M., Dravnieks, A., & Krotoszynski, B. K. (1970). Changes of vaginal odors of 6 patients under nitrofurazone treatment: A study in applied olfactronics. *Journal of Reproductive Medicine, 4,* 69–76.

Keith, L., Dravnieks, A., Krotoszynski, B. K., Shah, J., & England, D. (1973). A comparison of the effect of a suppository and two douches on vaginal malodorants. *Archive fur Gynakologie, 215,* 245–262.

Kelley, H. H. (1967). Attribution theory in social psychology. In D. Levine (Ed.), *Nebraska symposium on motivation* (Vol. 15). Lincoln: University of Nebraska Press.

Kelley, H. H. (1972). Causal schemata and the attribution process. In E. E. Jones, D. E. Kanouse, H. H. Kelley, R. E. Nisbett, S. Valins, & B. Weiner (Eds.), *Attribution: Perceiving the causes of behavior.* Morristown, NJ: General Learning Press.

Kennon, L. (1965). Some aspects of toiletries technology. *Journal of Pharmaceutical Sciences, 54,* 813–831.

Keverne, E. B. (1977). Pheromones and sexual behavior. In J. Money & H. Musaph (Eds.), *Handbook of sexology.* Amsterdam: Elsevier/North Holland.

Kiell, N. (1976). *Varieties of sexual experience: Psychosexuality in literature.* New York: International Universities Press.

Kirk-Smith, M. D., & Booth, D. A. (1980). Effect of androstenone on choice of location in others' presence. In H. van der Starre (Ed.), *Olfaction and taste VII: Proceedings of the Seventh International Symposium on Olfaction and Taste and of the Fourth Congress of the European Chemoreception Research Organization.* London: IRL Press Ltd.

Kirk-Smith, M., Booth, D. A., Carroll, D., & Davies, P. (1978). Human social attitudes affected by androstenol. *Research Communications in Psychology, Psychiatry, and Behavior, 3,* 379–384.

Kleck, R. E., & Strenta, A. (1980). Perceptions of the impact of negatively valued physical characteristics on social interaction. *Journal of Personality and Social Psychology, 39,* 861–873.

Klein, R. W. (1980). pH and perspiration. *Cosmetics and Toiletries, 95*(7), 19–24.

Labows, J. N., McGinley, K. J., & Kligman, A. M. (1982). Perspectives on axillary odor. *Journal of the Society of Cosmetic Chemists, 34,* 193–202.

Largey, G. P., & Watson, D. R. (1972). The sociology of odors. *American Journal of Sociology, 77,* 1021–1034.

Lawless, H. T., & Cain, W. S. (1975). Recognition memory for odors. *Chemical Senses and Flavor, 1,* 331–337.

Lawless, H. T., & Engen, T. (1977). Associations to odors: Interference, mnemonics, and verbal labeling. *Journal of Experimental Psychology: Human Learning and Memory, 3,* 52–59.

Levine, J. M., & McBurney, D. H. (1977). Causes and consequences of effluvia: Body odor awareness and controllability as determinants of interpersonal evaluation. *Personality and Social Psychology Bulletin, 3,* 442–445.

Liddell, K. (1976). Smell as a diagnostic marker. *Postgraduate Medical Journal, 52,* 136–138.

Lippman, L. G. (1980). Toward a social psychology of flatulence: The interpersonal regulation of natural gas. *Psychology: A Quarterly Journal of Human Behavior, 17,* 41–50.

Mace, J. W., Goodman, S. I., Centerwall, W. R., & Chinnock, R. F. (1976). The child with an unusual odor. *Clinical Pediatrics, 15,* 57–62.

MacFarlane, A. (1975). Olfaction in the development of social preferences in the human neonate. *Parent-infant interaction,* Ciba Foundation Symposium 33. Amsterdam: Elsevier.

Marks, L. E. (1978). *The unity of the senses.* New York: Academic Press.

McBurney, D. H. (1984). Taste and olfaction: Sensory discrimination. In I. Darian-Smith (Ed.), *Handbook of physiology: Section 1. The nervous system: Volume 3. Sensory processes, Part 2.* Bethesda, MD: American Physiological Society.

McBurney, D. H., Levine, J. M., & Cavanaugh, P. H. (1977). Psychophysical and social ratings of human body odor. *Personality and Social Psychology Bulletin, 3,* 135–138.

McClintock, M. K. (1971). Menstrual synchrony and suppression. *Nature, 229,* 244–245.

McClintock, M. K. (1983). Synchronizing ovarian and birth cycles by female pheromones. In D. Muller-Schwarze & R. M. Silverstein (Eds.), *Chemical signals in vertebrates 3.* New York: Plenum.

Michael, R. P., Bonsall, R. W., & Warner, P. (1974). Human vaginal secretions: Volatile fatty acid content. *Science, 186,* 1217–1219.

Montagna, W., & Parakkal, P. (1974). *The structure and function of skin* (3rd ed.). New York: Academic Press.

Morris, N. M., & Udry, J. R. (1978). Pheromonal influences on human sexual behavior: An experimental search. *Journal of Biosocial Science, 10,* 147–157.

Moskowitz, H. R., & Gerbers, C. L. (1974). Dimensional salience of odors. *Annals of the New York Academy of Sciences, 237,* 1–16.

Moulton, D. G. (1977). Minimum odorant concentrations detectable by the dog and their implications for olfactory receptor sensitivity. In D. Muller-Schwarze & M. M. Mozell (Eds.), *Chemical signals in vertebrates.* New York: Plenum.

Mulder, D. J. (1971). Dogs in diagnosis. *The Lancet, 2,* 555.

Muller-Schwarze, D., & Mozell, M. M. (Eds.). (1977). *Chemical signals in vertebrates.* New York: Plenum.

Mykytowycz, R. (1970). The role of skin glands in mammalian communication. In J. W. Johnston, Jr., D. G. Moulton, & A. Turk (Eds.), *Advances in chemoreception: Communication by chemical signals* (Vol. 1). New York: Appleton-Century-Crofts.

Mykytowycz, R. (1977). Olfaction in relation to reproduction in domestic animals. In D. Muller-Schwarze & M. M. Mozell (Eds.), *Chemical senses in vertebrates.* New York: Plenum.

Nemy, E. (1981, April 8). On the scent of what sells a perfume. *New York Times.*

Nesbitt, P. D., & Steven, G. (1974). Personal space and stimulus intensity at a Southern California amusement park. *Sociometry, 37,* 105–115.

Orbach, C. E., Bard, M., & Sutherland, A. M. (1957). Fears and defensive adaptations to the loss of anal sphincter control. *Psychoanalytic Review, 44,* 121–175.

Parlee, M. B. (1983). Menstrual rhythms in sensory processes: A review of fluctuations in vision, olfaction, audition, taste, and touch. *Psychological Bulletin, 93,* 539–548.

Porter, R. H., Cernoch, J. M., & Balogh, R. D. (1985). Odor signatures and kin recognition. *Physiology and Behavior, 34,* 445–448.

Porter, R. H., Cernoch, J. M., & McLaughlin, F. J. (1983). Maternal recognition of neonates through olfactory cues. *Physiology & Behavior, 30,* 151–154.

Porter, R. H., & Moore, J. D. (1981). Human kin recognition by olfactory cues. *Physiology and Behavior, 27,* 493–495.

Preti, G., & Huggins, G. R. (1975). Cyclical changes in volatile acidic metabolites of human vaginal secretions and their relation to ovulation. *Journal of Chemical Ecology, 1,* 361–376.

Preti, G., & Huggins, G. R. (1978). Organic constituents of vaginal secretions. In E. Hafez & T. Evans (Eds.), *The human vagina.* Amsterdam: Elsevier/North Holland.

Preti, G., Huggins, G. R., & Silverberg, G. D. (1979). Alterations in the organic compounds of vaginal secretions caused by sexual arousal. *Fertility and Sterility, 32,* 47–54.

Quadagno, D. M., Shubeita, H. E., Deck, J., & Francoeur, D. (1981). Influence of male social contacts, exercise and all-female living conditions on the menstrual cycle. *Psychoneuroendocrinology, 6,* 239–244.

Quatrale, R. P., Stoner, K. L., & Felger, C. B. (1977). A method for the study of emotional sweating. *Journal of the Society of Cosmetic Chemists, 28,* 91–101.

Rabin, M. D., & Cain, W. S. (1984). Odor recognition: Familiarity, identifiability, and encoding consistency. *Journal of Experimental Psychology: Learning, Memory, and Cognition, 10,* 316–325.

Rogel, M. J. (1978). A critical evaluation of the possibility of higher primate reproductive and sexual pheromones. *Psychological Bulletin, 85,* 810–830.

Roth, P. (1974). *The great American novel.* London: Transworld Publishers.

Rotton, J. (1983). Affective and cognitive consequences of malodorous pollution. *Basic and Applied Social Psychology, 4,* 171–191.

Rotton, J., Barry, T., Frey, J., & Soler, E. (1978). Air pollution and interpersonal attraction. *Journal of Applied Social Psychology, 8,* 57–71.

Rotton, J., Frey, J., Barry, T., Milligan, M., & Fitzpatrick, M. (1979). The air pollution experience and physical aggression. *Journal of Applied Social Psychology, 9,* 397–412.

Rozin, P. (1976). The selection of foods by rats, humans, and other animals. In J. S. Rosenblatt, R. A. Hinde, & C. Beer (Eds.), *Advances in the study of behavior.* New York: Academic Press.

Rubin, D. C., Groth, E., & Goldsmith, D. J. (1982, August). *Olfactory cuing of autobiographical memory.* Paper presented at the meeting of the American Psychological Association, Washington, DC.

Russell, F. (1981). *The secret war.* Chicago: Time-Life Books.

Russell, M. J. (1976). Human olfactory communication. *Nature, 260,* 520–522.

Russell, M. J. (1983). Human olfactory communications. In D. Muller-Schwarze & R. M. Silverstein (Eds.), *Chemical signals in vertebrates 3.* New York: Plenum.

Russell, M. J., Mendelson, T., & Peeke, H. V. S. (1983). Mothers' identification of their infant's odors. *Ethology and Sociobiology, 4,* 29–31.

Russell, M. J., Switz, G. M., & Thompson, K. (1980). Olfactory influences on the human menstrual cycle. *Pharmacology, Biochemistry, and Behavior, 13,* 737–738.

Rutowski, R. L. (1981). The function of pheromones. *Journal of Chemical Ecology, 7,* 481–484.

Sarnat, H. B., & Netsky, M. G. (1974). *The evolution of the nervous system.* New York: Oxford.

Sastry, S. D., Buck, K. T., Janak, J., Dressler, M., & Preti, G. (1980). Volatiles emitted by humans. In G. R. Waller & O. C. Dermer (Eds.), *Biochemical applications of mass spectrometry, First supplementary volume.* New York: Wiley.

Schleidt, M. (1980). Personal odor and nonverbal communication. *Ethology and Sociobiology, 1,* 225–231.

Schleidt, M., & Hold, B. (1982). Human axillary odour: Biological and cultural variables. In J. E. Steiner & J. R. Ganchrow (Eds.), *Determination of behaviour by chemical stimuli.* London: IRL Press.

Schleidt, M., Hold, B., & Attili, G. (1981). A cross-cultural study on the attitude towards personal odors. *Journal of Chemical Ecology, 7,* 19–31.

Schneider, D. J., Hastorf, A. H., & Ellsworth, P. C. (1979). *Person perception* (2nd ed.). Reading, MA: Addison-Wesley.

Shelley, W. B., Hurley, H. J., & Nichols, A. C. (1953). Axillary odor: Experimental study of the role of bacteria, apocrine sweat, and deodorants. *A.M.A. Archives of Dermatology and Syphilology, 68,* 430–446.

Sokolov, J. J., Harris, R. T., & Hecker, M. R. (1976). Isolation of substances from human vaginal secretions previously shown to be sex attractant pheromones in higher primates. *Archives of Sexual Behavior, 5,* 269–274.

Solis-Gaffar, M. C., Niles, H. P., Rainieri, W. C., & Kestenbaum, R. C. (1975). Instrumental evaluation of mouth odor in a human clinical study. *Journal of Dental Research, 54,* 351–357.

Stefanik, R. M. (1980, September 16). Odor strikes school where janitors are out. *Pittsburgh Post Gazette.*

Stoddart, D. M. (1980). *The ecology of vertebrate olfaction.* London: Chapman and Hall.

Sturm, W. (1979). Deosafe fragrances: Fragrances with deodorizing properties. *Cosmetics and Toiletries, 94,* 35–48.

Sulloway, F. J. (1979). *Freud, biologist of the mind.* New York: Basic Books.

Swift, P. (1979, December 2). Keeping up with youth. *Parade Magazine.*

The medicine show. (1980). Mount Vernon, New York: Consumers Union.

Turk, A., Johnston, J. W., & Moulton, D. G. (Eds.). (1974). *Human responses to environmental odors.* New York: Academic Press.

Uttley, M. (1972). Measurement and control of perspiration. *Journal of the Society of Cosmetic Chemists, 23,* 23–43.

Wallace, P. (1977). Individual discrimination of humans by odor. *Physiology & Behavior, 19,* 577–579.

Whitehouse, H. A., & Carter, O. (1968, February). Deodorant efficacy of toilet bars. *Soap and Chemical Specialties, 64,* 66, 68, 75, 76, 102.

Wiener, H. (1966). External chemical messengers. I. Emission and reception in man. *New York State Journal of Medicine, 66,* 3153–3170.

Wiener, H. (1979). Human exocrinology: The olfactory component of nonverbal communication. In S. Weitz (Ed.), *Nonverbal communication: Readings with commentary* (2nd ed.). New York: Oxford.

Winter, R. (1976). *The smell book: Scent, sex, and society.* Philadelphia: J. B. Lippincott.

IV DEVIANCE

9 Maturation and Social Behavior: A Framework for the Analysis of Deviance

Gregory Northcraft
University of Arizona

Albert Hastorf
Stanford University

> *according to folklore our appearance telegraphs more information about us than we would care to reveal on a battery of personality inventories, intelligence tests, and character scales. From flame-colored hair through flat feet, few aspects of appearance fail to provide kernels of folk insight into another's nature.''*
> —(Berscheid & Walster, 1974)

INTRODUCTION: STUDIED INDIFFERENCE?

Among those doing research in the area, it has been fashionable over the years to bemoan the paucity of work being done on the psychology of *morphology*—the physical constitution and appearance of the human body. Thus, thumbing through the literature it is not uncommon to run across comments like that of Berscheid, Walster, and Bohrnstedt (1973) that:

> While there is a long and rich tradition in social psychology about how we perceive others and ourselves, how we organize these perceptions of self and others, and finally how we behave in interactions as a result of these perceptions, it is baffling how seldom physical appearance has been included as a variable within this tradition. (p. 1)

Given the time-honored adage that "first impressions are lasting," the folk-wisdom-alleged potency of physical appearance variables, and the virtual certainty that first impressions are based, in part, on physical appearance considerations (see Miller, 1970), absence of research in this realm would appear at first

221

blush an unjustifiable mystery. Many psychological researchers, however, suspect this oversight may not be so unreasoned.

Specifically, Lindzey (1967) has suggested two reasons why research on the psychology of morphology traditionally may have been avoided. First, he notes that the focus of psychological research always has been social and behavioral *change,* or at the very least what is (in principle) *changeable.* Spending time researching an aspect of the human experience that is (within limits) as relatively fixed and immutable as physical constitution amounts to pursuing something of a theoretical dead end. From a more romantic orientation, Lindzey's point might be taken to imply that researching implications of that which cannot be changed violates the scientist's deep-seated self-image as instrument of change and savior.

Lindzey also notes (and others agree; see Hammond, 1957) that avoidance of this area of research might well be a consequence of what he terms the *spectacular failure* of past models of the relationship between morphology and behavior to produce a viable and fruitful tradition of exciting research. Included in this list of ill-fated formulations would be the work of Gall and Spurzheim (1809), that of Kretschmer (1936), and Sheldon's work on somatotypes (1940).

Fortunately, these comments belie the amount of psychological research that has been done on physical appearance and constitution, or morphology. For instance, in one 6-month index for *Psychological Abstracts* in the late seventies, there were a whopping 52 citations for papers on obesity alone. Similarly, the last decade has seen a growing concern for quality research on disability and handicap as variables in social interaction. Finally, there exists in the psychological literature a strong tradition of research on physical attractiveness as a psychological variable (Berscheid & Walster, 1974.)

On the theoretical side of the coin, a more recent approach to the relationship between morphology and behavior that *has* generated some interest in psychological circles (see for instance Moriarity, 1974; Richardson, 1976) is Goffman's (1963) notion of "stigma." Summarized briefly, the "stigma" model consists of three basic propositions. First, all members of society have internalized a common belief system that dictates what is normal and what is deviant. Second, individuals alter their normal patterns of behavior when interacting with a morphologically deviant individual. Third, morphologically deviant individuals have negative self-concepts, manifested in the form of defensive, self-conscious styles of self-presentation. Essentially, this view sees the "stigma" (a handicap, for instance) as a stimulus to which *both* the possessor and his fellow-interactants respond.

Coming from what is now recognized as an ethnomethodological orientation, Goffman conceived the responding on *both* sides of the interaction to be *rule* governed, with the rules dictated by the common belief system. It would be the rules that tell interactants (on *both* sides of the interaction) just how to react to deviance. It is the belief system that make the possessor of a stigma and fellow-interactants agree that there is something to be reacted to.

That the "stigma" model would warrant a better reception than a "body-type-yields-behavior-type" theory like Sheldon's should come as no surprise. As Hall and Lindzey (1957) have noted, research that supports any *direct* link between physiology and behavior appears dangerously supportive of genetic determinism. And again, because of the scientist's attachment to "change-ability," genetic determinism and its aura of inevitability have never really been welcome visitors in the social behavior circles of American psychology. Goffman's stigma doctrine, on the other hand, undercuts the directness of the link between morphology and behavior by interposing normative considerations between the stigma stimulus and its associated responses.

The stigma doctrine further constitutes an improvement on theories like Sheldon's in that it has implications that go beyond the behavior of the possessor of the stigma. It posits an effect on fellow interactants, namely adjustment or disruption of behavior according to rules dictated by the belief system.

The stigma doctrine clearly has its drawback, however. The central notion that reactions to deviance are rule governed, with the rules being somehow a simple function of the common belief system, would appear in part misleading. Whereas some research has demonstrated *negative* reactions to the deviant, such as behavioral rigidity and inhibition, and escape (Kleck, Ono, & Hastorf, 1966), other work has demonstrated that rules may prescribe *positive* responding, such as a "norm to be kind" (Hastorf, Northcraft, & Picciotto, 1979). In fact, rules could be in conflict, or the rules might simply dictate *unspecified* differential treatment for the different, resulting in ambivalent (Richardson, 1976) and even unpredictable and inconsistent interactions with the handicapped. Thus, the discomfort and avoidance or disruption of behavior that Goffman construes as simple rule-following could instead be a manifestation of confusion or uncertainty as to how to act appropriately.

This seems especially likely in view of research by Freedman and Doob (1968) utilizing *contrived* forms of deviance. By creating artificial forms of unspecified deviance, they were able to recreate the avoidance behavior in others and self-consciousness in "deviants" found in interactions with real deviants. That these outcomes could be obtained with *contrived* forms of deviance suggests that whatever rules there are could hardly be specific, and that reactions to deviance probably occur as a function of interactional consequences of general social beliefs about deviant individuals.

Furthermore, "rule governed" suggests a consistency and uniformity of reactions over time. However, research has shown (Langer et al., 1976) that mere exposure to a deviant individual even in the absence of interaction may attenuate the avoidance and discomfort effects usually characteristic of interactions between normals and stigmatized individuals. This has led to a "novel stimulus" hypothesis, which contends that some of the avoidance and discomfort responses of fellow-interactants may simply be an involuntary arousal reaction to an unusual visual stimulus (Langer et al., 1976) or violated expectations of what a person should be like (Richardson, 1976) rather than rule following. As an involuntary response to the *visual impact* of a stimulus, initial reactions to deviance may be subject to habituation over time (Tighe & Leaton, 1976). At least part of the usual reaction to deviance in social interaction therefore might be subject to attenuation over time unless other forces serve to maintain it (Moreland & Zajonc, 1976).

Finally, the stigma doctrine casts reactions to deviance in a potentially misleading short-scope time frame. It fails to address the question of how its two separate "main" effects (self-consciousness of the deviant individual, and alteration of behavior of fellow-interactants) might interact or reciprocally contribute to the development or maintenance of each other over time. In this sense, the stigma doctrine may be true, but only as far as it goes. It may be providing only a glimpse of the first stage of a complex interactional progression.

To put this last point in a more concrete perspective, consider the possibility of a recessive gene that gives one little boy in 100,000 green ears. Let us further suppose that knowing his ears to be so unusual, the possessor feels quite self-conscious and has an appropriately defensive self-presentation style. And finally, let us suppose that the deviance of the ears is not lost on others, and that they react in "appropriately" negative ways (such as avoiding eye contact and generally feeling and looking uncomfortable in the presence of the green-eared boy).

As far as this portrait goes, it seems to fit the stigma model quite well. But the example begs some important questions. Just as the negative self-presentation style of the green-eared boy and the "avoidance" behaviors of his fellow-interactants can be seen as responses to the stimulus of the green ears, those behaviors themselves in turn serve as stimuli in social interaction. The negative self-presentation of the green-eared boy becomes a stimulus to his fellow-interactants, and their avoidance behaviors become a stimulus to him. These stimuli then in turn generate more responses *cum stimuli* on *ad infinitum*. It is this interplay or interaction of main effects that the stigma doctrine seems to neglect.

AN EXTENDED PERSPECTIVE

The importance of interactional effects can be seen by considering the Symbolic Interactionist view of the self-concept (see for instance Manis & Meltzer, 1967), and the more recent Dynamic Interactionist and contextualist views of social interactions (e.g., Lerner, 1978). Tracing their roots back to Mead's notion of reflected self-appraisal (1934) and Cooley's "looking glass theory of the self" (1902), these interactionist views emphasize the alteration or determination of self-concept and social behavior via *internalization* of the reactions of others.

Traditionally, interactionist research has focused on the effects of overtly evaluative feedback in social interaction (see for instance Haas & Maehr, 1965). However, research on self-fulfilling prophecies has demonstrated that non-evaluative behaviors can have similar impact. Word, Zanna, and Cooper (1974) found that interviewers behaved somewhat differently when interviewing black and white job applicants (who themselves had been trained to behave identically). Some of the interviewers were then "trained" to demonstrate the behavior characteristic of interviewing blacks. Later, some naive white job applicants were interviewed by both "trained" and untrained interviewers. Those job applicants interviewed by the "trained" interviewers (i.e., treated as if they were black applicants) performed less adequately and were more nervous. Apparently, the interviewers' behavior, which was by design a reaction to race of applicant, was reflected in the behavior of the applicant. In a similar study (Snyder, Tanke, & Berscheid, 1977), males talked over the phone with "target" females whom they had been told were either attractive or unattractive. These conversations were taped. Objective ratings of the "target" females' contributions to the conversations revealed that the females assigned to the "attractive" condition were judged to have sounded more attractive, even though they were of course blind to which "attractiveness" condition they had been assigned.

Applying these results to the example of the green-eared boy, the avoidance behavior of others in his presence may cause the green-eared boy to become even *more* self-conscious and more defensive. Similarly, his self-conscious defensive interaction style may cause others to increase their avoidance behavior in his presence. In this way, interactions between the green-eared boy and others begin to take on the properties of a feedback loop, or exacerbation cycle (Storms & McCaul, 1976). Negative behavior on each side of the interaction *elicits* negative behavior on the other, which then acts to render behavior on the first side of the interaction even more negative. Over time, behavior on *both* sides becomes progressively more negative.

One aspect of the exacerbation process not adequately explained by the symbolic interactionist camp is the mechanism by which internalization of the actions of others into the self-concept is accomplished. One candidate offered by Storms and McCaul is the attribution process. Faced with the negative behavior of another in his presence, the green-eared boy searches for a possible cause to which to attribute that behavior. If the attribution he comes up with entails some implicit evaluation (e.g., "he acts that way because he doesn't like me," hence I am not a likeable person) that evaluation might then be internalized, and assimilated into the self-concept.

The attribution process plays a similarly important role on the other side of the interaction. If, as suggested earlier, the discomfort and avoidance behavior of the fellow-interactant occur as a function of confusion and visual impact (rather than as simple compliance to belief system prescriptions), the fellow-interactant may find himself searching for an appropriate cause for his behavior. The defensive self-presentation style of the stigmatized individual (rather than the deviance itself) then becomes a handy hook on which to hang (i.e., rationalize) the avoidance behavior and discomfort of the fellow-interactant. This would be especially true if the fellow-interactant is unconsciously trying to avoid the correct attribution for fear of feeling himself prejudiced against morphologically deviant individuals.

The disturbing possibility herein is that *an exacerbation cycle can become independent of the stimulus that originally gave rise to it.* To return again to our example, an individual interacting with a green-eared boy may (wishing to avoid a self-attribution of prejudice) incorrectly label his initial discomfort as a reaction to the green-eared boy being cold and defensive. The green-eared boy's own initial discomfort would simply reinforce this attribution. And the avoidance behavior thereby elicited in the fellow-interactant would serve to reinforce the discomfort and self-consciousness of the green-eared boy. At this point, the self-consciousness of the green-eared boy would have become a function of the avoidance behavior he perceives in his fellow-interactant, whereas the fellow-interactant would have come to see his discomfort and avoidance behavior as a function of the negative self-presentation style of the green-eared boy. There would still be an exacerbation cycle, but now it would be independent of green ears.

This is important because of the previous suggestion that response to morphological deviance is *not* totally rule governed but is as well a product of confusion of how to act and visual impact of a novel stimulus. Because the confusion could presumably be cleared up with a little experience, whereas the visual impact (as has been shown) will attenuate naturally with exposure, negative responses to deviance should be short lived. On the other side of the interaction, a decrease in negative feedback might help repair the self-concept of the deviant. As a consequence, the defensiveness of self-presentation could be decreased, effectively initiating a *positive* feedback loop, resulting in increasingly more favorable interactions.

However, if an exacerbation cycle becomes established that is independent of the stigma stimulus, habituation to the visual impact of the stigma would have little effect, and whatever experiences do occur (assuming avoidance doesn't become escape) will be decidedly negative. In short, the negative nature of responses to deviance, once established, may be maintained even in the absence or dissolution of their original cause.

Perhaps even more unsettling is the possibility suggested by the self-fulfilling prophesy research that reaction to deviance is a *robust* phenomenon; that is, the *original* response need only occur on one side of the interaction to initiate the exacerbation cycle. Consider what would happen if our green-eared boy had longish hair that effectively masked his deviance. The stimulus value of his stigma would be lost on others, because they wouldn't be able to see the ears. However, he might, nevertheless, be self-conscious about his condition and therefore defensive, constantly fearing discovery of his deviance. His defensive interaction style might then *elicit* avoidance behavior and discomfort, whereas in the previous examples it simply *reinforced* them. Such a possibility could also be relevant when a fellow-interactant has simply habituated to the visual impact of the stigma as a stimulus. Or when the stigma has quite literally disappeared (as when an obese person loses an extraordinary amount of weight), but the negative self-concept, or perhaps the *expectation* of negative behavior in social interaction, remains.

In a recent study done by Strenta and Kleck (1979), subjects were led to believe *incorrectly* that a fellow interactant thought them to have some stigmatizing physical condition (a facial scar, an allergy requiring constant medication, or epilepsy). Following a taped interaction, subjects were asked to review the tape and enumerate which behaviors of their fellow-interactant were specific reactions to the stigma they thought themselves to possess. The results revealed a marked propensity for the subject to view the actions of the fellow-interactant as influenced by the supposed stigma. Such a self-conscious cognitive set could easily promote a defensive interaction style and thereby initiate the type of exacerbation cycle under consideration. It should come as no great surprise, then, that the negative impact of one form of morphological deviance (obesity) has been known to outlast the deviance itself by over 20 years (Stunkard, 1976).

On the other side of the interaction, if the possessor of the stigma for some reason fails to feel or act self-consciously, the self-fulfilling prophesy studies suggest that avoidance behavior and discomfort on the part of fellow-interactants again might *elicit* self-consciousness, where in previous examples it was only being reinforced.

In any of these cases, the final outcome would appear to be the same—an exacerbation cycle with a self-conscious, defensive interaction style on one side of the interaction, and avoidance behavior and discomfort on the other. What is important to note is the robustness and dynamism of this phenomenon. Not only can the negative nature of the interaction become independent of its cause—it can even establish itself where some of the original behaviors thought to contribute to its causation are absent. Once established, this exacerbation cycle then harbors the potential of augmenting the negative nature of the interaction far beyond the original reaction to the stigma stimulus. The interactionist perspective thus casts interaction with a deviant in a much more complex and dynamic light than the "stigma" doctrine.

The possibility of these robust interactional effects raises serious questions about the proper unit of analysis for examining interactions between deviant and normal individuals. Past efforts (e.g., Comer & Piliavin, 1972; Kleck, Ono, & Hastorf, 1966) traditionally have utilized a small scope methodology, choosing to focus on a stimulus (the stigma) and its apparently immediate effects (discomfort on one side of the interaction; self-consciousness on the other). Although this approach helps lay out the molecular components of complex interactions, it may miss the dynamic interaction of these components over time. In the Strenta and Kleck study just discussed, for instance, it would be interesting to know whether the predisposition of the subject to attribute behaviors of his fellow-interactant to his (nonexistent) stigma actually impacted the fellow-interactant's behaviors. Furthermore, the robustness of the negativity of interactions between deviant and normal individuals presents problems for a molecular-oriented analysis. Molecular research focusing on only one side of the interaction cannot adequately distinguish between true causation of an effect by a stimulus and misleading correlation of the stimulus and response, as when the behavior of a fellow-interactant (rather than the stigma) elicits a given set of behaviors in a deviant individual.

On the other hand, research might fit the other extreme and focus only on the long-term outcome of the dynamic, interactional processes. We could envision a study, for instance, that found that green-eared boys are less likely to go to college, less likely to get married, and more likely to choose professions where they work alone. Again, such studies really fail to elucidate the processes by which outcomes occur. In doing so, they might serve to invite the adoption of oversimplified models, by masking the manner in which molecular effects (such as negative self-concept) are complexly maintained or augmented by interaction over time. In a similar fashion, macro-outcome studies propagate a confusion between the permanence of a stigma and the immutability of its effects. Given the previously discussed possibility of maintenance of molecular effects over time by complex interactional processes and not simply reaction to a stimulus, macro-outcome studies misrepresent the power of the stigma stimulus to generate negative impact over time. In doing so, such studies disguise the potential dissolution (and even reversal) of these effects by intervention and disruption of the exacerbation cycle processes.

In sum, the level of analysis problem can be likened to answering the question of how a particular football game turned out. At the molecular level, which team kicked off, or who scored a touchdown are details that give no feeling for the "big picture" of the whole game. On the other hand, a final score is an outcome measure that contains little information of how that outcome came about, or in what ways it might have been otherwise. The only satisfactory response to such a question must be more than even just the two together—it must be an accounting of how the molecular details of the game added up to produce the final macro-outcome. The analogue to this answer in psychological research would be a methodology that extends the analysis of molecular effects over time. The fine-grained analysis characteristic of molecular research could be brought to bear on both sides of the interaction over time to help understand how dynamic and interaction processes produce macro-outcomes. This is what we might call an *extended molecular analysis.*

Extended molecular analysis offers to the study of morphology and behavior several distinct advantages. Where an area of research consists of scattered molecular findings and a few macro-outcome propositions, extended molecular analysis can help integrate a "pet" phenomenon into the theoretical mainstream. Insinuating mediating processes (where possible) between a variable's molecular effects and macro-outcomes serves to weave isolated findings into a larger theoretical fabric by relating the molecular effects and macro-outcomes to other *accepted* "building block" processes, as well as to each other. This weaving of the "pet" phenomenon into the theoretical mainstream then serves several further purposes. It lends credence to the relationship between a variable and an associated macro-outcome by casting the relationship in terms of accepted and understood processes. Further, by casting the "pet" phenomenon in a light relating it to mainstream theoretical principles, extended molecular analysis may help stimulate research interest in the area. Recall for a moment Lindzey's comment that previous formulations relating behavior and morphology have failed to generate a fruitful research tradition. One can imagine this resulting from researchers failing to see any connection between a "body-type-yields-behavior-type" model (like Sheldon's) and their own work. The suggesting of mediating links (such as feedback cycles and attributional processes) between morphology and its psychological and social impact may serve to highlight such connections. For example, studies by DeJong (1979) demonstrate the mediation of reactions to the obese by attributions of self-cause. This work may help bring research on obesity out of the weight-change clinic and into the cognitive social psychology mainstream.

In addition to integrating isolated findings into the theoretical mainstream, suggesting mediating links between a variable's molecular and macro-outcome impact provides an opportunity to understand paradoxes and puzzling exceptions that often surface at the macro-outcome level. Understanding the development and interaction of molecular effects over time allows insights into how causal paths might diverge. In effect, this constitutes a perspective on how paradoxes and exceptions might occur—and thereby helps the exceptions prove the rules. (As we see later, deviance in maturational timing presents its share of such puzzles: the failure of physical development to predict dating behavior in adolescence, and the existence of two contradictory behavior syndromes associated with late maturation in adolescent males.)

Finally, extended molecular analysis provides an opportunity for the scientist to flex his muscles as an instrument of change and savior. When a relationship is couched only in terms of a variable's molecular effects and macro-outcomes, the researcher is left with little room to maneuver. The only apparent way to preclude the impact is by doing away with the variable—an untenable alternative given the relative immutability of morphology. However, identification of mediating links between the molecular and macro impact of a variable provides opportunities for intervention, especially when these mediating links include cognitive processes such as attributions.

DEVIANT MATURATION: A CASE IN POINT?

One morphological variable that stands to profit greatly theoretically from the more thorough examination offered by extended molecular analysis is the timing of physical maturation during adolescence.

Medically, it is quite normal for adolescent growth to begin maturational acceleration anytime within a 6-year span (from 9 to 15 years of age for males; from 8 to 14 years of age for females). During puberty, hormonal changes within the body are reflected outwardly in weight gain, growth in height, and development of secondary sex characteristics, such as pubic hair. In fact, for many years pubic hair development was utilized to assess maturational development. More recently, however, more accurate assessment methods have been developed (Tanner, 1969) that account as well for development of other secondary sex characteristics (such as testicular enlargement in males, or breast development in females).

The normal maturational calendar for an adolescent features several years of progressive height and weight gain climaxed by an adolescent "growth spurt," which lasts about a year. Height and weight gains reach their peak velocity at this time. During peak velocity, males will gain (on the average) at the rate of 9.4 centimeters per year in height, and 9 kilograms per year in weight. For females, peak velocity gain in weight (on the average, 8.3 kilograms per year) occurs 6 months after peak velocity gain in height (8.3 centimeters per year). It should be stressed, however, that adolescent maturation is extremely variable. From a doctor's point of view, the span of "normal" timing is sufficiently wide that as little as 5 or 6% of adolescents would actually be classified as having physically deviant maturational timing (Barnes, 1976).

However, comparison of an adolescent's growth progress with peers' progress, or a standard for his or her chronological age, may reveal deviations within the medically "normal" range that, nevertheless, generate a certain amount of anxiety and unhappiness. Such unfortunate departures from the normal maturational schedule may include cases of development that is too slow or too fast, and can encompass as many as 16% of adolescents within a chronological age level (Dwyer & Mayer, 1968/1969).

Even where overall timing of the maturational process is normal, asynchronizations may develop when individual *parts* of the body develop physically at quite apparently disparate rates (Eichorn, 1975). In such cases, the resulting appearance of the adolescent may be *temporarily* freakish or deformed, again possibly resulting in a significant amount of psychological and social impact.

The possibility of psychological and social impact arising as a consequence of maturational timing makes it a particularly fertile research realm for a variety of reasons. First, and probably most obviously, variations in physical development may have important status consequences during the adolescent years (e.g., Faust, 1960) because of the fundamental role physical development plays in providing opportunities for social involvement. For boys, success *and even participation* in varsity athletics will be heavily determined by relative physical development within the peer group. For girls, attractiveness to the opposite sex and consequent social status and prestige similarly may be affected by physical maturation and development. For both boys and girls, peer-group visibility will be affected by maturational timing both for purely physical reasons. Through the aforementioned mediation of social involvement this visibility in turn may determine or contribute to accessibility of formal and informal positions of leadership within the peer group (Jones & Bayley, 1950). Finally, acceptance into the *adult* community, along with its consequent accessibility to *appointed* positions of leadership, responsibility, and even employment during adolescence may as well in large measure be determined by timing of physical development of the teenager (Peskin, 1967).

Perhaps more surprisingly, timing of maturation and development is also of interest because its social impact during adolescence is reflected in later life. For boys, timing of maturation has been linked to later life occupational status, informal social participation, supervision of subordinates, and even officership in organizations (Ames, 1957). For girls, age of menarche has been shown to be strongly related to age of marriage (Buck & Stavraky, 1967). Of course, the links between maturational timing and social status during adolescence and later life may not be at all independent. Research has shown that maturational timing is strongly related to both educational aspirations and expectations (Duke et al., 1979). Thus those variables that confer status and mediate extracurricular involvement (and perhaps even curricular achievement) in high school consequently may be playing a substantial role in determining which students go to which colleges, and even which students go to college at all. By thus mediating the accessibility of career training and development, timing of maturation may gain a measure of determination over later careers and behaviors.

Timing of maturation in the adolescent is also of concern because of its affect-laden nature during the teenage years. The apparent potency of this variable in ordering lives during the teenage years is not lost on the adolescent; self-evaluations reveal a greater preoccupation with physical characteristics than with either social or intellectual development (Frazier & Lisonbee, 1950). Additionally, the simple magnitude and salience of physical changes during adolescent development (such as menarche) may generate anxiety. Further, concern with the *permanence* of bodily changes that for the adolescent heretofore had been only temporary may prove difficult to deal with. Further, such basic physical development may be exacerbated by adolescents' being less emotionally mature and socially tactful in dealing with (and talking about) such changes both in the self and others.

Finally, timing of maturation during adolescence should prove fertile ground for psychological inquiry because of the unique research opportunity it represents. For instance, variations in rate of physical development are very democratic; maturational timing has not been convincingly linked to any demographic characteristics (except family size), thereby allowing examination of the psychological and social impact of a morphological variable relatively uncontaminated by other psychological effects. More importantly, if it is *change* that psychological research thrives on, study of the maturing adolescent should provide a welcome climate indeed. Because the variable under consideration entails morphological *change* and not just difference, it provides an opportunity to examine development of impact over time. Further, developments in pediatric endocrinology have even provided for the opportunity to gaining experimental control over both the timing (Barnes, 1976) and extent (Goldzieher, 1956) of an adolescent's physical development. Thus, coupled with its face-valid potency, the methodological "handiness" of maturational timing as an experimental variable should have rendered it quite an attractive arena in which to pursue research.

Happily, the attractiveness of this variable has not been lost on the psychological community. Many ambitious efforts have been mounted in the attempt to ascertain the psychological and social correlates of aberrations from normal adolescent physical maturation. Unfortunately, even the best of these have proven lacking in theoretical inquisitiveness and insight.

PAST EFFORTS: RESEARCH AT THE MACRO-OUTCOME LEVEL?

The California Adolescent Growth Study (Jones, 1943) proved the most fruitful of a series of large-scale research efforts. These studies consisted of examination and observation of a group of adolescents (usually longitudinally), in the hopes of dealing with a broad variety of developmental issues. The California Adolescent Growth Study in particular followed 180 adolescent males and females (pared down by attrition from 215 original entrees) over a 7-year period in the early 1930s. Data collected during this period included demographics, some behavioral records (such as activity levels and peer-reputation ratings), physiological and morphological data, and a psychological profile relating to abilities, interests, attitudes, activities, and status in the group. Where possible, follow-up data also was collected when the subjects reached age 33.

Less well known was a similar research effort undertaken by the Institute of Human Development at Berkeley. Known as the Guidance Study (McFarlane, 1938), this work appears to have focused on independent replication of the Growth Study findings, but from a decidedly more psychoanalytic perspective. Its methodology consisted of the TAT, some interviewing, and evaluation on motorific, cognitive, social, and emotional scales. Subjects were adolescents from Berkeley, born in 1928 and 1929. Follow-up was attempted when subjects reached age 30.

A less ambitious, non-longitudinal research program was conducted in the San Jose area of California, again in the 30s. This study (Stone & Barker, 1937, 1939) focused specifically on the implications of maturational timing in females. Examining 720 females ranging in age from 132 to 183 months, methods of evaluation and assessment included the Bernreuter Personality Inventory, the Pressey Interest–Attitudes Test, and the Otis Intelligence Test.

Finally, the National Health Examination Survey (e.g., Gross et al., 1979) represents the only significant data sample on the impact of adolescent maturation that does not consist exclusively of California adolescents during the 30s. The magnitude of this effort was substantial, entailing a national probability sample of 3600 males and 3500 females ages 6 to 11, and a similar number of males and females ages 12 to 17. This research program was carried on during the 60s; data collection included demographics and personal history, physical examination, several forms of objective testing, and interviews with school personnel.

These (and a few smaller) research efforts have reaped a harvest of effects of maturational timing during adolescence. For males, the early maturer has been found to be seen as physically more attractive and better groomed, more poised and matter of fact, and less attention-seeking (Jones & Bayley, 1950). However, he may also demonstrate higher manifest anxiety, more frequent and severe loss of temper, long-term reliance on social participation, and a relatively permanent avoidance and fear of impulses (Peskin, 1967). The late-maturing male, on the other hand, shows greater evidence of negative self-concepts, prolonged dependency needs, feelings of rejection by others, rebellious attitudes toward parents, and strong affiliative needs (Mussen & Jones, 1957). He also tends to rate higher in activity, intellectual curiosity, and exploratory behavior but lower in social submission (Peskin, 1973). Most recently it has been discovered that late-maturers are more likely to suffer from enuresis, especially if male (Gross et al., 1979). In general, early maturation for males appears to be a mixed blessing, offering certain competive advantages (for instance, earlier acceptance into the "adult" world) at nontrivial costs, such as a demand for overly rapid emotional adjustment and assumption of responsibility. For the late-maturing male, on the other hand, life probably seems like *all* costs with little compensation; at best adolescence probably prepares him for later life's capriciousness and inequalities.

In females, whereas early maturation spells better adjustment and a more favorable self-concept, it is the late-maturing females that are outgoing, assured, eager, animated, peppy, talkative, and confident (Jones & Mussen, 1958). As with males, early maturation in females surfaces as a mixed blessing providing some clear-cut advantages in social status and prestige (Faust, 1960), but often at the cost of isolation from age-mates. In general, however, the social and psychological impact of maturational rate appears to be much less striking for females, a point reflected in the fact that males requesting medical treatment for maturational timing problems outnumber females by 15 to one (Barnes, 1976).

Of course, it could be argued that the greater impact of late maturation for males (and, until recently, early maturation for females) may simply reflect a heightened *salience* due to males maturing later than females. (A late-maturing female could still mature earlier than most of her male friends, but a later-maturing male matures later than everyone; and in turn, the early-maturing female may be taller than even the tallest of her male friends.) However, that salience is the whole answer is doubtful in view of recent work that has demonstrated that dating behavior is much better predicted by age than sexual development (Dornbusch et al., 1979).

Interestingly, most of these studies of maturational timing have chosen only to compare the two extremes (late- and early-maturers), disregarding the advisability of including a "normal" comparison group. Where such precautions have been taken (Weatherly, 1964), the psychological picture painted is somewhat different. For males, the early maturers look much like "normals"—it is the late maturers that are the real outsiders. For females, differences between the extremes become even less distinct.

Unquestionably, these studies reveal that maturational timing during adolescence can have important psychological and social impact. What they do *not* reveal is how or why.

Significantly, the absence of work on the *process* by which the impact of maturational timing occurs is not simply a function of the correlational methodology that pervades the maturational-timing research tradition. One recent study (Rosenfeld, Northcraft, & Hintz, 1982) has taken the medical manipulability of maturational timing in hand and attempted to examine the effects of this variable prospectively and experimentally. In this study, late maturers have been randomly assigned to hormone treatment or nontreatment conditions. Physical, psychological, and social variables are being evaluated in a standard before/after design. Unfortunately, a little serious consideration suggests that in a very important sense, even experimental control over this variable will yield results that are little better than correlational in nature. Careful experimental control may help better delineate the precise profile of impact of maturational timing. But as long as the outcome variables are general macroimpact over an extended time period, the important *process* questions will remain unanswered.

That examination of process considerations is important for maturational timing is underscored by the existence of several puzzles at the macro-outcome level. First is the difference in effect between the sexes. Maturational-timing effects are generally less pronounced in females; further, whereas early maturation tends to render males the center of attention, it often isolates the early-maturing female (Jones & Mussen, 1958). Second, late maturation in males has become associated with two *contradictory* behavioral syndromes—heightened activity and social withdrawal (Jones & Bayley, 1950). No current theoretical formulation can explain both of these possibilities. Finally, as mentioned earlier, recent work has demonstrated that dating behavior in adolescence is much better predicted by age than sexual development—even breast-size development in females.

What is missing in the maturational-timing research tradition is, of course, extended molecular research. At the molecular level of analysis, researchers in this area have apparently accepted implicitly a simplified causal model. It is stated in Dwyer and Mayer (1968): "Marked variations in maturational timing may adversely influence how a person is treated by others, and how he thinks of himself'' (p 356).

Typically, then studies of the effects of maturational timing have focused only on the macro end product of the interplay and development of these presumed molecular effects, as if to suggest that what occurs in between is obvious or unimportant. From a theoretical standpoint, however, nothing could be further from the truth. Although previous outcome research has presented a convincing ''big picture'' of the effects of maturational timing, examination of interactional, dynamic processes that mediate the development of macro-outcomes offers the possibility of substantial theoretical advancements.

Notice, however, that even at this preliminary level, important underlying processes are at work. Unlike the deviance of handicap, the deviance of aberrant maturation may be *positive or negative*. As mentioned earlier, deviance does not produce effects in some ''self-evident'' manner—positive or negative affect becomes attached to deviance according to social belief systems. Whereas deviance of any sort may produce uncertainty of how to act, that uncertainty will have some ''feel'' (positive or negative) to it. Thus, the deviance of early or excessive growth in females may produce avoidance because of male rules concerning acceptable sizes of dating partners. In males, such excessive growth impacts positively because of the male preoccupation with success in competitive athletics. Physical deviance has no a priori psychological impact; it comes to have one through the larger social context. And contrary to Goffman's notion that the belief system dictates rules for social behavior, in some cases it may instead be rules for social behavior that determine when deviance is important.

This last point becomes important to the maturationally deviant because there may be instances where there are no important rules that apply, and where thereby the deviance has no positive or negative valuation. This seems plausible because maturational deviance falls on a continuum with normality—other kinds of deviance are more discreetly separated. Where a handicapped person would always be seen as different, a late maturer (for instance) might only be seen as different in those situations (like competetive athletics) that have rules that speak to his or her deviance.

The two different possible valuations of deviant maturation give rise to two different types of interactional consequences. On the negative side of the coin, the deviance will deflate the self-concept of the deviant and give rise to negative behaviors in fellow-interactants. This leads into the exacerbation cycle discussed earlier, where the negativity on both sides of the interaction becomes independent of the original stimulus. On the positive side of the coin, deviance could inflate the self-concept of the deviant (the early-maturing male, for instance) and generate positive behaviors in fellow-interactants (such as deference, rather than avoidance). This would lead to a feedback loop with positive consequences, where the positivity on both sides of the interaction would become independent of the original stimulus.

Of course, the independence of the exacerbation cycles or feedback loops is quite important if the deviance in question is maturational, for two reasons. First, maturation is a transient phase of life, and so the deviance as a stimulus eventually disappears. If a feedback loop is established that is *independent* of the stimulus, the original impact (positive or negative) should long outlive the disappearance of the deviance. This helps explain how maturational timing can still have life-style impact (as noted earlier) even 15 years later. Second and equally important, if there are situations where maturational deviance should have less impact, the independence of a positive or negative feedback loop will bring impact to those situations as well. Thus, for instance, the negativity established between a female and a late-maturing male in a dating situation (where the deviance is important) might easily carry over to a schoolwork setting (where the deviance is unimportant). Note that this is *more* than just generalization, which would eventually extinguish. It is establishment of responses that then maintain the effect over time.

These contentions become even more plausible given the robustness of interactional processes. Consider, for instance, the consequence of one side of the interaction not reacting to the deviance as a stimulus.

If the deviant's deviance is not a very salient component of his (or her) self-image, or if he (or she) does not have a strong internalization of the appropriate situational norm, the behaviors generally associated with the deviance may not be generated. The late-maturing male, for instance, may not feel himself to be very abnormal and may consequently not behave self-consciously. Similarly, the early-maturing male may not consider overwhelming physical presence to be important and may therefore not display the expected self-confidence. However, a fellow-interactant may nevertheless provide a stimulus in the form of reaction to the deviance, if the deviance and normal are sufficiently salient to the fellow-interactant. And this stimulus may elicit *as a response* in the deviant the very behavior appropriate to the deviance but not generated through the self-image. For instance, avoidance or rebuff of the late-maturing male in social interaction may *induce* self-consciousness even where self-perception does not. Furthermore, not particularly having any reason to expect the rebuff or avoidance, the late-maturing male will be faced with a classic attribution problem. In searching for a sufficient cause to explain the behavior of his fellow-interactant, he may well hit on his deviance, thus heightening (for him) its causal salience and increasing his internalization of the appropriate norm.

On the other side of the coin, the deviant's self-perception as deviant gives rise to behaviors that induce in fellow-interactants (even those who don't perceive the deviant as deviant) reactions toward the deviant that are commensurate with the deviant's self-image. In effect, the self-image of the deviant becomes a kind of self-fulfilling prophesy—sensitivity to his (or her) own deviance has caused the deviant to generate behaviors that insure that others will react to him (or her) *as a deviant.* Of course, their reactions then become a further stimulus for the deviant to evaluate. Being commensurate with the deviant's self-perception *as deviant,* the behaviors of others then serve to reinforce the deviant's self-perception, which in turn leads the deviant to generate more behaviors that ensure his (or her) treatment by others as deviant. For instance, the confident, self-assured presentation style of the early-maturing male may elicit respect or deference in social interaction. This respect or deference should further bolster his positive self-image, leading to a *more* confident, self-assured presentation style, and more consequent respect and deference in further social interaction. The prophesy of the self-image, therefore not only fulfills itself—it becomes self-reinforcing, leading to a positive spiral, heightening its effects over time.

Extended molecular analysis thus reveals the effects of maturational timing as extremely robust. Even where appropriate reactions to deviance are absent, social interaction effects will render the system highly self-correcting. Where "expected" behavioral reactions are missing, they will quickly be elicited indirectly. Where salience of the deviance, or feeling for the norm, are low, they may quickly be heightened, "telegraphed" through behavior in social interaction.

On a more general theoretical plain, extended molecular analysis has provided three distinct models to explain effects of deviance in maturational timing: reactivity initiated directly by both sides of the interaction, initiated directly only from the side of the fellow-interactant, or initiated directly only from the side of the deviant. Interestingly, recent research (Northcraft, 1981) may provide a way to choose among these alternatives in the case of deviant maturation. Explorations into perceptions of physical deviance (utilizing hierarchical-clustering-analysis techniques) have revealed that people seem to group their perceptions of physical diability into six categories: sensory defects, self-caused problems, cerebral disfunctions, internal disorders, permanent functional impairments, and "essentially normal" problems. The two most salient manifestations of deviant maturation (excessive and deficient stature) were placed in the "essentially normal problems" category and in fact were perceived as minimally deviant even within that category. (Given the previously noted probability of deviance in maturational timing, it may be assumed that this sample was comprised of almost entirely nondeviants.) This finding suggests, then, that the reactions may not be directly initiated by the nondeviant fellow-interactant, because manifestations of maturational-timing deviance do not elicit extreme "deviance" judgments from nondeviants. Consequently, maturational-timing effects are probably elicited by the behaviors of the maturational deviant.

Of course, feedback loops can also have "dampening" effects. Consider the possibility of a fellow-interactant who has not internalized the norm, or, to take a more realistic possibility, has the norm and notes the deviance but specifically chooses to behave as if the deviance of the deviant were not important. A well-meaning parent, for instance, might choose to treat a late-maturing male as his chronological, rather than physical, age dictates in sympathy for the youngster's plight. Again, the behavior, unexpected from the viewpoint of the deviant, gives rise to an attribution problem for the deviant, but one with a decidedly different twist. The deviant now finds himself being treated to behaviors normally accorded nondeviants *in spite of* his apparent deviance. Following the workings of a classic *negative* feedback loop, this treatment would be expected to *decrease* the deviant's perception of the causal salience of his deviance and weaken the deviant's internalization of the appropriate norm. In turn, this would redirect the deviant's own behavior toward more normal realms, thus promoting more normal reactions toward him (or her) in further social interaction. The result is a spiral that moves to *normalize* the deviant's perception of himself, thereby undercutting the primary cause of maturational-timing effects.

From the viewpoint of intervention strategies aimed at alleviating maturational-timing problems, this suggests that a little understanding and sympathy could go a long way. Specifically, a potentially destructive feedback loop can be interrupted by orchestrating reactions that serve to direct the deviant's self-image in more productive directions. Further, where orchestration of responses is not feasible, attribution therapy provides another way to interrupt a harmful exacerbation cycle. Key to the feedback loops discussed is the deviant's attribution of causality for his fellow-interactant's responses to his (or her) deviance. It is this *attribution* (rather than the behavior) that feeds the self-image of the deviant. Attribution-therapy literature (Valins & Nisbett, 1971) suggests that supplying the deviant with an attribution strategy that prevents internalization of the fellow-interactants' behaviors will also interrupt the feedback cycle. Although this may not dissolve a harmful self-image in the manner of a negative feedback loop, it may at least serve to attenuate spiralling feedback effects. Sympathetic responding can have its risks, however.

Consider the possibility of sympathetic feedback to a late-maturing male, as mentioned earlier. Sympathetic reaction not only bolsters a flattering self-image—it also encourages further interaction. And where reactions of other fellow-interactions prove less hospitable, it specifically encourages further interaction with the sympathetic party. This can be a problem where the perceived encouragement to further interaction is not well founded, or where such encouragement was meant to be situation specific. Thus, the prom queen may react positively to the late-maturing male out of sympathy. It may be the case, however, that she is doing so to *terminate* the interaction as pleasantly (and quickly!) as possible. Or it may be that she means to encourage further interaction on a *friendship* basis, but not at any romantic level of involvement. This would seem especially important if maturation deviance norms are situation specific. For instance, whereas the late-maturer's self-image may be the primary cause of reactions to him in friendship interactions, much stronger norms concerning acceptable physical characteristics of dating partners may overwhelm any self-image effects in romantic interactions.

Inappropriate responses by the late maturer to this limited encouragement (for instance, his or her overtures to further interaction) may quickly reveal the sympathetic response for what it really is. And this, in turn, may undermine the late-maturer's confidence in his accurate assessment of others responding to him. The result could be the internalization in the late maturer of a cognitive predisposition to interpret *all* feedback as essentially negative, much as the subjects in the Strenta and Kleck experiment (cited earlier) saw the majority of responses to them as reactions to their deviance. The adoption of such a predisposition would virtually ensure the miring of the late-maturing male in the mud of a negative self-image spiral.

Interestingly, the possibility of divergent feedback spirals in maturational-timing effects sheds some light on an important paradox noted earlier. That there are two distinct behavioral syndromes associated with late maturation in males may simply reflect the work of positive and negative feedback loops. Withdrawal may occur where self-perceived deviance and a commensurate negative self-image fuel a destructive feedback loop. On the other hand, the late-maturing male who somehow generates positive behaviors may find his confidence swelled by favorable reactions that belie even his own self-perception of his deviance. This alternative feedback scenario could even result in the late-maturer's admission into the social center of attention—a lofty realm normally reserved for his confidence-bolstered early-maturing counterparts.

CONCLUSIONS

Extended molecular analysis provides an important tool to the process of psychological inquiry. As shown in the application of this perspective to the effects of deviance in maturational timing, examining complex interactions of molecular processes can provide invaluable insights into the generation of macro-outcomes.

In the present chapter, extended molecular analysis has been developed within the framework of a thought–experiment methodology. This should not be thought of as a limitation; armchair theorizing only succeeds insofar as it is backed up by careful empirical validation of constituent principles and hypothesized relations. Extended molecular analysis thus should be seen not as a self-contained methodology, or a proposal for less empirical investigation. Rather, it is a frame of mind to bring to a problem like maturational-timing effects. Getting the "big picture" is certainly one aspect of the scientific endeavor, but understanding how the individual pieces of the puzzle interlock to yield the "big picture" is the essence of scientific understanding.

Extended molecular analysis is no stranger to the scientific scene. Gaining understanding into macroeffects by examining the interplay of their component molecular processes is as old as the practice of science. So in a sense, this chapter has at best done little more than re-invent the wheel. Hopefully, at worst it has re-invented a wheel that will help round out our understanding of the relationship between psychology and morphology.

As a final thought, this extended molecular analysis would be remiss in not summarizing the impact of adding interactional considerations to a stigma conceptualization of interaction with the deviant other. The stigma doctrine casts reactions to deviance in terms of two simple and isolated effects. The interactionist perspective adds several important dimensions to this description: namely, the augmentation and maintenance of the simple effects over time independent of the continued availability of the deviance as a stimulus. Unfortunately, persistence and generalization of simple effects often can prove empirically indistinguishable from the complex maintenance and augmentation of these same effects over time, leaving little to choose between these two views.

The real test of the interactionist amendments to stigma theory therefore must lie in another suggestion of the foregoing analysis—the possibility of interactional interventions that wash out the normal reactions to a form of deviance, despite its continued presence as a stimulus. This is an outcome that is clearly not compatible with the stigma doctrine.

This test could be achieved retrospectively by what we might call an analysis of deviant cases of deviance. These would be individuals whose morphological deviance would, by the stigma doctrine, *incorrectly* predict them to behave self-consciously and have negative self-concepts. By analyzing the processes by which certain cases have *avoided* the negative impact that stigma theory would expect them to have encountered, we can again utilize the exceptions to help prove (or in this case establish) the rules.

On the prospective side of the coin, a more exciting test of the interactionist amendments might lie in the *creation* of deviant cases of deviance. Armed with the insights of an extended molecular analysis, strategies could be designed to preempt the initiation of detrimental exacerbation cycles, thereby allowing habituation and adjustment to the deviance as a stimulus to run their natural course. In the case of maturational timing, several such strategies come to mind. First, by initiating interactions in situations where behaviors are highly structured, the deviant can (to some extent) help preclude behavioral confusion or uncertainty (and hence discomfort) in his fellow-interactant. Second, armed with an attributional set that minimizes internalization of negative responding on the part of the other, the deviant might successfully survive original negative responding without adverse effects. Finally, there would appear to be tremendous potential in the deviant "talking a good game" and not telegraphing his or her discomfort across interactions. In these ways, establishment of detrimental feedback loops might be prevented, and a little positivity substituted in its place.

Happily, this last possibility may have already successfully undergone a preliminary test. In the study mentioned earlier in which some late-maturing males received hormone treatments to speed up maturation, patients came in 1 year after entering the study, in order that the psychological and social impact of their participation might be assessed. One patient, during his 1-year follow-up interview, admitted that being in the study had lots of impact for him; he felt more confident, and saw himself as interacting better with both his family and friends. Significantly, he attributed the changes to his no longer being ashamed or defensive about his "problem," because he had been reassured by the doctors that it was nothing permanent or anything he should feel guilty about. Clearly these changes did not occur as a function of changes in morphology because this patient had been in the "control" group of the experiment—he had never received any treatment for his "problem," and had not grown in the interum. In his case, a favorable expectation set and a dose of reassurance had drastically altered the interactional consequences of his morphological deviance. It is through the understanding of just such outcomes that we will come to know the essence of interaction with a deviant other.

ACKNOWLEDGMENT

Work on this manuscript was supported in part by the Center for the Study of Youth Development, Stanford University; and by National Institute of Health Grant PHS 5 R01 MH29446.

REFERENCES

Ames, R. (1957). Physical maturing among boys as related to adult social behavior. *California Journal of Educational Research, 8,* 69–75.

Barnes, H. V. (1976). The teenager with pubertal delay. *Primary Care, 3,* 215–229.

Berscheid, E., & Walster, E. (1974). Physical attractiveness. In L. Berkowitz (Ed.), *Advances in experimental social psychology* (Vol. 7). New York: Academic Press.

Berscheid, E., Walster, E., & Bohrnstedt, G. W. (1973). *Body image, physical appearance, and self-esteem.* Paper presented to the American Sociological Meetings, New York.

Buck, C., & Stavraky, K. (1967). The relationship between age of menarche and age of marriage among childbearing women. *Human Biology, 39,* 93–102.

Comer, R. J., & Piliavin, J. A. (1972). The effects of physical deviance upon face-to-face interaction: The other side. *Journal of Personality and Social Psychology, 55,* 33–39.

Cooley, C. H. (1902).*Human nature and the social order.* New York: Scribner.

DeJong, W. (1979). *Reactions to the obese mediated by attributions of self-cause.* Unpublished doctoral dissertation, Stanford University.

Dornbusch, S. M., Carlsmith, J. M., Gross, R. T., Martin, J., Jennings, D., Rosenberg, A., & Duke, P. M. (1979). *Sexual development, age, and dating: A comparison of biological and social influences upon one set of behaviors.* Stanford University. Unpublished manuscript.

Duke, P. M., Carlsmith, J. M., Dornbusch, S. M., Martin, J. A., & Gross, R. T. (1979). *Behavioral correlates of early and late sexual maturation during adolescence.* Stanford University.

Dwyer, J., & Mayer, J. (1968–1969). Psychological effects of variations in physical appearance during adolescence. *Adolescence, 3,* 353–368.

Eichorn, D. H. (1975). Asynchronizations in adolescent development. In S. E. Dragastin & G. H. Elder (Eds.), *Adolescence in the life cycle: Psychological change and social context.* New York: Wiley.

Faust, M. S. (1960). Developmental maturity as a determinant of prestige in adolescent girls. *Child Development, 31,* 173–184.

Frazier, A., & Lisonbee, L. K. (1950). Adolescent concerns with physique. *School Review, 58,* 397–405.

Freedman, J. L., & Doob, A. N. (1968). *Deviance.* New York: Academic Press.

Gall, F. J., & Spurzheim, J. G. (1809). *Recherches sur le systeme nerveux.* Paris: Schoell.

Goffman, E. (1963). *Stigma.* Englewood Cliffs, NJ: Prentice Hall.

Goldzieher, M. (1956). Treatment of excessive growth in the adolescent female. *Journal of Clinical Endocrinology, 16,* 249.

Gross, R. T., Duke, P. M., Martin, J. A., Carlsmith, J. M., & Dornbusch, S. M. (1979). *Enuresis: multi-handicapping condition.* Paper presented to the National Meeting of the American Pediatrics Association.

Haas, H. J., & Maehr, M. L. (1965). Two experiments on the concept of self and the reaction of others. *Journal of Personality and Social Psychology, 1,* 100–105.

Hall, C. S., & Lindzey, G. (1957). *Theories of personality.* New York: Wiley.

Hammond, W. H. (1957). The status of physical types. *Human Biology, 29,* 223–241.

Hastorf, A. H., Northcraft, C. B., & Picciotto, S. R. (1979). Helping the handicapped: How realistic is the performance feedback received by the physically handicapped. *Personality and Social Psychology Bulletin, 5,* 373–376.

Jones, H. E. (1943). *Development in adolescence.* New York: Appleton-Century.

Jones, M. C., & Bayley, N. (1950). Physical maturing among boys as related to behavior. *Journal of Educational Psychology, 41,* 129–148.

Jones, M. C., & Mussen, P. H. (1958). Self-conceptions, motivations, and interpersonal attitudes of early- and late-maturing girls. *Child Development, 29,* 491–501.

Kleck, R., Ono, H., & Hastorf, A. H. (1966). The effect of physical deviance upon face-to-face interaction. *Human Relations, 19,* 425–436.

Kretschmer, E. (1936). *Physique and character.* New York: Harcourt.

Langer, E. J., Fiske, S., Taylor, S. E., & Chanowitz, B. (1976). Stigma, staring, and discomfort: A novel-stimulus hypothesis. *Journal of Experimental Social Psychology, 12,* 451–463.

Lerner, R. (1978). Nature, nurture, and dynamic interactionism. *Human Development, 21,* 1–20.

Lindzey, G. (1967). Morphology and behavior. In J. N. Spuhler (Ed.), *Behavioral consequences of genetic differences in man.* New York: Aldine.

Manis, J. G., & Meltzer, B. N. (1967). *Symbolic interaction: A reader in social psychology.* Boston: Allyn & Bacon.

McFarlane, J. W. (1938). Studies in child guidance: I Methodology of data collection and organization. *Monograph of the Society for Research in Child Development, 3*(6, whole).

Mead, G. H. (1934). *Mind, self, & society.* Chicago: University of Chicago Press.

Miller, A. G. (1970). The role of physical beauty in impression formation. *Psychonomic Science, 19,* 241–243.

Moreland, R. L., & Zajonc, R. B. (1976). A strong test of exposure effects. *Journal of Experimental Social Psychology, 12,* 170–179.

Moriarity, T. (1974). Role of stigma in the experience of deviance. *Journal of Personality and Social Psychology, 29,* 849–855.

Mussen, P. H., & Jones, M. C. (1957). Self-conceptions, motivations, and interpersonal attitudes of late- and early-maturing boys. *Child Development, 28,* 243–256.

Northcraft, G. B. (1981). *The perception of disability.* Unpublished masters thesis, Stanford University.

Peskin, H. (1967). Pubertal onset and ego functioning. *Journal of Abnormal Psychology, 72,* 1–15.

Peskin, H. (1973). Influence of the developmental schedule of puberty on learning and ego functioning. *Journal of Youth and Adolescence, 2,* 273–290.

Richardson, S. A. (1976). Attitudes and behavior toward the physically handicapped. *Birth Defects Original Article Series, 12,* 15–34.

Rosenfeld, R., Northcraft, G. B., & Hintz, R. (1982). A prospective randomized study of a testosterone treatment of constitutional short stature in adolescent males. *Pediatrics, 69*, 681–687.

Sheldon, W. H. (1940). *The varieties of human physique.* New York: Harper & Brothers.

Snyder, M., Tanke, E. D., & Berscheid, E. (1977). Social perception and interpersonal behavior: On the self-fulfilling nature of social stereotypes. *Journal of Personality and Social Psychology, 35*, 656–666.

Stone, C. P., & Barker, R. G. (1937). Aspects of personality and intelligence in postmenarcheal and premenarcheal girls of the same chronological ages. *Journal of Comparative Psychology, 23*, 439–455.

Stone, C. P., & Barker, R. G. (1939). The attitudes and interests of premenarcheal and postmenarcheal girls. *Journal of Genetic Psychology, 54*, 27–71.

Storms, M. D., & McCaul, K. D. (1976). Attribution processes and emotional exacerbation of dysfunctional behavior. In J. H. Harvey, W. J. Ickes, & R. F. Kidd (Eds.), *New directions in attribution research.* New York: Wiley.

Strenta, A., & Kleck, R. E. (1979). *Effects of an individual's salient physical characteristics upon social perception.* Dartmouth College, Unpublished manuscript.

Stunkard, A. J. (1976). *The pain of obesity.* Palo Alto: Bull.

Tanner, J. M. (1962). *Growth at adolescence.* Oxford: Blackwell.

Tanner, J. M. (1969). Growth and endocrinology of the adolescent. In L. J. Gardner (Ed.), *Endocrine and genetic diseases of childhood.* Philadelphia: Saunders.

Tighe, T. J., & Leaton, R. N. (1976). *Habituation: Perspectives from child development, animal behavior, and neurophysiology.* New York: Wiley.

Valins, S., & Nisbett, R. E. (1971). *Attribution processes in the development and treatment of emotional disorder.* New York: General Learning Press.

Weatherly, D. (1964). Self-perceived rate of physical maturation and personality in late adolescence. *Child Development, 35*, 1197–1210.

Word, C. O., Zanna, M. P., & Cooper, J. (1974). The nonverbal mediation of self-fulfiling prophecies in interracial interaction. *Journal of Experimental Social Psychology, 10*, 109–120.

10

The Measurement of Attitudes toward Physically Disabled Persons

Jerome Siller
New York University

Research and conceptualization in the area of disability has been strongly influenced by Lewinian field theory. Phenomenology and the interactive field of person and environment have characterized the approach of the most influential theorists and researchers in the area (Barker, Wright, Meyerson, & Gonick, 1953; Cruickshank, 1980; Dembo, 1969; Dembo, Leviton, & Wright, 1975; Meyerson, 1948; Wright, 1960, 1964). From this group of persons and their associates the term somatopsychology was coined to describe the social-psychological consequences of disablement. Somatopsychology is concerned with the relation between physique and behavior. Barker et al. (1953) stated: "This relation is concerned with those variations in physique that affect the psychological situation of a person by influencing the effectiveness of his body as a tool for actions or by serving as a stimulus to himself or others" (p. 1). Somatopsychological analysis stresses dynamic interactions and fluid evolving situations amenable to change and modification that reflects a potent rehabilitation orientation.

Many consequences follow from this particular field oriented emphasis. An immediate crucial point is that disability is a social event and that perhaps the most disabling aspect of the situation may be the orientation of those who are singling out "disability" as something special. Thus, Finkelstein (1979) in a radical attack upon all the research in disability contends that to even structure the situation in terms of the disability involved is prejudicial and invalid. Other works on the nefarious effects of labeling and the process of stigmatization support such concerns. From another vantage point, one must also be concerned about implications drawn regarding the supposed causative effects of the disability when, in fact, that may not be the salient feature. In any event, it is clear that a social psychological perspective reveals that disability is not within the person but can only be understood (aside from its purely physical aspects) in terms of the interactive context. Even what is to be defined as a disability has social determinants.

The emphasis on somatopsychology has had two direct consequences for the study of attitudes. There clearly is a distrust of the "artificiality" of laboratory-type research. In addition, there tends to be disinterest or at least considerable reservation regarding the usual attitude research employing self-report instrumentation. Both of these criticisms are based upon the objection beautifully considered by Dembo (1969) in terms of the "subject-object" orientation and the obvious preference for more phenomenological approaches.

Nonetheless, attitudes toward disabled persons have received considerable attention and a rather large body of literature on this subject exists. I characterize general trends in the overall research, discuss some of the methodological problems involved, describe principle instruments employed, and review some of the more systematic studies. Because of time and space limitations certain topics that deserve considerable explication such as parental and employment attitudes are only briefly dealt with. The latter is slighted because adequate recent treatments are available (Schroedel & Jacobsen, 1978) and the former because of the almost complete absence of significant research on such a vital topic.

The term *physically disabled* although adequate for certain purposes may not be of a sufficiently clear referent for many other purposes. As used in this chapter, "physically disabled" mostly focuses on the sensory conditions such as deafness and blindness, and on the skeletal and motor conditions such as amputation, poliomyelitis, and body deformations. However, skin disorders, burns, obesity, and other physical conditions that serve as a strong social stimulus clearly fall within our purview. Other conditions such as cancer, heart disease, epilepsy, muscular dystrophy, and the like are also considered here as there is a clear continuity of attitude orientation toward all these disabilities. One other definitional note: The presence of neurological involvement affecting one's cognitive/coping potential, e.g., cerebral palsy *with* cognitive dysfunction, substantially changes the stimulus picture for nondisabled respondents. We assume that any central nervous system involvement will affect motoric behavior without higher intellectual dysfunction unless otherwise noted.

MEASUREMENT CONSIDERATIONS

Relevant literature on attitudes toward the physically disabled is widely dispersed over many journals encompassing many different professional groups. No particular theoretical approach, aside from that of somatopsychology, has had much impact. For example, Kelley et al. (1960) discussed comparison level as a potentially valuable approach to understanding some aspect of disabled–nondisabled interactions but this has not proven to have stimulated research. (Interestingly enough, the Kelley group virtually ignored the more traditional attitude work as reported at that time). Other possible theoretical approaches such as attribution theory, derivations from the "just world" hypothesis, and the like all have received relatively minor attention with the possible exception of Freudian theory. Sociological influences as reflected in such concepts as stigmatization, marginality, and deviance have generated some research (Kutner, 1971; Safilios–Rothschild, 1970; Sussman, 1965) but the major thrust has been atheoretical in nature with most studies obtaining empirical correlations based upon instruments of dubious psychometric character.

Virtually all techniques generally employed in the measurement of attitudes have been used in relation to disability. Thus, questionnaires, social distance scales, sociometrics, interviews, semantic differentials, picture stimuli, physiological measures, story telling, interaction studies, and more have all been used in at least one study. Such a wide range of instruments and techniques makes evaluation of individual studies difficult due to the absence of adequate technical information to assess the measuring instruments and limits generation of results. Most instruments have been used only once with no follow-ups. The lack of a theoretical framework to guide scale development has been another major deficiency in attitude research as has been insufficiently sensitive and complex measures of children's attitudes. However, several systematic and programmatic approaches have been undertaken, and these are reviewed briefly in this section from the point of view of their methodological bases; their substantive findings are reported in the other content sections.

A basic conceptual division has been made as to whether attitudes toward the disabled are best represented as being along a single dimension of positiveness–negativeness (e.g., the Attitude Toward Disabled Persons Scale (ATDP) of Yuker, Block, & Younng, 1966) or as multidimensional in character (Schmelkin, 1985; Siller et al., 1967a, 1967b; Siller, 1970a, 1970b; Whiteman & Lukoff, 1964, 1965).

Unidimensional approaches typically derive a single score such as degree of acceptability, positiveness, or willingness to associate with. Even when multiple scores are obtained, as might be done on a sociometric or social distance scale, a single underlying dimension is assumed, the true meaning of which is only loosely suggested by the title of the scale. In practice, despite the name offered by the scales developer, and by different areas of content tapped, such scales usually intercorrelate fairly highly. Most of the single score measures probably tap a mixture of dimensions on an affective level (Siller et al., 1967b).

Some of the more widely used unidimensional attitudinal indices used in disability are described.

The ATDP (Yuker et al., 1966) is easily the most widely used disability attitude assessment scale. Developed to provide a brief and easily administered scale of verbalized attitudes directed toward disabled persons in general, it is applicable for both nondisabled and disabled users. Scale development was carefully thought through and well executed. Items follow a basic Likert-type format (e.g., "You should not expect too much from disabled people," "Most disabled people worry a lot," responded to along a 6-point scale). Considerable data on the psychometric properties of the ATDP, its factorial structure for various populations, and its correlates among numerous personological, demographic, and response set indices, have been reported by various researchers with much of that work summarized in an excellent monograph (Yuker et al., 1966). The original ATDP has 20 items for which a summated total score is obtained. Two new forms of the ATDP expanded the number of items to 30, but the improvement in reliability over that of the 20-item form was not substantial; the value of the new scales as alternate forms is limited by their median intercorrelation of .67. Various reliability estimates have been derived with an average in the mid-.70s, not dissimilar to other scorable measures of attitudes. A wide variety of sources for data on validation also were reported by Yuker et al. (1966) generally supporting the use of the ATDP for the general purpose of attitude measurement in this domain.

The ATDP has served as a spur to research in this area. For a number of years it was the only "reasonable" instrument of its type available. Its brevity, ease of administration, and supportive psychometric data encourages wide use. Offshoots such as those that substituted specific disability conditions for the more generalized term of disability (e.g., Bates, 1965) have appeared in a number of reports of research. It also has been translated into many languages.

As experience with the ATDP has accumulated, a number of recurrent concerns have been expressed regarding the scale. Strong doubts have been raised regarding the general term *disability* that raises too many referents for the respondent; e.g., is amputation or blindness or a cardiac condition being referred to? (Siller, 1966; Siller et al., 1967b). The scale also evokes connotations of emotional, social, and cultural possibilities for those using it (Smits, Conine, & Edwards, 1971). The reliability of the ATDP, although acceptable for research purposes in general, is somewhat on the low side. In all, this writer who has used the ATDP extensively in the past and has provided considerable data on its basic psychometric properties and correlates (e.g., Siller & Chipman, 1963, 1964; Siller et al., 1967a) regards the ATDP as the best developed of the "early" disability attitude indices but feels that its inherent limitations are serious enough to justify development of more powerful measures.

Cowen and his associates have provided unidimensional scales on blindness (Cowen et al., 1958, 1961) and on deafness (Cowen et al., 1967) that have received more than the usual peripheral development and usage. Although other unidimensional Likert-type scales are available, the Cowen and Yuker scales have been the more widely used ones with the latter by far the instrument of choice for most studies and the former sometimes preferred for studies on the specific conditions of blindness or deafness.

The semantic differential (Osgood et al., 1957) has been frequently used in one form or another in a number of studies (e.g., Whiteman & Lukoff, 1965) and particularly for doctoral dissertations (e.g., Haddle, 1973). A problem, to this writer, is that although the semantic differential successfully discriminates between populations or changes in a person in regard to the evaluative component, it does not contribute directly to an understanding of the content of the attitude.

Richardson (1971) and in association with others (e.g., Goodman and Richardson, 1963; Richardson et al., 1961) has examined values associated with children's interactions with the disabled by means of a set of picture stimuli. Subjects are shown pictures of six children, the same sex as themselves, in which all features of appearance are held constant except the presence or absence of a visible physical handicap and the type of handicap. The figures are ranked for preference and the average ranking for each type of condition for a population, or a child's preference in relation to his group's preference can then be determined. Numerous studies have used this approach. As a set of experimental stimuli rather than as a scale, customary indices of reliability and validity are not relevant and so have not been stressed. Some methodological issues regarding this procedure are raised later in the section on developmental factors.

A wide variety of social distance measures have been reported and are discussed throughout this chapter. To this writer the results of such studies are mostly uninteresting in that ratings are highly influenced by the other conditions concurrently being rated and that the empirical findings are virtually never tied up to a priori theoretical work. Psychometric sophistication usually is lacking and assumptions of dimensionality are sometimes inappropriately made (Siller et al., 1967a). The precise dimension upon which the social distance indices are taken (e.g., preference, seriousness for one's self) often differ from study to study making comparability difficult. However, by now a fairly consistent order of preference, as is described later, has emerged from use of this approach, and future work in this direction seems to be less productive than others to be described.

A strong relationship between a measure of disability attitude and non-disability indices is yet to be demonstrated (Siller et al., 1967a, 1967b). Does this mean that such relationships are absent or are extant instruments too insensitive? Pursuing the latter possibility as the more likely, it was suggested that methodological problems of measuring disability attitude are related to two theoretical issues (Siller, 1966). The first methodological difficulty has been mentioned earlier in terms of the vague referent of the general term "disability." This procedural problem reflects the theoretical issue of the extent to which attitudes of the public are general across disabilities and the extent to which they are specific to a disability. The second theoretical issue pertains to the dimensionality of attitude structure in this domain. Both the Cowen scales and the ATDP, by employing only a single summative score, treat this domain as one dimensional. Other work supports the contention of multidimensionality, and these are now discussed.

An important implication of the multidimensional approach is that one's definition, conceptualization, and measurement of the attitudinal domain becomes more differentiated and flexible. Major theoretical and empirical issues of this attitude domain were investigated in a series of studies under the writer's direction (Ferguson, 1970; Siller, 1970a, Siller et al., 1967a, 1967b; Vann, 1970). The purpose of these studies, which was fully realized, was to describe and to measure salient dimensions of attitudes toward the physically disabled by the nondisabled.

The latter measurement aspect is discussed here and the theoretical aspect of dimensionality and its empirical findings discussed in the following section on Structure of Attitudes.

Factor analytic techniques of scale construction represents a logical choice of method for determining whether an attitude domain is multidimensional. A direct answer is given to the question of dimensionality of attitude structure in a given area with the nature of the component attitudes suggested by interpretation of the resulting factors. Furthermore, factor analysis yields highly reliable scales with a minimum number of items. This writer and his associates developed a series of factor analytically based scales collectively called the Disability Factor Scales (DFS) that clearly demonstrate multidimensionality in this domain. Eschewing the general term *disability* separate questionnaires (Likert-type) have been developed on the conditions of amputation, blindness, cosmetic conditions (Siller et al., 1967b), deafness (Ferguson, 1970), Obesity (Vann, 1970), Cancer (Siller and Braden (unpublished), and a General Scale (Siller, 1970a) composed of the highest loading items from the specific disability conditions. The set of questionnaires together provide wide flexibility in assessing attitudes toward specific disabilities or toward the more general disability domain. Each questionnaire is scored for a number of dimensions (usually seven) that are described in the section on Structure of Attitudes. The scales are self-report, objectively scored, economically administered in terms of time (number of items for individual questionnaires range from 69 to 105, with scales ranging from as little as 4 to 23, with most about 10) and are comprehensible to adolescents. Reliability is very good particularly considering the small number of items per scale ranging with but few exceptions in the high .70s to some in the .90s. Various validity studies of factorial, construct, and concurrent group nature have proven to be very supportive. All but the cancer and obesity scales have received cross validation using fairly large numbers of cases, and results are uniformly very confirmatory of the basic attitude structure obtained and of the scales themselves (e.g., Kohler & Graves, 1973). Normative data are available for a variety of groups and various correlates obtained by the Siller group and from studies done by others. The technology of the DFS is such that new scales for different disability conditions can readily be constructed using the dimensional approach and existing item stems. The DFS has been widely used and often has proven to be discriminating even when other instruments do not (e.g., Marinelli & Kelz, 1973). Attempts to develop alternate forms so far have not been successful. Use of the DFS with disabled populations themselves has been done with a number of disability groups and a rewritten version for the deaf is being tested (Zuckerman, 1980).

Whiteman and Lukoff (1964, 1965) also have applied a components approach to the study of attitudes toward the disabled. Unlike my own approach where similar item format was deliberately used to minimize instrument variance, Whiteman and Lukoff used a diversified item format to minimize response set and to lend support to clusters or factors cutting across indices referring to common content but differing modes of presentation. Whiteman and Lukoff have provided valuable initial structuring of disability attitude dimensions and have suggested a number of potentially useful instruments of measurement. However, at present, the variety and complexity of tasks to which the subject must respond, and the level of vocabulary used, severly limit the general utility of their indices. The indices themselves have not been further developed nor reports of their further use made. The particular factorial dimensions obtained in their studies essentially can be subsumed within the set obtained in the Siller work that lends credence to both orientations and to the meaningfulness of dimensions obtained.

An interesting different multidimensional approach to attitude measurement in disability has been followed by Jordan in a series of studies extending over a number of years (Jordan, 1971). Following Guttman's facet theory approach, Jordan and various students studied physical-mental-social disability and racial ethnic differences. Defining attitudes as "a delimited totality of behavior with respect to something" (Guttman, 1950, p. 51), the orientation differs from most others that view attitudes as predispositions to behavior. Jordan developed a priori attitude behavior scales (ABS) guided by facet theory that deals with attitude subuniverses ranging through the following ordered levels: societal stereotype, societal norm, personal moral evaluation, personal hypothetical action, personal feeling, and personal action. Self-report items were then constructed by a priori methods following the aforementioned facets for the conditions of deafness, mental illness, black–white relations and mental retardation. Certain reliability and validity data are reported that are supportive of the approach. An interesting feature of the ABS has been Jordan's extensive use of cross-cultural samples.

Systematic examination of the relationship among the various measurement indices would be of considerable value in clarifying the degree of overlap among the various indices. The work of Jordan and of Siller also provide theoretical bases for further establishing the dimensionality of the attitude domain.

Jordan criticizes the usual approaches such as the factor analytic and unidimensional as being inconclusive or contradictory about predictor variables and suggests that confusion stems from items being derived from different subuniverses of the total attitude domain (1971). No formal correlational work has been done comparing the ABS of Jordan and the DFS of Siller. The former stemming from an a priori developmental approach and the latter from a systematic listing of possible content dimensions (e.g., direct contact relationships, general attitudes regarding treatment, subordinate–superordinate relationships) and then empirically through factor analysis reducing the total set of dimensions to a "basic" seven. An informal analysis of the item structure of the DFS by Jordan (personal communication) reveals a surprisingly wide diversity of item levels actually represented thereby implying that the ABS and DFS may with further development actually be examined analytically from the both positions.

Although the ATDP has been used in studies along with the DFS and the ABS, sample sizes have not been sufficiently large or representative to draw firm conclusions regarding their interrelationships. However, our contention, as indicated earlier, that the ATDP basically is a measure of general affect receives empirical support in that when the DFS and ATDP were used together what were identified as general affect scales on the DFS correlated most highly with the ATDP (Siller et al., 1967a). Elsberry (1975) found a differentiated pattern comparing the ATDP and DFS that did not follow the suggested affect interpretation; however, only 30 subjects vaguely defined as *nondisabled college students* were used. Other unpublished data of the writer's gives further support to the affect hypothesis, but a definitive resolution of this issue has yet to be made.

One final note! Considerable dissatisfaction has been raised in many quarters regarding the omission of situational factors in assessment of personality and attitudinal effects. Sloat and Frankel (1972) examined the contributions of subjects, disabilities, situations, sex of target persons, and items to the variations of attitudes toward persons with a disability, and their results strongly suggest the need for including the situational aspect within a multidimensional analytic framework, and for considering the interactional aspect of these variables. Grand, Bernier, & Strohmer's research (1982) reinforces the Sloat & Frankel conclusion by showing the importance of social context and specific disability for attitudes.

STRUCTURE OF ATTITUDES

Conceptualization of the dimensionality of the attitude domain in this area obviously has considerable practical and theoretical implication. The most direct and extensive research bearing on this question has been conducted by the present writer and his associates (Ferguson, 1970; Siller et al., 1967a; Siller, 1970a; Vann, 1970; and in considerable unpublished work). The work has been cross validated, used with a large variety of populations and with substantial numbers of persons, and confirmed by the work of others. In short, seven fairly comprehensive dimensions of attitude, along with scales to measure these dimensions, have been found for a wide range of conditions: amputation, blindness, cancer, cosmetic disfigurement, deafness, and obesity as well as for general or cross-disability dimensions. Although for certain conditions (cancer and obesity), the basic seven are not completely obtained, in general, the following are well descriptive of the findings on attitudinal components:

1. *Interaction Strain*—uneasiness in the presence of disabled persons and uncertainty as how to deal with them.

2. *Rejection of Intimacy*—rejection of close, particularly familial, relationships with the disabled.

3. *Generalized Rejection*—a pervasive negative and derogatory approach to disabled persons with consequent advocacy of segregation.

4. *Authoritarian Virtuousness*—ostensibly a "prodisabled" orientation, this factor is really rooted in an authoritarian context which manifests itself in a call for special treatment that is less benevolent and more harmful than it seems.

5. *Inferred Emotional Consequences*—intense hostile references to the character and emotions of the disabled person.

6. *Distressed Identification*—personalized hypersensitivity to disabled persons who serve as activators of anxiety about one's own vulnerability to disability.

7. *Imputed Functional Limitations*—devaluation of the capacities of a disabled person in coping with his environment.

The study of these components has led to a number of strong conclusions, some of which are noted here. The seven described represent an initial taxonomy of the attitudinal domain in disability and probably have implications for other deviant conditions. Attitude components are highly general across disabilities. Components of attitudes within a disability tend to be positively correlated, and a person favorable (unfavorable) toward one disability will have similar feelings toward others. Greatest consistencies in attitudes across disabilities ordinarily will be on the same component (e.g., Inferred Emotional Consequences on amputation with Inferred Emotional Consequences on any other condition). The structure of attitudes for physical disability is organized more strongly around attitude component than by specific disability condition.

Although attention to a specific attitudinal component might be justified for a particular purpose, careful thought should be given as to what one is really interested in and to pursuing the flexible and differentiated attitudinal path rather than using unnecessarily lesser differentiated ones. Marinelli and Kelz (1973), studying the relationship between attitudes toward disabled persons and state and trait anxiety supported this point. A form of the DFS (Cosmetic Conditions) served to discriminate subjects on the basis of heart rate and Manifest Anxiety Score whereas the ATDP did not. The more complex factorial structure of the

TABLE 10.1
Attitude Components Salient to Various Conditions

	Physical										
	Sensory			Ortho-pedic	Language		Cardiovascular			Neurological	
Attitude Components	Blind	Color Blind	Deaf	Ampu-tat'n	Sta-*bmer*	Apha-sia	Cancer	Stroke	An-gina	Cere. Palsy	Brain Damage
Interaction strain	√a	—	√	√	√	√	√	√	—	√	√
Rejection of intimacy	√	—	√	√	√	√	√	√	√	√	√
Generalized rejection	√	—	√	√	√	—	√	—	—	√	√
Authoritarian virtuouances	√	√	√	√	√	√	—	√	√	√	√
Inferred emotional consequences	√	—	√	√	√	√	√	√	—	√	√
Distressed identification	√	√	√	√	—	—	√	—	—	—	—
Imputed functional limitations	√	—	√	√	√	√	—	√	√	√	√
Intense personal aversion	—	—	—	—	—	—	—	—	—	—	—
Proximate offensiveness	—	—	—	—	—	—	—	—	—	—	—
Personal responsibility	—	—	—	—	—	—	—	—	—	—	—
Fat man stereotype	—	—	—	—	—	—	—	—	—	—	—
Positive stereotype	—	—	—	—	—	—	√	—	—	—	—

aChecks indicate found in studies by the Siller group or probable components, dashes signify not found or unlikely. Entries for all but amputation, blindness, deafness, obesity, and certain cosmetic conditions are hypothetical.
bBlank column indicates a number of conditions could be placed here or in other columns.

DFS and its orientation toward a specific attitude object were believed responsible for the discrepant attitude results.

Marinelli and Kelz used a total score for the DFS, as others have, which obscures the contribution of individual components. Some justification for this can be advanced as Siller et al. (1967b) performed what they called a "quasi-second order factor analysis" of the various scales on the DFS- Amputation, Blindness, Cosmetic Conditions combined and found four supraordinate factors labeled Net Affect, Authoritarian Virtuousness, Distressed Identification, and Cosmetic Aversion. These findings were replicated in a subsequent study by Kohler and Graves (1973). In effect, one can use the identified components individually, by division into the four quasi-factor structures, or even by summation of them all depending on one's purpose. All three approaches have been followed with fruitful results.

As more work is done on the structure of attitudes it is almost certain that various disability specific dimensions will emerge as has been found for cancer (Siller & Braden, unpublished) and obesity (Vann, 1970). It is less likely that a major general dimension will emerge using the same factor analytic approach, although that too is conceivable.

Our emphasis on the importance of recognizing the multidimensionality of attitudes toward the physically disabled derives from the expectation that under-

| Attractiveness | | Physical-Emotional | | | | | | | Special Groups | | | |
| Attractiveness | | Psychosomatic | | | | Emotional | | | Race | | | |
Comely	Ugly	Asthma	Psoriasis	Ulcer	Obesity	Neuroses	Psychoses	Charac. Disord.	White	Negro	Mental Retard.	Aged
—	√	—	√	—	√	—	√	√	—	√	√	√
—	√	√	√	—	√	—	√	√	—	√	√	√
—	√	—	√	—	√	—	√	√	—	√	√	√
—	—	√	√	√	√	—	√	√	—	—	√	√
—	√	—	√	√	√	√	√	√	—	√	√	√
—	—	—	—	—	—	√	—	—	—	—	—	—
—	—	√	—	—	√	—	√	—	—	√	√	√
—	√	—	√	—	√	—	√	√	—	—	√	—
—	—	—	√	—	√	√	—	—	—	√	—	—
—	√c	√c	√	√	√	√	—	√	—	—	—	—
—	√	√	—	√	d/	—	√	—	—	√	√	√
—	—	—	—	—	—	—	—	—	√	—	√	—

cCertain conditions may be seen as under the control of the person by some and not by others. This introduces confusion when both types are combined in a study.

dVarious conditions may be depicted sterotypically, e.g., "ulcer-type," "the blind."

standing of effective attitude change procedures, cues for developmental studies on the origins of specific components, differentiated analyses of the relation of personality structure to particular manifestations of attitudes, and the like will be enhanced. Elsewhere, (Siller, 1984) I report on a number of studies done under my supervision and by others that demonstrate the viability of this argument.

The preference for multidimensional content oriented work on our part transcends the empirical fact that more variance is accounted for in this manner. It also offers an opportunity to conceptualize and empirically test an extremely wide range of social groupings in terms of common and unique attitudinal components. Table 10.1 illustrates this point. Some of the entries are based on already existing data, whereas others are hypothetical. One might use the cross-corresponding components in many ways such as in the isolation of causative elements and the establishment of a psychologically meaningful taxonomy in contrast to medical or other physicalistic approaches.

ARE THE PHYSICALLY DISABLED REALLY DIFFERENT?

Before proceeding with discussion of specific research findings on the attitudes held by various groups toward the physically disabled, let us enjoin the issue as to what, if any, real features might exist that could promote differential treatment. As might be expected from the mention earlier of such attitudinal components as Interaction Strain and Inferred Emotional Consequences, the "kernal of truth" belief held by some could be used to shift responsibility for one's feelings or for change from themselves to the stigmatized person.

Nowhere has more work been done on differential factors in the disabled than with the blind. Witkin et al. (1968) hypothesized that because lack of vision is likely to hamper development of articulation and to foster dependence on others, congenitally totally blind children may be expected to show less differentiated cognitive functioning than their sighted peers. This hypothesis was confirmed. However, in addition to being inferior in analytic competence, the blind children were strikingly superior to the sighted in capacity for sustained auditory attention and about equivalent in verbal comprehension ability. The writers (Witken et al., 1968) concluded that "the picture of the blind is one of unevenness in level of functioning from one cognitive area to another" (p. 767).

A number of writers indicate that delays or deviations in development of the blind occur that are specific for blindness and do not have the same significance that such delays would have for a sighted child. (Fraiberg, 1968; Gillman, 1973; Jastrzembska, 1976). In effect, despite timing differences the standards for the blind should be based on that of the growth and development of the nonhandicapped average child. However, Sandler (1963) suggests ego development of the blind child will proceed along different lines than that of the sighted, whereas Burlingham (1964) holds that nothing in the life of the blind infant can make up for the missing interplay with the mother by means of looking and smiling at each other.

Regardless of whether profound developmental consequences do result for the blind, there can be no question that such things as mannerisms ("blindisms") and the stare of many blind persons do present stimuli with decided social effect.

Similar mixed reports have been made on the effect of deafness upon cognition. Whereas some report cognitive skills of congenitally deaf children to be unaffected (Furth, 1961; Lenneberg, 1967), others report a delay of 1 or 2 years in the emergence of certain aspects of logic, though subsequent emergence follows the usual developmental sequence (Oleron, 1961 as reported in Sarlin and Altshuler, 1978). Altshuler (1964) among others refers to the frequent finding of implusivity in the deaf, and Levine (1956) reports that deaf adolescent subjects had conceptual lags, deficient emotional adaptability, rigid patterns of response, egocentricity, and immaturity. Sarlin and Altshuler (1978) in a standardized setting obtained fantasies from 5-year-old deaf and other boys and found that the impact of deafness on cognitive functioning was "akin to—but apparently no worse than—the cultural deprivation phenomenon experienced by low socioeconomic-status children." There was no paucity of fantasy life found in the deaf children.

The possibility of actual systematic differences in social perception of the disabled has been raised by Schiff and Thayer (1974). In an analysis of the literature involving social perception and deafness they conclude that deaf persons lose key nonverbal information from the face—especially the eye region—because they concentrate peripheral and central visual attention on decoding linguistic information. Deaf and hearing persons also differentially weigh kinetic social information, and differences in perceived degree of several interactive characteristics result. As part of the different informational currents and emphases, impaired communication and resulting communication discomfort on both parts result.

Blau (1964) performed research to determine whether loss of one primary communicative channel would lead to compensatory sensitivity in the remaining channel and concluded that although blind people were more attentive to affective aspects of auditory communication, they were less accurate at judging the emotional characteristics of the communication. Schiff and Thayer (1974) couple the Blau study with their own on deafness and conclude that for neither condition does the compensatory process largely work. As they point out, ''this substitution leads to an overloaded visual system, and deaf-hearing differences appear which increase problems of social misunderstandings'' (p. 66).

Other studies also have directly concerned themselves with the question of the social perception of the disabled. Richardson (1963) directly asks the question as to whether handicapping has a blunting or sensitizing effect on a person, and, after reviewing relevant studies, concludes that the evidence is consistent in suggesting that *blunting* rather than *sensitizing* is the more likely consequence. Richardson, Hastorf, and Dornbusch (1964) using self-descriptions of 9–11-year-olds reaffirm the aforementioned and conclude that restricted access to direct experience in social interaction leads to impoverishment of perceptual categorization. Ingwell et al. (1967) comparing 12 women undergraduate students with orthopedic disabilities to 12 matched controls found the disabled women to be the less socially sensitive on their measures. Both the handicapped and nonhandicapped had significantly more difficulty in attempting to predict the behavior of handicapped subjects than that of nonhandicapped subjects.

Kleck in a series of studies has demonstrated experimentally how the behavior of a nonhandicapped person is modified in the presence of a handicapped person. Thus, in one study a standardized social situation was used to examine the behavior of high school students (previously unknown to each other) toward handicapped and nonhandicapped peers (Kleck et al., 1966). When contact was made for the nonhandicapped there was in comparison to their reactions to the handicapped more distortion of opinion, less variability in the opinions offered, shorter responses to questions, and much variability among the aforementioned. This and other such interactive studies clearly show that the attitudinal component of Interaction Strain operates to reduce spontaneity and comfort on the part of the handicapped and is reflected in many behavioral cues. Comer and Piliavin

(1972) examined the disabled person's side of the disabled–nondisabled interaction picture and found that encounters between patients with severe leg disabilities and physically normal persons affected the disabled persons so that they smiled less, reduced eye contact, inhibited their head and hand movements, terminated the interaction sooner, and reported more discomfort and liking for the normal other. As Schiff and Thayer (1974) observed, there is a pattern of mutual difficulty in disabled–nondisabled interactions.

Schoggen (1963) poses as a fundamental question whether the social-psychological living conditions of children with physical disabilities differ in systematic ways from those of comparable nondisabled children. Using an ecological approach employing specimen records ("a detailed sequential narrative of a long segment of a child's behavior and situation") Schoggen (1963) suggests that his data gives little support to the "widely held notions that children with physical disabilities are the objects of oversolicitous and rejecting behavior, that parents and teachers resort to 'unusual, ill-defined procedures' (Jordan, 1962) in raising handicapped children, and that children with disabilities are more dependent" (p. 17). Schoggen concludes that behavior settings more than physical characteristics of the child are determining outcomes, a position at variance with the tendency to identify the cause of difficult interactions within the individuals involved. The work cited earlier in this section obviously requires reconciliation with Schoggen's findings and conclusions, although no one would likely deemphasize the great importance of behavior settings for behavior in a specific situation.

Such nondisabled behaviors as staring, rude questions or actions, and devaluative and subordinating action precipitate resentment and anger in reaction to the unthinking and unempathic person. The disabled person's justified anger might then be misperceived by the outsider as an inevitable character distortion resulting from disablement (Inferred Emotional Consequences).

The use of various psychological defensive techniques by the disabled have been described but none seem unique to them. One defence, that of denial, seems to be particularly prevalent, e.g., Lipp et al. (1968) found that physically disabled subjects demonstrated extreme differences in perceiving slides of disabled people as opposed to normal people. The results were explained in terms of denial by the disabled. Our own experience using many different psychological instruments is highly confirming of the general proposition that denial is an important mechanism used by the disabled to deal with the implications, personal and social, of their situation. The degree to which the denial is unconsciously operating varies greatly among persons. A consequence for measurement is that when disabled populations rate themselves one cannot usually interpret whether the self-reports are based upon real feelings, what they wish were so, or fantasies of greater negativity than actually exist. I have obtained all three reactions in my own work, and the literature also provides conflicting data on this question (e.g., Comer & Piliavin, 1975; Dixon, 1977; Friend, 1971; Lazar et al., 1978;

Schroedel & Schiff, 1972; Weinberg–Asher, 1976). The interpretation of the results of such studies must also take into account related findings in the study of social stereotypes in racial attitudes where there is a tendency, particularly with campus populations, to express more positive sentiments about Negroes than about one's own racial group (e.g., Karlins et al., 1969).

Disturbances in nondisabled–disabled interactions also are attributed to an assumed "impairment in emphatic ability" due to the supposed different developmental tracks imposed by disability. Such feelings might be most strong regarding those with congenital conditions (Siller, 1976a). Black (1964) using a projective-type test involving the disabled in helping roles reported physically normal people found it difficult to think of a disabled person as a helper. Two more recent studies found quite opposite results in that nondisabled undergraduates responding to hypothetical counseling situations preferred disabled over nondisabled counselors (Brabham & Thoreson, 1973; Mitchell & Fredrickson, 1975). In the Brabham and Thoreson study an interesting additional finding was that the able-bodied students who appeared most maladjusted tended to reject the disabled counselor. This finding is very much in line with the theoretical position of the relationship between personality factors and attitudes toward the disabled to be discussed later. Mitchell and Fredrickson, who extended the earlier work of Brabham and Thoreson, interpret the general pattern of their results to support "an enhanced ability to understand and empathize" hypothesis, however, their assumption is inferential and does not derive directly from their data.

From the aforementioned review (which is fairly representative) one can infer that as soon as one departs from the direct fact of disability evidence can be provided to demonstrate that persons with disabilities do or do not have different developmental tracks, social/skills and perceptions, defensive orientations, empathic potential, etc. Much of the data suggests that if the disabled do present themselves as "different" this often enough is a secondary consequence of the social climate rather than inherent disability-specific phenomena. As Moriarty (1974) points out, "only when minority group members are stigmatized do they feel and act like social deviants" (p. 849). However, as the work of Schiff and Thayer (1974) and others demonstrates, there are real psychological consequences to disablement, particularly when the sensorium is affected, that also create interpersonal stresses. There can be no static "right" answer to the question of the degree to which an undefined person with an ambiguously preceived disability is "different": Different to whom and for what purpose?

From the point of view of research, there is a clear need to separate the real interpersonal consequences of deficiency conditions, such as absence of hearing, from rationalizations regarding these conditions. When one considers the real situation one can then propose viable aids, e.g., lip reading, signing, interpretors. When rationalizations predominate one has no basis for remediation. This becomes evident when examining the attitudinal component named Imputed Functional Limitations. This was found to be a clear affective dimension where supposed "real" limitations served to sweeten an obviously negative attitude orientation.

To the extent that certain disabilities create sensory deficiency states resulting in inadequate social perception and the like, programs of social skills training are indicated, I long have advocated that rehabilitation for the disabled should include enhancement of the coping capability of the disabled. Practically, this means supplementing such physical procedures as mobility, training, with specific training in dealing with help, curiosity, and dealing with the attitudes of others.

Developmental Aspects

The possibility that physical disability may interfere with the very course of development already has been indicated. Certainly, parents, peers, and other significant others as well as one's own self are confronted with something of great import (Richardson, 1969). Our knowledge of familial attitudes consists mostly of anecdotal and clinical-type reports. More research based studies generally are weak for such reasons as small numbers, limited nonrandom samples, poor instrumentation and methodologies, and inadequate or crude statistical handling. I attend here to two particular aspects of the developmental picture, that of origination of attitudes toward the disabled and values held by nondisabled children toward the disabled. Other research on attitudes of children toward the nondisabled is discussed in the section "Social Position of the Disabled."

Only a few studies report on the emerging perception of disability as seen in preschool-age children (e.g., Fine, 1978; Jones & Sisk, 1970; Weinberg, 1978). Weinberg (1978) examined 3-to 5-year-old children's awareness of physical impairment. The children were shown pictures of either a same sex, able bodied child sitting in a regular chair or the same child sitting in a wheelchair and were asked a series of yes–no questions to assess their attitudes toward the pictured child. She found a shift of understanding between ages 3 and 4. The younger children did not appear to relate to the disability whereas the 4-year-olds responded that what was different was that the child was in a wheelchair. It would seem that by age 4 children have learned something about physical disability and are attending to it as a distant but important element. Further, Weinberg reports that knowledge about disability does not have a significant effect on liking, willingness to share, or the child's perception of other's desire for him/her to play with the disabled child.

Jones & Sisk (1970) studied 230 nondisabled children between the ages of 2 and 6 who responded to a drawing of a same sexed child wearing a leg brace and to a drawing of an identical child without braces. Standard questions were asked regarding interpersonal acceptance and limitations imposed by orthopedic disability. At age 4 children began to perceive the limitations imposed by orthopedic disability with consistency. Responses to the two drawings were not significantly different (aside from five-year-olds greater rejection of the orthopedically disabled child in regard to the question "Would you play with him?"). Four and 5-year-olds perceived the disabled child as less likely to have fun. Five-and six-year olds, in general, qualified their responses by indicating conditions under which they believed the disabled would have fun or be acceptable.

Fine (1978) undertook to separate the age range at which nondisabled pre-schoolers began to perceive physical deviation in others from their attitudes toward this physical fact. A second facet of the Fine study was to explore the relationship of the preschool child's self concept and level of castration anxiety to the age of perceptual awareness of and attitudes toward physical deviance. It was hypothesized that preschool children who demonstrate developmentally early perceptual awareness of physical deviance will most negatively evaluate physical deviance, have greater castration anxiety and a more negative self-concept. Other hypotheses were that negative evaluations of physical deviance is associated with high castration anxiety and with negative self-concept. The total enrollment ($N = 125$) of two preschool programs with an age range from 3 years-6 months to 6 years-5 months was used to establish the age of perceptual discrimination of physical deviance. A modification of the picture series used by Richardson was employed. Fifty percent or more of an age group (in 3-month intervals) did not correctly identify the deviant picture (missing left arm) "different" from two others identical except for presence of left arm in four sets of pictures until the age interval of 5–6 to 5–8. Children at each of the age intervals studied were able to discriminate the perceptually different picture, however, as a group the majority did not do so until almost time for regular school entrance. In order to determine whether "early perceivers" were more negative than basal or later perceivers, 12 evaluative adjectives appropriate for preschoolers were embedded in sentences ("Which is the good one?") and ascribed by the child to either one of the physically deviant or physically normal referents in the stimulus picture. It was found that the base rate for negatively toned adjectives (ugly, bad, mean) for the disabled picture for the entire population was so high as to virtually preclude differentiation between early and nonearly perceivers. This would suggest that, although not meeting the rigorous criteria for correct perception of difference that on some functional level, awareness was there. The relationships of castration anxiety and self-concept to age of onset of perceptual discrimination was tested by comparing the 20 available "early perceivers" to 20 matched (age, sex, IQ) controls on the Children's Thematic Apperception Test and the Children's Self-Social Constructs Test for the variables in question. The results supported both hypotheses regarding castration anxiety: There were higher castration anxiety scores for early perceivers, and those with higher castration anxiety scores were more negative. However, only the hypothesis on the greater negative self-image of early perceivers received support as no relationship was found between attitudinal evaluations of physical deviation and self-concept.

The findings of Weinberg (1978) and Fine (1978) extended downward previous findings of Richardson (1970) regarding the negative attitudes toward the disabled held by first graders. That attitudes of elementary school and older children continue to be negative has been documented in many other studies. Adolescence in particular poses threats and increases negativity (Higgs, 1975; Siller et al., 1967a). The key position of the preschool years for subsequent attitude formation certainly deserves considerably more attention than it has received.

Important sustained research on developmental aspects of disability has been conducted by Richardson. A number of references to aspects of his work are made in various sections of this chapter. Richardson's basic measurement device has been a picture preference ranking method (see "Measurement Considerations"). Some of the essential findings of his research suggest: (1) widespread preference for the nonhandicapped over the handicapped with preference for children with certain disabilities over others, (2) a remarkably consistent ordering of disability conditions by groups of children with very different geographical settings and social backgrounds, (3) a period of close contact does not change preferences, (4) contact and having a disability oneself does not change the order of preferences (Richardson, 1969, 1970, 1971; Richardson et al., 1961, 1968, 1974).

Richardson (1970) maintains that positive or negative preferences for specific disabilities reflect widely held attitudes of society toward the handicapped and, as children become more socialized through aging, that their order of preference becomes similar to that of adults.

It is interesting to note that use of the picture preference technique has failed to support certain possible preconceptions, to wit: (1) an intense contact in a relatively short amount of time can overcome initial barriers (Kleck, 1969; Richardson, 1963); (2) greater contact facilitates personal knowledge of one's peers and thus affords greater opportunity to make judgments based on more than physical appearance alone (Richardson et al., 1974); (3) high sociometric status would lead one to express more normative values towards the handicapped whereas those in low sociometric positions would less often express normative values (Richardson & Friedman, 1973); (4) functional impairments are least liked (Richardson et al., 1961).

Certain criticisms of the methodology of picture preference technique (Alessi & Anthony, 1969; Matthews & Westie, 1966) and of the uniformity of preferences (Dow, 1965; Newfield, 1964; Yuker, 1983) have been raised. Uniformities of ranking are contingent upon the child's exposure to the value and ability to learn the value (Goodman et al., 1963). A response to criticisms of the interpretations of the studies using the picture preference technique has been made by Richardson (1983).

If one were to follow a components of attitude approach, then the relative emergence of individual components developmentally would be of interest. For example, the work by Fine (1978), which suggests the possible role of oedipal-like phenomena, might imply the emergence of something like the "Distressed Identification" component at that age whereas the "Interaction Strain" component as a later developmental emergence. The implication of such developmental differences are many including such matters as character structures associated with holding particular attitude components and resistance to change.

THE SOCIAL POSITION OF THE PHYSICALLY DISABLED AND PREFERENCE RANKINGS FOR TYPES OF DISABILITIES

Probably the most widely quoted summary of attitudes toward the physically disabled persons is that of Barker et al. (1953) to the effect that "public, verbalized attitudes toward disabled persons are on the average mildly favorable; an appreciable minority openly express negative attitudes. . . Indirect evidence suggests that deeper unverbalized attitudes are more frequently hostile" (p. 84). Twenty years of work in this domain and close review of the literature convince this writer of the continued truth of the aforementioned quote. Physical disability is in most instances a stigmatized condition with distinct social implications.

In this section some of the studies bearing on the social distance and social interaction of the disabled and the nondisabled are considered. Results for children are generally treated separately from that for adults.

Sociometry has been a major tool in examining the social status of handicapped children. In one early study it was found that the physically handicapped were not accepted by normal children in integrated classes and that few of these children had enough positive assets to offset completely the negative effect of being labeled as handicapped by their classmates (Force, 1956). Around the same time, Freeman and Sonnega (1956) found no basis for assuming that speech-handicapped children were socially rejected merely because of speech. Soldwedel and Terrill (1957) found similar sociometric status of disabled children to their normal classroom peers, whereas Elser (1958) found the sociometric status of hearing handicapped to be lower on the average than their classmates with the midly handicapped and those without hearing aids being least accepted. As Raskin (1962) noted regarding the blind, they tend to be liked but not well respected. A general pattern of findings of the early studies seems that despite the practice of placing exceptional children in regular classes on the basis that this enables them to maintain normal relations with their peers, this does not prevent segregation from their peers (Gronlund, 1959).

Later studies in the 1960s continue to support the findings of earlier reports. Thus, Centers and Centers (1963) with elementary school-age amputee children, Bansavage (1968) with orthopedically impaired adolescents, Marge (1966) and Gallagher (1969) with speech-defective children all report social status impairment for disabled children. Acceptability of speech-disabled children, however, was not found to be a factor in playground activities for the first- and third-grade children in those studies. Teachers' attitudes toward the speech deficiency were thought to be highly influential for the other children (Gallagher). Mothers of normal-speaking children did not differ greatly in attitude toward speech disorders than mothers of speech-handicapped children and there was a trend for teachers to prefer normal-speaking children (Marge). Richardson's work already cited also supports the differential situation of disabled children. Thus, whereas some differentiation according to specific activity involved might be a factor in the interactions of disabled and nondisabled children, a general orientation of status devaluation repeatedly emerges.

As the pressures for mainstreaming increase in the 1980s one would expect that the greater influx of disabled children into the regular school system would have an impact greater than in the past. Definitive studies in this respect have yet to be forthcoming, and, in fact, the complexity of the issues and the methodological problems are such that one would not expect single isolated studies based on small unrepresentative samples of students, teachers, administrators, and communities to really be the suitable medium for exploration of these problems.

We take but two of the many studies beginning to be reported as examples of the more recent research. McCauley et al., (1976) used an observation schedule of interactive behavior to compare the behavior of hearing-impaired and non-disabled children in a classroom setting and reported no significant differences. Disabled children did, however, rely more heavily on teachers as a source of rewarding social interactions whereas the nondisabled relied more on their peer groups. Reich et al. (1977) conducted a study of 195 hearing-impaired students in four programs that varied in their degree of integration. After controlling for relevant variables, Reich concluded that the results indicate that integration is beneficial to academic development, but that personal and social difficulties may result. Regardless of the type of program, students to be integrated must have highly developed oral skills, at least average intelligence, and supportive parents.

Implications for attitudes from studies such as those just cited evolve around the necessity to create a milieu that will maximize successful interactions as children demonstrably (leaving aside criticisms regarding specific studies or parts of studies) have pronounced early attitudes toward disability. These tend to be negative and are maintained and built upon with development, tend to isolate or at least lead to differential treatment of children with disabilities, and are highly influenced by parental and teacher attitudes. The actual performance of the disabled child may or may not influence interaction outcomes for the good, but can rather easily affect such interactions for the bad. Careful attention to setting the stage for constructive interactions is necessary as contact alone (see sections on "Developmental Aspects" and "Attitude Change") may have negative rather than positive consequences.

Studies with adults are spread over many areas such as professional–client attitudes, teacher attitudes, employment, etc. and are discussed elsewhere in this chapter.

Attention in research with adults has not been directed toward the sociometric status of disabled persons as much as it has been toward establishing perceptions of the general population toward different disabilities. Social distance-type studies have established consistent and stable relative rankings for adults of a variety of physical and other conditions (e.g., Harasymiw et al., 1976a, b; Jones, 1974; Shears & Jensema, 1969; Siller et al., 1967a; Tringo, 1970). Typical results find cerebral palsy, body deformations, and obesity among the most rejected whereas amputation and blindness are more favorably ranked with many other conditions falling at various points along continua. A consistent finding has been that relatively high degree of social acceptance is noted up to the point of marriage. A sharp decrease in percentages of subjects who would accept disabled persons occurs between the adjoining scale points of "Would Have As A Friend" and "Would Marry." In one representative study of amputees the percentages drop from approximately 80 to 18, for wheelchair it is from 79 to 7, the blind 77 to 16, harelip 69 to 8, stutterer 65 to 7, deaf mute 53 to 10 and cerebral palsied 38 to 1 (Shears & Jensema, 1969). A general order of preference is usually physically disabled first, sensory disabled second, and brain injured third. "Social" conditions such as mental illness, alcoholism, and delinquency are invariably rejected.

Shears and Jensema (1969) suggest that six dimensions probably combine and interact in the formation of stereotypes of anomalous persons-visibility, communication, social stigma, reversibility, degree of incapacity, and difficulty in daily living. Barker (1964) describes an "organic" and "functional" dichotomy. Siller (in preparation) identifies a set of primary variables that mediate between real aspects of a disability and the ultimate form in which components of attitude are structured toward that disability (transient–permanent, organic–functional, etiology, terminal–nonterminal, and personal responsibility). Each invididual condition also has the possibility to connote certain psychological qualities (e.g., paralysis-dependency, cerebral palsy-uncontrol, skin conditions-dirtiness, Siller et al., 1967a).

Earlier, in discussing the multidimensional nature of attitudes and our own components approach, it was mentioned that attitudes can be specific to a condition (e.g., fear of contagion) or more general encompassing many conditions (e.g., interaction strain). The question of which components are salient to a particular disability or set of disabilities becomes an empirical question some answer to which data have already been provided and is shown in Table 10.1. (Ferguson, 1970; Siller, 1970; Siller & Braden, unpublished; Siller et al., 1967a; Vann, 1970).

The findings of Siller (1970a and unpublished) are unequivocal in regard to the presence of attitude components across disabilities that were operationalized in the DFS-General measures.

Jones (1974) following up implications of the generality of attitudes toward the exceptional used hierarchial factor analysis to analyze responses to a social distance questionnaire (six interpersonal situations and 13 categories of exceptionality–nonexceptionality). The results revealed a general factor concerning attitudes toward the disabled cutting across type of disability and interpersonal situation. The general factor was differentiated into attitudes toward the physically disabled, psychologically disabled, and mildly mentally retarded-nonexceptional. Attitudes toward the gifted emerged as a separate factor. Tringo (1970) also found generally higher correlation of each disability variable in his social distance scale with the overall score than with other disability variables suggesting the usefulness of generalized measures such as the ATDP or the combining of DFS scores. However, Siller (1970) specifically demonstrated that organization of attitudes for physical disabilities is much more strongly based upon specific attitude component than for disability type. One might infer that the most useful approach to understanding of the attitudes of the general population would be a sensitive appreciation of whether one is interested in disability in general or in a specific disability, and whether one needs to approach the problem through an overall score or through measures of specific components. Conceptualization and instrumentation for proceeding in all necessary ways now are available.

Variables Affecting the Interaction of the Disabled–Nondisabled

A wide variety of factors has been identified as having import in the interaction process of the disabled with the nondisabled such as culture, social class, personality of the disabled and/or nondisabled, physical status of the person (as disabled or not), specific experiences, contact, itinerant class situation, achievement level of the disabled, coping style and acknowledgment or nonacknowledgment of the disability by the disabled, context of the interaction, and demographic factors such as age, sex, religion, race, and education of the nondisabled. Almost any variable identified for the disabled or for the nondisabled has its counterpart in the other. I undertake here briefly to characterize our impression of the general status of these factors referencing only those citations that are not likely to be found readily in other general sources or that are leads for further references.

Age, sex, and other demographic variables are important mostly in the manner in which attitudes toward the disabled are expressed rather than in their formation. Thus, women may have attitudes similar to men but will be more likely to express them in ways influenced by their sex role. Adolescents of both sexes tend to be more rejecting than are younger or older persons and persons better educated to be most accepting. Ethnicity (Richardson et al., 1961) and cultural bias (Dow, 1965; Jaques et al., 1970; Jordan, 1968) may also be implicated in reactions to the disabled. It is very difficult to make hard generalizations regarding the influence of these various demographic factors as their operations are complex and unlikely to be described in a direct and simple way.

The personality of the nondisabled person has been studied in relation to that person's attitudes toward the disabled (Siller, 1985). In general, significant but weak relationships have been found for a variety of personality dimensions with "favorable" variables such as ego strength, body image boundaries, nurturance and good adjustment, and social interaction measures correlating with acceptance and more "negative" variables such as anxiety, hostility, alienation, and authoritarianism correlating with rejection (Noonan et al., 1970; Siller et al., 1967a; Yuker et al., 1966). Particular ego defensive structures of the nondisabled have been shown to be related to negativity (Gladstone, 1977). The pattern of results from numerous studies suggests that "ego strength" and the ability to attain stable relations with others underly positive reactions toward the disabled. Ethnocentrism is clearly related to negative attitudes and is highly general in nature. Those who express ethnocentrism toward other outgroups tend to express negative attitudes toward the physically disabled.

Studies using the physical status (disabled or nondisabled) of the person as a variable are beginning to be reported but no trends are yet evident. Increasing attention is being paid to the attitudes of the disabled themselves, but results are as yet indefinite. The realism of perceptions of the disabled toward their own social position and of attitudes of the nondisabled toward them would profit from systematic research effort.

The context in which interactions take place usually is undefined or limited in the usual research study, yet there is evidence that context is an important element (e.g., Shurka & Katz, 1976; Sloat & Frankel, 1972). Certainly, one might expect that whether the disability will effect outcomes, such as in a competitive situation involving limitations assumed to involve the disability, would be a factor in interactions. In fact, Jones (1970) in an experiment on the effects upon verbal learning and associative clustering of the presence of a blind person found a greater tendency to believe that one's performance was impaired when interacting with a blind individual than when interacting with a sighted one, even though the objective evidence was to the contrary. Fear of negative social implications from others for the nondisabled also has been shown to be an element in their attitude orientation (Siller et al., 1967a).

A beginning is being made on specifying concrete operations which can enhance or retard disabled–nondisabled interactions. Thus, Bazakas (1977) in an experimental study of a person in a wheelchair interacting with a nondisabled person found that the former received the most favorable response only when presenting himself as both coping and with open acknowledgment of his condition. Either alone, coping or acknowledgment, was insufficient to promote positive response. Achievement level of the disabled person and the type of school service received also has been shown to influence acceptance (Havill, 1970). The search for more such variables that directly affect attitudes and consequent social interactions is clearly indicated.

Contact has been frequently considered as a key element influencing attitudes and this is discussed in the section on "Attitude Change."

Experimental Studies

In addition to the most widely used means of assessing attitudes (self-report devices of one sort or another), a number of more experimentally manipulated studies have been undertaken, a number of which already have been mentioned. Thus Kleck, Comer, and Piliaven, and Bazakas are but a few who have actually sought to manipulate the actual interaction experience between disabled and nondisabled persons.

To give the flavor of some other kinds of experimental research relevant to attitude structure a few random studies are mentioned. Wittreich and Radcliffe (1955) used distorting lenses in determining thresholds for apparently mutilated and normal figures and found the threshold for the mutilated figure to be significantly higher than for the normal one. This has implication for processes involved in initial perception of physical difference.

In a quite different area, Mesch (1976) studied the interaction quality between dyads of disabled–disabled, disabled–nondisabled, and nondisabled–nondisabled. Mixed dyads showed the most self-disclosure on a high intimacy topic. Least self-disclosure was shown by the nondisabled–nondisabled dyad at all levels of topic intimacy. Mesch's findings can be seen in a context with the two studies mentioned earlier regarding nondisabled preferences for disabled counselors.

Doob and Ecker (1970) examined the effect of stigma on compliance and found subjects were significantly more willing to complete and mail a questionnaire when the female requester wore an eye patch then when no eye patch was worn. They concluded that stigma increased compliance when subjects did not anticipate any further contact with the stigmatized person. Levitt and Kornhaber (1977) reexamined the Doob and Ecker study introducing methodological checks that led them to conclude that, although the basic finding was replicated, handicap need not be stigmatizing in order to increase compliance.

Thayer (1973) pursued a field experiment on helping behavior with the disabled (deaf) in Grand Central Station in New York examining the effects of race and sex on the part of both the helper and the one to be helped. Thayer concluded that no single explanation could account for the pattern of differences observed and that different combinations of racial and sexual perspectives were necessary to account for the behavior in each condition.

The research on helping behavior illustrates the value of breaking away from an exclusive disability directed framework and tuning into broader conceptual frameworks available from sociology, social psychology, psychodynamic systems, and elsewhere. The work on helping behavior can be seen as logical outgrowths of intense contemporary research interest on prosocial behavior involving help and altruism.

Interpersonal attraction has been another area of active research that has had impact on studies in disability. One aspect in particular—physical appearance—has direct disability implication. The basic relationship between "good" and "beautiful" has been well established. The converse of what is ugly is bad also seems to hold (Siller et al., 1967a) being what has been called an "emotional syllogism" (Franz Alexander). A recent study supports the syllogistic notion (Hansson, 1976).

Social psychological research on the "just world" concept ("people have a need to believe that their environment is a just and orderly place where people usually get what they deserve") would seem to have great significance for studying the effects of disability upon the nondisabled. Lerner & Miller (1978), the former of whom has been primarily responsible for the modern development of this concept, show many ways in which this concept can be used to understand the conditions of victimization. Application to attitudes toward the disabled is obvious.

An interesting demonstration of nonnaturalness in disabled–nondisabled interactions was provided by Hastorf et al. (1979). It was shown that handicapped individuals more than able-bodied ones received inaccurate feedback from able-bodied subjects. The difference in feedback was not because less was expected of the disabled confederate but rather, presumably, because of a "norm to be kind."

Attitude Change

Although physical disability has been the subject of some studies directly attempting to change attitudes toward the disabled, less than 20 have come to our attention. Unfortunately, despite a variety of approaches including emotional role playing (Clore & Jeffrey, 1972; Straus, 1975), television and other media presentations (Donaldson, 1976, Donaldson & Martinson, 1977; Sadlick & Penta, 1975), experimentally directed attempts to reduce interaction strain (Bazakas, 1977; Evans, 1976), assertiveness training (Glenwick & Arata, in press), hypnosis (Daniels, 1976), various short-term contact and information-giving experiences through workshops and the like (Harasymiw & Horne, 1976; Lazar et al., 1971), and even a systematic and intensive educational campaign (Sands & Zalkind, 1972), no really impressive fundamental and lasting positive reports have been forthcoming; that is, although a number of the studies mentioned earlier have reported positive findings, the total impact of any approach or study is not encouraging for broad programs of change.

Some of the useful themes that do emerge are that it would be helpful to train the disabled person in social coping skills, emotional role playing be encouraged in the nondisabled, contact and informational techniques be jointly used and not either one alone (Anthony, 1972), attraction toward a disabled person will increase if that person is seen as attitudinally similar (Asher, 1973).

One factor, that of contact, warrants some further consideration as it likely can be most significant for disabled–nondisabled interactions. Contact in itself is not a definitive concept as the consequences of the contact can be either favorable or unfavorable depending upon other contingencies. Generalizing from much research in the area of ethnic attitudes (e.g., Allport, 1954; Amir, 1969) factors favoring positive interactions between the disabled and the nondisabled include: (1) the contact involves status equals pursuing common goals; (2) the contact is perceived as instrumental to the realization of a desired goal; (3) contact is between members of a majority group and higher status members of a minority group; (4) when an "authority" and/or the social climate are in favor of and promote the intergroup contact; (5) when the contact is intimate rather than casual; (6) the contact is pleasurable; (7) when the members of both groups interact in functionally important activities or develop common goals or superordinate goals that are higher ranking in importance than the individual goals of each of the groups; (8) the contact is volitional; (9) the contact is selected over other rewards.

Factors strengthening prejudice are: (1) when the contact produces competition between the groups; (2) when the contact is unpleasant, tension laden; (3) when the prestige or status of one group is lowered as a result of the contact situation; (4) when members of a group or the group as a whole are in a state of frustration; (5) when the members of the minority group are of a lower status or are lower in any relevant characteristic than the members of the majority group.

It should be also noted that when change through contact occurs it may be in intensity rather than of direction, and that change may be limited to but one aspect of the situation. Amir (1969) also points out that most of the investigations reporting favorable attitude change through contact are conducted under favorable conditions that might not be true in real life. Finally, our own work points to the importance of the quality rather than the amount of contact (Siller et al., 1967a).

We believe that attitude change toward the disabled will be most successful when efforts are directed toward the affective state of the nondisabled person. Discovering the sources of the negative attitudes will better provide workers with cues for effective change procedures. Perceiving the multidimensionality of attitude structure should be helpful in pinpointing attitudinal components, suggesting differential change procedures, and supplying appropriate assessment of the effects of interventions. Attitude change efforts in physical disability are in their infancy, but need not remain so. Full utilization of the disabled themselves in these efforts should go without saying.

ATTITUDES OF PROFESSIONALS AND REHABILITATION WORKERS

Professional personnel in rehabilitation and teaching often are of considerable importance to the disabled person. In this section attitudes toward the disabled held by professionals in relation to education and rehabilitation are considered and some bases underlying these reactions explored.

ATTITUDES OF EDUCATORS

Not surprisingly, familiarity with a condition generally lessens negativity (Higgs, 1975; Siller et al., 1967b; Yuker et al., 1966) and teachers who have had specific experience with one kind of disability tend to prefer continuing to work with that kind (Murphy, 1960). Our own experience with numerous teachers and students of special education suggests that although many would willingly work with children of most any type of disability condition, many others have distinct preference for a particular type (unpublished data). One might expect the greater familiarity and knowledgeability would help to make teachers more comfortable in working with new populations (e.g., Warren & Turner, 1966). Elementary school teachers express attitudes similar to the general population (Conine, 1969) that should suggest the need for special training. Although some have found that attitudes of teachers toward the handicapped are mildly favorable (Murphy, 1960; Murphy et al., 1960; Warren & Turner, 1966), it is also possible that experience with the handicapped (at least for a retarded population) may increase teachers' rejection (Gottlieb, 1981; Major, 1961). Later, quality of contact is discussed as being important in the development of attitudes.

The question cannot be whether training for teachers should be undertaken, but rather, what would be the most effective training for helping all teachers regardless of special education status or not.

Harasymiw and Horne (1975a) examined the effect of a program designed to prepare teachers for integration of handicapped students into the regular class. Teachers from integrated and nonintegrated schools ($N = 352$) were examined for favorability of attitude with the former found to be the more favorable. Neither sex nor number of special education courses taken were related to favorable attitude. Younger teachers were significantly more favorable. One might wonder about the absence of a relationship between number of special education courses and favorable attitudes. If the finding is not due to measurement problems then the nature of what constitutes special education courses might be in question. Can one infer that course work geared to the cognitive dimension without dealing with the more affective aspects of disabled–nondisabled interactions is insufficient to effect favorable attitudinal growth?

Teachers, as do other populations, can view the disabled both in terms of the specificity of their conditions and in a more generalized way. For example, Wechsler, Suarez, and McFadden (1975) surveyed 547 teachers and found that children with asthma or heart conditions, and children requiring crutches and braces were viewed as more easily integrated into the regular classroom than children with visual and hearing problems, or children with histories of convulsions and seizures. Those teachers with previous experience teaching physically handicapped children were most optimistic about integrating these children into the regular classroom.

As Murphy (1960) has documented, teachers, principals, speech clinicians, freshman teachers-to-be as a group least prefer to teach the visually handicapped and hearing disabled when compared to other forms of exceptionality except the delinquent. Newman (1976) examining faculty attitudes at the college level toward the admission of the handicapped also found blindness to be the most handicapping for college work. Rates as second most handicapping was deafness with paralysis close behind. The disabilities of cerebral palsy and muscular dystrophy also were considered to be quite restricting. Amputation was seen as less of a problem and body deformation and skin disorder almost never.

Newman, however, also found that 98% of his faculty sample (based on a 57% return on a population of 816) were in favor of admitting handicapped students, at least on a restricted basis. Utilization of sensory aids for the blind and deaf and informing faculty about the potential of these aids obviously would be helpful. Newman (1976) properly makes the point that his findings "underscore again the fact that equal educational opportunity for the handicapped is more of a problem of the nonhandicapped than of the handicapped."

The Newman and Murphy findings regarding the negative reactions of educators toward blindness as presenting the greatest handicap for school work parallels the data of Siller et al. (1967a) and others that blindness is generally considered to be the worst disability that one could have. Newman, whose eight categories of disability types were taken from the Siller study, thereby permitting comparisons, found an apparent contradiction regarding deafness. Whereas Siller's group found mild and most favorable reactions to deafness, Newman's sample regarded deafness as the second most handicapping condition. The substantial difference I believe lies in the lack of knowledge about deafness that prevailed in our own 1967 study. That is to say, that although relatively large numbers of persons were involved, they were not educators and were quite ignorant of the very real difficulties created by deafness. Newman's sample was probably more sophisticated in this regard.

When general population groups rate various forms of exceptionality the physical disabilities as a whole do not fare too badly. In effect, it is conditions with social disturbance potential that seem to be reacted to most negatively. Thus delinquent, mental illness, hyperactive, and agressive conditions are most rejected. This finding seems to hold up with special educators who were found to be more favorable toward the mentally and physically disabled than toward alcoholics (Greer, 1975). However, the special education personnel in Greer's study were more demanding of the physically and mentally disabled and were more lenient with alcoholics, presumably because of the lesser effectiveness of rehabilitation programs for the latter.

Teacher attitude studies are becoming supplemented by appreciation of the role of educational administrators. Lazar, Stodden, and Sullivan (1976) compared attitudes held by male and female administrators toward instructional goals, personal adjustment, and the handicapped. Using three different attitude instruments, it was found that sex made no difference on the variables studied and that regardless of acceptance or nonacceptance of the handicapped instructional goals were the same.

In an earlier study Rickard, Triandis, and Patterson (1963) developed an instrument for measuring the extent of employer prejudice and examined prejudice towards a variety of disability groups. Results showed that employers were prejudiced against disabled job applicants, with similar patterns of prejudice found for both personnel directors and school administrators.

Policies governing the acceptance of physically disabled college students into teacher training programs were surveyed in 1291 colleges and universities (Bender et al., 1968). Responses from 678 schools (58% return) were analyzed by size, type of school, and type of disability. No consistent policy regarding acceptance emerged. Two major reasons advanced for those programs not accepting handicapped students into their programs were that they will not be permitted in the teacher training program, and schools in the field will not accept handicapped teachers. The authors make specific recommendations to disabled persons and educators regarding improvement of this situation including early contact by the applicant with administrators of teacher training programs that schools develop good communication with accepted students, increasing information relative to specific limitations to teaching imposed by various disabling conditions, and counseling programs.

As a reminder that one cannot facilely generalize from the attitude domain to the behavioral, Schoggen (1966) reported on extensive records of behavior and situation on matched pairs of children in everyday activities at home and in public schools. Analysis of the specimen records for intra-pair differences in treatment afforded by their mothers and their classroom teachers revealed no statistically significant differences on any of the 10 variables studied, e.g., amount of time spent with child, frequency of help giving, amount of conflict. The finding suggest that differential treatment by their mothers and teachers in everyday life cannot be assumed.

Although the finding of Schoggen makes sense and is a proper interpretation of the data, the present writer must enter a disclaimer if one is tempted to conclude that no behavioral effects of disability are to be observed. I was a fellow panelist when the Schoggen paper was presented and during the subsequent discussion one of our colleagues who was in the audience, herself severly speech and motorically affected, spoke at length supporting Schoggen's findings and affirming that she never had the experience of differential reaction and that the rest of the findings, including my own, were of dubious validity as they presumably were not behaviorally based. Unfortunately, my observation then, supported by others, was that many in a large roomful of rehabilitation psychologists were in evident discomfort as she continued to speak, thereby contradicting the very point being made. Generalizations on this subject obviously are most difficult to support. All disabilities do not have the same stimulus properties and have varying potential for eliciting disturbed reactions. When multiple and obvious conditions are involved the likelihood of untoward reactions is increased.

Attitudes of Rehabilitation Personnel

It is quite natural for those involved in any activity to want to feel that their actions will contribute to good effects. When one's efforts do not lead to much success, a resulting pessimism obtains. As a result, certain kinds of conditions traditionally have lesser "appeal" to professional workers than do others (e.g., Ort et al., 1965). Thus, aging, mental retardation, the dying, and chronic disability all seem to have relatively restricted interest for professionals in general. Professionals, like most, prefer working with the "beautiful people," those who are most like themselves intellectually, social class-wise, etc., and those who can be helped.

Thus, in one typical study the major reason given by rehabilitation counselor's preference not to rehabilitate particular kinds of disability was lack of speed and ease of success in achieving vocational rehabilitation (Goldin, 1966).

Stotsky et al. (1968) surveyed physicians regarding their knowledge of rehabilitation services and their attitudes with respect to various facets of rehabilitation. Questionnaires were mailed out to 1500 randomly selected physicians, 150 psychiatrists, and 30 physiatrists in the six New England States with a 32% response rate. Information concerning the existence of state rehabilitation agencies (the largest and most important purveyors of rehabilitation services) either was lacking (over half of the sample), or usually seriously incomplete. Stotsky et al. (1968) states: "Generally speaking, physicians were positive in their attitudes toward rehabilitation but did not relate to the institutionalized structures through which it is made available." Psychiatrists differed sharply from physiatrists and general practitioners for most responses. They related most closely to the rehabilitation process—particularly social and emotional aspects, whereas the others were concerned most with physical aspects. Although a decade old, there is no reason to believe that the results of this study would be substantially different if replicated now.

The relationship between expectations of the teacher and performance of the students ("Pygmalion effect") has been widely publicized. A rehabilitation study of this relationship used 26 blind adolescents and their houseparents (Mayadas, 1975). Support for the hypothesis that expectations of significant others would bear upon the performance of the institutionalized adolescents was obtained. Mayadas points out how important it is that significant personnel be carefully selected and receive continued training. In another study Mayadas and Duehn (1976) examined the behavior performance of 56 blind persons in view of the role expectations of significant others: "Findings suggest that there is a correlation between the expectation of significant others and the 'blind role' assumed by blind persons." The preceding findings likely are highly generalizable to all disability conditions and all rehabilitation professions as they are to most basic relationships between persons of discrepant statuses.

Some studies have been concerned with the comparison of different rehabilitation personnel groups. Thus, Crunk and Allen (1977) investigated differences in attitude (semantic differential) toward the severely disabled of five rehabilitation groups: 45 vocational rehabilitation counselors, 50 disability determination examiners, 25 facility workers, 32 graduate rehabilitation students, and 35 undergraduate rehabilitation students. Findings indicated that demographic factors of age, sex, employment, and education contributed only in a small way (10% of the variance) to the results. The group did differ from one another (ANOVA, $p < .01$) in attitudes toward the severely disabled. Disability determination examinees were most negative followed by facility workers. Least negative were the vocational rehabilitation groups. In a different report, other group differences were found when eight major disabilities (deafness, migraine headaches, ulcerated stomach, cardiac or heart condition, blindness, tuberculosis, amputated arm (above elbow), and amputated leg (above knee) were ranked as they might be disturbing of personally afflicted by 7 rehabilitation professors, 32 future rehabilitation counselors, and 50 Mensa members (Wilson et al., 1968). Both groups were significantly different from the seven experts (professors) whose attitudes were judged to represent a more objective view. Interestingly enough, although both the Mensa members and students ranked blindness (as usual) as most personally distressing, it was ranked fifth for the professors who ranked deafness as one. Migraine headaches was ranked number 2 for professors and students and 4 for Mensa members. Research of this type suggests exploration of attitudes of the special vocational groups involved in rehabilitation work so as to determine what preconceptions exist and to initiate work regarding them. As Wilson et al. (1968) indicate, "one may not take for granted that either highly intelligent or highly interested but relatively uninformed persons will view handicaps with the same objectivity as experts."

Goldin (1966) found that counselors prefer not to deal with certain kinds of clients because of their quest for successful cases. Of eight disability conditions most preferred were amputees (25%), visual (21.4%) and mental illness

(20.2%). Cases least preferred by counselors were mental retardation (25.6%), mental illness (25.6%), and intercurrent acute episode diseases, e.g., epilepsy (22.0%). Other conditions listed were neurological motor impairments, speech and hearing, and incapacity diseases none of which received either much favorable or unfavorable ratings. Goldin observed that predictability of client behavior is an important consideration in the counselor work preference.

Warren and Turner (1966) also provided data on the relative rankings of a variety of conditions of exceptionality by several groups of professionals. Subjects included 24 teachers of the mentally retarded, 22 social workers, 63 student nurses, 17 medical students, 27 graduate students in school administration, and 219 psychology and education students. In order, preferences for the total group were: academically talented, antisocial, sight handicapped, mildly retarded, hearing handicapped, brain injured, and severely retarded. With a few exceptions, the ranks were consistent across groups. Rankings also were obtained on the educational emphasis respondents felt this area was given in current training in one's field of specialization. The results of this ranking were almost identical to ranking of preference. When rankings for familiarity were compared with the other two rankings a highly similar pattern was obtained. The absence of much differentiation among the three categories would suggest that a common attitudinal element (net affect?) underlies all. Some other findings of interest were that reporting having relatives in one of the areas of exceptionality is highly correlated with preference for that area. The data on Preference and the subsections of the Familiarity scale suggests, according to Warren and Turner, that the less an individual cares about an exceptionality in terms of work preference, the less he bothers to find out about it, or that the less one believes that one knows about an exceptionality, the lower it is rated.

Schroedel (1976) summarized attitudes among 14 samples totalling 346 professionals and obtained from six studies using Cowen's Attitudes Toward Deafness Scale (Cowen et al., 1967) as "mildly positive." Other studies using the Siller groups' Disability Factor Scales-Deafness (Ferguson, 1970) with small groups of professionals suggested no significant differences in attitudes on the factor scales (Schroedel, 1972). Measurement of attitudes of professionals in the area of deafness is continuing and this is an area of active research using these scales.

Research based studies on attitudes of professionals toward cancer are beginning to appear in contrast to the more prevalent clinical writings. Tichenor and Rundall (1977), using two experimental attitude scales, found strong reactions and suggested the need for further information and guidance in the treatment of cancer patients. Siller and Braden (unpublished, 1976) developed a cancer form of the Disability Factor Scales that was then used in an attitude change experiment with physical therapy students. Three aspects of this study are particularly noteworthy. First, in the development of the scales where large numbers of health related professionals were used among other groups, the factorial structure was only partially reflective of the structure of attitudes repeatedly found for other disability conditions. Considering the robustness of the attitudinal dimensions across other disability types this is a most significant finding. Second, the factorial structure of a previously developed set of scales (Haley et al., 1968) that had rather good psychometric development but based on a narrow norm group (medical students) was not replicated in the Siller and Braden study. The most obvious explanation would seem to be the restricted nature of the Haley et al. population. Third, favorable attitude change was induced by the specific experimental program attempted as measured by the DFS-Cancer scales. Finally, Pinkerton and McAleer (1976) studying 34 practicing counselors used variations of the ATDP to assess attitudes toward people with cancer, heart disease, renal failure, and paraplegia. They also ranked these conditions in terms of threat to themselves. Counselors were then presented with case study formats and asked to make eight professional decisions regarding the four conditions.

> The results strongly support general conclusions in the literature that counselors are less likely to provide counseling and case services to cancer patients than to patients with other equally devastating disease-related disabilities. A relationship is demonstrated between case service, attitudes toward the cancer patient, and personal fear of cancer.

It is obvious that cancer has a unique quality that must be taken into consideration in the training of professionals both in terms of patient impact and on social perceptions including that of professionals.

We have reviewed briefly some of the literature on two specific conditions—deafness and cancer, as samplers for other disability conditions. A review of attitude studies on blindness in general may be found in Monbeck (1973). It would be accurate to conclude that the bulk of systematic work is yet to be done.

As a final note documenting the importance of professional attitudes for client outcomes the work of Krauft et al. (1976) and Cook et al. (1976) can be mentioned. In the latter study, counselors judged by superiors as the more effective counselors rated the disabled similarly to normals. In the Krauft et al. work counseling personnel holding more positive attitudes, as measured by the ATDP, experienced greater success than less positive S's when working with clients perceived to have those disabilities most different from the able-bodied. One cannot be mechanical in interpreting the results of studies such as these that use the ATDP. As Bell (1962) suggested one can more safely say that the ATDP scale provides a measure of the attitude that the physically disabled differ in certain ways from the general population than that the scale measures "degree of acceptance" of the handicapped.

The review of professional attitudes to this point has dealt mostly with descriptive studies without much insight into causative factors. It would be well to consider them at this point. Schofield and Kunce (1971) did a close study of six experienced counselors in relation to counselor perceptions and counselor treatments. They asked whether a specific disability would be perceived differently by different counselors, and would a specific counselor perceive various kinds of disabilities in different ways. Schofield & Kunce inferred from their findings that: (1) various perceptual styles and stereotypes exist; (2) counselor perceptions may be as descriptive of the counselor as they are of the client; and (3) perceptions may influence counselor–client interactions. What becomes evident from studies of this nature is that unless one enters into the inner life of the rehabilitation worker a dimension essential for the explanation of the phenomena observed is lacking.

The crucial nature of the personal element of the rehabilitation worker is also shown when one observes the frequency with which direct-care staff contribute to their own difficulties in dealing with clients around rehabilitation issues. Workers who attempt to "reassure away" depressed feelings may unwittingly reinforce denials and obscure the needs for dependency and appropriate mourning reactions (Shapiro & McMahon, 1966). Frustration and anger toward clients who do not improve are also evident. One also can observe anger and rejection by the staff toward clients who manifest hostility or passive–aggressive behavior.

As McKegney (1968), Siller (1969), and others have pointed out, medical personnel, particularly physicians, see themselves as healers and have been trained within an acute care frame of reference where passivity on the part of the patient is encouraged—if not even insisted upon. Wright (1969) found the need to emphasize negative aspects of disability among professionals who "needed to reassure themselves of the importance of their services and thereby of themselves" (p. 94). One cannot overly stress the crucial importance for those with chronic disabling conditions to be self-sufficient and active in their own behalf. One must be careful that rehabilitation workers' attitudes, such as those mentioned earlier and others to be discussed, do not actually intrude upon the rehabilitation process.

Olshansky (1974) wrote of feelings of "mutual resentment" that exist between counselors and their clients and described a number of causes of this supposed resentment. Olshansky holds that by increasing the self-esteem of the counselor in terms of status and financial rewards, as well as to allow him the freedom of expressing his feelings in an atmosphere of mutual support among members of his profession, his own resentment would diminish leaving him better able to help the client deal with his.

Olshansky (1974) points out that one aspect of client resentment is that in counselor–client relationships the latter is always in an "inferior" position. The topic of a status-differential between professional and client was the subject of a group of articles by Kerr, Frankel, and Siller. Frankel (1970) compares the professional–client relationship in rehabilitation to the relationship between teacher and student where the former holds all the power, knowledge, and "moral worth." The student learns to "play the game" while learning to "abdicate his personhood to his role as a student." Kerr (1970), writing from the perspective of a disabled professional, corroborates these assertions to a degree but allows that staff expectations of clients may be either helpful or harmful to the rehabilitation process depending on the attitudes and orientations of the professionals. Siller (1970) argues that the status differential is neither intrinsically "good" or "bad," and might be quite appropriate to a given situation. Siller attributes the primary significance of destructive status differential situations to "transference distortions" and countertransference that implies that one can structure such a relationship in many ways depending on the particular needs of the individual. Blank (1954) in about the only article on this issue describes certain prevalent attitudes based on transference and countertransference in working with the blind. He points out that workers with serious countertransference problems are usually regarded "as having blind spots, inept, hostile, too disturbed to work with clients, or lacking initiative (anxious and inhibited)." Blank indicates that many countertransferences are not deep-seated and, per se, are not pathognomic of personality disorder. Blank suggests the hypothesis that a great part of the "growth" of a worker attributed to "experience" actually represents his gradually and progressively solving his countertransference problems, principally on a preconscious level, in his interaction with his clients (and co-workers) so that he becomes continually better able to see the client's problem and the indicated line of help.

Earlier, the attitudinal dimension of Authoritarian Virtuousness was described. It was indicated that although ostensibly a "prodisabled" attitude orientation it was really reflective of a subordinating and negative tone. This dimension easily is the most robust and replicable of all the components failing to emerge only in our cancer study (Siller & Braden, unpublished). Authoritarian Virtuousness would seem to be particularly relevant in studying attitudes of professionals, support personnel, and volunteers toward client populations. The presence of this quality in such persons should be identified and corrective procedures implemented as it goes counter to basic rehabilitation goals.

In this section on professional's attitudes toward clients a wide variety of studies has been described and discussed. Although a few have written with some depth on this topic (e.g., Leviton, 1971, 1973; Parsons, 1951, Sussman, 1965; Wright, 1960) and its general importance is universally recognized, there has been a conspicuous absence of extended programmatic work whereby in-depth analyses and pursuit of concommitant variables are meaningfully pursued. Although we have been able to review only a portion of the available literature in this area, the total number of available studies and the quality of research dealing specifically with attitudinal aspects fails to reflect its real importance. In general, the level of research sophistication is relatively low with .dies mostly of small samples of nonrandomly selected professional populations assessed by weak instruments.

It is our recommendation that systematic research be undertaken in this area of both a quantitative and qualitative nature. The available data are quite adequate for most "nose counting" purposes. What is needed now is more work of an explanatory nature that could then be used to direct attitude change programs.

Final Remarks

Any inclination to consider disability outside of the larger social context and as something that resides only in the disabled person is destructively wrong. It is hoped that the aforementioned citations and analyses have served to convey the complexity and dynamic nature of the attitudinal situation as regards the physically disabled. Great continuities exist between the physically disabled and other deviant individuals, but, for that matter, even greater continuities exist between the physically disabled and all other persons.

In opting for wide coverage, we have had to sacrifice critical assessment of individual articles and chose to take most reports at face value. Actually, this writer is a highly critical of much of the past research literature on a variety of grounds, some of which were expressed. It is of considerable satisfaction to note that studies are becoming increasingly sophisticated and more appropriate to the complexity of the subject. I believe that we have sufficiently "tooled up" conceptually and methodologically to look forward to a new wave of significant research that will be of direct use to those involved in working with the disabled. It is to be hoped that systematic programs of research directed toward specific problems of need will be accompanied by attention to basic theoretical and measurement concerns.

REFERENCES

Alessi, D. F., & Anthony, W. A. (1969). The uniformity of children's attitudes toward physical disabilities. *Exceptional Children, 35,* 543–545.

Allport, G. W. (1954). *The nature of prejudice.* Reading, MA: Addison–Wesley.

Altshuler, K. Z. (1964). Personality traits and depressive symptoms in deaf. In J. Mortis (Ed.), *Recent advances in biological psychiatry.* New York: Plenum Press.

Amir, Y. (1969) Contact hypothesis in ethnic relations. *Psychological Bulletin, 71,* 319–342.

Anthony, W. A. (1972). Societal rehabilitation: Changing society's attitudes toward the physically and mentally disabled. *Rehabilitation Psychology, 19,* 117–126.

Asher, N. W. (1973). Manipulating attraction toward the disabled: An application of the similarity-attraction model. *Rehabilitation Psychology, 20,* 155–164.

Bansavage, J. C. (1968). Social acceptance in a group of orthopedically impaired adolescents. *Proceedings of the 81st Annual Convention of the American Psychological Association, 3,* 647–648.

Barker, D. (1964). Concepts of disabilities. *Personnel and Guidance Journal, 43,* 371–374.

Barker, R. G., Weight, B. A., Meyerson, L., & Gonick, M. R. (1953). *Adjustment to physical handicap and illness: A survey of the social psychology of physique and disability* (2nd ed.). New York: Social Science Research Council.

Bates, R. E. (1965). *Meaning of "disabled" and "handicapped": Their relation to each other and other specific defects.* Unpublished doctoral dissertation, University of Houston.

Bazakas, R. (1977). *The interpersonal impact of coping, dependency, and denial self-presentations by the disabled.* Unpublished doctoral dissertation, New York University.

Bell, A. H. (1962). Attitudes of selected rehabilitation workers and other hospital employees toward the physically disabled. *Psychological Reports, 10*, 183–186.

Bender, J. A., Kolstoe, P. O., & Kaplan, H. M. (1968). Acceptance of disabled college students into teacher training programs. *Exceptional Children, 34*, 685–691.

Black, K. V. (1964). *Attitudes toward the disabled acting in the helper role.* Unpublished master's thesis, University of Colorado.

Blank, H. R. (1954). Countertransference problems in the professional worker. *The New Outlook for the Blind, 48*, 185–188.

Blau, S. (1964). An ear for an eye: Sensory compensation and judgments of affect by the blind. In J. R. Davitz (Ed.), *The communication of emotional meaning.* New York: McGraw-Hill, 113–127.

Brabham, R. E., & Thoreson, R. W. (1973). Relationship of client preferences and counselor's physical disability. *Journal of Counseling Psychology, 20*, 10–15.

Burlingham, D. T. (1964). Hearing and its role in the development of the blind. *Psychoanalytic Study of the Child, 19*, 95–112.

Centers, L., & Centers, R. (1963). Peer group attitudes toward the amputee child. *Journal of Social Psychology, 61*, 127–132.

Clore, G. L., & Jeffrey, K. M. (1972). Emotional role playing, attitude change, and attraction toward a disabled person. *Journal of Personality and Social Psychology, 23*, 105–111.

Comer, R. J., & Piliavin, J. A. (1972). The effects of physical deviance upon face-to-face interactions: The other side. *Journal of Personality and Social Psychology, 23*, 33–39.

Comer, R. C., & Piliavin, J. A. (1975). As others see us: Attitudes of physically handicapped and normals toward own and other groups. *Rehabilitation Literature, 36*, 206–221, 225.

Conine, T. (1969). Acceptance of rejection of disabled persons by teachers. *Journal of School Health, 39*, 278–281.

Cook, D. W., Kunce, J. T., & Getsinger, S. H. (1976). Perceptions of the disabled and counseling effectiveness. *Rehabilitation Counseling Bulletin, 19*, 470–475.

Cowen, E. L., Bobrove, P. H., Rockway, A. M., & Stevenson, J. (1967). Development and evaluation of an attitudes to deafness scale. *Journal of Personality and Social Psychology, 6*, 183–191.

Cowen, E. L., Underberg, R. P., & Verillo, R. T. (1958). The development and testing of an attitudes to blindness scale. *Journal of Social Psychology, 48*, 297–304.

Cowen, E. L., Underberg, R. P., Verrilo, R. T., & Benham, F. G. (1961). *Adjustment to visual disability in adolescence.* New York: American Foundation for the Blind.

Cruickshank, W. M. (Ed.). (1980). *Psychology of exceptional children and youth.* (4th ed.). Englewood Cliffs, NJ: Prentice-Hall.

Crunk, W. A., Jr., & Allen, J. (1977). Attitudes toward the severely disabled among five rehabilitation groups. *Journal of Applied Rehabilitation Counseling, 4*, 237–244.

Daniels, L. K. (1976). Covert reinforcement and hypnosis in modification of attitudes toward physically disabled persons and generalization to the emotionally disturbed. *Psychological Reports, 38*, 554.

Dembo, T. (1969). Rehabilitation psychology and its immediate future: A problem of utilization of psychological knowledge. *Psychological Aspects of Disability, 16*, 63–72.

Dembo, T., Leviton, G. L., & Wright, B. A. (1975). Adjustment to misfortune—A problem of social-psychological rehabilitation. *Rehabilitation Psychology, 22*, 1–100.

Dixon, J. K. (1977). Coping with prejudice: Attitudes of handicapped persons toward the handicapped. *Journal of Chronic Disease, 30*, 307–322.

Donaldson, J. (1976). Channel variations and effects on attitudes toward physically disabled individuals. *AV Communication Review, 24*, 135–144.

Donaldson, J., & Martinson, M. C. (1977). Modifying attitudes toward physically disabled persons. *Exceptional Children*, 337–341.

Doob, A. N., & Ecker, B. P. (1970). Stigma and compliance. *Journal of Personality and Social Psychology, 14,* 302–304.

Dow, T. E., Jr. (1965). Social class and reaction to physical disability. *Psychological Reports, 17,* 39–62.

Elsberry, N. L. (1975). Comparison of two scales measuring attitudes toward persons with physical disabilities. *Psychological Reports, 36,* 473–474.

Elser, R. P. (1958). Social status of physically handicapped children. *Exceptional Children, 23,* 305–309.

Evans, J. H. (1976). Changing attitudes toward disabled persons: An experimental study. *Rehabilitation Counseling Bulletin, 20,* 572–579.

Ferguson, L. T. (1970). Components of attitudes toward the deaf. *Proceedings of the 78th Annual Convention of the American Psychological Association, 5,* 693–694.

Fine, J. A. (1978). *Castration anxiety and self concept of physically normal children as related to perceptual awareness of and attitudes toward physical deviance.* Unpublished doctoral dissertation, New York University.

Finkelstein, V. (1979). *Changing Attitudes & Disabled People: Issues for Discussion.* Monographs of the World Rehabilitation Fund.

Force, D. G. (1956). Social status of physically handicapped children. *Journal of Exceptional Children, 23,* 104–107.

Fraiberg, S. (1968). Parallel and divergent patterns in blind and sighted infants. *Psychoanalytic Study of the Child, 23,* 264–300.

Frankel, A. (1970). Uses and abuses of status in teacher–student relationships. *Rehabilitation Counseling Bulletin, 14,* 95–101.

Freeman, G. G., & Sonnega, J. A. (1956). Peer evaluation of children in speech correction class. *Journal of Speech and Hearing Disorders, 21,* 178–182.

Friend, E. (1971). *Social interaction of amputees and nonamputees as related to their attitudes toward amputation.* Unpublished doctoral dissertation, New York University.

Furth, H. G. (1961). The influence of language on the development of concept formation in deaf children. *Journal of Abnormal and Social Psychology, 63,* 386–389.

Gallagher, B. (1969). Teachers' attitudes and the acceptability of children with speech defects. *The Elementary School Journal,* 277–281.

Gillman, A. E. (1973). Handicap and cognition: Visual deprivation and the rate of motor development in infants. *The New Outlook for the Blind, 67,* 309–314.

Gladstone, L. R. (1977). A study of the relationship between ego defense style preference and experimental pain tolerance and attitudes toward physical disability. (Doctoral dissertation, New York University, 1977). *Dissertation Abstracts International, 37,* 77–5306.

Glenwick, D. S., & Arata, C. L. (in press). Assertiveness training in a college companion program: Effects on student volunteers and rehabilitation center clients. *Rehabilitation Psychology.*

Goldin, G. J. (1966). Some rehabilitation counselor attitudes toward their professional roles. *Rehabilitation Literature, 27,* 360–364, 369.

Goodman, N., Richardson, S. A., Dornbusch, S. M., & Hastorf, A. H. (1963). Variant reactions to physical disabilities. *American Sociological Review, 28,* 429–435.

Gottlieb, J. (1981). Mainstreaming: Fulfilling the promise. *American Journal of Mental Deficiency, 86,* 115–126.

Grand, S. A., Bernier, J. E., & Strohmer, D. C., (1982). Attitudes towards disabled persons as a function of social context and specific disability. *Rehabilitation Psychology, 27,* 165–174.

Greer, B. G. (1975). Attitudes of special education personnel toward different types of deviant persons. *Rehabilitation Literature, 36,* 182–184.

Gronlund, N. E., (1959). *Sociometry in the classroom.* New York: Harper & Brothers.

Guttman, L. (1950). The problem of attitude and opinion measurement. In S. A. Stauffer (Ed.), *Measurement and prediction.* Princeton, NJ: Princeton University Press.

Haddle, H. W. (1973). *The efficacy of automated group desensitization as a strategy to modify attitudes toward disabled persons.* Unpublished doctoral dissertation, Georgia State University.

Haley, H. B., Juan, I. R., & Gagan, J. F. (1968). Factor analytic approach to attitude scale construction. *Journal of Medical Education, 43,* 331–336.

Hansson, R. O., & Duffield, B. J. (1976). Physical attractiveness and the attribution of epilepsy. *Journal of Social Psychology, 99,* 233–240.

Harasymiw, S. J., & Horne, M. D. (1975). Integration of handicapped children: Its effect on teacher attitudes. *Education, 96,* 153–158.

Harasymiw, S. J., & Horne, M. D. (1976a). Teacher attitudes toward handicapped children and regular class integration. *Journal of Special Education, 10,* 393–400.

Harasymiw, S. J., Horne, M. D., & Lewis, S. c. (1976b). A longitudinal study of disability group acceptance. *Rehabilitation Literature, 37,* 98–102.

Hastorf, A. H., Northcroft, G. B., & Picciotto, S. R. (1979). Helping the handicapped: How realistic is the performance feedback received by the physically handicapped. *Personality and Social Psychology Bulletin, 5,* 373–376.

Havill, S. J. (1970). The sociometric status of visually handicapped students in public school classes. *Research Bulletin, 20,* 57–90.

Higgs, R. W. (1975). Attitude formation—contact or information? *Exceptional Children, 41,* 496–497.

Ingwell, R. H., Thoreson, R. W., & Smits, S. J. (1967). Accuracy of social perception of physically handicapped and nonhandicapped persons. *Journal of Social Psychology, 72,* 107–116.

Jaques, M. E., Linkowski, D. C., & Sierka, F. L. (1970). Cultural attitudes toward disability: Denmark, Greece, and the United States. *International Journal of Social Psychiatry, 16,* 54–62.

Jastrzembska, Z. S. (Ed.). (1976). *The effects of blindness and other impairments on early development.* New York: American Foundation for the Blind.

Jennings, M. (1951). Twice handicapped. *Occupations, 30,* 176–181.

Jones, R. L. (1970). Learning and association in the presence of the blind. *New Outlook for the Blind, 64,* 317–329.

Jones, R. L. (1974). The hierarchical structure of attitudes toward the exceptional. *Exceptional Children, 40,* 430–435.

Jones, R. L., & Sisk, D. (1970). Early perceptions of orthopedic disability. *Rehabilitation Literature, 31,* 32–38.

Jordan, J. E. (1968). *Attitudes toward education and physically disabled persons in eleven nations.* Latin American Studies Center, Michigan State University.

Jordan, J. E. (1971). Attitude-behavior on physical–mental–social disabilities, and racial–ethnic differences. *Psychological Aspects of Disability, 18,* (No. 1.), 5–26.

Jordan, T. E. (1962). Research on the handicapped child and the family. *Merrill–Palmer Quarterly, 8,* 243–260.

Karlins, M., Coffman, T. L., & Walters, G. (1969). On the fading of social stereotypes: Studies in three generations of college students. *Journal of Personality and Social Psychology, 13,* 1–16.

Kelley, H. H., Hastorf, A. H., Jones, E. E., Thibaut, J. W., & Usdane, W. M. (1960). Some implications of social psychological theory for research on the handicapped. In E. H. Lofquist (Ed.), *Psychological research and rehabilitation.* Washington, DC: American Psychological Association.

Kerr, N. (1970). Staff expectations for disabled persons: Helpful or harmful. *Rehabilitation Counseling Bulletin, 14,* 85–94.

Kleck, R. E. (1969). Physical stigma and task oriented interaction. *Human Relations, 22,* 53–60.

Kleck, R. E., Ono, H., & Hastorf, A. H. (1966). The effects of physical deviance upon face-to-face interaction. *Human Relations, 19,* 425–436.

Kohler, E. T., & Graves, W. H. III. (1973). Factor analysis of the Disability Factor Scales with the Little Jiffy, Mark III. *Rehabilitation Psychology, 20,* 102–107.

Krauft, C. C., Rubin, E. C., Cook, D. W., & Bozarth, J. D. (1976). Counselor attitude toward disabled persons and client program completion: A pilot study. *Journal of Applied Rehabilitation Counseling, 7,* 50–54.

Kutner, B. (1971). The social psychology of disability. In W. S. Neff (Ed.), *Rehabilitation psychology.* Washington, DC: American Psychological Association.

Lazar, A. L., Demos, G. D., Gaines, L., Rogers, D., & Stirnkorb, M. (1978). Attitudes of handicapped and nonhandicapped university students on three attitude scales. *Rehabilitation Literature, 38,* 49–52.

Lazar, A. L., Gensley, J. T., & Orpet, R. E. (1971). Changing attitudes of young mentally gifted children toward handicapped persons. *Exceptional Children, 37,* 600–602.

Lazar, A. L., Stodden, R. L., & Sullivan, N. W. (1976). A comparison of attitudes held by male and female future administrators toward instructional goals, personal adjustment, and the handicapped. *Rehabilitation Literature, 37,* 198–201.

Lenneberg, E. (1967). *Biological foundations of language.* New York: Wiley.

Lerner, M. J., & Miller, D. T. (1978). Just world research and the attribution process: Looking back and ahead. *Psychological Bulletin, 85,* 1030–1051.

Levine, E. S. (1956). *Youth in a soundless world.* New York: New York University Press.

Leviton, G. L. (1971). Professional–client relations in a rehabilitation hospital setting. In W. S. Neff (Ed.), *Rehabilitation psychology.* Washington, DC: American Psychological Association.

Leviton, G. L. (1973). Professional and client viewpoints on rehabilitation issues. *Rehabilitation Psychology, 20,* 1–80.

Levitt, L., & Kornhaber, R. C. (1977). Stigma and compliance: A re-examination. *Journal of Social Psychology, 103,* 13–18.

Lipp, L., Kolstoe, R., James, W., & Randall, W. (1968). Denial of disability and internal control of reinforcement: A study using a perceptual defense paradigm. *Journal of Consulting and Clinical Psychology, 32,* 72–75.

Major, I. (1961). How do we accept the handicapped? *Elementary School Journal, 61,* 328–330.

Marge, D. K. (1966). The social status of speech-handicapped children. *Journal of Speech and Hearing Research, 9,* 165–177.

Marinelli, R. P., & Kelz, J. W. (1973). Anxiety and attitudes toward visibly disabled persons. *Rehabilitation Counseling Bulletin, 17,* 198–205.

Matthews, V., & Westie, C. (1966). A preferred method for obtaining rankings: Reactions to physical handicaps. *American Sociological Review, 31,* 851–854.

Mayadas, N. S. (1975). Houseparents' expectations: A crucial variable in the performance of blind institutionalized children. *New Outlook for the Blind, 69,* 77–85.

Mayadas, N. S., & Duehn, W. D. (1976). The impact of significant adults' expectations on the life style of visually impaired children. *New Outlook for the Blind, 70,* 286–290.

McCauley, R. W., Bruininks, R. H., & Kennedy, P. (1976). Behavioral interactions of hearing impaired children in regular classrooms. *Journal of Special Education, 10,* 277–284.

McKegney, F. P. (1968). Emotional and interpersonal aspects of rehabilitation. In S. Licht (Ed.), *Rehabilitation and medicine,* Baltimore, MD: Waverly Press, 229–251.

Mesch, J. C. (1976). Content analysis of verbal communication between spinal cord injured and non-disabled male college students. *Archives of Physical Medicine and Rehabilitation, 57,* 25–30.

Meyerson, L. (Ed.). (1948). The social psychology of physical disability. *Journal of Social Issues, 4,* Entire issue.

Mitchell, D. C., & Fredrickson, W. A. (1975). Preferences for physically disabled counselors in hypothetical counseling situations. *Journal of Counselling Psychology, 22,* 477–482.

Monbeck, M. E. (1973). *The meaning of blindness.* Bloomington: Indiana University Press.

Moriarty, T. (1974). Role of stigma in the experience of deviance. *Journal of Personality and Social Psychology, 29,* 849–855.

Murphy, A. T. (1960). Attitudes of educators toward the visually handicapped. *The Sight-Saving Review, 30*, 157–161.

Murphy, A. T., Dickstein, J., & Dripps, E. (1960). Acceptance, rejection, and the hearing handicapped. *Volta Review, 62*, 208–211.

Newfield, W. F. (1964). *The effect of social desirability and birth order on the ranking of physical disabilities.* Unpublished master's thesis, Columbia University.

Newman, J. (1976). Faculty attitudes toward handicapped students. *Rehabilitation Literature, 37*, 194–197.

Noonan, J. R., Barry, J. R., & Davis, H. C. (1970). Personality determinants in attitudes toward visible disability. *Journal of Personality, 38*, 1–15.

Olshansky, S. (1974). Mutual resentment: An obstruction in the counselor–client relationship. *Rehabilitation Counseling, 35*, 36–43.

Ort, R. S., Ford, A. B., Liske, R. E., & Pattishall, E. G., Jr. (1965). Expectation and experience in the reactions of medical students to patients with chronic illness. *Journal of Medical Education, 40*, 840–849.

Osgood, C. E., Suci, G. J., & Tannenbaum, P. H. (1957). *The measurement of meaning.* Urbana: University of Illinois Press.

Parsons, T. (1951). Illness and the role of the physician: A sociological perspective. *American Journal of Orthopsychiatry, 21*, 452–460.

Pinkerton, S., & McAleer, C. A. (1976). Influence of client diagnosis-cancer-on counselor decisions. *Journal of Counseling Psychology, 23*, 575–578.

Raskin, N. J. (1962). Visual disability. In J. F. Garrett & E. S. Levine (Eds.), *Psychological practices with the physically disabled.* New York: Columbia University Press.

Reich, C., Hambleton, D., & Houldin, B. K. (1977). The integration of hearing impaired children in regular classrooms. *American Annals of the Deaf, 122*, 534–543.

Richardson, S. A. (1963). Some social psychological consequences of handicapping. *Pediatrics,* 291–297.

Richardson, S. A. (1969). The effect of physical disability on the socialization of a child. In D. A. Goslin (Ed.), *Handbook of socialization theory and research.* Chicago: Rand McNally.

Richardson, S. A. (1970). Age and sex differences in values toward physical handicaps. *Journal of Health and Social Behavior, 11*, 207–214.

Richardson, S. A. (1971). Children's values and friendships: A study of physical disability. *Journal of Health and Social Behavior, 12*, 253–258.

Richardson, S. A., & Friedman, M. J. (1973). Social factors related to children's accuracy in learning peer group values toward handicaps. *Human Relations, 26*, 77–87.

Richardson, S. A., Goodman, N., Hastorf, A. H., & Dornbusch, S. M. (1961). Cultural uniformity in reaction to physical disabilities. *American Sociological Review, 26*, 241–247.

Richardson, S. A., Hastorf, A. H., & Dornbusch, S. M. (1964). Effects of physical disability on a child's description of himself. *Child Development, 35*, 893–907.

Richardson, S. A., Ronald, L., & Kleck, R. E. (1974). The social status of handicapped and nonhandicapped boys in a camp setting. *Journal of Special Education, 8*, 143–152.

Richardson, S. A., & Royce, J. (1968). Race and physical handicap in children's preference for other children. *Child Development, 39*, 467–480.

Rickard, T. E., Triandis, H. C., & Patterson, C. H. (1963). Indices of employer prejudice toward disabled applicants. *Journal of Applied Psychology, 47*, 52–55.

Sadlick, M., & Penta, F. B. (1975). Changing nurse attitudes toward quadriplegics through the use of television. *Rehabilitation Literature, 36*, 274–278.

Safilios–Rothschild, C. (1970). *The sociology and social psychology of disability and rehabilitation.* New York: Random House.

Sandler, A. M. (1963). Aspects of passivity and ego development in the blind infant. *Psychoanalytic Study of the Child, 18*, 343–360.

Sands, H., & Zalkind, S. S. (1972). Effects of an educational campaign to change employer attitudes toward hiring epileptics. *Epilepsia, 13*, 87–96.

Sarlin, M. B., & Altshuler, K. Z. (1978). On the inter-relationship of cognition and affect: Fantasies of deaf children. *Child Psychiatry and Human Development, 9*, 95–103.

Schiff, W., & Thayer, S. (1974). An eye for an ear? Social perception, nonverbal communication, and deafness. *Rehabilitation Psychology, 21*, 50–70.

Schmelkin, L. P. (1985). Dimensionality of disability labels. *Rehabilitation Psychology, 30*, 130–149.

Schofield, L. F., & Kunce, J. (1971). Client disability and counselor behavior. *Rehabilitation Counseling Bulletin, 15*, 158–165.

Schoggen, P. (1963). *Environmental forces in the lives of children with and without physical disability.* Presented at the 1963 American Psychological Association Convention.

Schoggen, P. (1966). Observed behavior of mothers and teachers toward children with physical disabilities in natural settings. Paper presented at *American Psychological Association Annual Convention.*

Schroedel, J. G. (1972). *A study of behavioral validation of attitudes to deafness scales.* New York University Deafness Research and Training Center.

Schroedel, J. G., & Jacobsen, R. J. (1978). *Employment attitudes toward hiring workers with disabilities.* Albertson, NY: Human Resources Center.

Schroedel, J. G. (1976). Changing professional attitudes toward deaf people. In F. B. Grammatte & A. B. Grammattee (Eds.), *VII World Congress of the World Federation of the Deaf,* Silver Spring, MD: National Association of the Deaf.

Schroedel, J. G., & Schiff, W. (1972). Attitudes toward deafness among several deaf and hearing populations. *Rehabilitation Psychology, 19*, 59–70.

Shapiro, L. N., & McMahon, A. W. (1966). Rehabilitation stalemate. *Archives of General Psychiatry, 15*, 173–177.

Shears, L. M., & Jensema, C. J. (1969). Social acceptability of anomalous persons. *Exceptional Children, 35*, 91–96.

Shurka, E., & Katz, S. (1976). Evaluations of persons with a disability: The influence of disability context and personal responsibility for the disability. *Rehabilitation Psychology, 23*, 65–71.

Siller, J. (1966). Conceptual and methodological issues in the study of attitudes toward disability. Presented at the American Personnel and Guidance Association Annual Convention.

Siller, J. (1969). Psychological situation of the disabled with spinal cord injuries. *Rehabilitation Literature, 30*, 290–296.

Siller, J. (1970a). The generality of attitudes toward the disabled. *Proceedings of the 78th Annual Convention of the American Psychological Association, 5*, 697–698.

Siller, J. (1970b). The psychopathology of status. *Rehabilitation Counseling Bulletin, 14*, 102–107.

Siller, J. (1976a). Psychosocial aspects of disability. In J. Meislin (Ed.), *Rehabilitation medicine and psychiatry.* Springfield, IL: C. C. Thomas.

Siller, J. (1976b). Attitudes toward disability. In H. Rusalem & D. Malikin (Eds.), *Contemporary vocational rehabilitation.* New York: New York University Press.

Siller, J. (1984). The role of personality in attitudes toward those with physical disabilities. In C. J. Golden (Ed.), *Current topics in rehabilitation psychology.* New York: Grune & Stratton.

Siller, J., & Chipman, A. (1963). Response set paralysis: Implications for measurement and control. *Journal of Consulting Psychology, 27*, 432–438.

Siller, J., & Chipman, A. (1964). Factorial structure and correlates of the Attitudes Toward Disabled Persons Scale. *Educational and Psychological Measurement, 24*, 831–840.

Siller, J., Chipman, A., Ferguson, L., & Vann, D. H. (1967a). *Attitudes of the nondisabled toward the physically disabled.* New York: New York University, School of Education.

Siller, J., Vann, D. H., Ferguson, L. T., & Holland, B. (1967b). *Structure of attitudes toward the physically disabled.* New York: New York University, School of Education.

Sloat, W. L., & Frankel, A. (1972). The contributions of subjects, disabilities, situations, sex of target person, and items to the variation of attitudes toward persons with a disability. *Rehabilitation Psychology, 19,* 3–17.

Smits, S. J., Conine, T. A., & Edwards, L. D. (1971). Definitions of disability as determinants of scores on the Attitude Toward Disabled Persons Scale. *Rehabilitation Counseling Bulletin, 15,* 227–235.

Soldwedel, B., & Terrill, I. (1957). Sociometric aspects of physically handicapped and nonhandicapped children in the same elementary school. *Exceptional Children, 23,* 371–372, 381–383.

Stotsky, B. A., Goldin, G. J., & Margolin, R. J. (1968). The physician and rehabilitation. *Rehabilitation Literature, 29,* 295–299, 305.

Straus, A. (1975). Changing attitudes toward blindness: A role-playing demonstration for service blubs. *New Outlook for the Blind, 69,* 407–409.

Sussman, M. D. (Ed.). (1965). *Sociology and rehabilitation.* American Sociological Association.

Thayer, S. (1973). Lend me your ears: Racial and sexual factors in helping the deaf. *Journal of Personality and Social Psychology, 28,* 8–11.

Tichenor, C. C., & Rundall, T. G. (1977). Attitudes of physical therapists toward cancer: A pilot study. *Physical Therapy, 57,* 160–165.

Tringo, J. L. (1970). The hierarchy of preference toward disability groups. *Journal of Special Education, 4,* 295–306.

Vann, D. H. (1970). Components of attitudes toward the obese including presumed responsibility for the condition. *Proceedings of the 78th Annual Convention of the American Psychological Association, 5,* 695–696.

Warren, S. A., & Turner, D. R. (1966). Attitudes of professionals and students toward exceptional children. *The Training School Bulletin, 62,* 136–144.

Wechsler, H., Suarez, A. C., & McFadden, M. (1975). Teachers' attitudes toward the education of physically handicapped children: Implications for the implementation of Massachusetts Chapter 766. *Journal of Education, 157,* 17–24.

Weinberg–Asher, N. (1976). The effect of physical disability on self-perception. *Rehabilitation Counseling Bulletin, 20,* 15–20.

Weinberg, N. (1978). Examination of pre-school attitudes toward the physically handicapped. *Rehabilitation Counseling Bulletin, 22,* 183–188.

Whiteman, M., & Lukoff, I. F. (1964). A factorial study of sighted people's attitudes toward blindness. *Journal of Social Psychology, 64,* 339–353.

Whiteman, M., & Lukoff, I. F. (1965). Attitudes toward blindness and other physical handicaps. *Journal of Social Psychology, 66,* 135–145.

Wilson, M. E., Jr., Sakata, R., & Frumkin, R. M. (1968). Attitudes of some gifted adults, future rehabilitation counselors, and rehabilitation professors toward disabilities. *Psychological Reports, 22,* 1303–1304.

Witkin, A., Birnbaum, J., Lomonaco, S., Lehr, S., & Herman, J. L. (1968). Cognitive patterning in congenitally totally blind children. *Child Development, 39,* 767–786.

Wittreich, W. J., & Radcliffe, K. B., Jr. (1955). The influence of simulated mutilation upon the perception of the human figure. *Journal of Abnormal and Social Psychology, 51,* 493–495.

Wright, B. A. (1960). *Physical disability—A psychological approach.* New York: Harper & Row.

Wright, B. A. (1964). Spread in adjustment to disability. *Bulletin of the Menniager Clinic, 28,* 198–208.

Wright, B. A. (1969). Some psychosocial aspects of disability. In D. Malikin, & H. Rusalem (Eds.), *Vocational rehabilitation of the disabled.* New York: New York University Press.

Yuker, H. E., Block, J. R., & Younng, J. H. (1966). *The measurement of attitudes toward disabled persons.* Albertson, NY: Human Resources Center.

Zuckerman, W. B. (1980). *Deaf, blind, and nonhandicapped adults' attitudes toward each other as related to authoritarianism, alienation, and ego strength.* Unpublished doctoral dissertation, New York University.

V COMMENTARY

11 The Question of the Importance of Physical Attractiveness

Ellen Berscheid
University of Minnesota

It was precisely 20 years ago that Gardner Lindzey, in his presidential address to the Division of Personality and Social Psychology of the American Psychological Association, took his colleagues to task for ignoring the influence of morphological variables upon behavior. Lindzey (1965) used the term *morphology* broadly "to refer not only to the physical, structural aspects of the organism but also to any externally observable and objectively measurable attribute of the person . . . even aesthetic attractiveness" (p. 344). His remarks, some of which were scathing, enumerated many possible reasons for the then popular scientific belief that the study of morphological variables was an "unsanitary practice" and the resultant absence of information about their influence upon human behavior. A few years later, Elliot Aronson (1969) offered yet another reason why at least one of these appeariential variables, physical attractiveness, had been neglected. He suggested that, "It may be that, at some level, we [researchers] would hate to find evidence indicating that beautiful women are better liked than homely women—somehow this seems undemocratic" (p. 160). (Presumably, it would have been equally offensive to egalitarian philosophies to find that handsome men were better liked than homely men.)

If social psychologists were initially reluctant to confront the possibility that one morphological variable, physical attractiveness, plays a role in social interaction and thus in people's lives, they have overcome that reluctance with a vengeance in the past 2 decades. Beginning with the first systematic investigation of the impact of physical attractiveness on social interaction conducted by Walster, Aronson, Abrahams, and Rottmann (1966), interest in the impact of this variable has steadily increased. Today, the physical attractiveness literature is one of the largest within the interpersonal attraction area (for reviews, see

Adams & Crossman, 1978; Berscheid & Walster, 1974, Huston & Levinger, 1978). In just the period 1972 through 1976, for example, more than 40 studies investigating physical appearance were published (see Huston & Levinger, 1978). The fact that physical attractiveness is an important variable for the behavioral scientist to take into consideration when attempting to understand human social behavior is now amply documented by the results of hundreds of studies and the fact of this Ontario Symposium.

But just how important is it? This is undoubtedly the most common question people now ask about physical attractiveness. Practioners in a variety of professions not infrequently ask it; lawyers, for example. Those representing clients whose appearance has been irrevocably altered for the worse through the negligence of others often want to know how much we, the experts, think a particular decrease in attractiveness is "worth" in monetary damages. How much, they ask, should the manufacturer of a flammable nightgown be ordered to pay to the little girl whose face and body were burned beyond the remedial talents of plastic surgeons? How much should be awarded to the boy whose face was ripped beyond repair by a savage dog that escaped his owner's leash? What factors have to be taken into consideration? Will their physical unattractiveness affect their self-esteem? Will it influence their marital prospects, their job prospects? Will it influence their close relationships with their parents and siblings and peers?

On the basis of available evidence, social psychologists can now say "Yes, it probably will"; to assess damage, the judge and jury must consider *more* than the degree of impairment of physical function and the "mental anguish" precipitated by the single event that altered the person's appearance. "But how *much* will it affect their lives?" they ask. The judge and jury cannot duck the question with philosophical speculation and conjectural extrapolation from our empirical base. They must arrive at a very specific answer, one that can be expressed in dollars and cents.

Judges and juries aren't the only ones who have to make very concrete judgments about how important physical attractiveness is. Those in the dental and medical professions make such determinations everyday. The orthodontic surgeon, for example, has to decide whether breaking a jaw in order to achieve a perfect "bite" is worth lessening the person's physical attractiveness. Again, social psychologists can take some credit for the fact appearance is now more frequently considered by practitioners when treatments that will improve function but also will alter appearance are contemplated. But how *much*, they ask, is a specific increase or decrease in attractiveness level worth against a specific improvement of function?

Plastic surgeons and their clients, of course, also routinely make such concrete assessments and act accordingly. Sometimes the decision is easy for the client, even when the surgery considered is life threatening. A case in point is a young woman at the University of Pennsylvania hospital who was about to undergo surgery to correct facial disfigurements caused by the disease neurofibromytosis (the same disease suffered by "the elephant man," John Merrick, a 19th-century side-show freak who, despite his deformities or perhaps even because of them, became the toast of English high society). Interviewed by the Associated Press just before she went into the surgery that might cost her her life (Minneapolis Tribune, December 10, 1981), she said: "I can't take this abuse all my life and you'll never make me believe that most people will accept me for what I am. I don't want anybody to tell me that beauty isn't important, that just what I have inside is important." She went on to say that even if the surgery provided only 1% improvement in her appearance, she would go ahead with it anyway. Other prospective clients contemplating radical procedures to alter their level of physical attractiveness don't arrive at decisions so easily and, thus, not infrequently turn to the experts to help them decide how much appearance really matters.

No person, of course, escapes making decisions in his or her daily life about the importance of attractiveness. And so many ask the experts to help them make their decisions. Their queries go, "OK, you psychologists have demonstrated that my grandmother was wrong, that we *do* tend to judge books by their covers and people by their external wrappings. So now what? Just how important *is* appearance anyway? Is it important enough for me to _____ (fill in the blank: "lose weight," "undergo plastic surgery," "dye my hair," "buy new clothes instead of a new car," and so on)? We not only routinely make these decisions for ourselves but—perhaps even more difficult—for our children and others for whom we are responsible. And so, again, the advice of experts is sought.

For example, some years ago, as part of the craniofacial growth series of symposia held at the University of Michigan, I outlined what we social psychologists know about the influence of physical attractiveness on social interaction (Berscheid, 1981). To most people in the audience—dentists, orthodontic surgeons, anatomists, plastic surgeons, and so on—this information was new. Predictably, their comments after the lecture tended to be in the "but how important is it *really*?" category and had to do with the professional decisions they make as practitioners. However, as I was leaving the hall, I was stopped by a group of oral surgeons who had a more personal question of the "how important is it really" variety. They said that knowing what they now knew, they had been discussing what they themselves would do if their child was physically unattractive and if this state could be altered through expensive and painful oral or plastic surgery. "So, we've been wondering," they said, "what *you* would do? You're the expert. Do you think it would be worth it to put *your* child through that?

The question deserved a careful, judicious, scholarly answer or, at minimum, a straightforward "I don't know; it depends on too many things we don't know enough about." As it happened, however, I was running a fever, was numb with fatigue, and so was desperate to return to my hotel and not eager for a leisurely speculative discussion. Thus I heard myself blurting out, "If the unattractiveness was severe and if the child was not very bright, I would; if it wasn't and if the child was very intelligent, I wouldn't," and hurried on my way.

Later, I wondered why in the world I would have said something like that. In self-defense, I thought "Well, they asked a personal question and they got a personal answer." On the other hand, I realized that they were probably asking my opinion because they believed it to be an informed one. It wasn't. Furthermore, in reflecting upon my gut-level, knee-jerk response, I also realized that although that was indeed what I probably *would* do, I was implicitly making a number of assumptions.

The first assumption I was making was that a little physical unattractiveness never severely hurt anyone. This is probably not a bad assumption for several reasons, one of which is that we do not know even yet how physical attractiveness is distributed in the general population. The usual manner in which studies of physical attractiveness are done is to select, from college yearbooks or other materials, stimuli who represent a high physical-attractiveness level (usually as judged by peers), and also to select people who represent an average level of physical attractiveness as well as people who represent unattractiveness. We have no notion of the size of the populations from which we are selecting stimuli to represent those three general levels of physical attractiveness. It is possible, for example, that most people are slightly unattractive. It is equally possible that most everyone is "average." Or, it is possible that in our highly affluent and health-oriented society most people are physically attractive. In assuming that slight unattractiveness is not terribly handicapping, I was implicitly betting against this last possibility. I was doing so because it seems reasonable that the standards propagated by the media are very *high* standards and that, therefore, most people (considering all ages and the full range of socioeconomic status) fail to meet them; or, to put it another way, that the average and slightly unattractive have a good deal of company.

(In this regard, I recalled a comment made by an editor of a national news magazine. He and a visiting foreign editor had been waiting in a bus station and, so, "people-watching." After some time at this activity, the foreign editor asked him why it was the people in the United States seemed to be so "unattractive." "Is it," he asked, "because America is the melting pot of people of many ethnic and racial origins and that these mixtures are responsible for your being less attractive than Europeans?" To the editor's query to me about whether we Americans are less attractive than Europeans, I responded that if the European editor spent some time in a European bus depot, or even just standing on a street corner scrutinizing the physical attractiveness level of ordinary citizens in his country, he would probably find that they are not too much different on this dimension than Americans.)

In any event, there is some reason to guess that the physical attractiveness level of the man and woman on the street probably is not of the exalted level depicted on television programs and advertisements. Further, given that this level is constantly put before us, and also given contrast effects in judgments of physical attractiveness (Kendrick & Gutierres, 1980), it seems reasonable to assume that most of us are slightly unattractive or average at best. But, of course, all this is conjecture. There has been no systematic study of the distribution of physical attractiveness levels in the general population.

The second assumption I was making probably wasn't a bad one either, in retrospect, although my choice of a comparative variable surely would be subject to debate. In immediately focusing upon the child's intelligence, I was assuming that the question "How important is physical attractiveness?" is unanswerable in that form. First, we have to specify "Important *compared* to what?" I was comparing it to intelligence. And, here, I was assuming that intelligence is an extraordinarily valuable gift. (It also is one that, like appearance, appears to be heavily genetically determined. Furthermore, it seems to be "normally" distributed such that for every individual at the top end of the continuum who is blessed, there is another at the lower end who has been shortchanged—but people do not seem to lose sleep over the "undemocratic" nature of intelligence as they do about the undemocratic nature of attractiveness differences.) In any case, the assumption was that the gift of intelligence might do a great deal to make up for any deficit on the physical appearance dimension.

In addition, I was making a third assumption, specifically, that being physically attractive might actually *hinder* the development and full use of intellectual gifts. I was assuming that every individual is born with an array of potentials and that, furthermore, the existence of some potentials may inhibit the realization of others. For example, if a child is very intelligent, not only might he or she not need the benefits of physical attractiveness to get along in the world and to lead a happy and productive life, but, also, physical attractiveness actually might obstruct the achievement of his or her full intellectual potential.

As an illustrative case in point, Charles Steinmetz, the famous genius of electricity, comes to mind. One of his biographies, which I read when I was very young, had a picture of Steinmetz on the frontispiece and I was struck by how much he looked like Toulouse Lautrec, not only in facial appearance but in stature. He was barely taller than the chair his hand rested upon. One wonders, then, what Steinmetz's life would have been if he had looked like Rudolph Valentino, one of his contemporaries. Would we all still be lighting our houses with candles? What if Charles Steinmetz (whom, again as I dimly recall from the biography, was a shy withdrawn person) had been subjected to many strong social enticements and had become a social butterfly instead of contemplating the mysteries of electricity in the solitude of his study? Or, what if the growth hormones, yet to be discovered at that time, had been available and his parents had decided to have them administered to their son? Would greater physical stature have had the effect of reducing Steinmetz' mental stature? So how important was physical attractiveness to him?; to society?

We don't know. We never will in the individual case. And, in terms of generalities, we have not even begun to approach the question. In order to begin to answer the question of what difference a person's physical attractiveness makes in his or her life, we have to consider that appearance always lies embedded in the context of other personal qualities and potentialities, and that it lies embedded, as well, within an individual's physical and social environments. Given that there is not time enough and world enough for each individual to fully cultivate all of their potential along a variety of dimensions, appearance, in interaction with the person's other qualities and with environmental factors, will undoubtedly facilitate the development of some of these potentialities at the expense of others.

Not only do we have to consider the question of the importance of physical attractiveness in relation to other variables we know to influence the quality of people's lives, but we have to specify "Important *for* what?". Most people, when asked to specify *their* dependent variable of interest, say "happiness."

If the question is "How important is physical attractiveness for personal happiness," then we can answer. Studies of human happiness (e.g., Freedman, 1978; Matlin & Stang, 1978) indicate that most everybody is pretty happy. Not only are most people quite happy but most everyone thinks that they are going to be even happier tomorrow than they are today. One suspects, then, that there probably isn't too much variance in happiness to be accounted for by the physical attractiveness variable. But, then, we don't really know for sure. One of the reasons we don't know is because we rarely try to find the answer; that is, we have concentrated our studies on people's *reactions* to physically attractive and unattractive stimuli and seldom have attempted to find out how the stimuli themselves feel about their appearance and how *they* think it has influenced their lives, specifically what trials or glories they think it has brought them. And only recently have we begun to investigate how rapid increases or decreases in attractiveness level affect general happiness—and for how long.

In any case, and as the aforementioned suggests, the "How important is physical attractiveness" question is one that we, as researchers, can approach only obliquely even in the general case. The graveyard of rejected manuscripts submitted to professional journals, in fact, is littered with the corpses of those which purported to answer some variant of this general question directly. Even when the comparative independent variable is specified and even when the dependent variable is also clearly identified, the question how important Variable A is relative to Variable B with respect to influence upon Dimension C is not a question that can be definitively answered, even in the laboratory. For example, in his remarks as an outgoing editor of the *Journal of Applied Social Psychology*, Campbell (1982) outlined the major reasons for rejection of manuscripts for publication in that journal. One major reason was the form of the research question asked. One research question to be avoided because it "tend[s] to lead to studies that are not very useful! or that at least yield a very small return of information" (p. 697) is of the form:

> is variable A or variable B a more important influence on variable C? Some examples would be: Is job satisfaction or job commitment a more important deter-

minant of absenteeism or turnover? Is money or praise the more powerful reinforcer of certain behavior? Is motivation or skill a more important determinant of performance? The answers to these questions depends in large part on the range of values of each variable that is included in the study. Unless the investigator has a reasonably good idea of the relevant population variances and can interpret the sample variances accordingly, the results can be misleading. (pp. 697–698)

But if the question people most frequently ask us now is "How important is physical attractiveness in *my* life?" how can we help them? What we *can* do is what we have done—and are doing. We have shown that physical attractiveness is not irrelevant to a person's life. It makes a difference. It does need to be taken into consideration in making decisions whose consequences will affect physical attractiveness level for better or for worse. But because there are so many variables that also influence the quality of an individual's life, and because we know little about how they interact with physical attractiveness, and also because people differ so widely in what they want from their lives, the "how important is it" question will always be one that each individual has to answer for him or herself in the context of that individual's life.

People not only have to decide how important physical attractiveness is in making decisions that will affect their life and in making decisions that will affect other people as well, either people with whom they are in close relationship or people to whom they are providing professional services, but they also have to make a decision of how important the quality of physical attractiveness in *other* people is to them. For example, people have to decide how important physical attractiveness is as an attribute in a dating partner or a mate or an employee or with anyone with whom they are deciding whether to initiate, maintain, or terminate a personal relationship. Again, we have made a contribution in making people aware that, despite our collective protestations, most people *act* as though they think it important.

Even this information is not unuseful, as The People's Republic of China has recently learned the hard way. Concerned with the growing number of unwed persons, the Communist party sanctioned a nationwide campaign to "marry off" young men and women. Thus, the government sponsored official "night dancing parties," marriage introduction services, and organized singles outings. But the campaign has been a flop! According to the Associated Press (Minneapolis Star and Tribune, August 31, 1984), the Peoples Daily has pinpointed the reason: "men's and women's criteria for selecting mates are not practical. This situation is unsettling. When matchmaking workers ask a man what kind of mate he desires, he says, I want a beautiful woman. The result is they do not find anyone suitable." Apparently, physical attractiveness has been granted, at least amongst Chinese unmarried adults, preeminent importance. The government has learned that physical attractiveness is an important factor to consider in the achievement of their particular aims in this instance. But *how* important it is in relation to *other* relevant factors is something they will have to figure out given *their* resources, *their* social and environmental context, and the importance of *their* specific aim of marrying off their single people—a situation not unlike that faced by any individual who considers the question of the importance of physical attractiveness to him or herself.

REFERENCES

Adams, G. R., & Crossman, S. M. (1978). *Physical attractiveness: A cultural imperative.* Roslyn Heights, NY: Libra.

Aronson, E. (1969). Some antecedents of interpersonal attraction. In W. J. Arnold & D. Levine (Eds.), *Nebraska Symposium on Motivation* (Vol. 17). Lincoln: University of Nebraska Press.

Berscheid, E. (1981). An overview of the psychological effects of physical attractiveness and some comments upon the psychological effects of knowledge of the effects of physical attractiveness. In G. W. Lucker, K. Ribbens, & J. A. McNamara (Eds.), *Psychological aspects of facial form* (Monograph #11, Craniofacial Growth Series). Ann Arbor, MI: Center for Human Growth & Development.

Berscheid, E., & Walster, E. (1974). Physical attractiveness. In L. Berkowitz (Ed.), *Advances in experimental social psychology* (Vol. 7). New York: Academic Press.

Campbell, J. (1982). Editorial: Some remarks from the out-going editor. *Journal of Applied Psychology, 67,* 691–700.

Freedman, J. (1978). *Happy people: What happiness is, who has it, and why.* New York: Harcourt Brace Jovanovich.

Huston, T. L., & Levinger, G. (1978). Interpersonal attraction and relationships. *Annual Review of Psychology, 29,* 115–156.

Kendrick, D. T., & Gutierres, S. E. (1980). Contrast effects and judgments of physical attractiveness: When beauty becomes a social problem. *Journal of Personality and Social Psychology, 38,* 131–140.

Lindzey, G. (1965). Morpology and behavior. In G. Lindzey & C. S. Hall (Eds.), *Theories of personality: Primary sources and research.* New York: Wiley.

Matlin, M. W., & Stang, D. J. (1978). *The Pollyanna principle: Selectivity in language, memory, and thought.* Cambridge, MA: Schenkman.

Walster, E., Aronson, V., Abrahams, D., & Rottmann, L. (1966). Importance of physical attractiveness in dating behavior. *Journal of Personality and Social Psychology, 4*(5), 508–516.

Author Index

Numbers in *italics* indicate pages with complete bibliographic information.

A

Abrahams, D., 291, *298*
Abrahamsen, P., 103, *108*
Ackerman, C., 123, *136,* 145, 157, 168, *170*
Adams, G. R., 8, 11, 13, *19, 20,* 23, 25, 26, 36, 40, 43, 44, *47,* 81, *83,* 121, *136,* 145, 148, 150, *174,* 292, *298*
Addison, J., 18, *20*
Ago, Y., 103, *110*
Ahern, M., 30, *50*
Alessi, D. F., 67, 69, *83,* 262, *280*
Algozzine, B., 12, *21,* 27, *50*
Allen, J., 275, *281*
Alley, T. R., 24, *47*
Allon, N., 76, 77, 81, *83,* 163, *171*
Allport, G., 15, *20,* 270, *280*
Alperstein, L., 145, 148, 154, *171*
Altshuler, K. Z., 256, *286*
Ames, R., 231, *241*
Amir, Y., 270, *280*
Anderson, C. F., 73, *85*
Anderson, S. M., 30, *47*
Andes, S. E., 118, *138*
Angoli, M., 128, *138*
Anthony, W. A., 67, 69, *83,* 262, 270, *280*

Antons-Brandi, V., 72, *83*
Applebaum, S. L., 210, *212*
Arata, C. L., 269, *282*
Aronson, E., 17, *20,* 145, 148, 154, *175, 176*
Aronson, V., 291, *298*
Asch, S., 122, *136*
Asher, N. W., 270, *280*
Athanasious, R., 150, *171*
Attili, G., 193, *216*
Austin, M. C., 31, *47*
Avdzej, A., 81, *87*
Avis, W. E., 129, *137*
Azjen, I., 76, *84*

B

Babigian, H. M., 103, *110*
Black, K., 67, 68, 74, *85*
Baddeley, M., 72, *83*
Bailey, K. G., 132, 133, *136, 138,* 160, *173*
Bakeman, R., 42, 43, *51*
Baker, E. E., 124, *136,* 145, 157, 160, 168, 169, *171*
Baker, L., 103, *110*
Baker, M. J., 145, 150, *171*

299

Bakiewicz, T. A., 191, *211*
Balogh, B., 33, *50*
Bansavage, J. C., 263, *280*
Barash, D. P., 33, *47*
Barclay, S., 56, *62*
Bard, M., 199, *215*
Barker, D., 265, *280*
Barker, P., 122, *137*
Barker, R., 70, *85*, 232, *242*, 243, 245, 263, *280*
Barnes, B. M., 32, *49*
Barnes, H. V., 230, 232, 233, *241*
Barnlund, D. C., 14, 15, *20*
Barocas, R., 36, *47*
Baron, R. A., 150, 151, *171*, 203, 205, *208*
Barry, J. R., 267, *285*
Barry, T., 204, 205, *216*
Bassili, J. N., 8, 9, *20*
Bates, R. E., 248, *280*
Baudin, H., 149, *173*
Bayley, N., 231, 233, 234, *242*
Bazakas, R., 267, 269, *280*
Beach, F. A., 13, *20*, 89, *109*
Beauchamp, G. K., 182, 185, *211*, *212*
Beaumont, P. J. V., 106, *108*
Beigel, H. G., 129, *136*
Belfer, M. L., 53, 59, 60, 61, *62*
Bell, A. H., 277, *281*
Bell, R. Q., 23, 43, *47*, *51*
Beller, A. S., 89, 91, 93, *108*
Bem, D., 34, *47*
Bem, S. L., 30, *47*
Bender, J. A., 273, *281*
Benham, F. G., 248, *281*
Bennett, N. B., 94, *108*
Benson, P. L., 77, 78, *83*, 150, *171*
Berger, J., 151, *171*
Berkowitz, L., 34, 35, 40, *47*
Berkowitz, W. R., 124, 125, *136*
Bernier, J. E., 252, *282*
Bernstein, N. R., 53, 61, *62*
Berscheid, E., 7, 8, 9, 12, 17, *20*, *21*, 23, 26, 27, 28, 29, 31, 32, 40, 43, 45, 46, *47*, *48*, *51*, 53, *62*, 69, 70, *83*, 92, 97, *108*, 128, 129, 130, *136*, *137*, 150, 152, 155, 158, 159, *171*, *172*, *173*, 221, 222, 225, *241*, *242*, 292, 293, *298*
Bevan, W., 126, *137*
Bickman, L., 28, *51*
Bieber, I., 187, *211*
Birch, M. C., 182, *211*

Birnbaum, J., 256, *287*
Biro, G., 118, *136*
Biron, C., 199, *211*
Black, H. K., 36, *47*
Black, K. V., 259, *281*
Black, S. L., 199, *211*
Blank, H. R., 279, *281*
Blass, T., 145, 148, 154, *171*
Blau, S., 257, *281*
Bleda, P. R., 126, *136*
Bleda, R., 126, *136*
Bleda, S., 126, *136*
Block, J. R., 247, 248, 262, 267, 271, *288*
Block, S. H., 145, 148, 154, *171*
Blommers, P., 114, *136*
Bobrove, P. H., 248, 276, *281*
Bogdonoff, M. D., 73, *85*
Bohrnstedt, G. W., 12, *20*, 92, 97, *108*, 159, *171*, 221, *241*
Bonkydis, C., 25, 39, *48*
Bonsall, R. W., 196, *215*
Booth, D. A., 198, 199, *214*
Borges, C. A., 131, 132, *137*
Borjeson, M., 69, 81, *83*
Boskind-Lodahl, M., 106, *108*
Boukydis, C., 10, *20*
Bozarth, J. D., 277, *284*
Brabham, R. E., 259, *281*
Bradley, A. C., 115, *136*
Bramble, W. J., 29, *49*
Branch, C. H. H., 105, 107, *108*
Bray, G. A., 66, *83*, 92, *108*
Brehm, J. W., 160, *171*
Brewer, C., 72, *83*
Breytspraak, L. M., 73, *83*, 158, *171*
Brierley, D. W., 31, *47*
Brigham, J. C., 7, 18, *20*
Brill, A. A., 179, 187, 188, *211*
Brodsky, C. M., 95, *108*
Brody, B., 187, *211*
Bromley, D., 16, *21*, 31, *50*
Brook, R. H., 66, 73
Brooksbank, B. W. L., 198, *212*
Brophy, J. E., 36, 40, *47*
Brothen, T., 130, *137*, 158, *173*
Brown, A. C., 145, 148, 149, *176*
Brown, T. J., 145, 148, 149, 154, *177*
Bruch, H., 103, 105, 106, 107, *108*
Brucken, L., 29, *49*
Bruininks, R. H., 264, *284*
Bruner, J. S., 126, *136*

Buck, C., 231, *241*
Buck, K. T., 188, 189, 198, 200, 201, *216*
Bull, R., 121, *137*
Burlingham, D. T., 256, *281*
Burns, D. S., 150, *171*
Burnstein, B., 161, *174*
Bush, I. M., 197, *213*
Byrne, D., 152, *171*

C

Cacioppo, J. T., 154, 167, *175*
Caffrey, J. V., 133, *136*
Cahnman, W. J., 72, 74, *83*
Caille, P., 103, *108*
Cain, W. S., 180, 185, 204, 208, *211, 212, 214, 215*
Calden, G., 92, *108,* 118, *136,* 159, *171*
Cameron, C., 130, 132, *137,* 159, 165, *171*
Cameron, E. A., 182, *212*
Campbell, J., 296, *298*
Campbell, J. D., 31, *51*
Canning, H., 76, 77, *83*
Canon, L. K., 152, *176*
Cantor, N., 114, *140*
Caplan, M., 133, *137*
Carli, L. L., 143, *172*
Carlsmith, J. M., 231, 233, 234, *241, 242*
Carter, O., 191, *217*
Casey, R. C., 37, *49*
Cash, T. F., 31, 32, *48,* 150, *171*
Caskey, S. R., 70, 71, *83*
Casper, R. C., 103, *108*
Cavanaugh, P. H., 191, *214*
Cavior, N., 27, 31, 42, 43, *48,* 145, 148, 166, *171, 174*
Celhoffer, L., 10, *20,* 25, 39, *48*
Centerwall, W. R., 188, *214*
Cernoch, J. M., 192, 202, *215*
Chaikin, A. L., 149, *171*
Chaiken, S., 150, 151, 153, 154, 155, 156, 158, 159, 160, 166, 167, 168, *171, 172, 173*
Chanowitz, B., 74, 83, *85,* 223, *242*
Cheremisinoff, P. N., 204, *212*
Chigier, E., 67, *84*
Chigier, M., 67, *84*
Chinnock, R. F., 188, *214*
Chipman, A., 247, 248, 249, 250, 252, 262, 265, 267, 269, 270, 272, *286*
Churchill, G. A., 145, 150, *171*

Clark, K., 89, *108*
Clifford, B. R., 121, *137*
Clifford, E., 119, *137,* 159, 165, *172*
Clifford, M. M., 25, 40, 41, *48,* 150, 155, *172*
Cline, A. L., 118, *138*
Clore, G. L., 269, *281*
Cochran, C. D., 132, *137*
Cochran, T. C., 53, 59, 61, *62*
Coffman, T. L., 259, *283*
Cohen, A. S., 25, 36, *47*
Cohen, S. H., 145, 148, *174*
Comer, R. J., 161, *172,* 227, *241,* 257, 258, *281*
Comfort, A., 182, 196, *212*
Conger, J. C., 73, *83,* 100, *112,* 158, *171*
Conine, T., 248, 271, *281, 287*
Conner, T. L., 151, *171*
Conrad, D. E., 103, *108*
Constable, J. D., 53, *62*
Cook, D. W., 277, *281, 284*
Cook, T. D., 154, *172*
Cooley, C. H., 224, *241*
Cooper, H. M., 143, 152, *172, 173*
Cooper, J., 225, *243*
Coopersmith, S., 119, *137,* 165, *172*
Corter, C., 10, *20,* 25, 39, *48*
Costanzo, P. R., 100, *112,* 157, *172*
Cowen, E. L., 248, 276, *281*
Cowley, J. J., 198, *212*
Cozby, P. C., 14, *21*
Crane, P., 11, *20,* 26, 40, *47*
Crisp, A. H., 93, 103, *108, 110*
Crossman, S. M., 292, *298*
Crouter, A., 35, *48*
Crouthamel, C., 134, *137*
Cruickshank, W. M., 245, *281*
Crunk, W. A., Jr., 275, *281*
Curry, W., 13, *20*
Curtis, J., 157, *172*

D

Dabbs, J. M., 32, *51*
Daniels, L. K., 269, *281*
Dannenmeir, W. D., 126, 127, *137*
Davenport, W., 196, *212*
Davis, H. C., 267, *285*
Davis, J. M., 103, *108*
Davis, R. G., 185, *212*
Davis, W. L., 150, *174*

Deck, J., 195, *215*
DeGarine, I., 67, *84*
DeHamel, F. A., 125, *137*
DeJong, W., 72, 74, 75, 76, 82, *84*, 114, *137*, 227, *241*
DeLa Mare, W., 113, *137*
Delaney, J., 196, *212*
Delin, P. S., 127, *139*
Dembo, T., 245, 246, *281*
Demos, G. D., 258, *284*
D'Ercole, A., 115, *140*
Derlega, V. J., 31, 32, *48*, 149, *171*
Dermer, M., 8, 9, 18, *20*, 28, 31, 32, *48*
Desor, J. A., 185, *212*
Deutsch, F., 103, *112*
Dibiase, W. J., 71, *84*
Dickstein, J., 271, *285*
Dillon, D. J., 118, *137*
Dion, K. K., 7, 8, 9, 10, 17, 20, 25, 27, 28, 31, 32, 34, 35, 43, *47*, *48*, 145, 148, 150, 155, *165*, *172*
Dipboye, R. L., 150, *172*
Distelheim, I. H., 189, *212*
Dixon, J. K., 258, *281*
Dokecki, P., 27, 31, *48*, 166, *171*
Dollard, J., 118, *137*, 179, *212*
Donaldson, J., 269, *281*
Donohoe, P., 145, 146, 161, 162, 164, *173*
Doob, A. N., 163, 164, 166, 169, *172*, *173*, 223, *241*, 268, *282*
Doob, L., 118, *137*
Dornbusch, S. M., 66, 67, *84*, *86*, 231, 233, 234, *241*, *242*, 249, 257, 262, 267, *282*, *285*
Doty, R. L., 182, 186, 188, 190, 194, 195, 196, 197, 198, 200, 201, 210, *211*, *212*
Dow, T. E., Jr., 262, 267, *282*
Downs, A. C., 23, 29, 32, 41, 42, 43, *49*, 155, *174*
Dravnieks, A., 184, 189, 191, 196, 197, *212*, *213*, *214*
Dressler, M., 188, 189, 198, 200, 201, *216*
Dripps, E., 271, *285*
Druss, R. G., 104, *108*
Duck, S. W., 27, 31, *48*
Duddle, M., 103, *108*
Duehn, W. D., 275, *284*
Duffield, B. J., 269, *283*
Duke, P. M., 231, 233, 234, *241*, *242*
Dukes, W., 126, *137*

Duncan, B. L., 79, *84*
Dwyer, J. T., 90, 92, 96, 97, *108*, 109, 159, 163, *172*, 230, 234, *241*

E

Eagly, A. H., 143, 145, 148, 150, 150, 151, 152, 154, 165, 166, 167, *172*, *173*
Ecker, B. P., 164, *172*, 268, *282*
Eckert, E. D., 103, *108*
Edwards, L. D., 248, *287*
Efran, M. G., 150, *173*
Eggins, L., 122, *137*
Ehrensing, R. H., 103, *109*
Eichorn, D. H., 230, *241*
Elkind, D., 31, *48*
Ellis, A., 202, 204, *213*
Ellis, H., 187, 200, *213*
Ellis, R. J., 8, 9, 17, *20*
Ellsworth, P. C., 210, *216*
Elman, D., 130, *137*, 145, 146, 156, 157, 158, 162, 163, 164, *173*
Elser, R. P., 263, *282*
Emerson, P., 67, *86*
Engel, R., 145, 150, *176*
Engen, T., 182, 183, 185, 204, 210, *213*, *214*
England, D., 196, *214*
Erskine, B., 102, *111*
Eurman, L. J., 105, 107, *108*
Evans, J. H., 269, *282*

F

Farb, B., 123, *137*
Fatoullah, E., 145, 148, 151, *174*
Faust, M. S., 230, 233, *241*
Fazio, R. H., 76, *84*, 150, 170, *177*
Feighner, J. P., 105, *109*
Feingold, A., 129, *137*
Feldman, J. J., 90, 96, *108*, 109, 159
Feldman, S. D., 129, *137*, 157, *173*
Felger, C. B., 191, *215*
Felker, D. W., 70, 71, *83*, *84*
Felson, R. B., 41, *48*
Fenwick, S., 103, *109*
Ferguson, L., 247, 248, 249, 250, 252, 254, 262, 265, 267, 269, 270, 271, 272, 276, *282*, *286*, *287*
Festinger, L., 163, *173*
Field, P. B., 162, *174*

Finch, M. D., 119, *139*
Fine, J. A., 260, 261, 262, *282*
Finkelstein, V., 245, *282*
Fisek, M. H., 151, *171*
Fishbein, M., 76, *84*
Fisher, S., 122, *137*, 157, *173*
Fiske, S. T., 17, *21*, 74, 83, *85*, 223, *242*
Fitzgerald, H. E., 10, *20*, 35, *50*
Fitzpatrick, M., 205, *216*
Flapan, D., 31, *48*
Flay, B. R., 154, *172*
Force, D. G., 263, *282*
Ford, A. B., 274, *285*
Ford, C. S., 13, *20*, 89, *109*
Ford, L., 10, *20*, 25, 39, *48*
Ford, M., 197, 198, *212*
Foust, L. A., 61, *62*
Fox, M. M., 103, *110*
Fraiberg, S., 256, *282*
Framer, E., 78, 80, 81, 83, *84*
Francoeur, D., 195, *215*
Frankel, A., 79, *86*, 252, 267, 278, *282*, *287*
Frauchiger, R. A., 71, *85*
Frazier, A., 231, *241*
Fredrickson, W. A., 259, *284*
Freedman, J. L., 123, *137*, 163, 164, 166,
    169, *173*, 223, *241*, 296, *298*
Freeman, G. G., 263, *282*
Fremouw, W. J., 100, 105, *111*
Frey, J., 204, 205, *216*
Friedman, L., 146, 162, 163, 164, *176*
Friedman, M. J., 262, *285*
Friend, E., 258, *282*
Fries, H., 93, *109*
Frisch, R. E., 93, *109*
Frodi, A., 34, 35, 40, *47*
Fromkin, H. L., 150, *172*
Frumkin, R. M., 275, *287*
Fulford, R., 23, *48*
Furth, H. G., 256, *282*
Furuya, T., 14, *21*

G

Gacsaly, S. A., 131, 132, *137*
Gagan, J. F., 277, *283*
Gaines, L., 258, *284*
Gall, F. J., 222, *241*
Gallagher, B., 263, *282*
Garbarino, J., 35, *48*

Garcia, J., 183, *213*
Garfield, E., 200, *213*
Garfinkel, P. E., 89, 90, 93, 98, 103, 104,
    105, 107, *109*
Garner, D. M., 89, 90, 93, 98, 104, 105,
    107, *109*
Gellert, E., 95, 96, *110*
Genders, R., 202, 204, *213*
Gensley, J. T., 269, *284*
George, G. C. W., 106, *108*
Gerard, R. J., 73, *86*
Gerbers, C. L., 180, *215*
Getsinger, S. H., 277, *281*
Giancoli, D. L., 67, *84*
Giberson, R., 210, *212*
Gillen, B., 150, 166, *171*, *175*
Gillis, J. S., 114, 124, 129, 132, 133, *137*
Gillman, A. E., 256, *282*
Girolami, C., 103, *108*
Gladstone, L. R., 267, *282*
Glass, D. C., 145, 146, 161, 162, 164, *173*
Glenwick, D. S., 269, *282*
Goffman, E., 65, 74, *84*, 222, *241*
Goldberg, S. C., 103, *108*
Goldblatt, P. B., 92, *109*
Goldin, G. J., 274, 275, *282*, *287*
Goldman, M., 133, *137*
Goldman, R., 100, *111*, 154, 167, *175*
Goldman, W., 114, *137*, 155, 166, *173*
Goldsmith, D. J., 185, *216*
Goldzieher, M., 232, *241*
Gonick, M. R., 245, 263, *280*
Good, T. L., 36, 40, *47*
Goodman, C. C., 126, *136*
Goodman, N., 66, 67, *84*, *86*, 249, 262, 267,
    282, *285*
Goodman, S. I., 188, *214*
Goodsitt, A., 103, *109*
Gordon, A., 100, *111*, 145, 146, 153, 161,
    162, 164, 165, *173*, *175*
Gordon, M., 134, *137*
Gordon, S., 104, *109*
Gordon, T., 92, *111*
Gottfried, N. W., 32, *49*
Gottlieb, J., 271, *282*
Graham, C. A., 195, *213*
Granberg, D., 152, *173*
Grand, S. A., 252, *282*
Grau, B. W., 44, *51*
Graves, W. H., III, 250, 254, *283*

Graziano, W., 78, 80, 81, 83, *84*, 130, *137*, 158, *173*
Gregory, W. L., 145, 148, *172*
Green, A., 67, *86*
Green, M. S., 161, *173*
Greene, P., 150, *171*, 201, *212*
Greenwald, A. G., 146, 152, *173*
Greer, B. G., 273, *282*
Gronlund, N. E., 263, *282*
Gross, R. T., 231, 233, 234, *241, 242*
Groth, E., 185, *216*
Guidubaldi, J., 29, *49*
Gunderson, E. K., 119, *138*
Gurin, J., 94, *108*
Gutierres, S. E., 33, *49, 295, 298*
Guttman, L., 251, *282*
Guze, S. B., 105, *109*

H

Haas, H. J., 224, *242*
Hackett, R., 102, *111*
Haddle, H. W., 249, *283*
Haley, H. B., 277, *283*
Hall, C. S., 223, *242*
Hall, E. T., 180, 200, *213*
Hall, K. P., 151, *174*
Halmi, K. A., 103, *108, 109*
Halstead, P., 91, 96, *110*
Halverson, C. F., 43, *48*, 51
Hambleton, D., 264, *285*
Hamid, P. N., 149, *173*
Hamilton, D. L., 15, 17, 18, *20*, 80, *84*
Hammond, W. H., 222, *242*
Hampton, M. C., 90, *110*
Hankins, W. G., 183, *213*
Hansson, R. O., 269, *283*
Harasymiw, S. J., 265, 269, 271, *283*
Harding, B., 103, *110*
Harnett, J. J., 132, 133, *136, 138*, 145, 148, 149, 160, *173, 175*
Harper, L. V., 23, *47*
Harrell, W. A., 145, 148, 149, *173*
Harris, M. B., 68, 71, 76, 82, *84*, 149, *173*
Harris, R. J., 117, *138*
Harris, R. T., 196, *216*
Harrison, A. A., 130, 132, *138*
Harrison, A. M., 53, 59, 60, 61, *62*
Hart, C. J., 70, 71, *86, 95, 112*
Hartley, C. S., 132, *138*, 160, *173*
Hartup, W. W., 26, *48*

Harvey, J., 145, 148, 152, *175*
Hassett, J., 186, *213*
Hastorf, A. H., 66, 67, *84, 86*, 210, *216*, 223, 227, *242*, 246, 249, 257, 262, 267, 269, *282, 283, 285*
Havighurst, R. J., 31, *48*
Havill, S. J., 268, *283*
Hay, G. G., 54, 59, *62*
Hayden, G. F., 188, 189, *213*
Heather, B. B., 54, 59, *62*
Hecker, M. R., 196, *216*
Heider, F., 152, *173*
Heller, J., 115, *138*
Hency, T., 145, 146, 161, 162, 164, *173*
Helson, H., 33, *48*
Hendricks, D., 32, *49*
Hensley, W. E., 128, *138*
Herman, C. P., 91, 92, 96, 98, 99, 100, 101, 102, 105, 106, *109, 110, 111*, 122, 123, *136, 138*, 145, 157, 159, 161, 162, 168, *170, 173*
Herman, J. L., 256, *287*
Herrick, C. J., 183, *213*
Heuneman, R. L., 90, *110*
Hibscher, J. A., 100, 105, *110*
Higgins, E. T., 160, *174*
Higgs, R. W., 262, 271, *283*
Hildebrandt, K. A., 10, *20*, 35, 37, *49, 50*, 81, *84*
Hinckley, E. D., 118, *138*
Hinsdale, G., 70, *84*
Hintz, R., 234, *242*
Hjelle, L. A., 71, *84*
Hold, B., 193, 194, *213, 216*
Holland, B., 247, 248, 249, 250, 254, 271, *287*
Hopson, J. L., 186, *213*
Horai, J., 145, 148, 151, *174*
Horne, M. D., 265, 269, 271, *283*
Hottes, J., 150, *174*
Houldin, B. K., 264, *285*
Hovland, C. I., 150, 152, *174*
Howard, C. R., 145, 148, *174*
Howard, L. R., 42, 43, *48*
Huggins, G. R., 186, 196, 197, 198, *212, 213, 215*
Hurley, H. J., 191, *216*
Huston, T. L., 8, *20*, 31, *49*, 155, 166, *174*, 292, *298*
Hutton, H. E., 103, *110*
Hymel, S., 39, 40, *50*

I

Ikeda, A., 14, *21*
Ikemi, Y., 103, *110*
Ingwell, R. H., 257, *283*
Insko, C. A., 31, *51,* 151, *174, 176*
Iwawaki, S., 72, *84*

J

Jacklin, C. N., 32, *49*
Jackson, D. N., 8, *20,* 155, 166, *174*
Jacobs, B. M., 185, *213*
Jacobsen, R. J., 246, *286*
Jakobovits, C., 91, 96, *110*
James, W., 258, *284*
Janek, J., 188, 189, 198, 200, 201, *216*
Janis, I. L., 152, 162, *174*
Jaques, M. E., 267, *283*
Jarvie, G. J., 78, 80, 81, 83, *84*
Jastrzembska, Z. S., 256, *283*
Jeffrey, K. M., 269, *281*
Jellinek, J. S., 202, 203, *213*
Jennings, D., 234, *241*
Jensema, C. J., 265, *286*
Johnson, A. L., 198, *212*
Johnson, P. A., 95, *110*
Johnston, J. W., 204, *216*
Jones, D. J., 103, *110*
Jones, E. E., 246, *283*
Jones, H. E., 232, *242*
Jones, M. C., 231, 233, 234, *242*
Jones, R. A., 114, *138*
Jones, R. L., 260, 265, 266, *283*
Jordan, J. E., 251, 267, *283*
Jordan, T. E., 258, *283*
Jourard, S. M., 118, *139,* 159, 165, *174*
Juan, I. R., 277, *283*
Jung, F., 200, *213*
Jungermann, E., 191, *213*

K

Kahn, A., 150, *174*
Kahneman, D., 29, *51*
Kalogerakis, M. G., 187, 199, *213*
Kalucy, R. S., 103, *108, 110*
Kane, R. L., 66, *86*
Kannel, W. B., 92, *111*
Kaplan, H. M., 273, *281*
Karabenick, S. A., 119, *138,* 150, *171*

Karlins, M., 259, *283*
Karlson, P., 182, *213*
Karris, L., 157, *174*
Kassarjian, H. H., 124, *138,* 157, *174*
Katz, E., 122, *138*
Katz, R. A., 182, *213*
Katz, S., 267, *286*
Kaufman, M. R., 103, *112*
Keesey, R. E., 114, *138*
Kehle, T. J., 29, *49*
Keith, L., 196, 197, *213, 214*
Kelley, H. H., 78, *84,* 152, *174,* 209, *214,* 246, *283*
Kelley, L., 91, 96, *110*
Kelman, H. C., 147, 150, 151, 152, 153, 167, *174*
Kelz, J. W., 251, 253, *284*
Kendrick, D. T., 33, *49,* 295, *298*
Kennedy, P., 264, *284*
Kennon, L., 191, *214*
Kerr, N., 278, *283*
Kestenbaum, R. C., 200, *216*
Keverne, E. B., 182, *214*
Keyes, R., 114, 124, *138*
Kiell, N., 187, *214*
Kiker, V. L., 71, *85*
King, M., 152, *173*
Kirk-Smith, M. D., 198, 199, *214*
Kleck, R. E., 12, *20,* 27, 29, *49,* 69, 70, 78, 79, 82, *84, 85, 86,* 210, *214,* 223, 227, 242, 243, 257, 262, *283, 285*
Klein, R. W., 190, 191, *214*
Klienke, C. L., 149, 154, *174*
Kligman, A., 191, 194, *212, 214*
Knapp, J. R., 70, 71, *85*
Koch, J., 145, 148, 152, 154, *175*
Kohler, E. T., 250, 254, *283*
Kolstoe, P. O., 273, *281*
Kolstoe, R., 258, *284*
Korn, S. J., 95, *110,* 158, *174*
Kornhaber, R. C., 268, *284*
Kort, J., 19, *21*
Koster, E. P., 202, 203, *213*
Koulack, D., 128, *138*
Krantz, D., 163, *174*
Krauft, C. C., 277, *284*
Kretschmer, E., 222, *242*
Krisberg, B., 116, *138*
Krotoszynski, B. K., 191, 196, 197, *213, 214*
Krupka, L. R., 73, *86*
Kuehn, L., 121, *138*

Kuhn, D., 29, *49*
Kunce, J. T., 277, *281, 286*
Kurland, H. D., 72, *85*
Kurtz, D. L., 123, *138*
Kutner, B., 247, *284*

L

Labows, J. N., 191, *214*
Lahey, B., 78, 80, 81, 83, *84*
Laird, J. D., 146, 161, 162, *176*
Landy, D., 150, *174*
Langer, E. J., 74, 83, *85,* 223, *242*
Langlois, J. H., 8, 10, 12, 13, *20, 21,* 23, 25, 26, 28, 29, 32, 33, 35, 37, 39, 40, 41, 42, 43, *49, 51,* 155, *174*
Largey, G. P., 187, 199, 203, 204, *214*
Larkin, J. E., 77, *85*
Lass, N. J., 118, *138*
Lavin, D. E., 145, 146, 161, 162, 164, *173*
LaVoie, J. C., 145, 148, 150, *174*
Lawless, H. T., 180, 185, *214*
Lawson, M. C., 95, *110*
Layton, B. D., 31, *51,* 151, *174, 176*
Lazar, A. L., 258, 269, 273, *284*
Leaton, R. N., 224, *243*
Lechelt, E. C., 128, *138,* 160, *174*
Lefebvre, A., 56, *62,* 59
Lehr, S., 256, *287*
Leifer, H., 100, *112*
Lenneberg, E., 256, *284*
Lerner, J. V., 27, 29, 36, 40, 41, *50*
Lerner, M. J., 269, *284*
Lerner, R. M., 23, 27, 29, 36, 40, 41, *49, 50, 70,* 71, 72, *84, 85,* 95, 96, *110,* 119, 127, 130, *138,* 150, 158, 159, *171, 174,* 224, *242*
Lester, D., 136, *138*
Levine, E. S., 256, *284*
Levine, J. M., 74, *85,* 191, 208, 209, *214*
Levinger, G., 292, *298*
Leviton, G. L., 245, 279, *281, 284*
Leviton, L. C., 133, *138*
Levitt, L., 268, *284*
Lewis, P., 114, *137,* 155, 166, *173*
Lewis, S., 265, 269, *283*
Leyden, J., 194, *212*
Liddell, K., 188, *214*
Lieb, W. E., 191, *213*
Liederman, V., 67, 68, 73, 74, *85,* 158, *175*
Lindquist, E. F., 114, *136*

Lindzey, G., 222, 223, *242,* 291, *298*
Linkowski, D. C., 267, *283*
Lipp, L., 258, *284*
Lippman, L. G., 200, *214*
Liske, R. E., 274, *285*
Lisonbee, L. K., 231, *241*
Little, B. R., 31, *50*
Livesley, W. J., 16, *21,* 31, *50*
Lockheed, M. E., 151, *174*
Loddengaard, N., 77, 78, *83*
Loftus, L., 122, *138*
Lomonaco, S., 256, *287*
Lorenz, K., 24, *50*
Louderback, L., 76, 77, 82, *85*
Lowry, L. D., 186, *212*
Lukoff, I. F., 247, 249, 251, *287*
Lundy, R. M., 92, *108,* 118, *136,* 159, *171*
Lupton, M. J., 196, *212*
Luscher, M., 182, *213*
Lynn, M., 130, *138*
Lyons, A. S., 98, *110*

M

Maccoby, E. E., 32, *49*
Mace, J. W., 188, *214*
MacFarlane, A., 201, *214*
MacGregor, F. C., 59, 60, *62*
Mack, D., 99, 105, *109*
Maddox, G. L., 67, 68, 73, 74, *85,* 158, *175*
Maddux, J. E., 145, 148, *175*
Madowy, R., 114, *139*
Maehr, M. L., 224, *242*
Mahoney, E. R., 119, *139*
Major, I., 271, *284*
Malerstein, A. J., 30, *50*
Manchester, W., 89, *110*
Manis, J. G., 224, *242*
Manusco, R. P., 160, *174*
Marge, D. K., 263, *284*
Margolin, R. J., 274, *287*
Marinelli, R. P., 251, 253, *284*
Marks, G., 152, *175*
Marks, L. E., 182, *214*
Marliss, E. B., 102, *110*
Martin, J., 231, 233, 234, *241, 242*
Martinson, M. C., 269, *281*
Maruyama, G., 36, 39, 40, 41, 44, 46, *50,* 166, *175*
Maslow, A. H., 116, *139*
Mason, E. J., 29, *49*

Masterson, J. F., 103, *110*
Matlin, M. W., 296, *298*
Matsubara, H., 103, *110*
Matthews, V., 262, *284*
Mayadas, N. S., 275, *284*
Mayer, J., 72, 74, 76, 77, *83, 85,* 90, 96, *108, 109,* 114, *139,* 159, 163, *172,* 230, 234, *241*
Mayhew, P., 145, 146, 161, 162, 164, *173*
McA5, 146, 161, 162, 164, *173*
McAleer, C. A., 277, *285*
McArthur, L. Z., 15, 16, 17, 18, 19, *21,* 161, *174*
McBurney, D. H., 74, *85,* 181, 183, 191, *213, 214,* 208, 209, *213, 214*
McCaul, K. D., 225, *243*
McCauley, C., 135, *139*
McClintock, M. K., 195, *214*
McCauley, R. W., 264, *284*
McFadden, M., 272, *287*
McFarlane, J. W., 232, *242*
McGee, J., 73, *83, 158, 171*
McGinley, K. J., 191, *214*
McGrew, W. C., 195, *213*
McGuire, C. V., 120, *139*
McGuire, W. J., 120, *139,* 152, 165, 166, 170, *174*
McKegney, F. P., 278, *284*
McKenna, R. J., 100, *110*
McKinney, J. P., 125, *140*
McLaren-Hume, M., 73, *86*
McLaughlin, B., 43, *51*
McLaughlin, F. J., 192, 202, *215*
McLean, R. A., 78, *85*
McMahon, A. W., 278, *286*
McNair, C. D., 118, *138*
Mead, G. H., 224, *242*
Meltzer, B. N., 224, *242*
Mendelson, M., 80, *86*
Mendelson, T., 192, *216*
Merton, R. K., 12, *21*
Mesch, J. C., 268, *284*
Meyerson, L., 245, 263, *280, 284*
Michael, R. P., 196, *215*
Michela, J., 28, *50*
Miller, A., 8, 17, *21,* 146, 162, 163, 164, *176*
Miller, A. G., 29, *50,* 166, *175,* 221, *242*
Miller, A. R., 71, *85*
Miller, D. T., 269, *284*
Miller, N., 36, 39, 40, 41, 44, 46, *50,* 118, *137,* 166, *175*

Milligan, M., 205, *216*
Millman, M., 76, 82, *85*
Mills, J., 145, 148, 152, *175*
Milord, J. T., 16, *21*
Mims, P. R., 145, 148, 149, *175*
Minde, K., 10, *20,* 25, 39, *48*
Minton, H. L., 8, *20*
Minuchin, S., 103, *110*
Mitchell, D. C., 259, *284*
Mitchell, B. W., 90, *110*
Moldofsky, H., 103
Monbeck, M. E., 277, *284*
Monzell, M. M., 182, *215*
Moon, M., 78, *85*
Moore, J. D., 192, *215*
Moore, J. T., 73, *83, 158, 171*
Moore, M. E., 92, *109*
Moore, T., 127, 130, *138,* 158, 159, *174*
Moreault, D., 115, *140*
Moreland, D. B., 71, *85*
Moreland, R. L., 224, *242*
Morf, M. G., 113, *139*
Morgan, H. G., 103, *110*
Mori, S., 103, *110*
Moriarity, T., 222, *242,* 259, *284*
Morris, N. M., 197, *215*
Moskowitz, H. R., 180, *215*
Moulton, D. G., 181, 182, *211,* 204, *215, 216*
Mowrer, O., 118, *137*
Muesser, K. T., 44, *51*
Mugford, R. A., 182, *211*
Mulder, D. J., 189, *215*
Muller-Schwarze, D., 182, *215*
Mulliken, J. B., 53, 59, 61, *62*
Munic, D., 102, *110*
Munoz, R., 105, *109*
Munro, I., 59, *62*
Murphy, A. T., 271, 272, *285*
Murray, J. E., 53, 59, 60, 61, *62*
Murroni, E., 145, 148, 152, 154, *175*
Murstein, B. I., 31, *50*
Mussen, P., 70, *85,* 233, 234, *242*
Mykytowycz, R., 182, 203, *215*

N

Naccari, N., 145, 148, 151, *174*
Nackman, D. M., 75, *84*
Nakagawa, S., 103, *110*
Nash, S. C., 29, *49*

Nay, W. R., 145, 148, 149, *175*
Nebel, J. C., 124, *136*
Neimeyer, G. J., 67, *84*
Neisser, U., 34, *50*
Nelson, D., 152, *171*
Nemy, E., 203, *215*
Nesbitt, P. D., 203, *215*
Newfield, W. F., 262, *285*
Newman, J., 272, *285*
Netsky, M. G., 181, *216*
Nicolle, G., 103, *110*
Nichols, A. C., 191, *216*
Niles, H. P., 200, *216*
Nisbett, R. E., 29, 34, *50*, 79, *85*, 153, 165, *175*, 238, *243*
Noonan, J. R., 267, *285*
Northcraft, G. B., 75, *85*, 145, 148, 151, 152, *175*, 223, 234, 237, *242*, 269, *283*
Nowak, C. A., 23, *51*
Nylander, I., 92, 104, 105, *110*

O

Olmstead, M. P., 93, 105, *109*, 145, 161, 162, *173*
Olshansky, S., 278, *285*
Olson, J. M., 8, 9, 17, *20*
Ono, H., 223, 227, *242*, 257, 262, *283*
Orbach, C. E., 199, *215*
Orbach, S., 93, 94, 106, *110*
Orndorff, M. M., 194, *212*
Orne, M. T., 134, *139*
Orpet, R. E., 269, *284*
Ort, R. S., 274, *285*
Osborn, P. R., III, 125, *139*
Osgood, C. E., 249, *285*
Oskamp, S., 130, 132, *137*, 159, 165, *171*
Ouellette, P. L., 59, 60, *62*

P

Pack, S. J., 129, *140*
Padawer-Singer, A., 120, *139*
Page, R., 145, 148, 149, *176*
Pallak, S. R., 145, 148, 152, 154, *175*
Palmer, R. L., 103, 106, *108*, *111*
Parke, R. D., 38, 39, 40, *50*
Parlee, M. B., 186, *215*
Parsons, T., 279, *285*
Patterson, C. H., 273, *285*
Pattishall, E. G., Jr., 274, *285*

Pecora, M. C., 118, *138*
Peeke, H. V. S., 192, *216*
Penner, B. E., 151, *174*
Penta, F. B., 269, *285*
Perrin, F. A., 149, *175*
Peskin, H., 231, 233, *242*
Petrucelli, R. J., 98, *110*
Petty, R. E., 154, 167, *175*
Pfaffmann, C., 185, *213*
Phillips, J., 60, 61, *62*, 149, *171*
Piaget, J., 30, *50*
Picciotto, S. R., 223, *242*, 269, *283*
Piers, E. V., 54, *62*
Piliavin, J. A., 227, *241*, 257, 258, *281*
Pines, H. A., 77, *85*
Pinkerton, S., 277, *285*
Pliner, P., 102, *110*, 161, *177*
Polivy, J., 91, 92, 98, 99, 100, 101, 102, 105, 106, *109*, *110*, 111, 145, 159, 161, 162, *173*
Pool, K. B., 70, 71, 72, *85*
Popper, J. M., 125, *139*
Porter, R. H., 192, 202, *215*
Portnoy, S., 122, *139*, 145, 146, 157, 160, 165, 168, *175*
Post, E. M., 134, *137*
Powdermaker, H., 67, 82, *85*
Powell, G. E., 70, 71, 81, *85*, *86*
Power, T., 35, 39, 40, *50*
Preti, G., 188, 189, 196, 197, 198, 200, 201, *212*, *213*, *216*
Prieto, A. G., 126, 133, *139*, 165, *175*

Q

Quaade, F., 65, *85*
Quadagno, D. M., 195, *215*
Quatrate, R. P., 191, *215*

R

Rabin, M. D., 185, *215*
Radcliffe, K. B., Jr., 268, *287*
Radlove, S., 166, *175*
Rainieri, W. C., 200, *216*
Ram, C., 201, *212*
Randall, W., 258, *284*
Rapoport, R., 132, *139*
Raskin, N. J., 263, *285*
Raymond, B. T., 149, *175*

Redding, W. C., 124, *136,* 146, 157, 160, 168, 169, *171*
Rees, L., 157, *175*
Regan, D. T., 150, 151, *175*
Reich, C., 264, *285*
Reitman, J. W., 124, *136*
Rethlingshafer, D., 118, *138*
Revelle, R., 93, *109*
Rhodewalt, F., 161, *172*
Rich, J., 25, *50*
Richardson, S. A., 12, *20,* 27, 29, *49,* 66, 67, 68, *84, 85, 86,* 222, 223, 224, *242,* 249, 257, 260, 261, 262, 267, *282, 285*
Richman, R. A., 134, *137*
Rickard, T. E., 273, *285*
Robbins, M. C., 133, *139,* 165, *175*
Roberts, J. V., 96, *111,* 126, 131, 132, *139*
Robins, E., 105, *109*
Rockway, A. M., 248, 276, *281*
Rodin, J., 80, 86, 145, 146, 156, 161, 162, 164, *175, 176*
Roe, D. A., 91, 96, *110*
Rogel, M. J., 182, *215*
Ronald, C., 27, 29, *49*
Rogers, D., 258, *284*
Rogers, R. W., 145, 148, *175*
Ronald, L., 12, *20,* 262, *285*
Roncari, D. A. K., 102, *111*
Rosenberg, A., 234, *241*
Rosenberg, L., 210, *212*
Rosenblatt, J. S., 24, *50*
Rosenblatt, P. C., 13, 14, *21*
Rosenfeld, R., 234, *242*
Rosman, B., 103, *110*
Ross, L., 19, *21,* 29, *50,* 79, *85,* 153, *175*
Ross, M. B., 25, *50,* 185, *213*
Roth, P., 199, *215*
Rothbart, M., 145, 148, 151, 154, *176*
Rottmann, L., 291, *298*
Rotton, J., 204, 205, *215, 216*
Royce, J., 67, *86*
Rozin, P., 183, *216*
Rubenstein, C., 70, *84*
Rubin, D. C., 185, *216*
Rubin, E. C., 277, *284*
Ruderman, A., 100, 105, *111*
Rudofsky, B., 67, *86*
Rump, E. E., 127, *139*
Rundall, T. G., 276, *287*
Rush, J., 102, *112*
Rusiniak, K. W., 183, *213*

Russell, F., 204, *216*
Russell, G. F. M., 102, 103, 105, 106, *110, 111*
Russell, M. J., 191, 192, 195, 201, 202, *216*
Rutowski, R. L., 182, *216*

S

Sadlick, M., 269, *285*
Saeed, L., 130, 132, *138*
Safilios-Rothschild, C., 247, *285*
Sagarin, E., 74, *86*
Sakata, R., 275, *287*
Sallade, J., 69, *86*
Salvia, J., 12, *21,* 25, 27, *50*
Sameroff, A., 24, 30, 45, *50*
Sampson, E. E., 14, *21*
Sandler, A. M., 256, *285*
Sands, H., 269, *286*
Sappenfield, B. R., 33, *50*
Sarlin, M. B., 256, *286*
Sarnat, H. B., 181, *216*
Sastry, S. D., 188, 189, 198, 200, 201, *216*
Sawin, D. B., 38, 39, *50*
Schachter, S., 100, *111,* 147, 161, 169, *176*
Schiff, W., 257, 258, 259, *286*
Schlafer, R. J., 92, *108,* 159, *171*
Schlafer, R. S., 118, *136*
Schleidt, M., 193, 194, *213, 216*
Schenker, C., 166, *175*
Schiavo, R. S., 149, *176*
Schmelkin, L. P., 247, *286*
Schneider, D. J., 210, *216*
Schofield, L. F., 277, *286*
Schoggen, P., 258, 273, *286*
Schopler, J., 150, *176*
Schroedel, J. G., 246, 259, 276, *286*
Schroeder, H., 145, 146, 156, 162, 163, 164, *173*
Schwartz, D., 89, 90, 98, 104, 105, 107, *109*
Schwartz, M., 145, 146, 156, 162, 163, 164, *173*
Scott, P. M., 151, *177*
Sears, R., 118, *137*
Seay, B., 32, *49*
Secord, P. F., 118, *139*
Secord, P. S., 159, 165, *174*
Sejwacz, D., 145, 148, *172*
Seltzer, C. C., 96, *109*
Selvini-Palazzoli, M., 93, 94, 103, 105, *111*
Severs, D., 77, 78, *83*

Shaffer, J. P., 125, *139*
Shah, J., 196, *214*
Shainess, N., 92, 93, *111*
Shaman, P., 210, *212*
Shantz, C. U., 32, *50*
Shapiro, L. N., 278, *286*
Shapiro, L. R., 90, *110*
Sheare, J. B., 12, *21*, 27, *50*
Shears, L. M., 265, *286*
Sheehan, D., 136, *138*
Sheehy, E., 53, *62*
Sheldon, W. H., 222, *242*
Shelley, W. B., 191, *216*
Sherlock, B., 149, *176*
Shorey, H. H., 182, *213*
Shoud, K. F., 151, *174*
Shubeita, H. E., 195, *215*
Shurgot, B. A., 130, *138*
Shurka, E., 267, *286*
Siegel, B., 71, *86*, 95, *112*, 158, *177*
Sierka, F. L., 267, *283*
Sigall, H., 28, *50*, 145, 148, 149, 150, 154, *174*, *176*
Sikes, S., 146, 161, 162, *176*
Sikorski, L., 210, *212*
Siller, J., 247, 248, 249, 250, 252, 254, 255, 259, 262, 265, 266, 267, 269, 270, 271, 272, 278, 279, *286*, *287*
Silver, R., 101, 105, *110*
Silverman, I., 31, *50*
Silverman, J. A., 104, *108*
Silverberg, G. D., 196, *215*
Singh, D., 146, 161, 162, *176*
Sirlin, J., 106, *108*
Sisk, D., 260, *283*
Sleet, D. A., 95, *111*
Sloat, W. L., 252, 267, *287*
Slochower, J., 80, *86*, 145, 146, 156, 161, 162, 164, *176*
Smart, D. E., 106, *108*
Smith, G., 145, 150, *176*
Smith, M. E., 118, *140*
Smith, S. D., 68, 71, *84*
Smits, S. J., 248, 257, *283*, *287*
Snyder, M., 12, *21*, 23, 45, 46, *51*, 79, *86*, 114, *140*, 145, 148, 151, 154, 161, *176*, 225, *242*
Snyder, P. J., 186, *212*
Sokolov, J. J., 196, *216*
Soldwedel, B., 263, *287*
Soler, E., 204, *216*

Solis-Gaffar, M. C., 200, *216*
Solomon, M. R., 150, *176*
Solow, C., 65, *86*
Sonnega, J. A., 263, *282*
Sontag, S., 99, *111*
Sorbye, B., 103, *108*
Sorell, G. T., 23, *51*
Sorlie, P., 92, *111*
Sours, J. A., 103, *111*
Sparks, W., 130, 132, *137*, 159, 165, *171*
Spencer, J. A., 100, 105, *111*
Spurzheim, J. G., 222, *241*
Staats, A. W., 151, *176*
Staats, C. K., 151, *176*
Stabler, B., 115, *140*
Staffieri, J. R., 69, 70, 71, *86*, 95, *110*, *111*, 158, *176*
Stalling, R. B., 146, 162, 163, 164, *176*
Stang, D. J., 296, *298*
Stavraky, K., 231, *241*
Stefanik, R. M., 204, *216*
Stein, S., 42, 43, *48*, 145, 148, 155, 165, *172*
Stephan, C. W., 8, 10, 12, 13, *20*, *21*, 23, 28, 33, 39, 40, *49*, *51*
Steven, G., 203, *215*
Stevenson, J., 248, 276, *281*
Steward, D. S., 14, *21*
Steward, M. S., 14, *21*
Stewart, A. L., 66, 71, 73, *86*
Stewart, J. E., 150, *176*
Stewart, R. A., 70, 71, 81, *85*
Stirnkorb, M., 258, *284*
Stitt, C., 135, *139*
Stoddart, D. M., 182, *216*
Stodden, R. L., 273, *284*
Stogdill, R., 123, *140*
Stokes, S. J., 28, *51*
Stolz, H., 119, *140*
Stolz, L., 119, *140*
Stone, C. P., 232, *242*, *243*
Stoner, K. L., 191, *215*
Storck, J. T., 150, *176*
Storms, M. D., 225, *243*
Story, I., 103, *112*
Stotland, E., 152, *176*
Stotsky, B. A., 274, *287*
Straus, A., 269, *287*
Strenta, A. C., 78, 79, 82, *84*, *85*, *86*, 210, *214*, 227, *243*
Stroebe, W., 31, *51*, 151, *174*, *176*
Strohmer, D. C., 252, *282*

Strongman, K. T., 70, 71, *86,* 95, *112*
Stuart, J. L., 119, *138*
Stunkard, A., 73, 80, *86,* 92, *109,* 102, *112,* 114, *140,* 227, *243*
Sturm, W., 191, *216*
Styczynski, L. E., 28, 29, 36, 41, *49, 51*
Suarez, A. C., 272, *287*
Suci, G. J., 249, *285*
Suematsu, H., 103, *110*
Sugita, M., 103, *110*
Sullivan, N. W., 273, *284*
Sulloway, F. J., 187, *216*
Sussman, M. D., 247, 279, *287*
Sussman, S., 44, *51*
Sutherland, A. M., 199, *215*
Swann, W. B., 23, *51*
Swift, P., 203, *216*
Switz, G. M., 195, *216*
Szyrynski, V., 103, *112*

T

Taka Lashi, N., 103, *110*
Tanke, E. D., 12, *21,* 45, 46, *51,* 225, *242*
Tannenbaum, P. H., 249, *285*
Tanner, J. M., 228, *243*
Tatgenhorst, J., 77, 78, *83*
Taylor, S. E., 17, *21,* 74, 83, *85,* 153, 176, 223, *242*
Tennis, G. H., 32, *51*
Terrill, I., 263, *287*
Thayer, S., 257, 258, 259, 268, *286, 287*
Theander, S., 103, *112*
Thibaut, J. W., 246, *283*
Thiel, D. L., 8, 9, 18, *20,* 28, 31, 32, *48*
Thompson, G. G., 31, *47*
Thompson, K., 195, *216*
Thompson, M., 89, 90, 98, 104, 105, 107, *109*
Thompson, S. C., 153, *176*
Thompson, V. D., 31, *51,* 151, *174, 176*
Thoreson, R. W., 257, 259, *281, 283*
Threlkeld, J., 102, *110*
Thumin, P. J., 126, 127, *137*
Tichenor, C. C., 276, *287*
Tighe, T. J., 224, *243*
Tinsley, B., 39, 40, *50*
Toth, E., 196, *212*
Touhey, J. C., 30, *51,* 134, *140*
Trehub, S., 10, *20,* 25, 39, *48*
Triandis, H. C., 273, *285*

Tringo, J. L., 265, 266, *287*
Trnavsky, P. A., 42, 43, *51*
Truhon, S. A., 125, *140*
Turk, A., 204, *216*
Turner, D. R., 271, 276, *287*
Tuthill, J. A., 128, *138*
Tutton, S. J., 70, 71, 81, *85, 86*
Tversky, A., 29, *51*

U

Udry, J. R., 197, *215*
Underberg, R. P., 248, *281*
Underwood, L., 115, *140*
Unger, R. K., 149, *175*
Urbanczyk, S., 132, *137*
Usdane, W. M., 246, *283*
Uttley, M., 191, *216*

V

Valins, S., 238, *243*
Van Dalen, D. B., 156, *176*
Vann, D. H., 75, *86,* 247, 248, 249, 250, 252, 254, 262, 265, 267, 269, 270, 271, 272, *286, 287*
Vaughn, B. E., 28, 29, 35, 40, *51*
Vener, A. M., 73, *86*
Veno, A., 133, *140*
Verillo, R. T., 248, *281*
Victor, J. B., 43, *48*
Vincent, L. M., 99, 104, *112*

W

Wagener, J. J., 146, 161, 162, *176*
Waldrop, M. F., 43, *51*
Walker, R. J., 122, *137*
Wallace, P., 191, 195, *217*
Waller, J., 103, *112*
Walster, E., 7, 8, 9, 12, 17, *20,* 23, 25, 26, 29, 31, 32, 40, 43, 46, *47, 48,* 53, *62,* 69, 70, *83,* 92, 97, *108,* 128, 129, 130, *136,* 150, 152, 155, 158, 159, *171, 172,* 221, 222, *241,* 291, 292, *298*
Walster, G. W., 31, 32, *47*
Walters, G., 259, *283*
Ward, C. D., 121, 125, *140,* 157, *176*
Wardle, J., 101, 106, *112*
Ware, C. L., 29, *49*
Warner, P., 196, *215*

Warren, S. A., 271, 276, *287*
Warsh, S., 102, *111*
Watson, D. R., 187, 199, 203, 204, *214*
Watson, R. A. R., 71, *85*
Watts, A. F., 31, *51*
Weatherly, D., 234, *243*
Wechsler, H., 272, *287*
Weinberg, N., 260, 261, *287*
Weinberg-Asher, N., 259, *287*
Weiss, W., 150, *174*
Weitzman, E. L., 103, *109*
Wells, W. D., 71, *86*, 95, *112*, 158, *177*
West, S. G., 145, 148, 149, 154, *177*
Westie, C., 262, *284*
Wetzel, C. G., 19, *21*
Whatley, J. L., 73, *83*, 158, *171*
Whitaker, L. A., 60, 61, *62*
White, H., 72, *83*
Whitehouse, H. A., 191, *217*
Whiteman, M., 247, 249, 251, *287*
Whitt, K., 115, *140*
Wiback, P., 150, *172*
Wicklund, G., 149, *176*
Wiener, H., 186, 187, *217*
Williams, J., 121, *140*
Wilson, G. T., 100, 105, *111*
Wilson, M. E., Jr., 275, *287*
Wilson, P. R., 127, *140*, 160, *177*
Wilson, T. D., 19, *21*, 34, *50*
Winokur, G., 105, *109*
Winter, R., 186, *217*

Witkin, A., 256, *287*
Wittreich, W. J., 268, *287*
Woodruff, R. A., 105, *109*
Woody, E. Z., 100, *112*, 150, 157, *172, 173*
Wooley, O. W., 82, *86*, 93, *112*
Wooley, S. C., 82, *86*, 93, *112*
Word, C. O., 225, *243*
Wright, B., 70, *87*, 245, 263, 278, 279, *280, 281, 287*
Wyden, P., 90, 96, *112*

Y, Z

Yankell, S. L., 201, *212*
Yarmey, A. D., 121, *140*
Yarnold, P. R., 44, *51*
Yarrow, M. R., 31, *51*, 151, *177*
Yoder, J., 149, *171*
Young, C. M., 91, 96, *110*
Young, R. A., 204, *212*
Young, R. D., 81, *87*
Younger, J. C., 102, *111*, 161, *177*
Youngng, J. H., 247, 248, 262, 267, 271, *288*
Yuker, H. E., 68, *87*, 247, 248, 262, 267, 271, *288*
Zajonc, R. B., 224, *242*
Zalkind, S. S., 269, *286*
Zanna, M. P., 8, 9, 17, *20*, 76, *84*, 129, *140*, 150, 170, *177*, 225, *243*
Zuckerman, W. B., 251, *288*

Subject Index

A

Academic ability, relationship to attractiveness, 41

Academic performance, *see also* Grade levels related to height, 126

Acceptance, social, 28

Activity levels, attractiveness and, 43

Adolescent(s), adolescence
male, self-image, related to height, 119
maturation, timing of, 229–232
role of attractiveness in, 31

Adult(s)
expectations, related to attractiveness in children, 10–12
treatment of unfamiliar children, 34–35

Age
acceptability of overweight persons and, 68
related to attractiveness stereotyping, 8, 17

Agent of social influence, *see* Social influence

Aggression, 41–42
appearance and, 42–43
effect of environmental odor on, 205
height and, 136

"Air pollution," 204

Alcohol, effect on restrained eater, 101

Alcoholics, educator's attitudes toward, 273

Amputee, attitudes toward, 250, 253, 254, 263, 265

Anal odor, 199

Animals, *see* Nonhuman species

Androstenol, response to, 198–199

Androstenone, response to, 199

Anorexia nervosa, 93, 94, 101, 102–104, 106–107
"Mild" or "forme fruste," 105

Anxiety, dietary restraint and, 100

Apgar scores, infant attractiveness and, 38–39

Apocrine sweat glands, 190

Appearance, *see* Physical appearance

Assertiveness, attractiveness and, 166

Attitude(s)
changes, identification-based, 153
defined, 251
related to disability, *see* Physical Disability
similarity, estimate of height and, 126
social, *see* Social attitudes

Attitude behavior scale (ABS), related to disability, 251–252

Attitudes Toward Deafness Scale, 272

Attitudes Toward Disabled Persons Scale (ATDP), 247–248, 249, 252, 253, 254, 266, 277
for cancer, 277

Attraction
heterosexual, related to attractiveness, 13–14
interpersonal, disability and, 269

Attractiveness, *see* Facial attractiveness, Physical attractiveness

Attribution process, related to deviants, 225–226
Attribution theory, 247
Attribution therapy, for maturational deviance, 238
Authoritarian Virtuousness, disability and, 253, 279
Autosomal dominant mutations, 55, 55t
Avoidance behavior, deviance and, 223–224, 225–226
Axilla, odor from, 190–191
  response to, 191–195

B

Ballerinas, anorexia nervosa among, 104–105
Behavior
  attractiveness stereotyping and, 12
  differential, development of, 40–43
  of disabled children, 264
  helping, differences in, 268–269
  influence of morphology on, 291
  interpersonal, see Interpersonal behavior
  nonverbal attribution and, 210
  odor and, 186–188
  parental, related to attractiveness, 37–40
  related to height, 135–136
  related to maturational deviance, 240
  social, see Social behavior
  toward disabled, 257–258, 273–274
Behavioral confirmation, as function of attractiveness, 45
Behavioral dominance, see Dominance
Behavioral expectations, 23, 32
  attractiveness based on, mediating variables and individual differences in, 27–33
Behavioral reactions, maturational timing and, 237
Behavioral syndromes, related to maturational deviance, 239
Belief system, 222
"Bingeing," "binges," 100, 101, 106
Blacks, interviewing of, 225
"Blemishes of individual character," 74
Blind, blindness
  attitudes toward, 248, 250, 253, 254, 263, 265
    of educators, 272
    of rehabilitation personnel, 277
  development, 256

institutionalized, relationships, 275
interactions with sighted people, 267
Body shape, idealized, 93
Body image
  height and, 118–120
    self-description, 120–121
  related to dating, 130
Body weight, see also Overweight
  categorization, 145–146t, 146
  in context of other appearance and behavioral cues, 81–82
  importance of, compared to height, 114–115
  perception of, 66
    influence on physical attraction ratings, 158–160
  related to rating, 96
  social influence and, 154, 155–160, 166, 169, 170
  susceptibility to, 161–165
Boys, see also Males
  attractiveness, social acceptance and, 28, 29
  maturation and development, 230, 231
    deviance, 233, 234
Brain, proportion devoted to olfaction, 181
Breast odor, response to, 201–202
Breath odor, response to, 200–201
Bulimarexia, 106
Bulimia, 101, 105–106, 107

C

Cancer, attitudes toward, 253, 254
  of professionals, 276–277
Castration anxiety, related to disability, 261
Categorization, of physical attractiveness, 15
Cerebral palsy, attitudes toward, 265
"Changeability," 223
Character, individual, blemishes of, 74
Chemical messengers, external, 186
Children, see also Infants and children
  attractive, 23
  blind, 256
  disabled
    attitudes toward, 263–264
    behavior of, 264
    mainstreaming of, 264
    social-psychological living conditions, 258
  disposition toward physical deviation, 66–67
  interaction with disabled, 249

interpersonal behaviors, similarity in attractiveness and, 32
odor, identification by, 192
older, relationship with parents, physical attraction and, 39–40
perception of disability, 260–262
physical characteristics, peer behavior and, 12–13
stereotyping, 30–31
unfamiliar, adult treatment of, 34–35
Cleft lip and palate, 55, 55t
Cognition, effect of deafness on, 256
Cognitive mediators, in expectations as function of appearance, 29–31
Cognitive perspective, on attractiveness stereotyping, 15–17, 19
Cognitive processing, 34
Communication, social influence and, 167–168
Competence
    infant, related to attraction, 39
    parental, 8
    stereotyped views on, 25
Compliance, 154
    effect of stigma on, 268
    heightened, attractiveness and, 149
    weight and, 161, 162
Conceptualizations, related to attractiveness stereotyping, 18
Confidence, *see* Self confidence
Conformity
    physical attractiveness and, 150
    related to height, 122–123
    weight and, 161
Contact, related to disabled-nondisabled interaction, 270
Continuity of attractiveness, 43–44
Contrast effect, in attraction, judging by, 33
Control(s), 210
    internal, 166
    related to thinness, 93, 94
Coping capability, of disabled, 260
Corsets, 98–99
Cosmetic conditions, attitudes toward, 250, 253, 254
Counselors, attitudes toward disabled, 277–278
Countertransference, disability and, 279
Craniofacial deformity patient
    appearance ratings
        after surgery, 57–58, 60
        before surgery, 56–57, 60
    diagnostic criteria, 55–56
    global study, 53–54
    pilot project-self-esteem ratings, 54, 59–60, 61
    psychological adjustment, 53, 62
        following surgery, 58–59, 60–61
Culture
    related to attractiveness stereotyping, 14
    related to attitudes toward overweight, 67

D

Date selection, height and, 129–130
Dating partners, similarity in levels of attractiveness, 32
Deaf, deafness
    attitudes toward, 248
        of educators, 272
        of rehabilitation personnel, 271, 275
    effect on cognition, 256
    –hearing differences, 257
    social perception and, 257
Decision making, importance of physical attractiveness in, 297
Defensive techniques, in disabled, 258–259
Deformity(ies), 74
    craniofacial, *see* Craniofacial deformity patient
Denial
    in disabled, 258–259
    pathological, 59–60
Dental profession, importance of physical attractiveness, 292
Dependence. *see* Field dependence
Depression, clinical, effect on restrained eater, 101
Development
    in blind person, 256
    physical attractiveness and, 46
        theoretical overviews, 23–24
    physical disability and, 260–263
    variation in, 230–231
Deviance, 222
    contrived, 223
    maturational, *see* Maturational deviance
    perception of, 237
    perspective
        extended, 224–227
        weight-influencability, 164
    reactions to, 223, 224, 226

Deviance (cont.)
  self-consciousness related to, 227
  studied indifference, 221–224
Diet, dieting, 90–91
  habits, prevalence of, 114
  magazine articles on, 90
Dietary chaos syndrome, see Anorexia nervosa, Bulimia
Dietary restraint, disinhibiting, 100
"Differential attention" hypothesis, height and, 127
Differential behavior, development of, 40–43
Differential treatment, socialization and, 34–43
Disability, see Physically disabled
Disability Factor Scales (DFS), 250–251, 252, 253, 254, 266
  cancer, 277
  deafness, 276
Discomfort effect, of deviance, 223, 226
Discrimination
  axillary odor and, 194
  toward overweight, 76–77
Distressed Identification, disability and, 253, 254, 263
Doctor, see Physician
Dominance, related to height, 122–123, 157

E

Earnings, see Income
Eating, restrained, 106, 107
  consequences of, 99–102
"Eating Attitudes Test, The," (EAT), 104–105
Eccrine sweat glands, 190
Ectomorph, stereotyping, 70, 71, 72
Educators, attitudes toward disabled, 271–274
Ego deficits, in anorexia, 103
"Ego strength," attitudes toward disabled and, 267
Emotional consequences, inferred, disability and, 253, 256
Employer, employment
  discrimination, toward overweight, 77
  prejudice toward disabled, 273
Endomorph, stereotyping, 70, 71, 72, 95
Environmental factors, related to attractiveness stereotyping, 19
Ethnic background

disabled-nondisabled interactions and, 270
status-related, height perception and, 128
Exacerbation process, related to deviants, 225, 226, 236
Expectations
  behavioral, see Behavioral expectations
  differential, 44–47
    related to attractiveness tn children, 24–27, 44–45
Experience, 8
Extended molecular analysis, maturational timing and, 228–229, 237, 239–240
"External chemical messengers" (ECM), 186

F

Facial attractiveness, effect on susceptibility to social influence, 165–166
Facial deformity, see Craniofacial deformity patient
Facial stimuli, 16
Factor analysis, related to attitudes toward disabled, 250, 260
Fathers, see also Parents
  involvement with infant, related to attractiveness, 39
Fatness, see Overweight
Fecal odor, 209
  response to, 199–200
Feedback loops, in maturational deviance, 236, 237, 238, 239, 240
Females, see also Girls
  attractive, 17–18
  body type preferred, 95–96, 97
  dieting among, 90–91
  ideal shape, 90, see also Thinness
  interviewing of, 225
  self-esteem, body size and, 97
Feminism, related to thinness, 93
Field dependence, social influence and, 161–165, 166
First impressions, 221–222
  impact of physical appearance on. 8–9, 17, 19
Flatus odor, response to, 199–200
Food-related disorders, 94
Forced-choice procedure, related to stereotyping of over. weight, 70–71, 72
Functional limitations, imputed, disability and, 253
"Fundamental attribution error," 19

G

Gender
  related to acceptance of overweight, 67–68
  related to attractiveness stereotyping, in children, 11
  social advantage of attractiveness and, 28
Genetic determinism, 223
Genital spots, *see* Genitalstellen
"Genitalstellen," 187
Gifted, attitudes toward, 266
Girls, *see also* Females
  attractiveness, social advantages, 28, 29
  maturation and development, 230, 231
    deviance, 233, 235
    timing of, 232
Grade levels, *see also* Academic ability
  attractiveness and, 36

H

"Halo effect," 19
Hand odor, 195–196
Happiness, importance of physical attractiveness in, 296–297
Harvard Group Scale of Hypnotic Susceptibility, 161
Hay's Standardized Rating Scale of Appearance, 54, 56
Health professionals, *see also* Specific professional
  stereotyping of overweight, 73
Height, 113–114, 133–134
  attractiveness and, 128–132
  body image and, 118–120
    self-descriptions, 120–121
  categorization, 145t–146t, 146
  definitions, 116–118
  difference between short and tall people, 121–126
  future research directions, 134–136
  impact on social influence, 154, 156–158
  importance of, compared to weight, 114–115
  own, correlated to estimates of population means, 121
  perception of
    influence on physical attractiveness ratings, 158–160
    in others, 124–126
    social status and, 126–128

personal space and, 132–133
power and income and, 123–124
social influence and, 134, 158, 159–160, 160–161, 168–169
stature and, 115–116
stereotype, 135
target, 165, 166
  effect on susceptibility to social influence, 165–166
Helping behavior, differences in, 268–269
Heterosexual attraction, related to physical attractiveness, 13–14
Hormone treatment, for maturational deviation, 240–241
Hyperactivity, 43

I

Illness, related to thinness, social attitudes as cause of, 98–99, 107
Income
  height and, 123–124
  weight and, 78
Identification
  distressed, *see* Distressed Identification
  preverbal, of odors, 185
Identity, social, 210
Importance
  perceived, related to height, 125
  of physical attractiveness, 291–298
Impressions, *see also* First impressions
  formation, 44–47
  management, 210
  related to attractiveness stereotyping, 19
Indifference, related to study of maturational deviance, 221–224
Individual, versus group, attractiveness stereotyping and, 14
Individualism
  self-contained, 14
  valueing, 14
Infants and children
  attractive and unattractive, differential expectations, 24–27
  attractiveness
    adult judgment on, 10–12
    influence on parental treatment and behavior, 37–40
  response to mother's breast odor, 201–202
Influence, *see* Social influence
Information-processing strategies, 30

Instructions, "Nonobjective" versus "subjective," 9
Intellectual potential, attractiveness and, 295
Intelligence, 295
  attitudes toward disabled and, 275
  correlated to height, 121–122
Interaction, 222
  disabled-nondisabled, variables affecting, 266–268
  social, see Social interaction
Interaction Strain, disability and, 252, 256, 257, 263
Interactional effect, of deviance, 227
Internalization, 224
Interpersonal behavior
  attractiveness stereotyping and, 12
  children, similarity in attractiveness and, 32
Intimacy, rejection of, 253
IQ scores, relationship to attractiveness, 41

J

Jealousy, 32–33
Judgments
  of attractiveness, 9
    in infants and children, 10–12
    confidence ratio, 9
  conforming to, height and, 157
"Just world" concept, 269
  derivations from, 247
Juvenile delinquents, 42

L

Lateral Facial Dysplasia" (LFD), 55, 55t
Likability, 153
Living conditions, social-psychological, in disabled children, 258
Locus of control, 166

M

Males, see also Boys
  attractiveness
    height and, 159
    stereotyping of, 9
  body type preferred, 95, 96–97
  maturational deviance, 236
  self-esteem, body size and, 97
  self-image, related to height, 119
Male-taller norm, 129

Manipulative influence strategies, 42
Marital partner, selection, 14
Maternal behavior, nonhuman, 24
Maturational deviance, 229–232, 239–241
  intervention strategies, 238–239, 240–241
  research at macro-outcome level, 232–239
"Meanness," peer-nominated, 43
Medical profession, see Physician
Medical treatment, for overweight, seeking of, 73
Men, see Male
Menarche, age at, 231
Menstrual cycle
  breath odor during, 200–201
  vaginal odor and, 197
Mentally retarded, 276
Mesomorph, stereotyping, 70, 71, 95, 97
Miss America Pageant contestants, 89, 90
Moebius syndrome, 55
Molecular analysis, see Extended molecular analysis
Morphology, influence on behavior, 221–222, 291
Mother, see Parent
Mouthrinse, 200
Mutations, autosomal dominant, 55, 55t
"Mutual resentment," disability and, 278

N

Nonhandicapped-disabled interactions, 257–258, 259
Nonhuman species
  responses to physical characteristics of infant, 24
  social olfaction, 182
Nose, "genitalstellen" in, 187

O

Obesity, see Overweight
Occupational status, height estimation and, 128
Odor, 179–190, see also Smell sense
  attributional analysis, 209–210
  "basic," stereotype, 209
  categories, 180
  children, identification by, 192
  descriptions for, characterizing of, 183, 184t, 185
  human behavior and, 186–188

localization, 209
recognition of, 185
response to, 185–186
  of abnormal body odor, 188–189
  of artificial odor, 202–204
  of environmental odor, 204–205
  of normal body odor, 190–202
smell sense and, 181–185
suppression of, 180
Olfactory system, 181, *see also* Odor, Smell
  sense
Outcomes, *see* Social outcomes
Overeating, 101
Overweight, 65–66, 92
attitudes toward, 66–69, 253
disposition toward, antecedents and consequences, 82–83
fat-person stereotype, 69–73, 94
social influence and, 169
social outcomes and, 76–78
self-perception, 78–80
stimulus of, 81
susceptibility to social influence, 161
unresolved issues, 80–83

P

Parent(s)
competence, expected, 8
expectancies and attitudes, infant attractiveness and, 33, 46
rating of appearance, craniofacial deformity
  and, 56, 57
treatment and behavior, related to attractiveness, 37–40
Partner, desirable, height and, 129
Peer(s)
attractiveness stereotyping and, 12–13
expectations, related to attractiveness in
  children, 26–27
social behavior with, related to attractiveness, 41–43
Perception, *see* Social perception
Performance
social, related to height, 126
stereotyped view, 25
Perfumes, 200–201, 209, 211
Personal space, height and, 132–133
Personality(ies), 8
factors in attitudes toward disabled, 259
traits, height and, 121–124

Persuasion, persuasiveness, 170, *see also* Social influence
height and, 157–158
related to attractiveness, 148–149, 150–151,
  152–154, 155
weight and, 164
"Pet" phenomenon, 228–229
Pheromones, 182, 197
synthetic hypothetical, human female sexual, 197
Physical appearance, role in social influence,
  see Social influence
Physical appearance rating, related to craniofacial deformity, 56, 57–58
Physical attractiveness
categorization of, 145t–146t, 156
continuity of, 43–44
height and, 128–132
importance of, 291–298
social influence, 147–150
  mediation of agent attractiveness effects,
    150–151
  underlying psychological pressures, 151–
    155
  stereotyping based on, *see* Stereotyping,
    based on physical attractiveness
Physical development, *see* Development
Physical deviance, *see* Deviance
Physical resemblance, effect on expectations
  and behavior, 32–33
Physically disabled, disablement
attitudes toward, 245–246, 280
  changes in, 269–271
  differential feelings and, 255–263
  measurement considerations, 246–252
  of professionals and rehabilitation work-
    ers, 271–280
  relationship to non-disability, 249
  structure of, 252–255
developmental aspects, 260–263
-nondisabled interactions, 259
  variables affecting, 266–268
psychological consequences, 259
preference rankings for types of disabilities,
  263–271
social position of, 263–271
Physician
attitudes
  toward disabled, 278
  toward rehabilitation, 274
importance of physical attractiveness, 292

Physician (*cont.*)
-patient relationship, effect of overweight
stereotyping on, 73
Physique
satisfaction, related to height, 118–119
social influence and, 165, 166, 167, 169–
170
Picture preference technique
disability and, 260, 261, 262
overweight and, 67–69
Piers-Harris Self-esteem Inventory, 54
Plastic surgeons, 292–293
Play, 41–42
Playboy Magazine centerfold, 89
Playboy playmates, 93
Political candidates, height, voting intention
and, 124–125, 157
Power
height and, 123–124
Preference
rankings, for types of disabilities, 263–271
societal, for thinness, 89–90
Prejudice
status-related, height preference and, 128
toward disabled, 270
of employer, 273
Pressure, *see* Social pressure
"Problem of visibility," 15
Process consideration, for maturational timing,
234
Psychiatric patient, eating disorders, 101
Psychiatrist, attitudes toward rehabilitation,
274
Psychologically relevant variant, physical attractiveness as, 46
Psychosocial adjustment, following cra-
niofacial surgery, 58–59, 60–61
"Public self," 15

R

Racial ethnic differences, in attitude toward
disability, 251
Rank preference position, of overweight child,
67
Ratings, attractiveness, 32
Rehabilitation, attitudes toward, 274
Rehabilitation personnel, attitudes toward dis-
abled, 274–280
Reinforcement, 11

Rejection, 258
related to disability, 253
social, 28
Resemblance, *see* Physical resemblance
Resentment, mutual, disability and, 278
Responses, submissive, 133
Rule following, 224
"Rule governed," 223

S

Salience, related to attractiveness stereotyping,
17
Scale construction, factor-analytic techniques,
related to attitudes toward disability,
250
Scents, *see* Odor
School achievement, *see also* Grade levels,
Academic achievement
relationship to attractiveness, 41
Self, public, 15
Self-appraisal, 224
Self-assurance, maturational deviance and, 237
Self-centeredness, 8
Self-concept, 210, 224
persuasion and, 155
related to attitudes toward disabled, 261
Self-confidence, related to maturational de-
viance, 236
Self-consciousness, related to deviance, 223,
227
Self-disclosure, 15
Self-esteem
body size and, 97
height and, 119, 126, 165, 166
related to craniofacial deformity, 59
"Self-fulfilling prophecy effects," related to
attractiveness stereotyping in children,
11, 12
Self-image
following craniofacial surgery, 58
maturational deviance and, 236–237
Self-perception, height and, 135
Self-rating, of appearance, related to craniofacial deformity, 56, 57–58, 59–60,
60–61
Semantic differential, related to disability studies, 249
Sensitivity, compensatory, 257
Sensory deficiency states, 260

Sex, *see* Gender
Sex-role stereotyping, attractiveness liking
     and, 30
Sexuality, odor and, 187–188
Silhouette cutouts, related to overweight ster-
     eotyping, 70
Similarity in attractiveness, influence on ex-
     pectancies and behavior, 31–33
Skin odor, response to, 190–196
Skin tone, styles, 91
Slimness, *see* Thinness
Smell sense, *see also* Odor
  anatomical and phylogenetic considerations,
     181–182
  function, 180
  relationship to other senses, 183–186
Social acceptance, 28
Social attitude, related to thinness as cause of
     illness, 98–99, 101
Social behavior
  development, attractiveness and, 46–47
  olfaction in, 182
  with peers, related to attractiveness, 41–43
Social distance measures, related to disability,
     249
Social influence, role of physical appearance
     in, 143–144, 152, 166–168
  agent of, 143, 167
  as agent variable
     physical attractiveness, 147–155
     weight and height, 155–161
  of attractiveness, 167
  categorization of literature, 144–147
  functional theory of, 147
  of height, 168–169
  on susceptibility to, 169
     facial attractiveness and, 169–170
  target of, 143
  as target variable, 161
     height and facial attractiveness, 165–166
     impact of weight in susceptibility, 161–
     165
Social interactions, 224
  impact of physical attractiveness on, 291–
     292
  related to maturational deviance, 236, 237–
     238
Social learning perspective, on stereotyping
     based on physical attractiveness, 10–
     17, 18

Social outcomes, overweight and, 76–78
  self-perception, 78–80
Social perception
  body size and, 95
  of disabled, 257, 260
Social performance, related to height, 126
Social position, of disabled, 263–271
Social pressure, for thinness, consequences of,
     99–107
Social rejection, 28
Social skills, assertiveness and, 166
Social status
  height and, 126–128, 134
  related to thinness and dieting, 91, 92
Socialization
  differential treatment and, 34–43
  factors, related to stereotyping based on
     physical attractiveness, 10
  process, influence of appearance on, 46
Society, preference for thinness, 89–90
Sociocultural factors, related to stereotyping
     based on physical attractiveness, 13–15
Sociocultural pressures, for thinness, 91–95
Sociometry, disability and, 263
Somatopsychology, related to disability, 245,
     246–247
Space, personal, height and, 132–133
Spectacles, 131
Speech-handicapped children, attitudes toward,
     263, 264
Stature
  height and, 115–116, 117, 132
  stereotypes associated with, 135
Status differential situations, disability and, 279
Steinhauer's Family Assessment Measure, 61–
     62
Stereotyping, stereotype, *see also* Sex-role
     stereotyping
  based on physical attractiveness, 7
     implications, 17–19
     research, 7–10
     social learning perspective, 10–17
  body size, 95–98
  children, 30–31
  height, 135
  overweight, 69–73, 94
  of thinness, 94
Stigma, categories of, 74
Stigma doctrine, 223, 224, 240
  interactionist amendments to, 240

Stimuli, facial, 16
Strain, *see* Interaction Strain
Subject-object orientation, 246
"Submissive" responses, 133
"Subtle reinforcement," 11
Sweat glands, body odor from, 190
Sympathetic reactions, to maturational deviance, 238–239
"Synthetic hypothetical human female sexual pheromone" (SHHFSP), 197

T

Target of social influence, *see* Social influence
Teacher
    attitudes, student height and, 131
    behavior to children, related to attractiveness, 36
    expectations, related to disability, 275
Thermoregulation, 180
Thinness, 89–91
    body size stereotypes, empirical evidence for, 95–98
    social attitudes as a cause of illness, 98–99
    sociocultural pressures, 91–95
        consequences of, 99–107
    stereotypes, 94
"Transference distortions," disability and, 279
"Tribal stigmata," 74

U

Unattractiveness, 294–295
    social influence and, 155
Underarm, *see* Axilla
Urinary odor, response to, 198–199

V

Vaginal odor, response to, 196–197
Vanity, 8
Verbal cues, attribution and, 210
Virtuousness, *see* Authoritarian Virtuousness
Visibility, problem of, 15
Vocational rehabilitation groups, 275

W

Weight, *see* Body weight, Overweight
Western society, preference for thinness, 89–90
WISC, verbal scale, 41
Withdrawal, 239
Women, *see* Female

Y

Youth, quest for, 93